SATIRE AS THE COMIC PUBLIC SPHERE

Humor in America

Edited by
Judith Yaross Lee, Ohio University
Tracy Wuster, The University of Texas at Austin

Advisory Board
Darryl Dickson-Carr, *Southern Methodist University*
Joanne Gilbert, *Alma College*
Rebecca Krefting, *Skidmore College*
Bruce Michelson, *University of Illinois at Urbana-Champaign*
Nicholas Sammond, *University of Toronto*

The Humor in America series considers humor as an expressive mode reflecting key concerns of people in specific times and places. With interdisciplinary research, historical and transnational approaches, and comparative scholarship that carefully examines contexts such as race, gender, class, sexuality, region, and media environments, books in the series explore how comic expression both responds to and shapes American culture.

SATIRE AS THE COMIC PUBLIC SPHERE

Postmodern "Truthiness" and Civic Engagement

James E. Caron

The Pennsylvania State University Press
University Park, Pennsylvania

Library of Congress Cataloging-in-Publication Data

Names: Caron, James Edward, 1952– author.
Title: Satire as the comic public sphere : postmodern "truthiness" and civic engagement / James E. Caron.
Other titles: Humor in America.
Description: University Park, Pennsylvania : The Pennsylvania State University Press, [2021] | Series: Humor in America | Includes bibliographical references and index.
Summary: "Examines the work of satirists through the lenses of humor studies, cultural theory, and rhetorical and social philosophy, arriving at a new definition of the comic art form"—Provided by publisher.
Identifiers: LCCN 2021011109 | ISBN 9780271089867 (hardback)
Subjects: LCSH: Political satire, American—History and criticism. | Public sphere—United States. | Postmodernism—United States.
Classification: LCC PN6149.P64 C37 2021 | DDC 320.97302/07—dc23
LC record available at https://lccn.loc.gov/2021011109

Copyright © 2021 James E. Caron
All rights reserved
Printed in the United States of America
Published by The Pennsylvania State University Press,
University Park, PA 16802–1003

The Pennsylvania State University Press is a member of the Association of University Presses.

It is the policy of The Pennsylvania State University Press to use acid-free paper. Publications on uncoated stock satisfy the minimum requirements of American National Standard for Information Sciences—Permanence of Paper for Printed Library Material, ANSI Z39.48–1992.

slapstick laughs at the imperative of the bladder and demands lunch before social justice
snark mocks the public sphere and nurtures partisan truthiness
satire laughs at public sphere vice and folly and enables silly citizenship
—JEC

Contents

Acknowledgments ix

Introduction 1

Part 1: Satire and the Public Sphere

1. Defining Satire 19
2. The Public Sphere 36
3. Truthiness Satire and the Comic Public Sphere 52

Part 2: Doing Things with Satiric Words

4. Satire and Speech Act Theory 85
5. Satire as Speech Act, Part One 89
6. Satire as Speech Act, Part Two 117
7. The Limits of Satiric Ridicule 155
8. Satiric Intent and Audience Uptake 189
9. Find the Punchline 208

Notes 231

Index 263

Acknowledgments

I begin my rounds of thanks with the students in a 2017 Senior Honors Seminar on postmodern satire. Discussions over the semester with the extraordinary group that made up the class helped me to think through a number of issues presented in this book.

I want next to thank Ryan Peterson for his invaluable editorial suggestions and all the Penn State University Press staff for their support in the process of bringing the book to publication. Thanks also to the editors of the series Humor in America, Judith Yaross Lee and Tracy Wuster, for seeing the potential in the book. They have been my steadfast colleagues over the years in the collective investigation by scholars of cultural artifacts that make people laugh, an enterprise usually designated as "humor studies."

A special thanks goes to Judith Lee, with whom I have shared many conversations over the years about humor in America as well as about all manner of comic cultural artifacts and comic laughter. Her invitation to speak at Ohio University on my idea about speech acts in the comic public sphere provided the genesis of the project, and when we spoke about elaborating the talk into a book project for the Humor in America series, she supplied needed encouragement and also sound advice about how to proceed, all in her usual generous fashion.

My wife Michelle (as always) deserves thanks as my best and most faithful interlocutor as I ramble through ideas and try out formulations.

Portions of the book are excerpted from the following: "Satire and the Problem of Comic Laughter," *Comedy Studies* 11, no. 2 (2020): 171–82, DOI: 10.1080/2040610X.2020.1729485; "The Quantum Paradox of Truthiness: Satire, Activism, and the Postmodern Condition," *Studies in American Humor*, ser. 4, vol. 2, no. 2 (2016): 153–81; and "Comic Belles Lettres and a Literary History of the American Comic Tradition," *Studies in American Humor*, ser. 3, no. 29 (2014): 13–34.

Introduction

In January 2017, a protester from the activist group Code Pink, Desiree Fairooz, was arrested for laughing during the confirmation hearing for Senator Jeff Sessions to become the next attorney general of the United States. While introducing Sessions, the other senator from Alabama, Richard Shelby, stated that his colleague had a "clear and well-documented" record of "treating all Americans equally under the law." Fairooz found that claim laughable—so she laughed. A rookie Capitol Hill police officer, who before the incident had never made an arrest nor guarded a congressional hearing, decided to take Fairooz into custody for disorderly conduct.

In May, Fairooz was convicted, but Judge Robert E. Morin tossed out the guilty verdict in July because the government had improperly argued that her laughter alone was enough to convict. In September, numerous news organizations reported that Fairooz would be retried when she refused a plea bargain, but shortly before the new trial date, the Department of Justice announced it was dropping the charge.[1]

If there was any doubt that laughter could be construed as comic political speech, the actions of the government in this incident prove otherwise. In effect, Fairooz's laughter registered as an unruly gesture within the staged civil disobedience of Code Pink and as another sign of its dissent, one understood as disruptive of official proceedings and therefore subject to the criminal code.

The fear implied in the government's actions, especially in its decision to retry Ms. Fairooz, suggests that some force still remains in the claim that "Against the assault of laughter, nothing can stand," famously expressed in an unfinished story by Mark Twain.[2] Although the implication of radical change in that assertion surely counts as a rhetorical overreach, comic laughter obviously worried the Department of Justice. The assault of laughter may not blow "a colossal humbug . . . to rags and atoms at a blast," as the passage from the story claims, but it obviously can disturb in significant ways. Otherwise why respond with criminal charges? This incident dramatizes the role of comic laughter as a fundamental social gesture signifying how comic political speech might operate in the twenty-first-century public sphere. Moreover, the incident underscores how forcefully satire might function as the comic form of what the ancient Greeks called *parrhēsia*, speaking truth no matter the consequence—but via laughter-provoking mockery and ridicule. No wonder that Donald Trump attacked *Saturday Night Live* (*SNL*) and Alec Baldwin for his impersonation of the president; the parody rattled the White House. Mr. Trump claimed *SNL* has terrible ratings when the facts demonstrate exactly the opposite: the skits featuring Baldwin as Trump practically revived the show, a meta-joke engendered by the impersonation. The repeated sketches on *SNL* featuring Baldwin as Trump so enraged the president that he wondered in a tweet, "how do the Networks get away with these total Republican hit jobs without retribution?"[3] Trump's demand for retribution against a television show airing satirical sketches reiterates the Desiree Fairooz debacle that attempted to repress the laughter of citizens as a danger to the state. Whether in print, broadcast, streamed, or staged in public places with guerrilla tactics, satire and its comic laughter can be logged as assaults on the follies and vices of civic society, what Jürgen Habermas famously called the public sphere.[4]

Satire as the Comic Public Sphere: Postmodern "Truthiness" and Civic Engagement examines the relationship between satire and the public sphere, a relationship that creates the comic public sphere, a parodic counterpart to Habermas's classic articulation of a particular kind of discourse and set of social practices first associated with Enlightenment values and technologies. The core thesis of the investigation can be simply stated: satire functions as comic political speech and signifies the presence of the comic public sphere. Even in its postmodern forms down to the present day, satire bears the legacy of the Enlightenment's values of reasoned debate, facts and evidence, accountability, and transparency that characterize Habermas's concept of the public sphere. Satire signifies the comic public sphere because it implicitly advocates for those values, no matter how aggressive its laughter-provoking presentation.

Whatever critiques have been leveled against Habermas's concept, the public sphere and its digital format today remain a fundamentally discursive realm. Satire understood as the public sphere's comic supplement, when viewed from the long historical perspective since the Enlightenment, underscores the crucial civic quality of accurate information and the narrative form generally called *news*. The role of news narratives anchors the eighteenth-century version of the public sphere first identified by Habermas; moreover, that crucial role has continued into the twenty-first century's version. However, under the pressure of digital technologies, the word *news* today does not necessarily signify a factual basis for reasoned debate but rather indicates a contested site in which counternarratives circulate and political spin doctors offer "alternative facts," as a White House aide, Kellyanne Conway, famously did to describe the initial press briefing of Sean Spicer, the first White House press secretary for the Trump administration.

Political discourse in the US—adversarial and dominated by television performances—often shows the same desire to push counternarratives to support alternative facts. For example, in April 2018, a handful of House Republicans wrote a letter to the Department of Justice demanding the prosecutions of Hillary Clinton and other Democrats to match the Russia investigation by special counsel Robert Mueller and the FBI. As Matthew Yglesias put it, "The point here is almost certainly not to generate any actual prosecutions so much as it is to try to muddy the waters in the media."[5] Websites such as the Drudge Report, Breitbart, and Infowars routinely construct narratives about current events to counter traditional news outlets, which have been tagged scornfully as the "lamestream media." *News* as a reference to reporting events now signifies not just a range of newspapers and broadcasts on TV and radio, as well as cablecasts or online dissemination, but a discursive space in which alternate realities compete.

There could hardly be a better example of consequences implied in Jean-François Lyotard's famous dictum about the delegitimizing of metanarratives that characterizes the postmodern condition. In his analysis, the question now asked about knowledge by "the State, or institutions of higher education is no longer 'Is it true?' but 'What use is it?'"[6] This shift in attitude about knowledge presents the fundamental problem for news reporting and thus the public sphere, for "use" can be turned any number of ways by the doctrine of alternative facts dispensed by spin doctors and public relations experts. Arguably, the most famous and far-reaching example of alternative facts to create a false narrative that circulates in the public sphere denies climate change, but Trump's demonstrably false assertion about *SNL*'s terrible ratings suggests the ubiquitous use of alternative facts to support even the most trivial claims. Supposedly, "May you live in interesting times," voices an old Chinese curse, with "interesting" apparently standing in for "tumultuous" and "disruptive." There can be little doubt that we do indeed live in interesting times. We have a president who rattles off falsehood so routinely that a major newspaper has published as a book a series of editorial opinions titled *Our Dishonest President*.[7]

The doctrine of alternative facts mounts a potentially deadly challenge to the idea of consensus built into Habermas's public sphere, for it attacks the Enlightenment's basic narrative of progress both scientific and social. The danger arises by exchanging the meaning of *consensus*—an agreement reached through dialogue and among free agents with reasoning intellects—for a consensus extracted from a media ecosystem, one that can be harnessed to political and economic apparatuses only interested in maintaining and improving their performances—that is, one in service to power. If enough people circulate those alternative facts and the conspiracies they foster, what Jean Baudrillard would call a simulacra of public sphere consensus appears, wherein appearance devolves into simulation.[8]

This threat has helped propel satire as a comic form of pushback in a bid to adapt the public sphere to the more recent phases of the postmodern environment. As though proving the second law of thermodynamics in social and political terms, the more that public sphere debate and discussion based on accurate news reporting have been attacked, the more satire has been employed as an equal and opposite reaction. The recent production of satire in the United States has thrived under these conditions. Rachel Caufield and Rob King each argue that American culture currently features a golden age of satire, an assertion that strikes a clear note, given the unrivaled ascendency of Jon Stewart, Stephen Colbert, Bill Maher, Samantha Bee, and John Oliver as pop culture satirists.[9] The popularity of comic work by Tina Fey, Amy Poehler, and Amy Schumer, for example, like the 2016 addition of Samantha Bee's *Full Frontal* (TBS) to the weekly line-up of cablecast shows, indicates the strength of gender-inflected satire. Larry Wilmore's *The Nightly Show* (Comedy Central, 2015–16) briefly brought an African American sensibility to the cultural scene memorably expressed earlier by *Chappelle's Show* (Comedy Central, 2003–6) and more recently by *Key & Peele* (Comedy Central, 2012–15). Trevor Noah's current version of *The Daily Show* (Comedy Central, 2015–present) features an international as well as person of color's satiric point of view, enabled by Noah's South African background. The addition in 2017 of Jordan Klepper's short-lived *The Opposition* to this formidable line-up indicated Comedy Central's basic belief that satire continues to sell.[10]

These examples suggest an unprecedented diversity to accompany satire's unprecedented visibility. A survey of satire in a stand-up format would easily elaborate this televisual hint of its ubiquity and of its reach in popular culture. Moreover, satire's visibility is truly international.[11] The literary scene in the United States over the past decade or so offers a long list of writers, some more well known than others, working in comic modes—Paul Beatty, Alison Bechdel, Robert Coover, Lydia Davis, Amy Hempel, Chuck Palahniuk, Guy Portman, Thomas Pynchon, Phoebe Robinson, George Saunders, David Sedaris, David Foster Wallace, Alexander Weinstein, Colson Whitehead, Gerald Vizenor—to round out this picture of satire's robust presence in contemporary American culture.

This ubiquity has occurred, in part, via the newest mass medium, the internet, with its progeny YouTube, a video world unto itself. Podcasts and streaming take their place as new formats in older media, existing alongside social media platforms that have a potential for comic presentation. These communication platforms blur genres in unforeseen ways through what Geoffrey Baym calls "discursive integration," which can be read, along with Baudrillard's regime of simulacra and its doctrine of alternative facts, as symptomatic of a postmodern condition, or, at the least, of the regular collision of modernism and postmodernism, or as an interweaving of the "political normative" and the "aesthetic-expressive." For Baym and other scholars, discursive integration has become a key factor in analyses of twenty-first-century satire because the "fundamental blurring of conceptual categories and media discourses . . . has created both the conditions *and the need* for the emergence of comedy [i.e., satire] as a site of political conversation."[12]

Satire in the United States of the twenty-first century, then, bears the marks of a postmodern aesthetic even as it continues to display Enlightenment intellectual roots not just in its efforts to inform in order possibly to reform but in its efforts to educate American citizenry. Being made aware of and educated about civic issues stands out as a theme as well as a goal of much contemporary satire. That goal implies a philosophical underpinning for satire today that contradicts or at least revises the deep irony of early postmodernism, an irony that questions foundational assumptions about knowledge and spurns metanarratives in which consensus values might be anchored. That early version of a postmodern condition would seem to preclude any satire at all, for how can the reformist impulse of satire as a comic mode operate in an aesthetic and cultural environment in which all ethical and moral values are said to be contingent? Nevertheless, the death of satire in the twenty-first century has clearly been exaggerated, for satire is not just surviving but thriving in a new cultural and aesthetic moment, as the list rehearsed above indicates.

The rise of fake news outlets such as the Drudge Report, Breitbart, and Infowars has been paralleled by satire in mock news formats.[13] The agonistic dynamic of news and mock news and fake news that permeates public discourse demonstrates the complicated discursive integration already in place even as it suggests a satiric battle already in progress. The assault on the Enlightenment's values of facts, evidence, and reasoned debate underpinned by good information in newspapers and other periodicals has propelled the mock news format to prominence, particularly since the advent of *The Daily Show with Jon Stewart* (1999–2015).[14] However, the defining moment for the satiric mocking of fake news and its correlative habits of pushing alternative facts and denying scientific research came with *The Colbert Report* (2005–14), a spin-off from *The Daily Show with Jon Stewart*, hosted by Stephen Colbert, when Colbert coined the term "truthiness" to describe the turn against facts and evidence.[15]

These parodic shows as well as other satiric endeavors have been fruitfully examined from a media studies perspective concerned with refuting the argument that mock news shows and their ironic satire encourage disengagement from and even cynicism about politics. Several studies argue that the entertainment television of the mock news shows represents instead innovative political engagement, countering apathy or cynicism by encouraging a participatory culture for their audiences, in effect, a new public sphere, or deploying the "ironic authenticity" of a postmodern satire to create counterpublics.[16] Moreover, this positive argument has been vigorously reinforced by an assertion that contemporary satire might constitute a kind of political action called "satiractivism," a level of citizenship performance beyond any discursive and affective engagement one might usually claim for satiric texts. This multipronged counterargument includes dissecting the studies upon which others have made the disengagement/cynicism argument, while offering empirical evidence refuting earlier empirical evidence.[17] Within this media studies framework, the satire in formats that play with the news—Stephen Colbert's or Jimmy Kimmel's late-night monologues or Samantha Bee's *Full Frontal* segments—is conceptualized as political communication.

I want to both extend this line of argument and turn it from media studies about political communication to what is conventionally called *humor studies*[18] by investigating how a certain kind of satiric text operates via a comic aesthetic within postmodern culture, and thus demonstrating how a parodic relationship to Habermas's idea of the public sphere enables comic political speech. This angle emphasizes poetics over politics, aesthetic expression over political communication. The alternative view that satire functions as political communication can be discerned, for example, in the statement that "two sharp-witted comedians—Bill Maher and Dennis Miller—[were] granted . . . the license to bend the inherited rules of entertainment talk and craft a new model by melding politics with humor."[19] This analysis works within a history of television from the disciplinary viewpoint of media studies, but humor studies would say that satire always melded politics with comic techniques, including humor, so "new model" makes little sense. What happened from the humor studies point of view was that postmodern aesthetics and the post-network environment provided an enormous cultural opening for satirists to do what they always did, critique social and political habits, albeit in new media formats. Similarly, arguing that mock news shows starring Jon Stewart and Stephen Colbert function as "the vanguard of a new kind of public affairs media [or] political journalism" and in doing so create "various political narratives" implies that satire is political speech.[20] Within humor studies' framework of investigating cultural comic artifacts, this line of thinking misreads the satire being deployed because it misapprehends the nature of satire as *comic discourse*; moreover, it provides an opening for the all-too-common argument that satire fails completely to be effective as a change agent.

I argue for conceptualizing satire as a form of aesthetic communication *supplementing* political discourse with its mode of comic discourse. It must be admitted, however, that understanding satire's function in the public sphere is not clear-cut. Though Amber Day calls her satiric examples "instances of political discourse," her project employs multiple theoretical angles—performance studies, communication studies, and literary studies as well as media studies—and so she stands closer to humor studies privileging aesthetics rather than politics. Day underscores the hybrid nature of the comic cultural artifacts being discussed so that a "clear separation between safely detached satire and real political life is often not . . . neatly identifiable [while] there is plenty of discursive exchange that takes place in the form of the seemingly 'irrational'—in the registers of parody, satire, fiction, and nonsense."[21] My concept of the *comic public sphere* encompasses these claims by theorizing its parodic relationship to the public sphere. I am not claiming that media studies analyses are without their virtues. In fact, I would agree that what counts as political engagement has been profoundly altered by a variety of new cultural artifacts rated as laughter provoking. Rather, I am asking what might be learned about such cultural artifacts, many accessed primarily on television, when examined from another theoretical angle.

The prominence of the news format for satiric purposes has been maintained and enhanced by an alumnus of *The Daily Show with Jon Stewart*, John Oliver, and his mock news magazine show *Last Week Tonight with John Oliver* (2014–present). Oliver uses most of his weekly half hour to dive deep into a single civic or social issue in a fashion that apparently often fits easily into the concept of satiractivism. As I argue, specific episodes of *Last Week Tonight* mark an explicit turn toward satiractivism, a turn that can also readily be seen in another relatively new and popular satiric show, *Full Frontal with Samantha Bee* (2016–present).[22] Both shows exhibit a distinct penchant for directly encouraging citizens to act in the public sphere. Thus, not only does satire project a thriving aesthetic as well as power a commercial enterprise, not only has it of late asserted itself as a notable force within the public sphere, but some satiric efforts have ratcheted up public sphere involvement with a turn toward an overt activism, a turn that threatens to blur my claim of a basic distinction from satire's function as comic political speech, as supplement to serious political speech.

This turn has altered what might be expected from contemporary satire, not only transforming at least sections of it to a laudatory effort to engage citizens in the ongoing conversation that constitutes a living democratic society, but also demanding participation in civic affairs to alter public policy on specific issues—insisting, in effect, that citizens exercise their most basic rights of free speech and access to the ballot box. Thus satire as comic political speech now apparently metamorphoses into political speech routinely in its satiractivist strain. More precisely, satire as a kind of comic activism presents itself as a rhetorical monster, part public sphere essay and part comic public sphere jokes and insults. Television shows like *Last Week Tonight* and *Full Frontal* illustrate the particular focus this study takes, zeroing in on satire that plays with news as media format and narrative form. This satiric playfulness upholds via comic means the ideal of communicative rationality the public sphere represents and so explicitly counters what might be called *the anti-public sphere* represented by fake news outlets like the Drudge Report, Breitbart, and Infowars. This study has as one of its goals the investigation of satiractivism's place in the contemporary moment of proliferating satire in order to understand how it helps to fuel the discursive dynamic in the digital age between the comic public sphere and the public sphere that intends to counter the anti-public sphere.

Satire has the baseline status of a particular comic mode functioning as comic political speech—that is, as a particular kind of speech act that supplements the public sphere with the possibility of effecting *metanoia*, a change of mind in its audience. Satire operates as a comic public sphere because any specific instance of satire has an embedded intent to promote discussion and debate and thus encourage the possibility of civic reform.[23] While that definition could be tabulated as transcendental, two historical overviews of satire indicate a crucial pivot that stresses the private and conservative side of satire that appears in Western classical and medieval and neoclassical satire, before the Enlightenment. However, overlapping the conservatism of neoclassical satire in the eighteenth century is the beginning of the public sphere idea of inquiry into public affairs that can include all citizens.[24] Thus satire as the sign of the comic public sphere appears as more modern and postmodern than otherwise. My broad formulation, then, should be revised: satire since the Enlightenment, as part of the project of modernity, functions most clearly as the sign of the comic public sphere, even in postmodern forms.

Specific topics important to any investigation of satire are explored in particular. One has been suggested already: the efficacy of satire. A bastion of mockery, satire has been mocked for having no discernible effect within the body politic or social. A second issue links author intention and the audience for satire. It would seem that, for satire, authorial intention often must give way to audience interpretation: a reader could say that a text might have been intended as a satire, or simply can be read as such regardless of any intention by the author.

The context of the Trump administration, some might say, calls for harsh forms of satire: the body politic under Trump's leadership has become so morally corrupt that blistering satire often feels required. When Juvenal about 110 CE wrote that "it is difficult not to write satire," he apparently felt that living in a social environment of mendacity and vulgarity, who could resist exposing its folly in the most obvious genre available, satire? Nearly twenty centuries later, the United States finds itself in conditions similar to Rome, replete with mendacity and vulgarity and satire. A third theme asks, therefore, when is satire so caustic that it should be classified as screed or rant powered by the low invective David Denby calls *snark*—that is, when does the ridicule and comic insults endemic to the comic public sphere devolve into the mere snarkiness of the anti-public sphere?[25]

Denby's analysis produces doubts about Juvenal as a satirist; the Roman writer's poems were largely motivated by revenge against individual butts: lampoons, not satires. Denby thus invokes Samuel Johnson's definitions of satire and lampoon in his *Dictionary*. Satire is a "poem in which wickedness or folly is censured," and "proper satire" should be distinguished from a lampoon, "which is aimed at a particular person." Moreover, a lampoon is a "personal satire; abuse; censure written not to reform but to vex."[26] Jonathan Swift put it this way: "There are two ends that men propose in writing satire, one of them less noble than the other, as regarding nothing further than personal satisfaction, and the pleasure of the writer; but without any view toward personal malice [i.e., lampoon]; the other [satire proper] is a public spirit, prompting men of genius and virtue to mend the world as far as they are able. And as both these ends are innocent, so the latter is highly commendable."[27] *Snark* is slang for the low invective that powers mere lampoons. In the analysis I develop, *snark* understood as the degenerate invective of mere lampoon signals the presence of the anti-public sphere, while proper satire in service to civic virtue indicates the comic public sphere. One of the goals of *Satire as the Comic Public Sphere* is an exploration of how to distinguish the ridicule that animates both discursive spheres and so distinguish satire from screeds and rants.

The arc of the argument for *Satire as the Comic Public Sphere* begins with "Defining Satire," which situates satire as one of the oldest aesthetic modes having the potential for provoking laughter. This first chapter offers a definition meant to provide a durable framework for understanding satire at its most basic level and thus to aid scholarly exploration of satire in any cultural environment at any historical moment; it also offers the idea of *The Comic*, the book's most radical theoretical idea: all laughter-provoking cultural artifacts constitute a separate discursive realm. In addition, this chapter advances the theory of *a–musement*, or the satire two-step—that is, satire rhetorically asks its audience to muse on or ponder the topic presented after laughing. Finally, the chapter broaches the problem of ridicule being used for civic reform.

The second chapter, "The Public Sphere," acknowledges the Enlightenment as the major pivot in a historical account of satire. Though "Defining Satire" presents a definition meant to aid in explorations of satire at any historical moment and in all cultures, the rise of the public sphere in specific European countries profoundly alters the role satire might play in the civic life of modern nations. This pivot becomes significantly visible in the assertion—for example, in Samuel Johnson's definition—that satire explicitly intends reform, whether social or political, an intention mostly confined to private behavior before the ascendancy of Enlightenment ideals. Thus my basic claim that satire signifies the comic public sphere, strictly speaking, emphasizes satire since the Enlightenment.

"The Public Sphere" provides historical context for understanding satire today as comic public sphere within a postmodern aesthetic, with two goals: first, that postmodernity does not erect a barrier to satire today, as some have argued. Embedded in that goal is a second, showing the ground of that claim, namely, that postmodernity constitutes a phase of what Habermas calls "the project of modernity" first expressed by Enlightenment thinkers.[28] Understanding the Enlightenment as the birth of modernity and understanding postmodernity as a later phase shows that, while satire displayed a specific negative quality at the height of early postmodernity, its intent to participate comically in the public sphere was never in doubt. Postmodernity, then, appears not as a rejection of Enlightenment ideals but as a profound modification, a relationship that Richard Bernstein presents with the metaphor *constellation* to capture the paradox of optimism and skepticism in the resulting amalgamation of principles. This chapter presents in brief what I take to be the most important historical and philosophical background for contemporary satire: postmodernity's relation to the Enlightenment, a relation that, in addition to creating a constellation of values for the contemporary cultural scene, enables the comic public sphere with satire as its sign.[29]

The next chapter, "Truthiness Satire and the Comic Public Sphere" highlights Steven Weisenburger's idea of generative and degenerative satire while tying it to the claim that within postmodern satire—even in its more caustic examples that threaten to cancel itself—proper satire still survives, pushing back against the argument that postmodernity precludes satire. According to Jonathan Greenberg, the opposite is true: postmodernists revive satire as a dominant literary phenomenon, though the term *black humor* is often used rather than *satire*.[30]

The key to that pushback for an important slice of contemporary satire is Stephen Colbert's neologism *truthiness*. The public sphere and satire depend upon news narratives and the journalistic imperative to report events as accurately as possible: *public sphere* names a discursive site for the conversation that ideally furthers democracy via rational communication. Postmodernity may have sapped the power of Truth as a transcendental concept, but accuracy in the news still greatly matters for the conversation of the public sphere. Thus, what I call *truthiness satire* does not mock postmodernity's skepticism toward transcendental truth; instead, truthiness satire mocks those who misapprehend that skepticism for a moral relativism in which anything goes, for an environment in which facts do not matter against the gut feeling of mere opinion.[31] In its reverse discourse form, truthiness satire operates as emblematic comic supplement to the postmodern public sphere; it appears to accept the validity of opinion over fact when its purpose insinuates exactly the opposite: to bolster the pursuit of accuracy in the news and in public sphere discourse. Truthiness satire as a comic maneuver often uncovers the stake in today's public conversation about civic issues: the informed citizen functioning as the lifeblood of a vibrant democracy.

That stake is precisely why in this study I have limited the examples examined to comic artifacts that play with the news. The informed citizen depends upon accurate news narratives to understand civic issues of the moment and the various points of view that debate on them necessarily generates. Truthiness, the degraded and cynical form of a postmodern skepticism about the validity of metanarratives, targets journalistic accuracy as irrelevant and threatens the very existence of the informed citizen.

The role of satire in the contest of truth claims and facts (public sphere) versus truthiness (anti-public sphere) defines the core object of my analysis. That clash invokes the Enlightenment's ideals of rationality and puts the spotlight on news narratives as the (post)modern and mass means of making truth claims in the service of the public sphere. Linking truthiness to the anti-public sphere perhaps registers as obvious enough. Understanding that truthiness satire in a reverse discourse dynamic has become a tactic of some postmodern satire perhaps sounds not so obvious. Within that dynamic, the through-the-looking-glass effect of truthiness becomes a clear satiric target.

My bricoleur use of Jean Baudrillard's regime of simulacra, Geoffrey Baym's discursive integration, and Steven Weisenburger's degenerative satire, along with Alan Kirby's notion of digimodernism, provides context for how truthiness satire demonstrates the embeddedness of the comic public sphere within the public sphere during the current cultural moment of Donald Trump's presidency, while also making visible its discursive antagonist, the anti-public sphere. The theoretical context does not describe all satiric efforts in that cultural moment, only those that have as their basic mode of operation a playfulness with news narratives and news formats.

Having emphasized theoretical and historical background in Part One, *Satire as the Comic Public Sphere* in Part Two examines in more detail specific examples of contemporary satire. "Satire and Speech Act Theory" begins the second half of the book by suggesting how satire fits into J. L. Austin's theory about speech acts before moving on to satiric artifacts playing with the news to highlight instances of what I take to be the most consequential satire of the day in the next two chapters, "Satire as Speech Act, Part One" and "Satire as Speech Act, Part Two."[32] Austin's concepts of *locutionary*, *illocutionary*, and *perlocutionary* speech acts sort contemporary examples of satire in a postmodern condition, with its potential for a truthiness mash-up of news reporting, into three categories that range across a spectrum—from news reporting resembling satire (locutionary) to satire resembling political speech (illocutionary) and even to satire resembling political action—that is, satiractivism (quasi-perlocutionary).[33]

In the next chapter, "The Limits of Satiric Ridicule," I am explicitly concerned with the aesthetics of the comic critique embedded in satire. Thus the question of satire being too caustic arises. When does satire, as its playfulness diminishes and its aggressiveness accumulates, cross a stylistic border and morph into mere rants or screeds, the low lampooning invective of snark? This chapter acknowledges that satire's playful insults have a perennial penchant to become the insults of mere snark. Thus the ethical dilemma for satire: Does its brand of critique, its form of speech replete with mockery and ridicule, interfere with the everyday mutual understanding necessary in the public sphere? The next chapter, "Satiric Intent and Audience Uptake," explores the issue of audience and intention by examining how speech acts by President Trump have been interpreted in the public sphere. Finally, "Find the Punchline" offers conclusions.

Satire as the Comic Public Sphere traces frontiers—not only between comic public sphere and public sphere, between satires and screeds (the limits of comic license), between satire and satiractivism, but also among different kinds of laughter and different phases of postmodernity—in order to acknowledge nuance in its attempts at granular analysis of specific examples. In probing the limits of concepts and ideas, this study demonstrates its own debt to Lyotard's description of postmodern knowledge making.

In the account of contemporary satire offered here, *truthiness* signifies the effects of discursive integration and a regime of simulacra that contribute to the postmodern aesthetic within which many contemporary satirists operate. Satire today has many specific targets, but its most significant comic butt must be the potential for a truthiness effect arising from misunderstanding the postmodern condition. *Truthiness satire*, then, ridicules even as it employs some effects of postmodernity, its discursive integration and regime of simulacra, to fashion a comic *parrhēsia* meant to supplement the debate and discussion of the public sphere.

A word about what this study is not: it does not move outside the realm of American culture in its specific examples, though I intend the definition of satire offered in the first chapter to be theoretically useful elsewhere and in other historical moments. Nor does *Satire as the Comic Public Sphere* pretend to be describing the totality of what constitutes the public sphere in the United States or all the satire that might belong in the comic public sphere. Rather, the primary goal centers on demonstrating how the postmodern aesthetic of truthiness satire operates within the dynamic between the two discursive spheres. The significance of truthiness satire resides not in its being the predominant kind of satire in the current cultural moment inflected by President Trump's administration, but in the way its postmodern aesthetic of playing with the news enables a comic critique of truthiness in that cultural moment. That critique makes truthiness satire the most ambitious and potentially consequential kind of satire today.

Finally, some words about words: *laughable* and *a–musement*. The peculiar orthography of *a–musement* is my way to defamiliarize the usual meaning of *amusement* as simply signifying pleasure: muse on the implicit thought after laughing at the comic presentation. *Laughable*, like *funny*, has two connotations, with one taking precedence in most usages. *Laughable* most often is taken to indicate not just something risible, worthy of laughter, but merely ridiculous, as though that is the only kind of laughter possible, but what of an amiable laughter signaling camaraderie? Are not cultural artifacts built to induce laughter *laughable* in nuanced ways? Similarly, *funny* most often is taken to indicate something risible but with the idea of pleasure, of fun, uppermost. However, *funny* also indicates something peculiar, as in *what's that funny smell?* The point here is that *The Comic*, signifying a discernible discursive realm, encompasses all these connotations. The Domain of the Laughable or the Domain of the Risible names The Comic. *Laughable* means ridiculous, but also laughter provoking or laughter inducing. As Stephen Halliwell demonstrates, even the Greeks had lots of discussion about other types of *to geloion*, the laughable, with adjectives added: e.g., mild, cheerful, good-natured, self-deprecating.[34]

One more point on this topic: Johnny Carson once said, "I just don't feel Johnny Carson should become a social commentator.... If you're a comedian, your job is to make people laugh. You cannot be both serious and funny."[35] Colbert and Stewart and Bee and Oliver are routinely called *comedians* or *late-night comedians*, not *satirists*. Carson was right in that not all comedians are satirists, though I venture to say that most satirists think of themselves as comedians too, in the sense that they have entertainment as one of their goals. However, he is wrong about being both serious and funny, which might be the bumper-sticker definition of a satirist. Curiously, commentators often seem to go out of their way to not use *satire* or *satirists*. Thus "political humorists" often serves as a tag for *satirists*, while phrasing like "opinionated comedy" or "a form of serious comedy" denotes *satire*. Often, Carson's term subsumes both: "Maher, of course, realizes that his *role as a comedian* on an uncensored public stage gives him special license and privilege to ridicule and satirize the powerful."[36] Jon Stewart at the "Rally to Restore Sanity" or Stephen Colbert in character testifying at a congressional hearing—these public performances are executed, we are told, by "comedic actors," not satiric actors.[37] Although these examples suggest that *satire* and *satirist* apparently are the Rodney Dangerfield of basic terms to describe certain comic artifacts—*they can't get no respect*—I use them as the predominant labels in what follows.

PART I

Satire and the Public Sphere

Satire ... is meant to make us scratch our heads, think, do a double-take, and then think again.
—Maajid Nawaz

Defining Satire

1.

At the most general level, satire should be defined as a comic mode lodged within a discourse called *The Comic*. In that discourse, all comic artifacts function as comic speech acts, as a subset of J. L. Austin's claim that fiction is parasitic speech, not full normal speech, with the usual rules of reference suspended, a point I will explore later. In order to provide a more elaborate definition of satire, its poetics, and its operation within the public sphere of a body politic, I first theorize its distinctiveness among all cultural artifacts that cause or intend comic laughter within the discourse of The Comic.

The Idea of The Comic

As an initial way into understanding the relationship between comic artifacts and civil society, consider this claim advanced by Sarah Bishop as part of her discussion of *The Colbert Report*: "We must set aside the view of humor as innocent relief and instead take up an examination of the ways humor's ability may exceed that of serious communications, providing access into previously off-limits contexts for the sake of deliberation, advocacy, and exchange."[1]

Bishop questions *humor* signifying only "innocent relief," a relief innocent in that it allows people to be less than serious. Bishop thus implies that *humor* should signify two forms of comic artifacts, neither the same as Freudian *witz*, tendentious or aggressive utterances involving smut or obscenity: the less-than-serious (innocent) and the more-or-less serious, the latter of which possesses an ability to access serious discourse ("off-limits contexts"). This wish for a doubled referent for *humor* arises from a confusion with fundamental terms to describe comic artifacts, though Bishop correctly insists on the need to sort comic artifacts into basic categories. Revising her wish for a doubled referent, I would stipulate instead that *humor* signifies the more light-hearted and whimsical and mostly entertaining side of all instances of comic artifacts. That formulation will allow me to claim that *satire* signifies those instances of comic artifacts that can "exceed . . . serious communications . . . for the sake of deliberation, advocacy, and exchange," that is, for the sake of the comic public sphere, for surely Bishop's triad of "deliberation, advocacy, and exchange" invokes Jürgen Habermas's public sphere. Satire as the sign of the comic public sphere clearly moves beyond the innocence of simple entertainment as well as the pleasure of Freudian psychic relief from internal censorship.

Bishop's confusion is unfortunately endemic in discussions about comic laughter and comic artifacts, especially when commentators want an umbrella term that will cover the entire field of investigation. *Humor* no doubt functions as the number one of the two favorite words for this umbrella function, *comedy* being the other. However, both terms have long histories in which they were used much more narrowly: the first has meanings rooted in medieval medical theory; the second referred, from Western classical antiquity to at least the Renaissance, only to a specific genre: dramas performed on stage. Thus neither usefully covers all examples of cultural artifacts designed to make people laugh. So I will use *The Comic* as my umbrella term.[2]

The Comic refers to a general discourse of and about the discursive domain of *the laughable*—that is, the domain of comic artifacts and comic laughter. (I am using "laughable" in this most general way to signify anything that induces or generates laughter of all kinds, not simply derisory.) Neither a discipline nor a science, The Comic as a discourse theoretically encompasses not just the comic artifacts of fine arts, literature, and folklore but also a manifold of everyday behaviors—such as banter, teasing, joking relationships—in the service of producing a specific response: comic laughter. The art of producing comic laughter has many modalities that begin in the street, the home, and the workplace and then reach toward profound and enduring examples in various artistic media. The Comic encompasses cultural artifacts both textual and performative—that is, writing of all sorts designated as comic—as well as comic practices without texts—for example, slapstick pratfalls or practical jokes: this aspect encompasses discourse *of* The Comic. In addition, The Comic contains the set of theoretical statements in the Western tradition, starting with Plato and Aristotle, as well as from other traditions, that explore the nature of comic laughter as well as comment on and analyze the myriad examples of comic artifacts: this aspect encompasses discourse *about* The Comic. The Comic thus has two aspects. One aspect includes a set of practices that may be everyday informal or may instead be artistically formal in conception and execution, in either case generating comic artifacts. These practices are complemented by a theoretical aspect, one that can be logically separated from commentary about art in general or aesthetics. Moreover, The Comic—discourse creating and denoting what the ancient Greeks called *to geloion*, the domain of the laughable—should be understood as part of an even larger discourse about human nature.[3]

All cultural artifacts within The Comic fall into two large classes: *the ridiculous* and *the ludicrous*. The ridiculous and the ludicrous represent the poles of comic laughter understood as affect. The former produces a comic laughter designed with the potential to improve its object; the latter produces a comic laughter designed to tolerate and even appreciate the object as is. *The ridiculous* laughs at its object, indicates emotional distance and potential antagonism. This class of artifacts often employs satire for topics concerned with civic issues and social institutions. *The ludicrous* laughs with its object, indicates emotional proximity with a measure of tolerance and sympathy. *The ludicrous* often signifies what one means when saying *what a character* in referring to an individual, and of course humorous eccentricities remain handy for writers creating comic characters. Specific comic artifacts should be understood as usually displaying a mix of the ludicrous and the ridiculous; specific comic artifacts that are purely ludicrous or purely ridiculous would be rare in this scheme of two primary classes of The Comic.

Within the broad discursive domain of The Comic, satire occupies a particular neighborhood. I take it as axiomatic that all comic artifacts play with social codes. Sometimes that play intends only entertainment, as in the nonsense, "did gyre and gimbal in the wabes," or when staging a slapstick pie fight in a silent two-reeler of Charlie Chaplin. An audience knows intuitively that people do not talk like the speaker in Lewis Carroll's "The Jabberwocky," just as one knows that good manners and proper decorum demand one should not throw food at other people. This primary knowledge, built-in via childhood socialization, is what Umberto Eco has in mind when he implies that The Comic always employs social codes surreptitiously.[4] Notably, nonsense rhymes and pie fights have minimal subversive intent against those codes. All comic artifacts with their inherent playfulness have a potential for critique or even subversion, but often this destabilizing force remains inactive or at a low level of social disturbance because mere entertainment remains the goal: humor. Nevertheless, the comic playfulness with these social codes sometimes foregrounds values or behaviors to remind the society (community, social body) of its faults, follies, vices, and absurdities. In those instances, the potential for comic critique (and possibly subversion) becomes activated. *Satire* names those comic artifacts that actualize the potential and distill it within a laughter-provoking presentation. Thus *satire* names a mode of comic speech associated with the ridiculous, while humor signifies a mode associated with the ludicrous. Bishop reaches for the word *satire* to name what comic artifacts do when they supplement serious communication—that is, when they parody the public sphere by creating a comic public sphere.

Two Paradoxical Structures

Satire as a particular *mode* within The Comic cuts across genres rather than existing as a form embedded in a literary history. This move has a historical warrant because evidence suggests that *satire* named a proper genre only for the Romans, who gave the Western comic tradition many classic examples, while also indicating a catch-all quality—a poetic and prose medley—with the phrase *lanx satura*, a mixed dish of fruits and nuts.[5] Given how broadcast, cablecast, and online outlets now serve up news, satire as mock news, politics, and entertainment as a generic mélange, one could still illustrate satiric presentations of that mélange using the image of a mixed dish. This mixed or mashed-up quality correlates with a basic assumption of scholars in several disciplines investigating satire in all media and with various methodologies: thinking of satire as simply a literary genre has outlived whatever usefulness it might have once had.[6] Thus satire should be understood as a particular kind of speech act that signals a particular kind of comic attitude.

Satire as a particular kind of comic speech act manifests two structuring paradoxes. First is its dual nature of being both serious and nonserious speech, usually referencing actual events, issues, and people but with comic techniques. This duality enables satire's potential for real-world impact well beyond other forms of comic artifacts, despite the skepticism of the postmodern condition. Second is satire's methodological paradox: committed ethically to promoting the process of social change, yet also committed comically to using the symbolic violence of ridicule and artful insult. Thus the enterprise of producing satire always remains ethically fraught, as the furor over Michelle Wolf's comic routine at the 2018 White House Correspondents' Dinner demonstrates, an event to be examined later. Moreover, the postmodern condition exacerbates the dilemma of how to construct an ethical ridicule.[7] This dilemma has concerned Western thought for centuries, and postmodernity's apparent lack of centering norms or standard values for making comic judgments inevitably complicates the contemporary production and reception of satire. Satire's paradoxical nature as a comic (nonserious) speech act that nevertheless also registers as serious has an analogy in the way that light behaves in a quantum state, as both wave and particle. Satire can be counted as both serious and nonserious speech, a paradox that causes confusion about how to judge the efficacy of satire. That confusion stands out as a particularly notable problem when examining examples of satiractivism, a topic to be explored later.

Within the contemporary cultural scene, a significant segment of its satire resists, even as it resides in, a postmodern condition, a segment mixing irony and earnestness to create a hybrid structure of affect. This structure retains the postmodern problematic of unstable representation but supplements it with an undaunted belief in creative rescripting. The process establishes a strategy of comic *parrhēsia* substituting localized narratives and truths for socially or philosophically outdated metanarratives and transcendental truths: *truthiness satire*. Stephen Colbert originally coined "truthiness" as a mocking reference to the discourse of divisive partisanship that signifies an anti-public sphere. Truthiness satire acknowledges the corrosive impact of fake news and conspiracy theories on the public sphere while at the same time insisting on its own civic yet comic engagement. Truthiness satire has the potential to function as a reverse discourse, rescripting anti-public sphere discourse into comic public sphere discourse.[8]

The Elements of Satire

A specific kind of comic speech act structured by two paradoxes—these qualities might define satire most succinctly. To further elaborate a definition, I borrow and revise a model from George Test, who has suggested that satire always has four elements: play, judgment, aggression, laughter.[9] Examining these elements will uncover how the paradoxes that structure satire operate and provide more details about what satire as comic speech act does and does not entail.

In my revision of Test's definition, *play* must be logically the first element in conceptualizing satire as a comic speech act. Theoretically, a cue for playfulness always exists for comic artifacts, something within a text regardless of the medium or something that frames the speech or event or behavior to signal the playful quality separating comic speech from earnest, serious speech. Recognizing cues does not always happen in a straightforward manner, particularly with informal instances of The Comic, such as bantering and teasing, when the playfulness of comic speech can emerge and then disappear multiple times in quick succession in the course of everyday conversation, as an application of discourse analysis methodology would reveal. Because an individual cannot always easily discern the play aspect inherent in comic speech, audience members can find themselves asking, *Are you kidding?*—or an interlocutor may take a joking statement as earnest and respond earnestly. Worse: discerning the play frame or play quality does not guarantee that an interlocutor or an audience (or a reader) will accept the play element. Worse still: like other forms of mock aggression, bantering or teasing can all too easily lose its play aspect and transform from comic insults into snarky insults in an effort simply to bully or degrade the butt.

Judgment must be next, for that element most clearly marks satire's connection to the public sphere and distinguishes it from other examples of The Comic. I change *judgment* to *critique* to clarify the nature of this element and in order to harness some of the philosophical meaning of *critique* as a negative move in a language game that always nevertheless implies affirmation. Given that *play* must be the first condition for satire, insisting on *critique* next returns to the first of satire's structuring paradoxes: its quantum state of being both serious and nonserious. Along with play, an earnest aspect to satire always exists in that it involves itself with social and political issues of the moment. Another way to say it: in the midst of the laughter-inducing, playful elements of satire, an explicit Public Service Announcement (PSA) moment frequently exists (a rhetorician would call the moment a *paralipsis*) that moves the comic quality of the example from the merely entertaining or the merely snarky to the satirically *a–musing*—that is, moves from thoughtless laughter to thinking about, or musing on, the embedded civic issues. Even if no explicit paralipsis exists, satire as critique creates its distinctive *a–musement*, which Maajid Nawaz describes in the epigraph to part 1, a process that warrants referring to satire as the sign of a comic public sphere.

The third element is *aggression*, what in classic terms scholars of satire usually call *ridicule* and/or *mockery*: satirists always build mockery and ridicule into their satire as a comic mode of communication. Test starts his analysis with this element, suggesting its importance for him. In his view, saying that satire constitutes "an attack is probably the least debatable claim that one can make about it."[10] Plato probably had this quality in mind when he spoke of the "playful malice" of laughter, and it raises an important issue: Can there be ethical ridicule?[11]

Even if one agrees with Lord Shaftesbury's famous 1709 defense of raillery and ridicule, this ethical dilemma exists, for there always remains an irreducible quality of unruliness to comic speech and its formal artifacts, the *paidia*, or deep play, noted by Roger Caillois.[12] Thus the ethics of satire remains fraught, disclosing the second structuring paradox. The common assertion that *comedy* and *humor* are inherently subversive glosses the capacity of comic speech to mock and comically denigrate, or stated more positively, its potential for comic critique, but not every comic artifact always employs that capacity. Moreover, despite popular consensus that proper satire always punches up—that is, its comic *parrhēsia* always speaks its truth to power—satire can also serve power and the status quo.[13]

Rolling together *play*, *critique*, and *aggression* as necessary conditions for the presence of satire demands a look at implications before focusing on the final element, *laughter*. Notable first: play in an ethological sense as a most basic behavior of birds and mammals becomes tied to human rituals and games of ritual insult, demonstrated in Robert Elliott's examination of preliterary forms of satire.[14] Trying to understand the basic nature of satire necessitates acknowledging its analogy to mock aggressive displays in animals, acknowledging that satire presents a symbolic form of ritualized aggression. Such behavior has been identified as the root of ancient Greek *kōmōdia* in its oldest form, as the plays of Aristophanes demonstrate. Moreover, the existence today of ritual clowns in Native American and Polynesian societies testifies to the profound nature of ritualized forms of comic aggression as well as their persistence. Within the discursive domain of The Comic, these practices and art forms constitute with satire a family of comic artifacts.[15]

Like ritual clowns, satirists operate as privileged speakers within a body politic, licensed to say what society otherwise represses or obscures.[16] Obscenities together with insults are permitted; in theory, this license to abuse means that it is forbidden to forbid certain forms of speech, an attitude that clearly has animated the French periodical *Charlie Hebdo*. For traditional societies ancient and contemporary, the ritual form licenses such a carnivalesque, anything-goes attitude. For modern societies, rhetorical and literary conventions have evolved to signify, at least in part, that license, conventions meant to conjure an imagined print or digital community sharing specific values that provide the metric for the comic ridicule. That metric in effect identifies comic butts by naming perceived wrongs—follies, foibles, vices—within the community. The ridicule directed at the comic butts ostensibly carries an intent to reform an individual or even heal the body politic, which gives rise to medical metaphors for satire: a caustic applied to the body politic. Satire evokes other specialized language besides medical metaphors. In keeping with the aggressive nature of satire, violent metaphors are used too. Thus the satirist aims ridiculing shafts or arrows at the butt, evoking the primary meaning of *butt* as an archery target, or the satirist tongue-lashes the body politic, as though summary punishment with cat-o'-nine tails on a man-of-war ship provides the appropriate analogy.

Given the above commentary, one might summarize by saying that *satire presents a symbolic mock aggression designed to cure or at least mitigate the ills of society via comic techniques*, but closer to the mark would be to claim that *satire's power lies in its rhetorical potential to change minds, to effect metanoia via its a–musement*. This rhetorical potential corresponds with what Dustin Griffin calls the "open-ended" design of many satires, a design "to discover, to explore, to survey, to attempt to clarify."[17] Moreover, satire has the capacity to move an audience from resting in the comic public sphere to acting in the public sphere proper, digital or otherwise—that is, an instance of satire *might* move an audience from enjoying its aesthetics to engaging in political activism. That action can take different forms. Amber Day has argued that satiric documentary films "have successfully nurtured the creation of oppositional political communities, or counterpublics, which are anchored by the films but then sustained by books, websites, interviews, and other media appearances," which function as "nodes . . . affecting the direction of wider public debate."[18] Thus a film's satiric critique might inspire participation in a particular kind of political community, an outcome any traditional satire might accomplish with its potential for metanoia, but Day's insight is that the counterpublic in the context of contemporary multipronged marketing can be sustained in many media formats, providing momentum as many individuals decide to become actively involved. Here the change of mind is not about switching one's position on a civic issue for another, the radical example of metanoia, or even altering one's position, but rather deciding to act on values or principles already held. *Satiractivism* names those instances of satire that go beyond the implicit exhortation to experience metanoia within the poetics of the comic public sphere and make an explicit call to direct action in the public sphere.

Specific comic artifacts should be understood as usually displaying a mix of the ludicrous and the ridiculous. For many creators of comic material, the question often becomes how can the ludicrous serve the goal of entertainment. For satirists, the perennial ethical problem becomes how to deliver ridicule with the right amount of laughter-provoking force, for they always risk the danger of allowing the comic anger of satire to become a mere rant or screed, or even to express the degenerate invective of the anti-public sphere—snark, in David Denby's analysis. At one end of a spectrum of ridicule, one finds satires that register bitterness and absurdity, dark satires employing black humor. At the other end, one discovers examples of satire the ridicule of which is mild, tempered by ludicrous humor that might even include whimsy or the purer silliness of slapstick. Joseph Addison and Richard Steele explicitly demanded such toned-down satire as far back as 1710: satirists should "rail agreeably," in their view. Their particular aesthetic for satire enjoyed a great vogue through the eighteenth and well into the nineteenth century, spawning locutions such as "sweet sarcasm" as descriptors for the tone of a supposedly friendly satire. However, even examples of such satire must have a comic butt, a target for ridicule however humorously mild, in order to be satire.[19]

As a demonstration of how the idea of agreeable raillery might operate in contemporary satire, consider the sketch by Keegan-Michael Key and Jordan Peele entitled "I Said Bitch." Daryl (Key) and Craig (Peele) are middle-class married men who clearly act stereotypically hen-pecked despite Craig's claiming, "I am the man of the house." The initial scenario begins as Daryl and his wife arrive at the home of Craig and his wife. As the hostess takes her counterpart on a tour of the house, Daryl apologizes to Craig for being late, blaming his wife. Recounting his admonishment for her egregious dallying, he claims to have addressed his wife as "bitch." (Performed as "biiitch.") Clearly impressed yet doubtful about Daryl's display of black masculinity encoded in "bitch," Craig questions him about using the word and makes him reaffirm it more than once. Each time Daryl says the word, both men look around to be sure that the wives cannot hear, comically undercutting the reason Daryl tells the story: to assert that he is the man in charge at home.

The sketch then proceeds by unfolding a variety of scenes, each one placing the men farther away physically from the wives, as they exchange their tales of being the man of the house. The comic quality of the sketch mainly resides in the greater distance from the wives dramatized in each successive scene—basement, tree in the front yard, nearby field with no houses visible, outer space—that nevertheless does not prevent the men looking around to see if the wives can hear each time one of them utters "bitch." In the scenes in the basement and in the field, the wives' presence actually does interrupt the exchange of putative manly control, the first time when they barge into the basement, the second time when Daryl's phone rings and he tells his wife that Craig is "giving him the neighborhood tour." The escalating exaggeration of the men's fear, dramatized by their repeatedly scouting for the whereabouts of the wives, reaches its climax when Craig exits a space capsule for a space walk before he utters "bitch" one last time. Each instance when the men assert that they have "laid it out" while looking directly into the eyes of their wives, each body gesture and voice inflection say otherwise. The men appear hilariously and immoderately feeble and foolish as they try to convince each other—and themselves—that they rule the domestic roost.[20]

While surely laughter at the characters' increasingly silly behaviors happens, the exaggerated distancing from the wives gives the sketch a whimsicality and absurdity more ludicrous and humorous than ridiculous and satiric. Nevertheless, satiric butts can clearly be discerned as the middle-class men code-switch their speech, the pivot being "bitch," and yet conspicuously fail to perform a stereotypical black masculinity. The sketch comically questions such versions of masculinity as it insinuates the role of class in the failure, creating an example of post-soul satire that examines what it means to be black (or "blackish") in the era of President Obama.[21] The sketch displays the symbolic aggression of satire in its mockery of stereotypical black masculinity, but its comic tone relies on a large admixture of light-hearted humor—"sweet sarcasm"—to create a twenty-first-century instance of satirists railing, or ridiculing—agreeably.

The Role of Comic Laughter

The last of Test's elements, *laughter*, requires the biggest modification. *Play* must be understood as entailing cues about playfulness, *critique* must reference social or political issues germane to the society, *aggression* must be the mock aggression of comic ridicule, and *laughter* must be specified as *comic laughter* to distinguish it from pathological forms.[22] However, the truly complicated part of adding laughter to the list of necessary conditions for satire happens because *comic laughter* implies the audience of a comic performance or the reader of printed comic material, and theorizing about audiences for comic artifacts is notoriously messy and inconclusive.[23]

The Comic understood as the domain of the laughable implies an aesthetic. To declare something laughter-provoking implies that someone made an aesthetic judgment, which simply but insistently states in another way the crucial nature of an audience or a reader for any sort of comic artifact. Without that aesthetic judgment, a comic quality cannot be discerned. For Sigmund Freud, the joke teller, the missing butt of the joke, and the third person who hears the joke exist in an affective dynamic; for rhetorical theory, the classical formula triangulates the rhetor, the message, and the audience. However, rhetorical and communications theory now present a more sophisticated idea of how the audience and the speaker interact in an exchange; for example, James Carey's argument that communication is a cultural phenomenon concerned with symbolic interaction through speech, rather than simply the transmission of information, implies an active role for the audience.[24] Regardless of differences in these models, comic laughter from an audience always constitutes an act of evaluation.[25]

However, theorizing about the audience for a comic artifact that insists on vocal laughter, as Test does, presents special problems. First of all, the issue of a joke not understood or the comic irony not discerned complicates analysis. Audience members can be routinely sorted in this manner, so treating *audience* or *readers* as the label for a monolithic entity always mistakes the process. Second, one might find a joke or comic artifact funny ha-ha and entertaining or even a–musing—and yet still not laugh. Moreover, some examples of comic artifacts exhibit a premise so grim or acerbic or cynical that no laughing out loud happens, yet the audience *gets* the premise of the comic artifact, or in Austin's terms, has "a proper uptake." Who laughs out loud at Jonathan Swift's "A Modest Proposal" or the ending of either Thomas Pynchon's *The Crying of Lot 49* or Stanley Kubrick's *Dr. Strangelove*?[26] More recent similar examples are easily found. A 2018 movie, *Anon* (as in *anonymous*) satirically presents the dystopic effects of technology, yet only one clearly comic scene exists. *Anon* might remind audience members of the series *Black Mirror* (2011–present), which also satirically presents the dystopic effects of technology, though its episodes vary widely in their comic moments (e.g., "Hated in the Nation" versus "Nosedive"). Theoretically, *Black Mirror* episodes and *Anon* could be tagged satiric because they present trenchant critiques of technology in a vein reminiscent of Swift or Pynchon or Kubrick.

All such examples might perhaps be logged as more *funny peculiar* or *funny absurd* than *funny ha-ha*, but literary and film scholars routinely hold up the examples from Swift and Pynchon and Kubrick as obvious instances of the comic artifact usually called *satire*. Clearly, some kinds of comic artifacts do not make audience members or readers laugh out loud. Those artifacts register as infrared light does—below the visible red end of the spectrum—below audible comic laughter yet still part of the conceptual spectrum of laughter-inducing phenomena that constitute The Comic.

Such examples suggest positing a silent laugh-on-the-inside response to complement the expected laugh-out-loud response: LOI to go with LOL. Laugh-out-loud comic artifacts would be analogous to the visible part of the light spectrum. In addition, scholars studying comic artifacts ought to recognize a deranged form of laughter, what might be called *cringe laughter*, a response part embarrassment and part pleasure that happens when a listener half-laughs at a bit of comic foolery in spite of his or her better ethical self. An even more complicated phenomenon along these lines of thought occurs with what Michael Billig has called "unlaughter"—that is, the audience member's reaction of nonlaughter even though he or she understands that a joke was intended and understands the premise of the joke but nevertheless refuses, for whatever reason, to laugh.[27] Theorizing about audience reactions to comic material beyond Freud's speculation about what mood the person is in who listens to an instance of *witz*, or beyond general speculation about the politics or social values of the audience, leads one directly into a region of sociological or psychological data gathering that I leave to others with the proper disciplinary camels to traverse. Similarly, comic laughter as an object of study has been claimed by neuroscientists armed with MRIs. Such studies must find a place within discourse about The Comic, but that terrain too exists beyond my concern here.[28]

Analyzing comic material becomes notoriously problematic when rhetorical or communications models attempt to theorize the audience. The problem can be especially knotty for satiric artifacts, which link to specific social or political issues of the day and thus imply extratextual referents that can be difficult to resurrect and situate. No way exists to guarantee which individual found which part of a given comic artifact laughable—LOL or otherwise—short of interviewing each and every studio audience member of, say, a TV sitcom (and how would that work with a movie or a book or the sitcom's broadcast audience?). This problem appears obviously enough when analyzing satire from the past, but, as noted earlier, a very recent example also demonstrates the issue: witness the paroxysm of misunderstanding about Michelle Wolf's performance at the 2018 White House Correspondents' Dinner.[29]

Nevertheless, scholars in the human sciences should not ignore comic laughter when trying to understand the cultural artifacts constructed to cause it. Rather, the empirical existence of comic laughter—which after all each and every human being has the physical equipment to produce—should function first as the premise for theorizing about comic art, and then second as the sign of the problem entailed in understanding audience and readers. Comic laughter in the first and theoretical instance should be conceptualized as the metaphorical zero in a hypothetically systematic accounting of comic artifacts and their social effects. This way of theorizing comic laughter resembles Wolfgang Iser's idea of "the imaginary," an inchoate matrix from which what he calls "the fictive" generates its representations.[30] The existence of comic laughter in every culture on the planet signifies such a generative matrix for all comic artifacts and therefore a radical starting point for all commentary about comic art forms. Georges Bataille's philosophy of non-knowing (*non-savior*) presents a similar scheme: comic laughter exceeds logic and reason and meaning, occupying a position outside the systematizing of philosophy yet producing effects within the system. This move by Bataille to understand comic laughter's function in a fashion similar to my idea of a metaphorical zero or to a "blank originary scene" has at least one other notable counterpart to name the metaphorical zero for The Comic, or in Bataille's terms, "That which is laughable may simply be *the unknowable*."[31] Sigmund Freud's tracing of the mental sources for *witz* names the unconscious as the generative matrix for joke processes. These various names for the metaphorical zero signify an irreducibly unknown quality of comic laughter axiomatic for understanding comic art forms of all kinds.

Comic laughter as the fourth element of satire thus signifies a basic philosophical issue within The Comic, but its more obvious function signifies the problematic of the audience—it shows that an audience member or a reader does not necessarily experience a laugh-out-loud LOL moment for a text or performance of any kind to be understood as comic. The absence of comic laughter in the audience that some strains of satire provoke points to the metaphorical zero for theorizing. All the individual artistic examples within the domain of The Comic have at their base a quality that effectively escapes a single definition even as the zero invokes a productive emptiness. Comic laughter—even deranged as cringe laughter or silent yet not absent in an LOI laugh-on-the-inside version or in unlaughter form—can function as a symbolic as well as literal manifestation of that quality.

Although it is conspicuously the case that the particular comic artifacts generally called satiric are not necessarily accompanied by laugh-out-loud comic laughter, they surely manifest an unruliness meant to perturb the body politic. Roger Caillois's concept of *paidia* as fundamentally unruly could be understood as naming this particular feature of the deep play found in comic art forms. John Morreall's survey of traditional objections to laughter per se suggests that it has long been understood in the West as profoundly unruly. In addition to diminishing self-control and fostering sexual license as well as anarchy, laughter signals someone insincere, idle, hedonistic, irresponsible, hostile, and foolish.[32] For the Department of Justice, Desiree Fairooz's laughter signified a civic unruliness deserving criminal prosecution.

The poet has furnished the traditional cultural image of the writer as one who creates, and writing creatively in the West up to the age of the novel mostly meant writing poetry; writing satire from the time of ancient Greece and Rome meant writing as a scold, a comic gadfly. The satirist, then, is a poet of sarcasm and cheeky insults in defense of civic virtue. Thus the idea that satire must include LOL comic laughter is surely a modern notion. Insofar as ridicule provides a tool for comic artifacts, satire might entail that comic laughter. However, ridicule is not comic laughter, or, rather, it implies comic laughter of a very specific kind.

Physical LOL comic laughter signifies audience reaction but not all reactions, and thus Test's unadorned term *laughter* in a formula for defining satire works best on a theoretical and symbolic level: the metaphorical zero signifying satire as a comic mode, not as a clear indication of audience reaction. Because satire always uses the symbolic violence of ridicule, friendly it is not—that would signify the relative tolerance of humor. Though both mild and harsh examples of satire exist, mixed with humor, as the Key and Peele sketch demonstrates, if the aggression of ridicule operates as a necessary condition for satire, there must be a limit to how mild a satire can be.

The Theory of A–musement, or the Satire Two-Step

As a specific mode of comic speech, satire represents the surplus that exceeds serious communication, a surplus meant to generate a particular kind of fun, what I have been calling *a–musement*—that is, a pleasurable reflection on the civic issue at hand. Though one of the first dictionary meanings for "amuse" is "entertain," other synonyms and related words include "consider," "contemplate," "ponder," and "meditate." Comic laughter engendered by satire, then, entails two steps for the audience: be entertained but then be thoughtful about the critique embedded in the satire. As Stephen Colbert said during an appearance on stage at Michael Moore's one-man Broadway play, *The Terms of My Surrender*: "'When you're laughing, you're not afraid, and if you're not afraid you can think. . . .' Referring to the Trump presidency, he added: 'We felt our way into this thing, and we have to think our way out of it.'"[33] Satire as a comic mode, then, has a double aim and presents its ethically salutary possibilities via a saltatory process: the satire two-step of a–musement.

Satire has a double aim because its elements create a basic paradoxical structure: as both serious and nonserious speech, satire enables a potential for social impact well beyond other forms of comic artifacts. In effect, satire can function as comic political speech, but it cannot, strictly speaking, function as political speech per se. Satire's intent to aid in reforming the body politic through ridicule, its claim to comically pursue truth as an act of *parrhēsia* (speaking truth regardless of consequence), even its apparent real-world impact, does not place it into the realm of the serious speech acts of policy statements and civic actions, a distinction to be developed later.

The Problem of Ridicule in the Name of Reform

An ontological paradox of being both serious and nonserious speech marks satire. Satire displays a methodological paradox too, one committed ethically to promote the process of social change, yet also committed comically to use the symbolic violence of ridicule and artful insult for such change. The second paradox and its ethical implications require a second look.

This second look concerns the aesthetics of a comic critique, its manner or style, which does not simply invoke rational argument and debate to probe weaknesses and expose assumptions and prejudices; in addition, it performs symbolic dismemberment. Thus the ethical dilemma for satire: Does its brand of critique, its form of speech replete with mockery and ridicule, interfere with the everyday mutual understanding necessary in the public sphere?—or as Jürgen Habermas puts it: "the vulnerable forms of innovation-bearing, reciprocal and unforcedly egalitarian everyday communication."³⁴ Because its use of ridicule and artful insult partly defines it, satire as comic mode constantly runs the risk of descending into the snarky insult and degenerate invective of the anti-public sphere, transforming even into hate speech. However, does satire's habit of using comic insult to power its ridicule necessarily result in polarizing citizens in the public sphere? Satire as the sign of the comic public sphere can be understood as a positive force for the communicative rationality necessary to democracy—its ongoing conversation—but does its recourse to ridicule always put it in danger of being read/received as polemic, rant, or diatribe?

The best answer has to be that satire can only be accused of being mere polemic if one forgets about its element of play. Its laughter-provoking, playful quality means that mere earnestness cannot create satire; indeed, mere earnestness can lead to tirades and harangues as well as good arguments. Earnest and unrelenting presentation of ideology torpedoed one effort to be satiric, *The Half Hour News Hour*.³⁵ And while satire always displays symbolic aggression, and thus can disrupt social situations, laughing at an instance of satire is not physical force or terrorist threats, so any claim reducing satire to its polemic coerciveness should be met with skepticism. The problem of snarky insults versus comic insults raises the issue of audience again. When Stephen Colbert represents political operative Karl Rove as Ham Rove, using an actual canned ham to suggest Rove's facial features, does that constitute an instance of comic insult or snarky insult? The context of one's politics surely matters for such judgments, but so does one's imagination. If an individual's imagination can find enough resemblance between face and ham, the tactic should register as comic insult in its absurdity. However, if one's politics block an imaginative discovery of resemblance, the tactic probably registers as the low invective of snark insult.³⁶

The real problem may be prior to the comic critique wielded via satire—the discourse of the public sphere already too often interferes with the means of mutual understanding. Thus the most profound satire today would be that which ridicules such everyday interference, for example those who claim the existence of "alternative facts," what Habermas calls "systematically distorted communication."³⁷ As noted before, the agonistic dynamic of news and mock news and fake news that permeates contemporary public discourse already demonstrates a satiric battle in progress.

That dynamic and satire's negative (i.e., ironic) support for communicative rationality points toward the potential for satire embodying (demonstrating, dramatizing) a kind of practical knowledge, what the ancient Greeks called *phrónēsis*, which can inform its critique. *Comic phrónēsis* means knowing what deserves ridicule. This knowledge leads to metanoia—maybe even satiractivism. Clearly, the satirist has a complicated task to produce worthwhile satire; just as clearly, the audience for a satiric performance or a reader of a satiric novel also has a complicated task, not just to discern the comic mechanisms of the satire, or to possess the requisite background knowledge of why a satirist targets a particular comic butt, but also to maintain enough of an open mind to be a–mused and thus capable of experiencing a metanoia.

Summing up this chapter's effort to define satire yields these assertions. *Satire* signifies a comic attitude and a comic tactic and names a mode within the discourse that constitutes The Comic. Satire entails a critique based on an implicit or explicit (ethical) value often made with an intent to aid in reforming the comic butt (target) of a ridiculing presentation. *Reform* does not reference a real-world social or political policy change but rather entails a potential metanoia, a change in thinking, perception, or belief, even a repentance of the old way of thinking, perceiving, believing. As with all comic artifacts, satire must be understood within a play frame. However, satire displays paradoxical structures. Analogous to light in a quantum state, behaving as both wave and particle, satire registers as both serious speech and nonserious (comic) speech—apparently stepping out of and back into its play frame. In addition, satire displays paradox in its design of using ridicule for an ethical goal.

At least in its modern and postmodern contexts, satire performs as the most public of comic modes, always a parodic part of the public sphere conversation within a body politic. Satire functions as the comic mode most involved with civic issues and so is most likely to have extratextual references to current social and political events. Satire since the Enlightenment signifies a supplement to the public sphere, namely, the comic public sphere, because it implicitly advocates for the Enlightenment's values of reasoned debate, facts and evidence, accountability, and transparency that characterize Habermas's concept of the public sphere, no matter how much or what kind of laughter is implied by its presentation.

The Public Sphere

2.

Satire as a specific kind of comic speech act that signifies the presence of the comic public sphere necessitates an understanding of what defines the public sphere. Above all, *public sphere* signifies a concept born of the Enlightenment and its modern belief in the rational capacity of people. Moreover, that Enlightenment concept has spooled across time, tying then to now as the thread from which the proper context can be woven for understanding how satire as a comic mode inevitably references external events and has a capacity to participate in comic fashion in the conversation of modern forms of democracy.[1] The Enlightenment ferment of ideas about science and society signals the birth of modernity. The public sphere is a feature of modernity, and many significant instances of satire in English, particularly in the eighteenth century, are shaped by the emergence of the public sphere in England. The public sphere in effect modernizes satire, creating the possibility of its functioning as the comic public sphere. Moreover, because postmodernity revises but does not reject the Enlightenment ideals that created modernity, the discursive arena of the contemporary postmodern public sphere retains satire's function as the comic public sphere.

Jürgen Habermas first introduced the concept of the public sphere in his 1962 book *The Structural Transformation of the Public Sphere: An Inquiry into a Category of Bourgeois Society*, translated into English in 1989. In a later formulation, Habermas defined the public sphere as

> a realm of our social life in which something approaching public opinion can be formed. Access is guaranteed to all citizens. A portion of the public sphere comes into being in every conversation in which private

individuals assemble to form a public body. They then behave neither like business nor professional people transacting private affairs, nor like members of a constitutional order subject to the legal constraints of a state bureaucracy. Citizens behave as a public body when they confer in an unrestricted fashion—that is, with the guarantee of freedom of assembly and association and the freedom to express and publish their opinions—about matters of general interest.[2]

Habermas employed the concept of the public sphere as a normative category to enable critique of twentieth-century democracies. His book explores "the prerequisites for democracy, which for him [are] linked to the implementation of reason, truth, morals and justice in political life . . . [in] true enlightenment fashion."[3]

Though Habermas originally conceptualized the public sphere as a category of the bourgeois class, scholarship subsequent to his book has shown that many of those who participated in its discursive realm were not bourgeois: nobles and government officials as well as academics featured prominently early on. James Van Horn Melton renames it the "Enlightened Public Sphere," and understands it to be "a realm of communication marked by new arenas of debate, more open and accessible forms of urban public space and sociability, and an explosion of print culture in the form of newspapers, political journalism, novels, and criticism."[4] "Enlightened Public Sphere" names a liberal ideal of a reasoning and democratic body politic. Discussion in the public sphere "should be embedded in communicative rationality, rather than in strategic/instrumental rationality, in order to achieve mutual understanding."[5]

The Digital Public Sphere

Given that the original Enlightened Public Sphere as discursive space had its expression via new literal spaces of social communication enabled by print technology, clearly today's digital technology has again created new discursive spaces for social communication: the digital public sphere is the Enlightened Public Sphere 2.0. Axel Bruns posits new digital spaces as public spheres that challenge the standard mass-mediated (think print and television) idea of a modern public sphere by including bloggers and citizen journalists, for example, as new creators of Habermas's "virtual stage" that is the public sphere.[6] Thus innovative communication technology once again mediates the public sphere.

The question now: What differences have been created between the Enlightened Public Sphere and the Enlightened Public Sphere 2.0, the digital public sphere, due to current digitized communications media? For Micheline Frenette and Marie-France Vermette, the characteristics of the digital public sphere that have created difference include personalized feedback, instantaneous interaction, participation potentially 24/7, and no geographic limitations. Discussion and debate are "relentlessly constituted, dismissed, or displaced," although, replicating the original public sphere, there exists a built-in oppositional stance to traditional politics so that "debates in regard to expertise most often oppose citizens to official institutions, the former not wanting to defer to the latter."[7] Moreover, the modalities of the digital public sphere (its ICTs: information and communication technologies) are legion in that the internet not only provides access to alternative media and other putatively informative sources such as blogs but also reroutes traditional media to online venues, creating what media scholars like Geoffrey Baym call the "post-network" era.[8]

The popularity of video-sharing sites such as YouTube, a feature specific to the internet, highlights this enlarged range of ways for information and points of view to be shared, as though the coffeehouses and salons of the original eighteenth-century public sphere had been transformed into tens of thousands of videos by thousands of citizens expressing opinions and critiques of any social or aesthetic topic while also sharing information about topics mundane or of the political moment. Furthermore, the speed of the new technologies, their nearly instantaneous ability for worldwide connections, collapses space as one surfs the internet. This move toward ICT's functioning as social media blurs the public sphere and the private sphere in their original forms described by Habermas. Moreover, professionals no longer monopolize the privilege of publishing because ICTs have spawned a host of amateurs.

As far back as the 1980s, Lyotard understood these technological changes as part of the process he refers to as "re-writing modernity." *Bits* have transformed from free forms of thinking or imagination to *bytes*, "units of information conceived by computing engineering . . . and made into a system."[9] Not just writing but all forms of inscription in any medium—sounds, speeches, and music as well as visual images—are subject to this machine systematizing. Lyotard resists saying that the resulting communication system necessarily amounts to a network of simulacra, as Baudrillard claims, but the potential can be easily glimpsed. Dubbing this new cultural phase "digimodernism," Alan Kirby in 2009 reiterated

Lyotard's insistence on computerization as the most pertinent material fact for postmodernity after the advent of television. "The forms of Web 2.0 [wikis, blogs, social-networking, open-source, open-content, file-sharing, peer production] are the most globally important cultural development of the twenty-first century so far, and they lie at the heart of digimodernism as we currently know it."[10]

While digimodernism as a specific element of postmodern aesthetics helps to frame the current production of satire in the United States in the early twenty-first century, the public sphere as a feature of democracy continues its demand that citizens remain informed on the issues of the day. Thus good citizenship requires good information. For the print culture of the original public sphere of the eighteenth century, the emerging marketplace of news sheets provided a basis for obtaining that information, and in England in particular, the coffeehouse provided a notable physical space for discussing and debating issues implied and evoked by the news. For the digimodernism of Enlightened Public Sphere 2.0, social media, online streaming services, broadcast, and cablecast media provide virtual discursive spaces to complement print. The idea of the public sphere, then, puts an enormous burden on a citizenry to persistently fact-check and consistently do its homework. The public sphere implies an informed citizenry; in market terms, citizens behave, ideally, as active consumers.

Satire today has taken the measure of the enormous changes that theorists such as Lyotard, Baudrillard, and Kirby have noted about existing technologies, in some cases imagining future technologies. Noted before, the movie *Anon* (2018) presents the dystopic effects of technology as though Baudrillard's sign-generating machine dominates human behavior. The totalizing recording capability that functions as the premise of the technology in that future storyworld creates at once the realism of a documentary and the illusion of a theater, the ultimate Reality as TV program in which consciousness and experience become data for instant playback. In digimodernist terms, this data creates texts as "systematic bodies of recording meaning."[11] This theme has also been explored in episodes of the satiric series *Black Mirror*, for example, "The Entire History of You" (Season 1, #3), which features a character who defies social convention by choosing not to replace the implant that records everything after its illegal removal.

The satire of the comic public sphere today demonstrates the impact of digitalization and social media on public discourse in the twenty-first century. Digits tapping on a keyboard suggests the possibility of a new kind of activist promoting a political or social agenda in new ways—in

#flashmob ways, for example, or the #MeToo movement. Such participation does not just indicate digimodernism; it also implies a new kind of citizen, instantly mobile and ready to coalesce into consensus, with a postmodern penchant for irony and parody. Another episode of *Black Mirror*, "Nosedive," satirizes the way in which social status via social media likes and dislikes rules everyone's life, suggesting the downside of #flashmob activism. Notably, that cautionary fictional tale about the negative potential of instant discussion and debate in the public sphere has been superseded by an actual instance of the state manipulating social media to create a compliant public. Echoing the technology in "Nosedive," China tested a tracking system for all citizens: baseline points are assigned and then taken away for social miscues or petty crimes with a goal to "purify society." Reality imitates art—or just an example of satire as crystal ball?[12]

From Enlightenment to Postmodernism: Satire and the Public Sphere

Habermas's argument locates the public sphere at the birth of modernity during the Enlightenment. This assertion has important consequences for understanding contemporary satire because satire in its modern form—that is, satire that routinely critiques institutional power as the comic public sphere—conspicuously appears at roughly the same time. As Stephen Bronner says, "The republic of letters [that defined the Enlightenment] rendered everything subject to criticism; nothing was sacred, least of all sacred things." Moreover, Enlightenment intellectuals "employed satire and wit to demolish puffery and dogma ... [to reach] a general audience of educated readers."[13] Satire as the comic form of criticism has had a role to play in any vibrant public sphere ever since.

Before the eighteenth century, satire could be mostly divided between the Horatian reformer who aspires to cure human folly and the Juvenalian misanthrope who wishes "to wound, to punish, to destroy."[14] John Gilmore notes that Roman satire in general takes a conservative stance, an attitude replicated as late as 1597 when the poet Joseph Hall produced the first substantial body of verse satires in English modeled on the Romans. Though Hall explicitly stated the possibility of satire changing moral behavior, his work shows that he considered satire to be a conservative force, targeting human folly rather than institutional power.[15] Nevertheless, the English impulse to satirize only grew after Hall's landmark work. "In traditional literary histories, English-language satire produces its greatest works in the late seventeenth and the early eighteenth," says Jonathan

Greenberg—that is, during the birth of the Enlightenment. Vic Gatrell emphasizes the long-lasting literary effects: "Satire occupied a central place in polite eighteenth-century culture [and] morally corrective satire retained an honoured place in the literary pantheon from the Restoration until the 1820s."[16] Gilmore offers this generalization about all the satirists of this fertile period: they are "united by the idea that their society as a whole, if not the individual targets of some satire, could, in fact, be improved, and that their own work might contribute to this [goal]."[17] This canonical image of a golden satiric age, fashioned by scholarship "in the 1950s and 1960s," asserts that the best satirists were conservatives and proponents of neoclassical values (order, decorum, refined wit) and that they "relied on a set of shared norms whose violations could be easily recognized and ridiculed."[18] As W. H. Auden puts it, "Satire flourishes in a homogenous society where satirist and audience share the same views as to how normal people can be expected to behave, and in times of relative stability and contentment."[19]

The view of more recent scholarship complicates that image of conservatism and shared values. Rather than stable in a way that clearly cements satirists to their audiences, this time period was "full of political contest, religious controversy, changing morality, even new understandings of human nature."[20] Moreover, satire is not necessarily pushing a moral purpose; social or political or intellectual as well as ethical failings may be targeted. Even if the satirist avows moral purpose, satire rarely spurs tangible reform, and it is thoroughly inadequate in the face of vice and corruption and evil. The focus on moral purpose "overstabilizes satire, eliminating its volatility, misrepresenting its emotional dynamics, and occluding our understanding of it."[21] Satire may be more about irreverence rather than morality, or it may degrade its butt more than morality demands. Contra Auden, satire thrives not in stable times but in uncertain ones.

In short, the late seventeenth and the eighteenth century's Janus-faced production of satire in England, looking back to the Romans using conservative verse satire and looking forward to modernity using subversive, mock journalism satire, marks a historical pivot. The public sphere transforms the context for satire: civic issues of the moment now circulate in print as well as in conversation, in comparison to the earlier, handwritten work passed around by court wits; the rise of parliament induces politicians to appeal continually to a public citizenry; literate citizens exchange ideas in coffeehouses; theaters, until the licensing act of 1737, could be freewheeling in their productions of political satire. Thus satire at this crucial moment found "a natural home in a public sphere saturated with polemic."[22] People read plays as coded social satires. The subgenre of satiric pamphlets, enmeshed in a discourse that was "topical, political, journalistic,"[23] produced Daniel Defoe's *The Shortest Way with Dissenters* (1702) and Jonathan Swift's "A Modest Proposal" (1729). These works exemplify a new variety of mock arguments to challenge the dominance of verse satire. *The Shortest Way with Dissenters* exemplifies a turn toward an exercise of the subversive potential of satire as comic public sphere, so disruptive to the political and religious establishment that Defoe had to stand in the pillory for it. Mark Rolfe's argument that satirists in democratic countries are "agents participating in politics" also reaches back to the Augustans of the eighteenth century.[24]

The entanglement of satire with the public sphere at the dawn of the Enlightenment shows at a basic level. The Enlightenment assertion of a universal human capacity to reason and thus to be educated underpins and amplifies the critiquing function of satire that has always existed, its a–musement effect, as well as its impulse toward a metanoia, just as surely as that universal capacity underpins the communicative rationality of the public sphere. That formula may be evident enough with satire in the eighteenth century, when the public sphere provided social energy for the emergence of representative democracy, or possibly even for satire in its modernist forms, but what of satire in the postmodern era? Layne Neeper bluntly states the complicating, even corrosive, effect on satire in a culture saturated with truthiness, the degraded form of postmodern skepticism: "The postmodernist project would, of course, seem wholly at odds with satire. Satire depends upon stable shared values that find wide acceptance across a given culture's social imaginary [so that] [p]ostmodern fiction's renowned distrust of ontological certainty or any meaningful metanarrative authority would seem to render it radically antagonistic to the stable codes so apparently necessary to the functioning of satire."[25] As we have seen, Jonathan Greenberg argues that even in the golden age of English satire, this assertion of widely shared and stable values is overstated. Nevertheless, the (in)famous postmodern distrust of metanarratives has meant that Theodor Adorno, for example, can doubt the possibility of satire in the immediate post–World War II environment in which the cultural shift that would be labeled postmodern began. In his view, the holocaust and the crazy possibility of nuclear annihilation left no conceptual and emotional space for irony and thus no space for satire. For Adorno, satire's use of irony presupposes a "compelling consensus of subjects," a community with shared values, ratified by comic laughter, that no longer holds sway.[26]

I think this line of argument is wrong. Nothing exists in the postmodern condition that rules out satire. That much should be apparent with the so-called black humorists of the 1950s and 1960s, though a good case can be made that the strain of satire they produced had its own peculiar qualities in the social and political environment Adorno cites, and that topic will be explored later. The postmodern condition not only allows satire but also encourages it. A brief look at two essays on the topic of "What is the Enlightenment?," one by Immanuel Kant and the other by Michel Foucault, suggests how the philosophical attitude of skepticism that characterizes postmodernity can be traced to Enlightenment ideals. That attitude fosters satire, with its element of critique. Moreover, satire generating laughter-provoking critique as the comic public sphere aligns with the public sphere, which was "inherently oppositional in its thrust, since its critical range extended inexorably to individuals and institutions traditionally exempt from scrutiny."[27]

The key idea from Kant is that *enlightenment* implies liberation from an intellectual immaturity, from the self-imposed shackles of "laziness and cowardice" that stand out as the chief causes for not being able to use one's own reason.[28] Crucially, Kant uses *public* in a sense that clearly foreshadows Habermas's ideas of a public sphere and communicative rationality, for the chief mechanism to achieve emancipation from immaturity rests upon the "freedom for man to make *public use* of his reason in all matters" (136, original emphasis). The mise-en-scène for achieving enlightenment for the public understood as "the great unthinking mass" (136) evokes guidance from someone already enlightened, namely, a citizen "in the quality of a scholar" (137). Thus a reasonable and educated person addressing the public through a dialogue engendered by the written word (i.e., the discursive public sphere) will necessarily enlighten "the true public, which is the world" (138).

Understanding Michel Foucault's meditation on the same question that prompted Kant's essay—"What is Enlightenment?"—entails recognizing Foucault's insistence that the metaphor of escape from immaturity used by Kant in presenting the liberating spirit of the Enlightenment "has determined, at least in part, what we are, what we think, and what we do today." Moreover, as an exit or escape from self-imposed shackles, enlightenment requires "an ongoing process."[29] Enlightenment as a *process* of change opens the door to apprehending a continuity between Enlightenment self-reflection and the possibility of self-reflection today. Basic philosophical questions such as humanity's relation to the present, humanity's historical being, and the way the self is understood as an autonomous subject are all "rooted in the Enlightenment, . . . [not in] faithfulness to doctrinal elements, but rather [in] the permanent reactivation of an attitude—that is, of a philosophical ethos that could be described as a permanent critique of our historical era" (44). This principle of permanent critique amounts to an "attitude of modernity" (39), and it is "at the heart of the historical consciousness that the Enlightenment has of itself" (44) and has bequeathed to posterity. Foucault returns to Kant's specific meaning of the public use of reason in the ideal sense of being free and universal: reasoning done by a reasonable being, as a member of reasonable humanity, for no other reason than reasoning's sake.

Because Foucault insists that the Enlightenment initiated modernity, its philosophical ethos of a permanent critique of human thought and action means that he remains bound to critique the Enlightenment, a critique in which one can discern a turn toward a cultural moment tagged as *postmodern*. Foucault describes the critique this way: "In what is given to us as universal, necessary, obligatory, what place is occupied by whatever is singular, contingent, and the product of arbitrary constraints?" (45). The phrasing suggests paradox: What within the universal is singular? Foucault wants to shift the focus of the always-ongoing critique "in the sense that it will not seek to identify the universal structures of all knowledge or of all possible moral action, but will seek to treat the instances of discourse that articulate what we think, say, and do as so many historical events" (46).

This reorientation of philosophical inquiry from the necessary to the contingent means that in the public sphere, when discovering the places where change is "possible and desirable," one must, as Foucault says, "turn away from all projects that claim to be global or radical" and prefer "partial transformations" (46). Lyotard speaks of a "local determinism" and the "pragmatics of language particles" that result from the postmodern dispersal of metanarratives into "clouds of narrative language elements."[30]

Enlightenment for Foucault, then, names a way of philosophizing that he carries on in his genealogical design and archaeological method. As a process of emancipation, enlightenment creates an always-now critique of the present moment, a process that engenders the signature attitude of modernity and makes necessary the dialogue of the public sphere. With satire operating as the sign of the comic public sphere, the Enlightenment spirit of an always-now critique takes shape as the theory of a–musement: muse on the critique that gave one the occasion to laugh.

From Enlightenment to Postmodernism: Rewriting Modernity

Here's the rub: the epochs named *Enlightenment* and *Postmodern*, with *Modern* supposedly sandwiched temporally between them, appear as a historical time line, antecedent or successor. However, they are also understood not as chronology signifying social and aesthetic ruptures but as cultural projects that alternate or coexist within what Habermas calls the larger cultural "project of modernity formulated in the 18th century by the philosophers of the Enlightenment."[31] To return to the phrasing of Foucault, we can note that modernity features a "mode of relating to contemporary society," a mode rooted in the Enlightenment's "philosophical ethos that could be described as a permanent critique of our historical era."

Lyotard in his short essay "Re-Writing Modernity" echoes Foucault's insistence on linking the Enlightenment with modernity and even postmodernity in the attitude and process of a philosophical ethos. Lyotard also understands postmodernity as "a promise with which modernity is pregnant."[32] Modernity in some sense contains within itself postmodernity as a potential unfolding. Lyotard uses the metaphor of "re-writing" to name this process, and like Foucault, he insists that there can be no transcendent end to it, no *telos*. More specifically, Lyotard borrows an idea from psychoanalysis to describe the process as a "working through." The project of modernity itself must be worked through. "Postmodernity is not a new age; it is the re-writing of some features modernity had tried or pretended to gain, particularly in founding its legitimation upon the purpose of the general emancipation of mankind" (8–9). Thus the rewriting of modernity already occurs as a part of the writing of modernity and its Enlightenment legacy. In this formula of a double gesture, Lyotard discloses the postmodern. He underscores this double gesture by highlighting double meanings: *fin* in French can mean *end* or *purpose*; *putting down* in English can mean *inscribing/writing/recording* or *silencing/repressing/discrediting*. To have *an end in sight* rather than *a purpose in mind* potentially evokes the problem of a totalizing impulse within Enlightenment universals, while the stakes in the doubled meaning of *putting down* are no less than the possibility and dangers of writing a history.

Through the device of the pun, Lyotard shows how the postmodern operates as a rewrite of modernity, an iteration that does not just display a difference but necessarily also binds the two so-called cultural moments as rewrites are materially and intellectually bound to an initial draft, the draft known as *Enlightenment*. The *post* of *postmodern* thus might be figured with the metaphor of a palimpsest. Other metaphors to imply this relationship so as to elide temporal succession would include a suture or a fusion. The task of rewriting would presumably entail marking differences in the rewrites, but more importantly, the rewriting must be wary of having a transcendent endpoint and wary of silencing as it inscribes—that is, wary of what is being put down in the rewrite. Here the psychoanalytic model serves Lyotard's rewrite metaphor. The working through must be more like free association than remembering, so that the rewrite possesses "the ability to let things come up, whatever they are" (8). Lyotard invokes an idea from Theodor Adorno, "micrologies," to name the result, which echoes a postmodern preference for local narratives inscribing knowledge rather than metanarratives with their implicit ideal of complete and definitive knowledge, a preference dramatized in the postmodern satire of the black humorists, as we will see. "Micrologies" also echoes Foucault's preference for "partial transformations." The postmodern unfolding from within the modern rewrites modernity while trying to avoid making the mistakes of a systematizing impulse that some extrapolated from Enlightenment thinking, or trying to avoid the more recent neoliberal market-driven insistence on optimizing performance for a system, and thus to insist instead on no particular goal or endpoint to the process. Rather, the *post* in *postmodern* signifies a working through with no end, with no purpose in the sense of having a specific end, but nevertheless having a purposiveness. That purposiveness can be defined as the spirit of the always-now critique, the necessity, as Lyotard puts it, to let each moment, "each 'now' be an opening" (8).

Habermas also argues that the project of modernity should ultimately be tied to Enlightenment ideas and aesthetics. In the expectations of Enlightenment thinkers such as Nicolas de Condorcet, progress in understanding the natural world through science also meant progress in improving the social world for morality and justice. Although that optimism evaporated with the wars and traumas that characterized the first half of the twentieth century, Habermas asks if the intentions of the Enlightenment, admittedly enfeebled, nevertheless are worth holding onto, while noting that modernity in all its phases develops out of the Enlightenment project of emancipation based on reason. Modernity begins with the Enlightenment and (for Habermas) can be continued with "adherence to a criterion of communicative rationality," that is, a process of dialogue and debate among free citizens in the public sphere that can facilitate consensus.[33]

The postmodern also entangles itself in significant ways with the Enlightenment via its numerous critiques of modernity, a move that already implies the project of modernity working out Enlightenment principles, as Foucault demonstrates in his analysis of Kant. In another example of critique as rewrite, Lyotard argues against following Habermas's idea of consensus because postmodernity questions the apparent totalizing effect of consensus as well as the "unitary end of history" it implies. Nevertheless, Lyotard asserts that a work of art "can become modern only if it is first postmodern," suggesting that the postmodern and the modern should not simply be opposed in a way that cancels each other out but rather should be understood to exist simultaneously.[34] Richard Bernstein provides a way out of this conundrum. Though he laments that Habermas uses the concept of consensus too conspicuously, Bernstein would save it from the charge of a potentially oppressive totality by shifting from that goal to the purposive process necessary for reaching it—that is, communicative rationality. To speak like Jacques Derrida, one must in Bernstein's model endlessly defer full consensus for the sake of a communicative rationality that defines process in the public sphere.

Thus the project of modernity according to Habermas remains in force, but only if it is first postmodern—that is, deferred with differences manifested by increments of agreement moving toward the horizon of consensus. In Lyotard's terms, the language game of consensus must be about the rules that enable agreement as well as the topics that might be agreed upon, while the knowledge gained must be transmitted in localized narratives (because it accrues in increments), not in a metanarrative of utopia that would extinguish all difference. Bernstein echoes Lyotard's paradox of simultaneity, speaking of the relationship of modernity/postmodernity not as a matter of either/or but as a constellation of operations or an overarching mood because they are "inextricably interrelated and entwined with each other."[35] Quoting Simon Malpas, Linda Hutcheon pithily notes the argument for conceptual simultaneity by saying that postmodernism "has persisted . . . as a 'space for debate.'"[36]

Amid any attempt to historicize and to conceptualize both the public sphere and the current cultural moment, what remains as most important for understanding satire as the sign of the comic public sphere is the persistence of Enlightenment ideals within a discursive domain privileging dialogue and debate. That domain enabled modern liberalism with its prime directive claim of universal rights: the cosmos gives every individual the birthright of equal treatment. When Thomas Jefferson wrote in the Declaration of Independence, "We hold these truths to be self-evident, that all men are created equal, that they are endowed by their Creator with certain unalienable Rights, that among these are Life, Liberty and the pursuit of Happiness," he turned an Enlightenment ideal for normative behavior (people in a society ought to act as if everyone was created equal) into a proclamation of universal rights as the basis for a just government. The claim for universal rights—along with the claim of a universal capacity for reason and its correlative that everyone can be educated—these assertions remain bedrock for the emergence and maintenance of a public sphere.

Postmodern liberalism, arguably born in the 1960s, has added "a politics of recognition" to the claim for equality within a "Universal Declaration of Human Rights," adopted by the General Assembly of the United Nations in 1948—that is, added a supplemental ethical goal to the prime directive command that one should act as though all individuals were created equal—also act as if all differences are respected.[37] This second directive has its own discourse separate from yet related to the universalizing of the Enlightenment. Thus postmodern liberalism implies a polity that respects sameness and difference at once and implies a belief in both equality before the law and affirmative action. The paradox in this constellation of values resembles light's behavior in a quantum state—wave and particle both—which means that the modern liberalism born in the Enlightenment advocates a set of basic values that have always underpinned modern satire—and continue to do so in the midst of the postmodern condition. Modern satire and thus the comic public sphere have accompanied the original public sphere discerned by Habermas from its birth. Far from satire being stifled by postmodernity, once one understands postmodernity as a rewriting of modernity that provides a constellation of values, that constellation (palimpsest, suture, fusion) provides a positive condition for the production of contemporary satire.

Satire in the Enlightenment assumed an ethos of dialogue and debate based on rational argument and conducted in a discursive domain Habermas named the public sphere. This generalized conception of audience and reader above all entailed an assumption of reasonableness, as Molière's *homme raisonnable* characters dramatize in literary fashion and as Kant's educated citizen addressing the public with the printed word demonstrates in a political mise-en-scène. Today, an ethos of pseudo-debate dominated by truthiness exists in a public sphere transformed by media saturation and simulacra, a public sphere always in danger of descending into an anti-public sphere. The hyperreality of simulacra in the form of polls all too often dominates political discourse. Nevertheless, the Enlightenment assumption of humanity's capacity for reasonableness necessarily undergirds contemporary satiric production.

Satire only needs to be rescued from the postmodern condition if one assumes that in postmodernity, no values, no norms are possible. However, such totalizing claims are exactly what postmodern theory abhors. Postmodernity presents a persistent critique of totality, totalization, and system as a closed entity. Postmodernity instead cultivates and champions difference and pluralism, not relativism. Values and rules and norms always remain discernible, but the postmodern critique has demonstrated that its localized values, paralogic rules, and evolving norms cannot be about conceptual stability but rather exist in tension with the Enlightenment's insistence on universality and rationality. The quantum state paradox of that tension entails the process of an always-now critique yoked to desire for emancipatory progress. Thus postmodernity does not enable the chaos of anything goes. As Lyotard says, incredulity toward metanarratives does not result in barbarity.[38] Another way to say it: just because no one can guarantee that an operating room is 100 percent sterile, it does not follow that an abattoir or a sewer presents an equally good space for performing surgery.

If universals must be tempered, if localized knowledge names the cultural game of the moment, satire will still appeal to values and norms while using rules within that game. When certain values appear as transcendental (e.g., greed is always bad), modernity becomes most visible: some appeal to an ideal human nature can be made as *an ought*. Postmodernity becomes most visible when identities are at stake, when difference is at stake. Only if by *post* one simply means *temporally after* instead of *supplement* or *constellation* does the current cultural moment threaten satire with extinction.

Postmodernism features a rigorous intention of being dialogic, also a basic feature of the public sphere. The always-now critique implied by Foucault aligns with rather than diverges from the Enlightenment ethos. From this angle of always being a potential disturbance in the social system, postmodernism should nurture the contemporary satire that constitutes the comic public sphere and thus should still be, potentially, part of the public sphere.

Admittedly, the potential tyranny of so-called enlightened reason and its instrument, the rational public sphere—as well as the potential for the public becoming a mass subject, the mob or a #flashmob—remain postmodern concerns, as Foucault and Lyotard demonstrate. Reason in a postmodern schema cannot simply invoke a regime of universals. Instead, reason remains contingent, and one must guard against its claim to an imperial nature by using (wait for it) reason. Hence the value of the constellation metaphor that seeks to salvage a claim to universal reason as long as the always-now critique remains as an accompanying force.

Lyotard says that an "incredulity" toward metanarratives characterizes the postmodern turn. The resurgence of satire in the contemporary moment suggests that incredulity does not mean dismissal; that did not happen with the Enlightenment metanarrative of emancipation and its unfolding in the various stages of modernity. Not incredulity as dismissal, not a failure to believe, but incredulity as skepticism, as a way to register provisional belief. The metanarrative of scientific progress, for example, does not warrant incredulous dismissal by Lyotard's own account; rather, knowledge in a postmodern condition signals a shift to an investigation about the limits of knowing. Today's public sphere and its parody, the comic public sphere, do not merely hold onto the intentions of the Enlightenment metanarrative of potential progress toward emancipation; rather, they refigure them, reappropriate them in a strategy of creative rescripting to adapt to today's conditions. True, the buoyant optimism destroyed by the twentieth century cannot be recovered. Lyotard says no one mourns that loss. The task becomes how to proceed with those results via the always-now critique.

Satire today implies support for both parts of the conceptual constellation: the universalism of human rights supplemented by an insistence on respect for difference. Satire's most profound cultural role today, then, employs in comic fashion the basic ethos of modern/postmodern liberalism as part of the aesthetic-expressive rationality of Habermas.[39]

Summing up differences between Enlightenment thinking and the latest form of modernity, usually called *postmodernity*, yields these claims. First, Enlightenment thinking centers on an assumption of universal human nature stripped of historical differences, as well as a cosmopolitan citizenship stripped of particular identities. In some formulations, Enlightenment thinking also constructs a scientific method designed to formulate laws for its processes with a *telos* of unity—the single key of knowledge that would unlock and thus dispel all mystery. Second, the poststructuralist thinking that powers postmodernity centers on understanding human nature in its historical unfolding as well as understanding the scientific method as one more form of human expression, a new suburb of language, in Ludwig Wittgenstein's phrase,[40] rather than the unitary paradigm for all cultural thought. Third, postmodern thinking maintains a skepticism about science as the single key to a utopia free of mythologies as well as a skepticism about *telos* per se—a radical sense of contingency. Fourth, that radical contingency is not the same as a claim to alternative facts within a world of ideological spin doctors whose statements ignore signifieds, who think of language not as a means to understanding the world but as an instrument for manipulating others so that they will believe what they want them to believe, reality becoming a matter of political taste narrated by an ideology. Moreover, any narrative must be subject to the always-now critique within a vital public sphere, supplemented by the satire of the comic public sphere.

Summing up similarities among Enlightenment thought and its rewrites as modernity and postmodernity provides these claims. First, humanity can be partially defined by a capacity for rational conversation and self-reflection (i.e., critique). Second, satire operates as the comic mode for that conversation and critique. Third, satire implicitly endorses the values behind that capacity, a capacity that underwrites normative ideals of the public sphere and so enables the comic public sphere: "full disclosure, willingness to provide reasons, openness to experience, an arena for systematic criticism," in the words of James Carey.[41] No one offers this capacity for conversation and critique as a ground for a metanarrative privileging the two spheres under scrutiny. The capacity may be a centering device, only a function, but even Jacques Derrida says that such functions are "absolutely indispensable."[42] The trick will be historically situating that centering device. The speech act comically supplementing that situating will be satire.

Why are these similarities and differences important? To understand the most important historical and philosophical background for contemporary satire: postmodernity's relation to the Enlightenment. Modernity, modern satire, and the public sphere all appear roughly at the same time via Enlightenment ideals. Postmodernity as a rewrite of modernity represents not a break that impedes the production of satire, but rather a revision that resituates satire in its contemporary moment.

Truthiness Satire and the Comic Public Sphere

3.

Defining satire remains a fraught and difficult enterprise in part because the term signifies an attitude and tactics that can inflect a myriad of discursive forms and literary genres. Nevertheless, a basic function always exists: satire operates as comic political speech, not political speech, in the public sphere. This fundamental distinction means that satire is best approached as a playfully aesthetic object rather than as political communication: understand its poetics first, then its politics. Moreover, because truthiness satire displays a postmodern poetics, it is important to be clear what a postmodern comic poetics entails.

The stakes involved with these three interlocking concepts—satire as comic political speech, satire as an aesthetic object, truthiness satire as an example of postmodern comic poetics—can be apprehended by contrast with Geoffrey Baym's excellent historical analysis of television journalism. Baym offers three phases since the advent of televised news based on Raymond Williams's well-known cultural categories: the *residual* names network news, "public service journalism" (e.g., Edward R. Murrow and Walter Cronkite); the *dominant* names multichannel news, commercial journalism, a "corporate product, focus-grouped and advertiser-approved" (e.g., Brian Williams); and the *emergent* designates post-network news, a "hybrid media that blends news and entertainment in unprecedented ways" (e.g., Jon Stewart and Stephen Colbert).[1] Network news features a "high-modern style," while multichannel and post-network news both employ a "postmodern style," based on Baym's signature insight of discursive integration.

Most importantly for my purposes, *The Daily Show with Jon Stewart* and *The Colbert Report* exemplify for Baym a particular hybrid of post-network television news: "the vanguard of a new kind of public affairs media, . . . a still developing *neo-modern* paradigm of news, one that *uses the style of postmodernism to pursue the high-modern ideals* of public information and democratic accountability that motivated news of the network age" (20, my emphasis).

Baym categorizes these two mock news shows as a hybrid form of political journalism. In my reading, they are instances of the playfully comic mode of satire, and when Baym says that they might function as "a new kind of public affairs media," they do so as speech within the comic public sphere. The hybridity of *The Daily Show with Jon Stewart* and *The Colbert Report* is the hybridity of all satire, its signifying a comic supplement to the public sphere, not the public sphere itself. In Baym's analysis, *The Colbert Report* "functions as a kind of neo-modern public sphere" (133), but I also take issue with "neo-modern." Baym uses that term because, like the so-called high-modern news of the Cronkite network era, *The Colbert Report* has as its ultimate goal the promotion of the public sphere, its deliberative discussion and rational debate. For Baym, the apparently cynical and unstable irony of postmodern television in general, what he understands as the postmodern *style* of both the multichannel and the post-network phases, undercuts the high-modern paradigm; however, the ultimately stable irony deployed in Colbert's show returns audiences to high-modern ideals, earning it the tag "neo-modern." While this designation serves to link the network and post-network phases to the public sphere, it also exposes the narrow and negative way Baym uses *postmodern* to describe the discursive integration of the multichannel and post-network phases of television journalism. In my view, *The Colbert Report* does not develop a neo-modern public sphere but rather serves as a reminder, in postmodern style, that the public sphere, as part of Enlightenment ideals, should be situated in the project of modernity, a project initiated during the Enlightenment and carried on today in phases that include both modernity and postmodernity, as Lyotard and Habermas argue.

A postmodern style for television news leads to cynicism, Baym argues, and thus would apparently preclude satire. However, that characterization of postmodern style stems from a misapprehension of postmodernity, one implying that postmodern philosophy's skepticism about universal values and transcendent truth translates into *anything goes*, the clarifying critique of radical skepticism becoming the lazy attitude of radical relativism. Satire has always been skeptical in its critiquing function, an attitude deepened in its postmodern phase but not inevitably indicative of cynicism. The postmodernism that clarifies, that enlightens, like its satire, harbors instead an idealism within its skepticism: always-now critique yoked to desire for emancipative progress.

Postmodernity for Baym, nevertheless, becomes a whipping boy because it supposedly enables a nothing-means-anything attitude; rhetorical hot air, unvarnished bullshit, and Colbert's idea of *jacksquat* are thus "effects of postmodernity" (142). Colbert's neologisms *wikiality* and *jacksquat*, like the more well-known *truthiness*, "provide *modernist* points of agitation against dominant political inclinations to reject objective inquiry and intellectual engagement in favor of hollow political spectacle" (141, my emphasis)—that is (in my terms), they agitate against the anti-public sphere. Baym's analysis ranges the sensible modernist paradigm enshrined in Cronkite-era network news against what he presents as a confused and confusing postmodern style of multichannel news and even most post-network news. Baym follows Harry Frankfurt's elaboration of *bullshit* as a rhetorical tactic, which is supposedly inseparable from the "various forms of skepticism which deny that we have any reliable access to an objective reality." Thus *postmodern* undermines "disinterested efforts" to determine truth and stands against "the notion of objective inquiry" (quoted in Baym, 142). This argument conflates anti-public sphere truthiness with postmodern skepticism about claims to be disinterested and objective.

Baym refers to *The Daily Show with Jon Stewart* and *The Colbert Report* as "neo-modern political journalism" because they apparently revive high-modern ideals and because the postmodern as he presents it is "too often incoherent, scattered, and disorienting" (171). While that stylistic characterization works for describing television news in the multichannel era, it does a disservice when applied to the philosophical positions of postmodern theorists whose skepticism ends up caricatured as a lack of "continuous faith in fact and accountability and the belief that words can, and should, mean something" (173). That description severs the postmodern from the Enlightenment ideals that underpin a notion of news reporting in a democratic environment. A better formulation to describe those shows would be, first, to understand them as postmodern instances of satire that imply, via their comic postmodern aesthetic, the ideal of accurate and reliable news reporting derived from the Enlightenment principle of transparency. That aesthetic is firmly grounded in a postmodern philosophy that does not discard facts and accountability and a belief that words "mean something," but does apply the Enlightenment criterion of critique to any claim by news reports of describing in disinterested fashion a transcendental objective reality. The rootedness in the Enlightenment of *The Daily Show with Jon Stewart* and *The Colbert Report* also appears in the very idea of the public sphere they serve so that *neo-Enlightenment* might be more apt to describe the shows' playfully ironic commitment to journalistic integrity, but that is as much to say a comic commitment to the *modern* idea of journalism as a feature of the public sphere. I agree with Baym that both shows reinforce the reasoned discourse of the public sphere, but they do so as its comic supplement: as comic political speech, not political speech, or even as political journalism, which misreads at a basic level. In addition, my objection entails understanding how postmodernity rewrites modernity, not as a return (neo-modern) but as a difference: *post* as *supplement* or *constellation*.

Satire is dissent, as Amber Day skillfully demonstrates, but my argument insists that its dissent is of a different order from political speech, one playfully aesthetic. Examining in some detail that playful aesthetic in the digital public sphere, within a more positive view of postmodern poetics, is the goal of this chapter. Oversimplifying somewhat, the digital public sphere or Enlightened Public Sphere 2.0 has been dominated by cultural politics, which tends to transcend national borders and to result in micropolitical or cause-oriented actions. In addition, the digital public sphere has enabled a postmodern style of politics, one "that celebrates the possibility of ironic, humorous and contradictory political actions."[2] Thus the classic Habermasian public sphere, with its rationality implicit to argumentation and debate, in its digital form "has lost the exclusivity of discursive practices, thus incorporating new modalities ranging from satire to humor, also including irony and sometimes with speeches approaching incivility."[3] These new modalities bring satire as the comic version of the always-now critique to the forefront, make it more visible than before, perhaps even more than in the eighteenth century and its original enlightened public sphere discerned by Habermas. Their virtues line up with basic features of the postmodern attitude: irreverence, mimicry, sarcasm.[4] Moreover, citizenship in the digital public sphere has morphed into John Hartley's concept of *Silly Citizenship*.

The silly citizen thinks of comic artifacts—especially satire—as "the go-to source for civic understanding."[5] Hartley understands citizenship as a discursive practice that evolves, and he develops a typology of citizenship in historical moments, though he says that in the current postmodern moment all of these types can be experienced at once. For my purposes, the last in his list works as the key: the Do It Yourself (DIY)/Do It With Others (DIWO) model. Citizenship at this level thus provokes "consumer productivity" and exhibits affinities with Alan Kirby's concept of digimodernism: choice-based affiliations and self-organized associations tap out silly citizenship with nimble digits on keyboards. Citizens in this mode proclaim and demonstrate their rights in social-network markets.

Digital technologies enable ordinary folks to self-represent as citizens in ways not possible before, and Hartley emphasizes the role of play or silliness in those self-representations.[6] The silly citizen places into a comic mode the idea of the informed citizen. In that model, people express their citizenship as "an individualised, private, rational calculus, based on objective information conveyed by a dispassionate press to a reading public that is also the Republic":[7] in short, the citizen in Habermas's public sphere.

The Enlightened Public Sphere 2.0 exhibits a mashed-up quality caused by discursive integration: "news, politics, entertainment . . . melded into previously unimagined combinations."[8] This melding has contributed to the condition necessary for the idea of satiractivism. Hence the relevance of the argument by Jeff St. Onge for the "engaged levity" and "absurdist critique" found in *MAD* magazine.[9] *MAD* enables what St. Onge calls the low-level end of the political engagement demanded in satiractivism—that is, the magazine's brand of satire creates a perception of the absurdity of politics, potentially uniting all citizens in a *communitas* of laughter that enacts Kenneth Burke's comic frame of acceptance.[10] For St. Onge, *MAD* engenders "true" satirists and "true" versus pseudo satire, wherein the satirist's comic speech demonstrates not an "easy nihilism" but the active posture of engaged levity. Thus "silly citizenship" and "engaged levity" indicate the discourse that articulates the comic public sphere, and the single most visible mode for that discourse is satire.

Lining up the attributes of the public sphere with the comic public sphere reveals informed citizenship with its parody, silly citizenship. Imagining an anti-public sphere, one can posit partisanship instead. For the public sphere, there is sense; for the comic public sphere, comic sense; for the anti-public sphere, nonsense. For the public sphere, there is rationality and transparency; for the comic public sphere, irony; for the anti-public sphere, obscurity as well as the gut feeling of what Stephen Colbert calls "truthiness." For the public sphere, there is data, information, news, and evidence; for the comic public sphere, mock news performed satirically; for the anti-public sphere, fake news, alternative facts, and uninformed opinion. For the public sphere, there is conversation; for the comic public sphere,

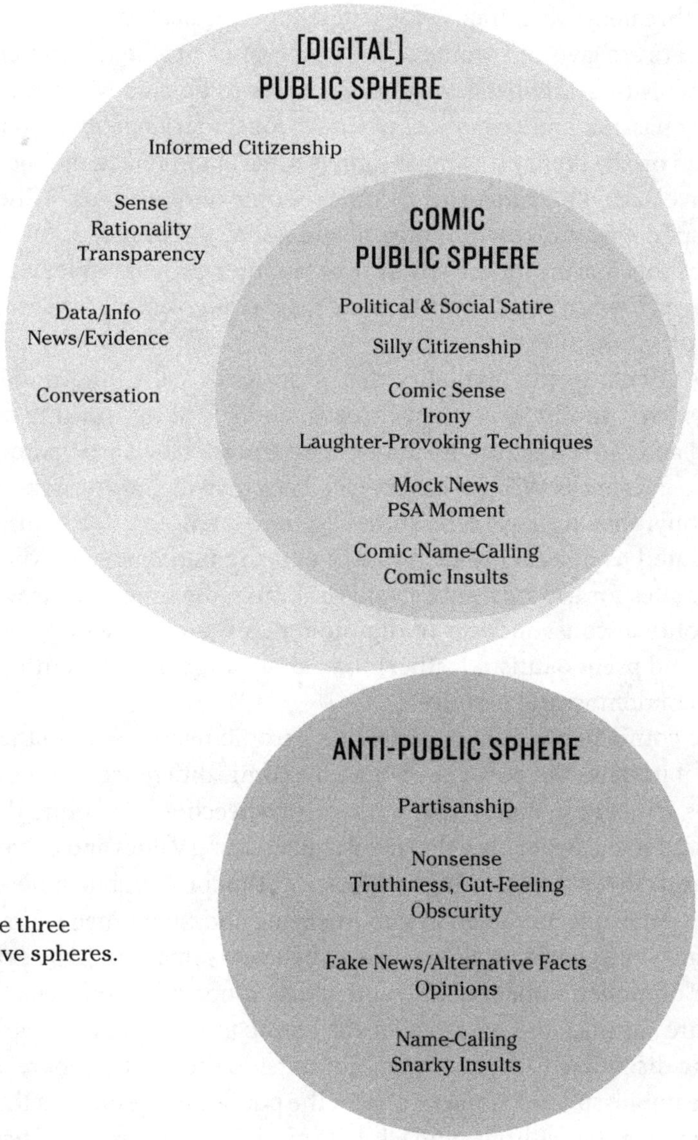

[DIGITAL] PUBLIC SPHERE

Informed Citizenship

Sense
Rationality
Transparency

Data/Info
News/Evidence

Conversation

COMIC PUBLIC SPHERE

Political & Social Satire

Silly Citizenship

Comic Sense
Irony
Laughter-Provoking Techniques

Mock News
PSA Moment

Comic Name-Calling
Comic Insults

ANTI-PUBLIC SPHERE

Partisanship

Nonsense
Truthiness, Gut-Feeling
Obscurity

Fake News/Alternative Facts
Opinions

Name-Calling
Snarky Insults

FIG. 1 The three discursive spheres.

comic name-calling and comic insults in service to educating its silly citizens and furthering their conversation of engaged levity; for the anti-public sphere, name-calling and snarky insults designed to deform, forestall, or even halt the conversation of democracy (see fig. 1). The anti-public sphere manifests what John Courtney Murray, after Lyotard, calls barbarism, which "threatens when men cease to talk together according to reasonable laws. There are laws of argument, the observance of which is imperative if discourse is to be civilized. Argument ceases to be civil when it is dominated by passion and prejudice; when its vocabulary becomes solipsistic, premised on the theory that my insight is mine alone and cannot be shared. . . . Conversation becomes merely quarrelsome or querulous."[11] The comic public sphere features satire, political and social. Other names for the variations of this discursive activity and its laughter-provoking format might be: *charged humor, citizen-satire, comic soapboxing, comic parrhēsia, laughtivism,* or *satiractivism.*

The advent of the textuality that Alan Kirby calls "digimodernism" in blogs, chat rooms, comment threads, and social networking sites has enabled and nurtured the anti-public sphere in that the participatory quality of the internet as Web 2.0 has spawned negative digital #flashmob action and anonymous hate speech. These digitized platforms for communication, touted as enhancing democracy and the public sphere, thus often become sites for the anti-public sphere at the same time. As Kirby puts it, "The political consequences of digimodernism are likely to be desocialization and pseudoautism [rather] than an upsurge in eighteenth-century notions of democratic practices."[12]

The comic public sphere exists in a parodic relationship to the public sphere; it imitates the public sphere with a comic difference, and not necessarily as a mocking counterpart. Its satiric speech acts critique the body politic and social over issues that involve fluctuating values and current civic events and current social fashions. Moreover, the comic public sphere's satire critiques persisting moral sentiments involving undesirable behaviors such as greed and vanity and moral corruption, behaviors that should be expunged in favor of moderation, empathy, and ethical if not moral behavior.[13]

Satire signifies the presence of the comic public sphere, a parodic or parasitic discourse that sits inside, not outside the public sphere, as does the anti-public sphere. Metaphorically, the public sphere engulfs the comic public sphere but without rendering it invisible. The comic public sphere resembles a benign cyst within real-world discourse, a funny-looking bump. Perhaps a better—that is, prettier—image exists to analogize the relationship of the comic public sphere to the public sphere that captures the crucial feature of being surrounded yet visible. In any case, the cyst image fits Aristotle's observation that *kōmōdia* (*comedy* used here as the umbrella term), displays the ridiculous, "which is a species of the ugly . . . something ugly and distorted without causing pain"[14] (see fig. 2).

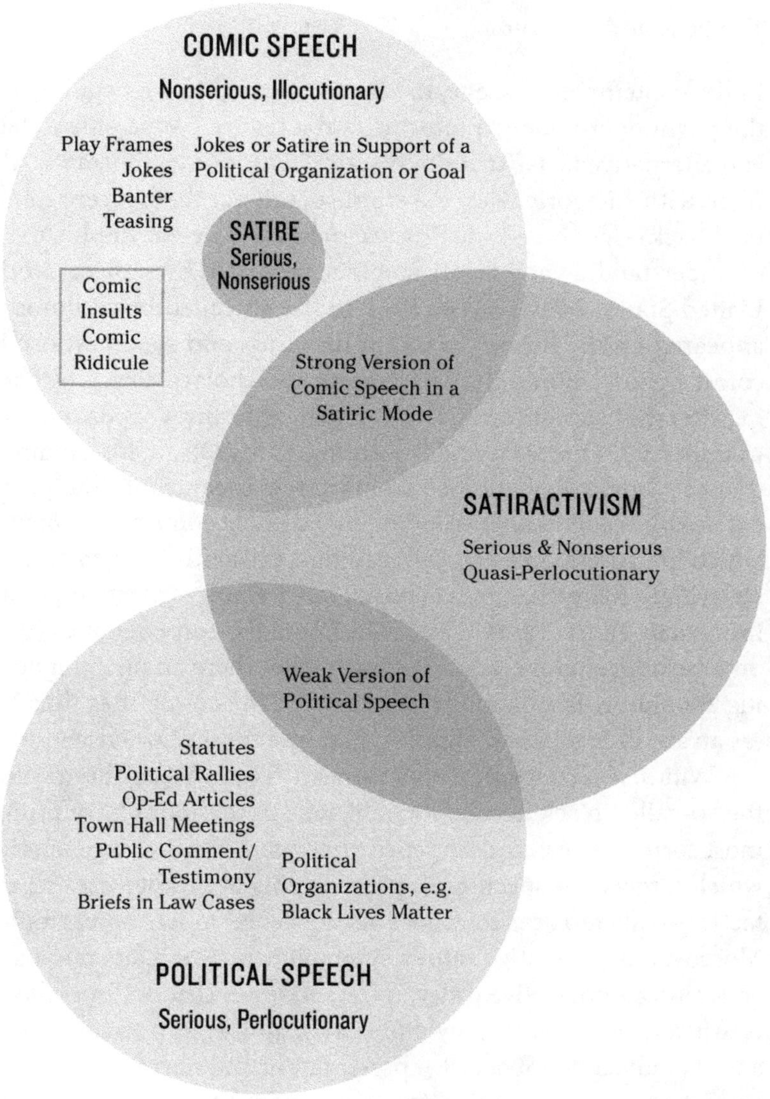

COMIC SPEECH
Nonserious, Illocutionary

Play Frames
Jokes
Banter
Teasing

Jokes or Satire in Support of a
Political Organization or Goal

SATIRE
Serious,
Nonserious

Comic Insults
Comic Ridicule

Strong Version of
Comic Speech in a
Satiric Mode

SATIRACTIVISM

Serious & Nonserious
Quasi-Perlocutionary

Weak Version of
Political Speech

Statutes
Political Rallies
Op-Ed Articles
Town Hall Meetings
Public Comment/
Testimony
Briefs in Law Cases

Political
Organizations, e.g.
Black Lives Matter

POLITICAL SPEECH
Serious, Perlocutionary

Comic Speech as Satire: Not an argument or statement of public policy, but instead mocking or ridicule with an intent to create metanoia about a public policy issue, but not an intent to create actual reform or initiate change.

Satiractivism • Laughtivism • Charged Humor • Comic Parrhesia: Comic speech in a satiric mode that explicitly intends to cause actual reform in public policy or civic life.

FIG. 2 Satiractivism's relationship to comic speech and political speech.

The Postmodern Comic

In the contemporary scene, the trajectory of satire's recent history within the postmodern comic points toward a reality TV president, fake news, and alternative facts. Truthiness satire in mock news formats, what I will trace with categories derived from speech act theory, represents comic pushback—laughter-inducing *parrhēsia*. However, the historical roots of understanding any comic laughter produced by satirical works in the United States today reaches back to the so-called black humorists that appeared on the literary scene in the 1950s and 1960s, whose brand of comic fiction embraced a dark edginess.[15] Scholars surveying comic writing after the black humorists have employed features of postmodern theory to understand the texts under scrutiny. Kirby Olson, for example, asserts that the "curious phenomenon of humor is central to the postmodern enterprise."[16] For Gillian Pye, "*the comic* has become a dominant mode in which to express, amongst other things, existential absurdity and human suffering."[17] Many examples of postmodern comic artifacts, especially in the immediate aftermath of World War II and the consequent Cold War, play on a lack of coherence, discovering a joke where an unambiguous meaning should be. In postmodernist theory, "the comic" has thus been seen "as an antidote to the totalitarian state and the authoritarian individual."[18]

Within this conceptual environment, Steven Weisenburger argues that the so-called black humorists notorious in the 1960s have produced the most corrosive postmodern satiric style, what he calls "degenerative satire," which targets not specific people or events but rather uses its ridiculing tactics to call into question codes of knowledge understood as foundational. Moreover, degenerative satire's symbolic violence offers no possibility of generating a normative order; its postmodern skepticism eschews norms or universals. Informed by a poststructuralist embrace of contingency and its radical doubt about representation and narrative *telos*, degenerative satire encapsulates significant aspects of the postmodern condition.[19]

This aesthetic revises the traditional view of satire as an avowed generative social force, one that dramatizes psychic energy (e.g., anger and disgust) cathected onto a target and repurposed to support a normative order. In contrast, the degenerative satire of black humor dramatizes psychic energy (e.g., fear, anxiety, and despair) as a free-floating and subversive displacement into laughter, a disruptive subversion potentially without end: no *telos* yet displaying comic purpose. Weisenburger understands comic techniques in the service of black humor as part of a strategy to master discourse about anxiety concerning the most serious of issues, starting with its treatment of the problem of representation: "any degenerative satire displays language as an enclosed, self-reifying system constantly in need of demolition through laughter from positions further and further outside" (136). Black humor subjects modes of expression and codes for social practices, as well as the resources for interpretation, to a satiric critique.

The black humorists complement their parodying of philosophical comic butts with a ridiculing of pop culture that functions as a caricature of all representation—that is, pop culture presents a mediation of experience through preexisting, mechanically generated signs. Degenerative satire draws attention to the processes of semiotic production, their technological apparatuses, and their circulation in the pop culture machine (110). The enabling technology historically starts with television and arcs to the internet. Television and computer screens become not just the material site of the postmodern sign machine but also the metaphor for a pop culture play of meaning: surface only, no depth, signifiers on a glowing screen with signifieds obscure or irrelevant.

The black humorists, therefore, map artistically what Roland Barthes presents analytically in *The Empire of Signs*, a regime with signifieds apparently AWOL, foretelling Jean Baudrillard's culture of simulacra.[20] Postmodern degenerative satire parodies James Agee's famous modernist dictum about "the cruel radiance of what is"[21]—what Weisenburger calls "the transcendent importance attached to everyday secular moments" (136)—by displaying a world radiant not with the metaphysical presence Agee posits, but instead displaying in the glow of the screen only the banality of an unremitting sign machine.

The project of traditional generative satire entails a comic process of teaching "how to bring power seekers and sanctimonious hypocrites down off their pedestals," while postmodern degenerative satire deflects that turbulent process into not-so-simple comic laughter. Such laughter—schizoid laughter in Weisenburger's analysis and "strangely fluid" like desire in Olson's—succeeds because it exceeds the grid of rationality, eliding the need for a hierarchy of masters and minorities.[22] Such profound subversiveness aligns with the habit of radical critique that characterizes the postmodern attitude, the always-now critique advocated by Foucault.

This harshest strain of postmodern satire, the degenerative satire of the so-called black humorists, behaves as if a black hole commands its conceptual center, so that satire very nearly crosses an event horizon that cancels out its status as satire. In its unyielding postmodernity, degenerative satire offers no explicit answers to the social and ethical problems its philosophical critique of language uncovers: an ever-more-persistent consumerism, a trajectory of technological innovation that seems to offer more freedom as it enchains consciousness to its gadgetry, not to mention the cold war threat of thermonuclear destruction (think *Dr. Strangelove*). No clear *paralipsis* or PSA moment apparently can exist. These features have laid the black humorists open to the contradictory charges from its contemporary critics that Weisenburger so ably demonstrates of both being beyond satire and not being satiric enough.

Comic laughter in this context signifies the aforementioned black hole energy that threatens satire in both Weisenburger's and Olson's accounts of postmodern satirists—that is, a strangely fluid schizoid laughter. To tag that energy as *laughter* is to understand degenerative satire within a psychological dynamic; its chronic use of gallows humor performs the double gesture of acknowledging yet denying the felt depth of anxiety in the Western social psyche during the first decades of post–World War II.

Displaying a structural affinity with the always-now critique of Enlightenment reason by a reasonable postmodern subject, this double gesture constitutes the legacy of the black humorists for contemporary satire and marks the tension in the new constellation of philosophical thinking that characterizes the postmodern condition.[23] That strange and strained double gesture registers as comic, maybe even laughably silly, certainly absurd, the critique of foundational concepts and norms implying the necessity to turn and twist to look at one's backside, to imagine looking at the back of one's head. Nevertheless, this doubled gesture of the postmodern condition perhaps suggests why satire in fact now flourishes. Far from crippling the production of satire and the comic public sphere, the postmodern condition with its convoluted laughter nurtures it.

Contemporary satirists, insofar as they imply serious values in their comic antics, necessarily uphold as prime directive the universalism of human rights supplemented by an insistence on respect for difference, a dynamic that Stephen Bronner insists is operational from the beginning of the Enlightenment.[24] Though the satire of the black humorists nearly zeroes out any sense of a stable ground for values, values are nevertheless implied in the comic butts they target: not just the corruption of social institutions and the problem of representation but also the technologies used for representation and their intense commodification. These comic butts signify public sphere issues that remain as potential topics for the ridicule of today's satirists.

Those satirists thus have the capability to retain the basic modernist quality born in the Enlightenment and revised in the postmodern moment. The contemporary satirists I examine represent a certain kind of postmodernist, one writing satire that has not given up on the potential efficacy of the always-now critique even if they practice their art from a philosophical position that refuses to accept social norms and values as transcendental. The satire they produce can therefore be called *generative within a postmodern contingency*. The contemporary satirists examined here should be distinguished from the postmodernist who writes degenerative satire, a satire implying that the universe contains only self-contradictory knots, ruptures, and fragments. In that regime, foundational concepts are ruthlessly questioned and persistently shown to be less than stable. However, even in that harshest of comic environments, values associated with Enlightenment and modernity are implied and persist, thus enabling the later postmodern form of satire, truthiness satire. Historical continuity is attenuated, not ruptured. Mere anarchy is not loosed. As Charles Jencks says, "Post-modernists are partly still-modernists who accept the Enlightenment as important."[25]

Though truthiness satire does not claim that Truth exists, in effect it decides what to do with degenerative satire's exposure of the problematic, maybe impossible, nature of a universal Truth. Truthiness satire thus incorporates the instability of the postmodern critique into its poetics yet claims a generative function for its art. Truth still matters, but truthiness satire locates it in new ways, in the local forms of reverse discourses, for example, maybe in particular within comic inversions of racial and gender stereotypes in a bid to insist on the postmodern dictum of respect for all differences.

Hyperreality and Truthiness

Donald Trump believes that if enough people retweet and share what he tweets, if enough people consume his Twitter statements by retweeting them or passing them along in other social media, such sharing validates his statements. Trump does not care that his statements can be fact-checked and exposed as lies; he only cares that they can be and will be digitally reproduced to generate the truthiness of the anti-public sphere.

Such digitized communication circulates with its faux aura of truth because of what Jean Baudrillard calls *hyperreality*.[26] New technologies shape and create new cultural and social conditions. At the birth of modernity, print culture changed European societies and their colonies in the Enlightenment and enabled Habermas's discernment of the original public sphere.[27] For the early phase of the postmodern condition, video and film technologies were the focus—television and cinema. In the postmodernity of Web 2.0, technologies associated with the computer and the internet form and deform cultural practices.

In Baudrillard's analysis of this brave new world, image supersedes and replaces the real because the endless repetition and reproduction and circulation of the image by television and computer—"from miniaturized cells, matrices, and memory banks"—might efface any sense of historical context.[28] Within societies in a postmodern condition, many cultural artifacts consist of images, which coded models produce (and reproduce) via technologies functioning as sign machines, pumping out signifiers that seem to have no signifieds, appearance devolving into simulation. A flood of signs represents the world, such that a common-sense view of reality becomes obscured if not lost, drowned by plenitude: hyperreality. The technological mediation of experience, which passes as reality, appears as a network of images and signs without a clear external referent. The real devolves into the hyperreal, "an operational effect of symbolic processes ... as images are technologically generated and coded before we actually perceive them."[29] The Kantian subject no longer produces a sense of reality by synthesizing concepts and intuitions with perceptions; rather, technological mediation threatens to replace that process.

Within the regime of hyperreality, communication technologies provide experiences more intense and engaging than the banality of everyday life. People experience media simulations of reality (think reality TV) or amusement parks (think Disneyland and Disneyworld) as more real than reality because they are inundated by simulacra. The availability and ubiquity of a stream of instantaneous images overexposes an individual in an "ecstasy of communication" in which subjectivity apparently has no extrinsic ground, producing the media-saturated consciousness of the individual constantly posting on Facebook or constantly tweeting and retweeting. In Baudrillard's analysis, representation entailing referents evaporates, leaving only images, spectacles, and the play of signs functioning as icons and simulacra with the potential to disappear the referent.[30]

People can construct their identities in the hyperreal as they perceive themselves within the play of signs detailing how others perceive them: Facebook and other social media such as Twitter hashtags.[31] In Baudrillard's pessimistic view of technological determinism, people lose contact with the real and even with their own imaginary in the endless play of signs that technologies now present as the dominant form of the symbolic order. Society today resides within the postmodern digital sphere 2.0 and thus potentially within a regime of simulacra and simulation—its hyperreality—insofar as people behave as unthinking consumers of signs the worthiness of which resides not in a use value but instead in their value of being reproducible—not in representing some idea or recording some event but rather in their multiplication in (re)tweets and (re)postings on social media platforms. When enough people consume Trump's Twitter statements by retweeting them or passing them along in other social media, hyperreality reigns. Trump remains indifferent to whether his statements contain facts or lies as long as citizens reproduce them and thus participate in the truthiness of the anti-public sphere.

In an episode of *Last Week Tonight*, John Oliver explicitly shows the Donald as such a very willing cog in the sign machine described by Baudrillard, using Trump's claim that millions of illegal votes were cast in the 2016 election. Trump consumes a statement in the media ecosystem that fits his worldview—in this case, a tweet by Greg Philips@jumpvote, who originally makes the claim about illegal voting—certainly does not fact-check it, half remembers it, yet passes it along as fact, prompting millions of others to pass it along as fact in a variety of communication sites, at which point the claim "takes on a life of its own and so validates itself." After tracing the genesis of the false claim, Oliver shows that it nevertheless circulates as accurate by showing a video clip of a woman who restates the claim several months later to a reporter in a focus group, and when challenged about where she obtained the so-called information, says, "from the media."[32]

Oliver, in that episode of *Last Week Tonight*, analyzes Trump's shaky relationship with reality and mocks his cable news mentality that focuses on Fox News—with the Drudge Report, Breitbart, and Infowars in supporting roles—all of which have a demonstrably tenuous relationship with facts. Oliver breaks down Trump's pathological lying and the problem of making actual policy with alternative facts. "Any policy discussion has to begin with a shared sense of reality," Oliver declares, stating the basic foundation for the public sphere. After working through a number of obvious lies told by Trump, including that it did not rain during his inauguration and that the crowds were bigger than for Barack Obama's inauguration, Oliver goes on to enumerate so many examples of Trump lying that he caps the list with a video clip in which a reporter laments the difficulty in covering Trump: "What does he mean when he says words?"

Representing reality sounds like a punch line because Trump speaks simulacra, will stand in the rain and say it is a sunny day, or alter the official path of a hurricane with a sharpie.[33] In Trump's through-the-looking-glass world, his Twitter feed provides the only ostensible news and facts a true patriot needs to hear. The referent disappears. Thus, when challenged to prove the claim that thousands of Muslims in the US supposedly celebrated 9/11, Trump held up the front page of Breitbart that merely reiterated the claim as well as citing Infowars as another echoing source. Oliver in a different episode provides an even better example of how Trump enthusiastically embraces hyperreality when he traces the anti-public sphere process that Trump exploits with the example of the term "spygate" being injected into the simulacra machine of the media. Trump utters a statement and then when some media outlets reproduce it, he quotes the digital echo as if it is newly minted and independent: he notes that "some people" are saying "spygate" to reference his spurious claim that President Obama wiretapped Trump Tower during the 2016 campaign, yet "some people" means he used the word.[34]

Trump and communication sites like Fox News, the Drudge Report, Breitbart, and Infowars create an anti-public sphere of disinformation, conspiracy theories, and rumors so that any citizen who, like Trump, listens only to those broadcasts or reads their web pages, thinks that he is the first president to tell the truth, rather than realizing that he has no discernible relationship with the truth other than ignoring it. Trump places himself squarely in a regime of simulacra when, confronted with the fact that no proof of illegal voting exists, he responds by stating what for him really matters: millions of people agree with him. The public sphere thus degenerates into the anti-public sphere of a public opinion based on rumor, a through-the-looking-glass consensus.

As D. R. Tucker put it after Trump accused President Obama of illegally wiretapping Trump Tower and offered no evidence: "To his supporters, he doesn't need any evidence; his words are the only proof. Trump understands that through Twitter, he can invent his own truth." Tucker also reminds his readers that the hyperreality of Trump on Twitter was preceded by

> an operative (said to be Karl Rove) in the George W. Bush White House who infamously boasted to writer Ron Suskind about the Bush team's ability to create its own state of being: "The aide said that guys like me were 'in what we call the reality-based community,' which he defined as people who 'believe that solutions emerge from your judicious study of

discernible reality." I nodded and murmured something about enlightenment principles and empiricism. He cut me off. 'That's not the way the world really works anymore.'"[35]

Trump's TV lawyer, Rudy Giuliani, has taken Rove's dictum to heart with a serpentine defense of his client against the investigation of Special Counsel Robert Mueller into Russian interference in the 2016 presidential campaign. The core of that defense: "Truth isn't Truth" and different versions of the truth can be advanced because facts exist in the eye of the beholder.[36]

In the hyperreal realm, alternative facts, politically motivated counter narratives, and crazy conspiracy theories thrive. That realm convinced Edgar Madison Welch to "self-investigate" with an automatic rifle the claim by Alex Jones (Infowars) and others that Hillary Clinton was running a child prostitute ring in the basement of a Washington, DC, pizza restaurant called "Comet Ping Pong." An investigative report by Amanda Robb clearly shows how the truthiness of the simulacra works: the digital trail creating this conspiracy theory included ordinary people, online activists, bots, foreign agents, and domestic political operatives, many of the latter associates of the Trump campaign. At one point early in the saga, the Twittersphere registered roughly 6,000 tweets about the story, labeled "Pizzagate" by some media outlets. The next day, there were nearly 55,000.[37]

The production of this conspiracy theory within the realm (mostly) of the internet exemplifies digimodernism, "the effects of cultural forms of digitization.[38] For such cultural production, authorship has become anonymous, multiple, layered, and social. While original texts set parameters, readers downstream who consume those texts also (re)produce them. Although this process creates community, the variable of anonymity taints and vitiates it, generating openings for trolls and bots. In the end, communication itself has become the stake, or at the very least, civility. Twitter exemplifies the negative potential of digimodernism in the way that individuals can be harassed and abused in the hyperreality of a social networking realm, "a quagmire epitomized [for example] by the roving flocks of hateful, misogynistic, and well-organized 'Gamergate' communities that flooded people's feeds with hate speech and threats."[39]

This supreme emphasis on symbolic value and reproducibility rather than use value or validity forms part of the problem that journalists face in their reporting when it repeats what Trump or others say, no matter how foolishly or maliciously outrageous. Contemporary news reporting must grapple with the dilemma that the very media being used to represent events accurately and report the news responsibly also has a potential to deny representation its power, emptying out meaning and erasing the referent so that the simulation of mere reproduction rules. In M. W. Smith's totalizing and apocalyptic rhetoric: "As all referentials are liquidated in the field of visual circulation, the context and conditions of historical production simply no longer matter."[40]

Such assertions of chaos imply the barbarity Lyotard rejects. It is not that contexts for historical production no longer matter; rather, they are much, much more difficult to discern. One can turn Smith's rhetoric inside out and say that the slide toward simulation makes knowing the history of an image or a story's production and circulation matter more than ever, if the stakes are high enough. Witness the effort of reporter Amanda Robb, noted before, who tracked down the internet circulation of the rumor that Hillary Clinton was running a pedophile ring out of the basement of a restaurant in Maryland. Robb's effort does more than merely demonstrate how elaborate was the reproduction of image and text. Even if Robb could not with certainty discover the specific origin of the conspiracy, apparently confirming Smith's assertion that a regime of simulation liquidates all referents (at least clear referents to an origin), Robb uncovered enough of the history and context to discredit the tale and to show how thoroughly politics rather than journalism motivated its circulation. Full signification may be deferred, but it nevertheless matters what can be known, for useful conclusions can still be made. Robb's efforts thus demonstrate the constellation of modern/postmodern values: access to the truth may not be easy and may remain partial, but the results of efforts to establish the truth can contribute to public sphere deliberation.[41]

However, simulation threatens the difference between the false and the true, as Baudrillard argues, for example, if one simulates an illness by producing symptoms. Are the symptoms real or false? *Postmodern* in part functions to name that part of contemporary culture *"unhinged by simulation."*[42] Is 9/11 an act of terror by jihadists or a simulation by the American government to consolidate its authority for the war on terror? Was the moon landing simulated on a sound stage? Facts no longer necessarily trace a specific trajectory toward knowledge in modernist fashion but rather mark what Baudrillard calls the *precession* of a model—a postmodern wobbling about the axis of truth—that engenders multiple and even contradictory interpretations.

The logic of the hyperreal produces empty signifiers, or signifiers with scrambled signifieds: for example, *Jihotties*, a term used to refer to ISIS men recruiting brides online, to women with automatic weapons in full burkas, or to any Muslim woman deemed sexy by the faceless machine of the internet. The clash of meaning in these differences—a precession of truth—can be discerned in the image of a woman in a burka sporting an automatic weapon, eye make-up, and red fingernail polish.[43] The logic of the hyperreal predicts the reality TV presidency of Donald Trump, who speaks for the people of the political id, the denizens of the anti-public sphere.

Thus arises an important part of the postmodern critique of foundational concepts: the availability of the real. The modernist conception of reality is posited as a philosophical ground unproblematically accessed—that is, a singular state of affairs always exists to which one can appeal for validity and thus track down lies and expose mystifications as well as ideologies. The metaphor *surface/depth* captures this modernist view of reality in which the real can be found beneath a surface. For the postmodern condition, this opposition of real and appearance has become one of appearance and disappearance on the surface, the screen. Politics today often becomes not about a debate of ideologies but rather a question of rendering the opposition invisible and inaudible. This process might be as sinister as literally disappearing individuals or as simple as claiming that what the opposition says constitutes fake news, while individuals in the opposition are ridiculed with disparaging names—or perhaps even rhetorically demonized.[44] The very conditions of representation are thus always at stake, particularly in the faux events that constitute truthiness.

Politics and the law deal indirectly with the problem of representation exhibited by fake events.[45] However, satire could theoretically attack the problem more directly with its ridicule of phoniness or hypocrisy. The public sphere deals with the consequences of the perfect representation of a faked event; the comic public sphere deals with the fakery itself. This division of cultural labor lines up with the difference between what Kant called the "determining judgment" and the "reflective judgment." The former enables decisions that conform to rules and regulations in a system, what would work properly within a theory. The latter more appropriately suits aesthetic matters, a realm without definitive prescriptions. *Modernity* in a narrow sense elevates the determining above the reflective and thus has a tendency to build metanarratives. *Postmodernity,* in its distrust of metanarratives, favors the reflective judgment.[46] In this cultural regime, satire steps forward. If, as Baudrillard argues, Disneyland not only projects an escape from the routine of everyday life but also, in its explicit fantasy, functions to reassure by opposition that America's political, social, and cultural life is real, then the poetics of satire enunciates the aesthetic and reflective judgment that makes visible the absurdities and laughable practices in the so-called real world.

Satire therefore not only can and does survive in a postmodern environment, but it also thrives in this milieu, insisting on the project of modernity working through Enlightenment values as it supplements the public sphere. Satire thrives in the postmodern environment because it has the ability to take on its intellectual coloring as truthiness satire. A conspicuous strategy for truthiness satire signifying the comic public sphere today resides in its reverse discourse structure, apparently replicating yet undermining that aspect of the postmodern condition generated by technology that Jean Baudrillard has called a regime of simulacra and simulation. Truthiness satire as reverse discourse holds the possibility of rescripting anti-public sphere discourse into comic public sphere discourse. In particular, truthiness satire confronts the through-the-looking-glass effect in today's news world: a broadcast site called Fox News routinely operates as a fake news show while millions of citizens perceive the mock news show *The Daily Show* as a cablecast site that delivers the real news, though leavened with ridicule. "One must think instead of the media as if they were . . . a kind of genetic code that directs the mutation of the real into the hyperreal."[47] In other words, the news media always run the risk of aiding and abetting the anti-public sphere. Truthiness satire ranges its reflective judgment against this possibility: its incessant ridicule directed at the anti-public sphere creates the comic version of the persistent fact-checking that news organizations must perform to help maintain the public sphere.[48]

Truthiness Satire as Postmodern Comic *Parrhēsia*

The through-the-looking-glass effect in today's news world seems to preempt the possibilities for the comic fantasy of parody and satire. Baym's discursive integration concept exposes the porous border among representational narratives that results in generic mash-ups of news and entertainment, while Baudrillard's regime of simulacra exposes the porous border between the real and the hyperreal that results in the unmoored signifiers of the image machine. Even before any satiric critique can be mounted, reality already has the appearance and feel of a fantastic construction by a faceless technology. Professional comedians might therefore lament that those cultural conditions preempt their creativity, but in fact the comic fantasy of parodies and satires can take advantage of those conditions, in the first place by dramatizing their comically absurd qualities. In many ways, this part of the contemporary satiric environment replicates what American satirists have been doing at least since the advent of the so-called black humorists in the 1960s, as alluded to earlier and as Weisenburger's analysis reveals. Their satire first mapped the problem of simulacra and dramatized empty signifiers, the very basis for truthiness. However, unlike the black humorists who truncated or obscured their comic critique after dramatizing the underlying conceptual and philosophical conundrums for these cultural conditions and thus wrote degenerative satire, satirists now behave much more ready to assume those conditions as the conceptual opening for their comic rebuttal, critique as reverse discourse, the truthiness-satire pushback of which often features PSA moments and satiractivism.

The through-the-looking-glass effect in today's news world manifests in several ways. For example, Anderson Cooper, a reporter for CNN, features an opinion segment on his show, but he does it with lots of sarcasm to accompany video clips, as though he were Jon Stewart. Moreover, the title of the segment is "The Ridiculist." One example from the series has former UN Ambassador Nikki Haley promoting her new book "along sycophant street." During the promotion tour, Haley says that President Trump was always truthful when dealing with her, is a good listener, and was great to work with. When Cooper plays the video of Haley, part of the time there is a split screen, similar to Colbert with a segment of "The Wørd," the split screen ironizing the news footage, with Cooper making faces as she speaks: eye rolls and facial grimaces as opinion making. Cooper follows the video clip by saying that according to everyone else who has worked with Trump, he is famous for not listening. When he shows a still picture of Trump at a cabinet meeting, Cooper says that Trump looks like "a guy who wishes he had some meatloaf in front of him, the food or the singer, either would be more interesting than governing."[49]

In a second example, Jake Tapper, also a respected reporter for the cable news channel CNN, writes an introduction to a book published by *MAD* magazine, *MAD About Trump*. From the other direction, an issue of *MAD* mocks in a faux movie format the United States' weak aid effort for Puerto Rico after two hurricanes struck the island with its title, *Tyrants of the Caribbean*, "Trump's Response to Puerto Rico: Throwing in the Towels." The comic magazine references an actual event: Trump literally tossing rolls of paper towels to a crowd of Puerto Ricans. *MAD* supplements its parody's use of actual events in Puerto Rico with quotes of actual utterances by Trump during his visit (e.g., *now the budget is out of whack*; *Puerto Ricans want everything done for them*) presented as dialogue in the imagined movie. In both the CNN examples, the world of legitimate news travels into the world of satire. In the *MAD* example, the world of satire mixes bits of the news into a parody of official government actions. While these comic artifacts invoke the comic public sphere, they also indicate how easily traversed back and forth is the frontier between the comic public sphere and the public sphere, how the through-the-looking-glass effect can be an enabler of rather than an impediment to the creation of satire.[50]

In yet another example, the discursive movement from satire to news can travel back again to satire, normalizing Jake Tapper and Stephen Colbert as they zigzag from jokes and banter about the news to discussing political events seriously and back to jokes when Tapper appears on *The Late Show with Stephen Colbert*. Their conversation in effect creates an improvisational comic routine that supplements Colbert's opening comic monologue, even though Tapper is a professional journalist and Colbert is a professional funny-man.[51] Tapper and Colbert as a comic yet serious duo (satire that entertains too) embodies a postmodern discursive space at once both comic public sphere and public sphere. That back-and-forth cannot be a surprise, for the comic monologues night after night on *The Late Show with Stephen Colbert* feature the same zigzagging between the jokes of the comic public sphere and the serious presentation of events appropriate for the public sphere. That zig and zag demonstrate what Jon Stewart taught his *Daily Show* audiences to expect and what has propelled Colbert to the top of the ratings heap for late-night shows.

The basic tactic of *MAD* mixing bits of the news about actual events with comic fantasy presents a paradigm of contemporary satire created within news formats in what amounts to a parodic civic education for creating silly citizens. However, the frontier between public sphere and comic public sphere can be breached in another way, when late-night satiric monologues segue into presentations of serious policy issues.

For example, in an episode of his show *Jimmy Kimmel Live!*, Kimmel uses his comic monologue segment to comment seriously on President Trump's description of the events that were part of "The Unite the Right" rally in Charlottesville, Virginia, from August 11 to 12, 2017. As that description rippled through the media ecosystem, much of the public was horrified that he apparently defended the white supremacists in the march while ignoring the death of a woman during a countermarch, a reaction Kimmel epitomized. Moreover, on August 14, 2017, both Seth Meyers and Jimmy Fallon registered their horrified reactions too, as citizens rather than professional comics. Both men said very nearly the same thing in critiquing Mr. Trump for equating the protesters against the white supremacists with the white supremacists, while ignoring the death of a protester who was run down with a car driven by a sympathizer of the white supremacists. In effect, Meyers and Fallon retooled the comic speech of their monologues to deliver instead the sober speech that characterizes the public sphere. Joining Kimmel, Meyers and Fallon transformed their usual comic critiques via satire into the serious critiques of the government that Habermas identifies as endemic in the public sphere: denizens of the comic public sphere in these instances easily crossed over into the public sphere.[52]

These examples point to the postmodern environment in which satire today operates. The easy movement back and forth between discourse in the public sphere and its parodic counterpart demonstrates a basic reason why the production and consumption of contemporary satire in the United States have reached unprecedented levels. Moreover, within the postmodern environment, the mix of the comic public sphere with the public sphere, demonstrated in these examples, has created the possibility of a new strain of satire, satiractivism. In the postmodern environment of discursive integration and digimodernism, audiences have become better positioned than ever to be satirists themselves as they participate in the comic public sphere as silly citizens. Inevitably, such silly citizens are much more likely to understand themselves to be in dialogue with the professionals, and thus to experience metanoia and respond to calls for activism via satiractivism.[53]

This turn to a form of activism housed within the comic public sphere becomes most visible in satiric examples that engage at different levels with the dissemination of news in all formats, print, broadcast, cablecast, or narrowcast. Part two of this study will examine such satiractivism in some detail. By way of prelude, I first look at another way in which truthiness satire with its reverse discourse structure signifying the comic public sphere encourages metanoia and thus grooms audiences for silly citizenship.

The Civic Engagement of Reverse Discourses

A reverse discourse can be traced to an earlier discourse that uses nearly identical signifiers. However, the apparent reiteration employs those signifiers for a reverse semantic effect: the speaker produces, situates, and directs his or her discourse in clear opposition to the meaning of the original discourse.[54] The paradigmatic example for a comic reverse discourse could be Dave Chappelle's parodies of PBS's *Frontline* with his character Clayton

Bigsby.⁵⁵ Chappelle imagines a blind man, Clayton Bigsby, who does not know he is black and who has become a prominent spokesman for white supremacists. Bigsby spouts racial hate speech, but the clear satiric effect of the sketch undermines its ideology. Chappelle employs the signifiers of white supremacy but situates their use in a comic context that produces a clear opposition to their original meaning, reversing the original discourse. As Simon Weaver puts it, "The multiple meanings generated by the reverse comic discourse represent forms of sign-slippage via appropriation."⁵⁶

At first glance, the tactic of a reverse discourse appears as the unstable irony and degenerative satire strain of postmodernism, yet intends the stable irony and generative satire strain of postmodernism, a kind of rewriting or rescripting. Satirically employing a reverse discourse in the name of social justice, however, runs the risk of reinforcing the very conditions the satire critiques: "paradoxically, reverse discourses also contain a polysemic element that can, at times, reproduce racism."⁵⁷ Jessyka Finley and Lisa Guerrero present instances of satire that demonstrate the fraught nature of employing caustic ridicule in the name of social justice.⁵⁸ Satire's inherent ethical risks become particularly problematic when satirists package ridicule as parody, when their postmodern citation intends to rewrite, repurpose, and redirect racial and gender discrimination.

The structure of a reverse discourse initially accepts the postmodern environment as the name of the signifying game, but only as a gambit to challenge the premise of detached irony that would weaken or even deny postmodern satire as a force for promoting change. The civic engagement implied in the structure of a reverse discourse emerging from the detachment of a postmodern irony, similar to what Amber Day calls "ironic authenticity," suggests the supplement to the postmodern public sphere that characterizes truthiness satire. In this brand of satire, the postmodern condition's supposed hostility toward satire has not been left behind so much as its signature skepticism has been turned in a new direction.⁵⁹

Case Study: Colbert, #CancelColbert, and Comic Reverse Discourse

On March 26, 2014, Stephen Colbert notably presented a reverse discourse, always a fraught tactic, as Dave Chappelle knows and as the character Archie Bunker proved long ago: people miss the irony—or choose to ignore it. In this case, some audience members, in the name of undermining racism, chose to ignore Colbert's intent to mimic in comic fashion and thus undermine racism.

In a segment satirizing the racist implications of the name for a professional football team, the Washington Redskins, as well as owner Dan Snyder's creation a few days earlier of a charity, "The Washington Redskins Original Americans Foundation," Colbert introduced his parodic version, "The Ching-Chong Ding-Dong Foundation for Sensitivity to Orientals or Whatever."[60] The parody implies that Colbert's pundit persona cared about a minority as much as Synder, the phrase "or Whatever" being the clue to the ironic depth of his sympathy. Snyder's charity demonstrates an obvious attempt to blunt #flashmob activism about the racist implications of the team's name, and Colbert clearly intended his fictional charity to be a satirical parody. The segment, which originally aired on a Wednesday, does not present a particularly complicated tactic: the charitable organization for the benefit of a minority community uses a racial epithet for that same community in the organization's name—an absurd fictional extrapolation of Snyder's own logic. Presumably, everyone who hates racism and despises Daniel Snyder laughs. Suey Park, the social activist who created the hashtag "#CancelColbert," however, did not miss the irony but rather chose to take the joke seriously for her own agenda, which at first glance does not include satire as a tool for reform. Colbert's parody shows that he stands with Park insofar as both are denouncing racism, but Colbert playfully mimics as a reverse discourse the racist signifiers as the tactic of denunciation.

The ensuing scenario demonstrates the Twitter #flashmob doing its thing: Park's hashtag trends for the rest of the week and the weekend. The digital clash acquires its dramatic force in part because of the difference between the segment on the show that featured reverse discourse and the tweet that appeared next evening on the show's promotional Twitter account, which reproduced a sentence from the segment without context: "I am willing to show #Asian community I care by introducing the Ching-Chong Ding-Dong Foundation for Sensitivity to Orientals or Whatever." Crucially, that Twitter account is the network's account, not Stephen Colbert's personal Twitter account, another clue that the apparent slur was not his own thought. As Colbert joked in his rejoinder to the hashtag demanding his show be canceled, "Who would have thought that a means of communication limited to 140 characters would ever create misunderstandings?"

Colbert's on-air reaction featured a number of other good points.[61] For example, he references Jonathan Swift's "A Modest Proposal" and claims to be offended as an Irish-American after reading just the first line, the point being that reacting negatively to Colbert's parody entails reacting without context and essentially in response to the tweet rather than the segment—or as he quips, "When the twit hit the fan." Moreover, Colbert in a number of places in his response drops his conservative pundit persona, most notably when he says that the hashtag activist Park—"hashtavist" he jokes—has been viciously attacked on Twitter, and that if Colbert fans think such tweets justify the satire and defend Colbert, they should stop immediately because Park merely spoke her mind.

Part of the bantering attitude in Colbert's reaction stems from the way he plays with his conservative pundit persona playing another character, a stereotypically caricatured Asian American. The fictional layers allow for a postmodern joke about the comic truth of what Colbert's persona says and thus about the availability of the real. When referring to his caricature of an Asian, Colbert says, "Very important: he is a character. He is not me. This is the real Stephen Colbert [gesturing to himself]. I mean everything I say on this show. He [gesturing toward the inset image of himself playing the Asian character] means . . . well, you just have to ask him, and he's not returning my calls right now." However, even with context, the #CancelColbert partisans claimed Colbert promotes racism. Colbert's performance in his response stages a rhetorical dance between his true self (his self self?) and his pundit self, saying first, "I am not a racist" (apparently his true self), and then reverting to a standard joke he makes as his pundit self: "I don't even see race. Not even my own. People tell me I'm white and I believe them because I just devoted six minutes to explaining how I'm not a racist." Colbert thus performs a complicated joke by encapsulating some of the problem surrounding conversations about race in America: white folks defensive and often unaware; people of color always necessarily aware and always trying to "stay woke" while also getting white folks "woke."[62]

Colbert also takes the opportunity to mock the news media as "a small group of people who only get their news from Twitter." Recapping the entire process allows Colbert to satirize the media ecosystem, which too often only wants contentious content, even if the dust-up merely conjures a phantom event, a simulacrum of news: "A web editor I've never met posts a tweet in my name on an account that I don't control, outrages a hashtag activist, and the news media gets seventy-two hours of content. The system worked."

This mixture of so-called hashtag activism with a satiric television show not only instructs by allowing a closer look at comic reverse discourse; it also illustrates how reverse discourse mocks and ironizes the through-the-looking-glass effect of truthiness. If the through-the-looking-glass trope often operates as a controlling metaphor for the postmodern environment, spawning truthiness, it also enables individuals, both professional comics and not-professional comics, to zigzag with ease between the comic public sphere and the public sphere so that the two discursive zones appear as a blended entity. In this instance, Colbert makes that zigzagging obvious enough, but it turns out that much the same can be said for Suey Park, who initiated the campaign "#CancelColbert." Dubbed a veteran of so-called "hashtag activism" by the media, Park has started or facilitated several other successful hashtags and, for her efforts, she was named one of the *Guardian*'s "top 30 young people in digital media."[63]

Most interesting for my purposes, Park suggests that she too plays a role. Moreover, she plays it self-consciously, "satirizing what we might expect from a twenty-three-year-old hashtag activist. 'There's no reason for me to act reasonable, because I won't be taken seriously anyway,' she said. 'So I might as well perform crazy to point out exactly what's expected from me,'"[64] a strategy that sounds similar to a reverse discourse. In an interview shortly after the outburst of anger generated by #CancelColbert, Park again resembles Colbert, saying that she sees herself as "someone who is both a writer and an activist," one who uses satire and hyperbole to imply political commentary. "I write jokes about race all the time, but I think they're supposed to make a social commentary."[65]

A postmodern *mise en abyme* of comic playfulness exists here in that Park claims to be displaying a persona for public consumption, as Colbert does. She intends her persona to critique Colbert's faux pundit, which in turn critiques by imitating an actual conservative pundit, Bill O'Reilly. Moreover, in this particular instance of satire under scrutiny, the Colbert persona projects yet another character in order to ridicule an actual person, Dan Snyder, and the name of his foundation. Like Colbert, Park performed and for the same reason: to ridicule and undermine racism.

For Park, the problem centers not on the intent but the tactic, objecting to the reverse discourse Colbert uses:

> The difference [from white folks like Colbert joking about race] is that I didn't take away attention from Dan Snyder or the Redskins. Colbert did when he chose to ruin an opportunity to make a point about racism in America by using more racism. So he's the one that destroyed an opportunity to shed light on Dan Snyder and the Redskins the moment that he chose to use Orientalism and a foreign accent to make his point.

And so, I think in that sense, it's Colbert that lacks context. It's Colbert that doesn't realize how he's using racism as a vehicle to end racism, which is really just circular logic and doesn't lead to an end destination of liberation.[66]

As Colbert says, Park speaks her mind, and in doing so, she epitomizes the problematic of the audience for a comic utterance, whether a joke or an entire satiric performance, for example a segment within an episode of *The Colbert Report*. In the first sentence of the last quote, Park demonstrates a basic problem for the consumption of satire: deciding what or who is the comic butt. When Park says that Colbert has taken attention away from Snyder and the name of his team, the Redskins, she denies that Colbert targets them as comic butts. Instead, Park's attention falls on the racism embedded in the satire's parody rather than the parody itself. That attention short-circuits the possibility of comic laughter because Park refuses the parodic nature of the utterance, guaranteeing its uptake as satire will fail. Moreover, when Park charges that Colbert "doesn't realize how he's using racism as a vehicle to end racism, which is really just circular logic," she explicitly blocks comic reverse discourse as the mechanism for the parody.[67] Park's objection implicitly blocks all reverse racism satire, including Dave Chappelle's use of racism as a vehicle to ridicule racism with his Clayton Bigsby character. Perhaps, her objection also curtails sharply the legitimate use of parody, like Colbert's persona. In the end, #CancelColbert for Park meant "knowing it would make him just a little bit more aware of how that satire isn't actually even very funny."[68] The ultimate joke for anyone following the controversy perhaps centers on how the intent for a comic utterance can be lost in the joking mechanism, making adversaries of like-minded satirists.

The #CancelColbert effort vividly illustrates the problem of comic laughter and audience, and not just that individuals in an audience will not all respond to a comic performance in the same way. Comic artifacts all present structures of incongruity and thus have an inherent potential for ambiguity. The comic use of a reverse discourse only enhances that potential. Simon Weaver puts it this way: "As humour increases its structural polysemia through the material of reversal, ambiguity increases, fixed meaning becomes more unlikely to appear, and the potential for multifarious political and ethical interpretations" becomes more likely.[69] Even more than other comic artifacts, those that employ reverse discourse flirt with an audience's failure to have a properly felicitous uptake. Indeed, comic reverse discourse effectively calls into question the very notion of such a successful uptake for a comic utterance or performance. When truthiness satire has at its base a reverse discourse effort against postmodern simulacra, it significantly runs the risk of being confused with the anti-public sphere rhetoric it targets with its ridicule.

The #CancelColbert effort also highlights the supplemental role the satirist intends to play in the public sphere. "Well-intentioned racial humor doesn't actually do anything to end racism or the Redskins mascot," Park said. "That sort of racial humor just makes people who hide under the title of progressivism more comfortable."[70] Park thus provides a clear example of the critique that satire does nothing to affect the real-world policy issue at stake. As Jay Kang notes, "Over the past two days, much of the debate about #CancelColbert has been about the efficacy of hashtag activism and whether the act of dissent has been cheapened by the ease, and sometimes frivolity, of Twitter protests."[71] I will return to the issue of satire's efficacy in the public sphere. For now, the #CancelColbert example highlights how comic tactics might frustrate rather than enable the comic public sphere as supplement.

Truthiness Satire and Satiractivism

Two seemingly opposed strains of satire must be posited to acknowledge the continuing force of the postmodern condition. Despite the deep irony of early postmodernism that seems to block satire, *vide* Layne Neeper's analysis mentioned earlier, the satire of the so-called black humorists appeared at the beginning of the postmodern epoch. However, that initial strain of satiric critique often offered no explicit call to action and/or no clear PSA sense of value upon which to base that action because unstable irony dominates the aesthetics of postmodern satire, especially in its first wave of examples. Weisenburger's analysis shows that the comic butts targeted nevertheless imply values. The resulting satire appears unsure of its pedigree as an art form with an impulse not only to judge but to reform, a degenerative satire.

As a newer, second postmodern strain, truthiness satire wields its irony, ultimately, with more assurance of its intent, asserting its ability to reclaim—not our political and social institutions—but rather a positive discursive space within the truthiness of the (digital) postmodern public sphere. A potential for active resistance marks that space, a resistance that begins in comic form but might enable a serious pushback against the simulacra regime of anti-public sphere truthiness: the satire two-step. This push-back—comic *parrhēsia*—offers the possibility of imagining reverse discourses in the name of social justice. Such robust satire and the potential for an accompanying satiractivism place a focus on the audience, and so digimodernism's emphasis on the audience provides the proper conceptual frame. However, these audience members behave actively rather than passively, their collective digits ready to blog and tweet about the issues that matter to them as individuals and as groups, issues highlighted by their favorite satirists or satiric formats.

Truthiness satire reimagines postmodern irony with an inflection of earnestness and insists on the persistence of local truths in the current cultural atmosphere. Truthiness satire exploits the hyperreal saturation of simulacra to rescript and so realign, however partially, the postmodern condition. Facts still matter and thus satire can still operate with a generative intent reminiscent of its historical tradition; satire can still matter in the face of a regime of simulacra, even take advantage of the anti-public sphere logic of truthiness. "You must go on. I can't go on. I'll go on"[72] might be its motto. With its potential for an embedded activist intent, truthiness satire enacts Jeff St. Onge's "engaged levity": an absurd treatment of civic issues that constitutes an ethical stance. Moreover, its ridicule operates ethically in any effort to undermine and even reverse the direction of a corrupting institutional power.

Truthiness satire does not return to unproblematic ideas about representation or even to modernism's playful anxiety about it, illustrated, for example, in the fractured point of view of Pablo Picasso's *Les Demoiselles d'Avignon*. Rather, truthiness satire turns its attention from representation as a fun-house mirror of intertextuality and metafictional doubling to explore how reverse discourses can be mobilized within a play of signifiers. Such play—drawing upon deconstruction's *différance*—therefore does not necessarily present a maze that traps in order to question the very structures of knowledge and meaning making, as does the play of the black humorists, but instead offers an aesthetic opening within discourses of hegemonic power, an opening that provides maneuvering room to resist by constructing alternatives. Iteration provides both the stuff of self-replicating ideologies and opportunities to short-circuit that process. Thus performance matters very much in truthiness satire: performance means parodic iteration and citation but with *différance* to enable the possibility of modification that could strengthen into the overt mocking resistance of a reverse discourse—even displaying satiractivism. This process seems particularly relevant for issues of identity and subjectivity, for if the dynamic of the contemporary self demands one continual performance within the parameters of social and discursive practices, as Judith Butler has argued,[73] then the parodic citation of racial and gender stereotypes stands as paradigmatic of satire operating within a truthiness condition.

Truthiness satire does not claim that either its implicit or explicit (PSA) corrective should be tabulated as normative; its reverse discourses instead should be understood as local, not universal. Postmodernism marks a loss of faith in metanarratives, yet truthiness satire does not then say that truth or truth values cannot be located; they are, however, contingent and piebald, streaked with an indeterminacy that displays the heritage of the postmodern. However, truthiness satire disallows that contingency and indeterminacy the status of a necessary and sufficient condition. Truthiness satire argues instead for a saltatory process—the satire two-step of a–musement—a process of rescripting via performative iterations: not the radiant play of signifiers as focus, but what kind of laughter-inducing responses remain as possible in such a regime. Those responses employ satire to create "ha ha" moments that are also "aha!" moments.

PART 2

Doing Things with Satiric Words

Difficile est satyras non scribere.
(It is difficult not to write satire.)
—Juvenal

Satire and Speech Act Theory

4.

A key tenet of my argument claims that satire is best understood as a particular kind of speech act that signals a particular kind of comic attitude. In this chapter, I borrow ideas from speech act theory as a framework for how some comic artifacts operate in the social and political world. Treating comic artifacts as comic speech acts—that is, as a subset of what J. L. Austin calls parasitic speech as opposed to full normal speech—will help to understand how what I have been calling truthiness satire might operate as comic political speech within the comic public sphere. I rework Austin's model without meaning to endorse its broader implications or fate in discussions on the philosophy of language, pragmatics, or the methodological variations of discourse analysis.[1]

Speech Act Theory: The Basics

The first point from speech act theory involves the distinction between *constatives* and *performatives*. Austin defines constatives as statements of fact, reports, or descriptions that can be judged either true or false. Performatives entail not just saying something but doing something: "the idea of a performative utterance was that it was to be (or to be included as part of) the performance of an action"; thus, "there is something which is *at the moment of uttering being done by the person uttering*."[2]

Austin wants to make explicit the different communicative forces within utterances, how utterances are to be taken: they must "secure uptake" (138) from a listener or audience, which implies the many ways that an utterance might be misconstrued and thus fail to secure its uptake, its intended meaning. Performatives for Austin imply intent. Thus saying *I am sorry* performs an apology, while asking—*Is he really sorry?*—implies the intent of the performative even as it is questioned. In contrast, the utterance, *He said he was sorry* reports what was uttered, a constative.

Austin distinguishes three classes of speech acts: locutionary, illocutionary, perlocutionary. For all of them, "the occasion of an utterance matters seriously" (100)—that is, not just the meaning of the words but also the context in which they are spoken will define the level of communicative force. Utterances understood as speech acts must always be understood as existing in a web of context. When Austin references "the field of actions which we perform with words" (76), he is evoking the complexity of that web, which constrains as it enables meaning.

For Austin, saying something in what he calls a full normal sense (sound, grammar, meaning) is a *locutionary act*; it is the performance of the act *of* saying something (94). An *illocutionary act* is the performance of an act *in* saying something; there can be different kinds of communicative force in saying something (for example, one can promise, pronounce, command, question)—for a satire, one ridicules. The illocution "takes effect" (116) or must "secure uptake" (138) from the audience. A *perlocutionary act* will "produce certain consequential effects upon the feelings, thoughts, or actions of the audience, or of the speaker, or of other persons: and it may be done with the design, intention, purpose of producing them" (101). In short, a perlocution characteristically *produces* certain effects by saying something (117)—that is, there can be actual consequences—bringing about new states of mind or substantive changes in the course of events.

Satire as Comic Speech

Dividing a set of utterances into political speech (always serious) and comic speech (always nonserious and playful), one can say that a speaker always intends political speech as a perlocutionary act, with an intention to effect real consequences—that is, to bring about a change in public policy or civic life, or at least a change in the debates concerning public policy and civic life. In contrast, comic speech in a satiric mode always registers first as illocutionary: the utterance performs ridicule without the intent to produce direct, substantive changes in the course of events. Insofar as that ridicule might bring about change, insofar as satire can display some measure of perlocutionary force, that function in my theoretical view should be restricted to a change of mind in the audience, or of the speaker, or of other persons—a *metanoia*. The utterance *I hereby walk to the store* does not perform the act of walking. One cannot perform the act of walking by pronouncing certain words. Similarly, a satire as comic speech act supporting a street protest can never be the equivalent of a street protest; a stand-up comedy performance satirizing citizens opposed to the Black Lives Matter movement can never be equivalent to a rally about police violence organized by Black Lives Matter. The satire within the format of a stand-up performance should be understood as a comic political speech act; the street protest and the rally function as political speech acts. The uptake for speech acts of Volodymyr Zelensky as president of Ukraine cannot be the same as those uttered by Volodymyr Zelensky the host of a satiric TV program, *Servant of the People*.

Austin makes an important distinction about language used in special ways—statements made, for example, "by an actor on a stage, or if introduced in a poem" (22)—in short, fictional statements. The fundamental distinction of *constatives* and *performatives* remains, but he declines to examine statements within the pretense of storyworlds, which he calls a "parasitic" use of language. For Austin, when Ebenezer Scrooge asserts, "I promise to keep Christmas in my heart," no one needs to check up on him later to be sure he keeps that promise. Concerns about the felicity or infelicity of that fictional performative—that is, the performative registers as a success or a failure—do not worry the philosopher of language because the normal conditions of reference are suspended.

Keeping the distinction of parasitic versus normal use of language, I want to do what Austin refuses and allow significant focus on parasitic or fictionalized language for my purposes as an investigator of comic artifacts and, in particular, as an investigator of the nature and poetics of satire. Austin at one point says that joking or writing poetry is "remote" (104) from his three categories of speech acts—locutionary, illocutionary, perlocutionary; I later use the last category to explore how satiractivism apparently operates as a special kind of political speech act. Moreover, the focus on a parasitic use of language (fiction) operates in a way that surely would have caused Austin to protest because my scheme insists that satire displays both a normal and a parasitic use of language. The fantasy and grotesquerie and general silliness that can characterize satire all form part of satire's fictional and thus parasitic pretense, while its habitual references to actual events and people demonstrates, in Austin's terms, a normal use of language.

Another way to describe the paradoxical ontology of satire being serious and nonserious at once: it behaves both as a constative and as a performative. The obvious side would be its status as a performative, in that it could be badly executed and thus fail, or in Austin's terms, become infelicitous. Alternatively, the aesthetic execution of the satire could be done well yet members of an audience could reject the utterance as not funny, another kind of infelicity. Suey Park's negative reaction to Stephen Colbert's comic reverse discourse about the Washington Redskins provides a good example of this last possibility. However, like a constative, a satire also can be mistaken or declared void or false if an audience member or reader judges its underlying values as wrong. Satires entail, imply, or presuppose constative statements in the values they champion. If a satirist mocks Donald Trump and representatives of his administration as incompetent and his or her audience laughs, it does so because its laughing members believe that a presidential administration should be competent. In short, the uptake by an audience for a satire as a comic political speech act could apprehend the utterance's status as either a performative or a constative.

Nevertheless, once one acknowledges the fictional or parasitic dimension of satire as a speech act, its performative quality comes to the forefront, with both illocutionary and some perlocutionary force. What does it perform at the illocutionary level?—what all recognize as the *sine qua non* for a satire, a mocking ridicule of a comic butt. However, satire as a speech act has a (weak) perlocutionary force also—that is, it has the "purpose of producing . . . effects upon the feelings, thoughts, or actions of the audience or of the speaker" (101). Satire at its best effects a metanoia in its audience, a change in thinking, perception, or belief—even a repentance of the old way of thinking, perceiving, believing. However, some contemporary satire also exhibits at times a potential for the quasi-perlocutionary force of satiractivism. Distinguishing between those two levels of satire's performative force will be a chief concern in the next chapters, which establish the difference between the relatively weak perlocutionary force indicated by the idea of metanoia and the relatively stronger perlocutionary force indicated by the idea of satiractivism.

5.

Satire as Speech Act, Part One

Examples of contemporary satire come in many forms, but the class of satiric artifacts that displays most consistently a relationship with the public sphere are those instances that distinguish themselves by comically playing with the news. Playing with the news has led to the cultural moment today in which professional comics explain the news with jokes, daily and on multiple channels, a cultural moment in which journalists willingly collaborate with satirists, a cultural moment in which the comic public sphere and the public sphere often appear as one discursive domain.

Playing with the News

Satire that plays with the news highlights in boldface its basic structure of being both serious and nonserious. The first television show in the postmodern era that brilliantly exploited that structure was the British production of *That Was the Week That Was* (*TW3*), with David Frost, which regularly employed parodies of broadcast news presentations for satiric purposes.[1]

The signature song performed by Millicent Martin at the top of the show presented last week's headlines in the lyrics, usually followed by Frost sitting at a desk highlighting two or three more headlines. In both segments, images of actual newspaper clippings with the headlines would often be flashed, presumably to demonstrate the validity of the song lyrics and what Frost offered as headlines and to imply the attitude, *you can't make this stuff up*. *TW3* routinely mocked public figures, usually politicians, for what they had done and said. In one segment from the February 16, 1963, show, members of parliament who rarely spoke or gave speeches were ridiculed by reading out some of the few words they had spoken, which were starkly cliché-ridden and banal.

While *TW3* regularly employed actual news headlines as source material for its satire, Frost did not pretend to be a newsman reading the news, which was one of the innovations featured years later in the "Weekend Update" segment as part of *Saturday Night Live* (*SNL*). Though *SNL* might claim *TW3* as a forerunner, both shows using skits and show tunes for comic purposes, it changed Frost's tactic of merely presenting headlines to ridicule their absurdities to a complete parody of a broadcast news anchorman. "Weekend Update" managed that shift by simply adding a new visual component: mimicking a news program's staging with an anchor newsman desk, behind which a performer read mock news copy with a screen above him showing images relevant to the parade of stories. Ridicule in *SNL*'s short mock news segment early on was most often directed at events and celebrities, rarely at political figures in any satiric fashion, at least in the first year with Chevy Chase as the faux news anchor. President Ford's legendary clumsiness offered a frequent target, but the segment mostly left out his administration's policies: slapstick, not satire. The ridicule from "Weekend Update" was also directed at broadcast news media, with Chase's character often caught talking personal matters on a phone, supposedly prior to being on air, to mock journalistic gravitas. The parody of news broadcasts extended to having a special report from a faux field correspondent (Lorraine Newman initially). This early formula has remained remarkably stable over the years.[2]

The Daily Show (*TDS*) represents the turning point for the mock news format. The creators of *TDS* originally conceived of it as a satiric parody of a "a failing cable network."[3] They deliberately wanted to differentiate the new show from *SNL*'s "Weekend Update" and have it "operate like a newsroom, but be a comedy show" (xvi)—that is, be a full parody of a news show, be mock news. Thus the format "loosely tracked that of a conventional newscast" (xvii). Like "Weekend Update," *The Daily Show* in its first iteration with Craig Kilborn hosting did more pop culture and lifestyle bits than politics because that journalistic angle mimicked what local news did, and the *TDS* staff understood their principal satiric target to be those soft news broadcasts.

When Jon Stewart took over the hosting duties, he wanted the satire in *TDS* to "punch up" (6) and thus be more about the public sphere conversation. Stewart brought "a real desire to have a satirical point of view about the substance of the ideas, not just the actions of the people" (21). Part of the ensuing change entailed not just spoofing news headlines or local news fluff pieces but also making fun of the mainstream news media. Stewart and company satirically interpret the news—*here is the news but now here is what it means from a comic perspective*—and thus create a point of view active rather than reactive or merely descriptive.

TDS under Stewart expanded the original notion of operating like a comic newsroom by ramping up the machinery needed for being an actual news-gathering entity: cutting footage deals, acquiring feeds, caching B-roll. Jon Stewart describes this *TDS* mash-up, the show's discursive integration to build a satiric mock news outlet, this way: "We were serious people doing a very stupid thing, and they (the news media) were unserious people doing a very serious thing" (51). In other words, the news media itself became a very large satiric target—the bull's-eye of the mock news enterprise. Moreover, Stewart complemented the material backbone of an actual news organization by hiring Chuck O'Neil from ABC, who as director promptly made *The Daily Show* set and graphics look like *World News Tonight*, and then hiring Jim Margolis from *60 Minutes* to become head of the field correspondents' production. *TDS* had a research chief, Adam Chodikoff, who read newspapers and websites daily, scoured the *Congressional Record* and reports from the Congressional Budget Office, and created a stable of academic policy experts as consultants, all to generate ideas and vet the accuracy of *TDS* segments. Over time, *TDS* became not just "the scourge of phonies but the nation's fact checker," as Emily Nussbaum put it (quoted in Smith, 157).

The legitimate news organization infrastructure served comic purposes. Steve Carrell indicates that mix of the serious and the silly when describing the basic persona of the faux field correspondents: "You're not really a reporter. You're pretending to be one. You're not really in character but kind of have to be. So you're improvising all day and pretending to be a correspondent, which none of us had any background in. So we were all sort of winging it. My character was a guy who took himself pretty seriously, but wasn't really up to the task" (23). David Javerbaum (the first writer hired by Ben Karlin, whom Stewart tapped to be head writer) refers to this persona as an "unreliable narrator" (42), which captures the liminal quality of the faux correspondent that Carrell describes, a topic I explore later with examples of Jordan Klepper's field correspondent reports. Stewart says that both Carrell and Stephen Colbert had a gift for using the faux correspondent persona to improvise with the person being interviewed so that they were not "just roasting this person. They were taking a walk with them" (66).

The competition in the early days of *The Daily Show with Jon Stewart* for doing mock news was only *SNL*'s "Weekend Update," which was much shorter and thus could not parody and satirize with any depth a particular subject, a difference *TDS* staff and Stewart understood and exploited. John Oliver's *Last Week Tonight* would be the next logical step once *TDS* had stamped its version of mock news on the cultural scene: an even longer comic focus on a specific topic. Thus the first important contribution of *The Daily Show* to developing the genre of mock news was its lengthening the "Weekend Update" segments, which were never more than a few minutes long, into a sit-down comic monologue that opened the show. The monologue featured satiric commentary on news events, but its duration indicated the prominence of satire and signaled a genre switch, from a variety-style show with skits and songs to a full-blown mock news format. Moreover, *The Daily Show* signaled its true genre as mock news not only by elaborating its parodic set, courtesy of Chuck O'Neil, but also by routinely adding multiple reports from so-called field correspondents. The look of the show along with its structure mimicked network news, with Stewart as the anchor at his desk and his faux correspondents reporting on specific stories.

What truly distinguished *The Daily Show with Jon Stewart* as mock news, however, was the way that Stewart often turned the interview segment, a feature of late-night talk shows, into something more closely resembling the Sunday political talk shows, such as *Meet the Press* and *Face the Nation*. When Stewart hosted Hollywood guests for the interview segment, he played the usual talk show host's role of burnishing celebrity. When politicians featured as the guests, the interview segment mirrored the news/discussion/public affairs hybrid format of the Sunday shows. Stewart also hosted guests writing serious books about public affairs so that in any given episode Comedy Central morphed into the Public Broadcasting System or C-SPAN for ten to twelve minutes. *TDS* became the place to go for a portion of the electorate who wanted to escape from the talking-head pundits (mostly the shouting-head pundits), those citizens who wanted to find support for their view that the public sphere had become absurd and/or who enjoyed being educated via comic tactics about important civic issues of the moment.

The Daily Show with Jon Stewart presents the phenomenon of the satirist explaining the news with darts of ridicule and mockery hurled at a variety of comic butts, sometimes the news media itself being one of those butts. The fourth estate supposedly acts as a check on government, operates as the watchdog for democracy. However, because, as Geoffrey Baym details, mainstream news on cable as well as legacy channels has seemed unable to keep up with the volume of bunkum streaming from the White House and Congress as well as other elected officials, citizens in the twenty-first century have turned in unprecedented numbers to satirists who speak truth to power: comic *parrhēsia* needed in extra-large portions.

As the brief genealogy of comically playing with the news suggests, the basic structure of satire as both serious and nonserious has enabled a generic mash-up that has blended in varying degrees news with mock news as comic pundits mock the punditry offered by news shows, while sit-down or standup comedians mock talk show hosts as well as the hosts of the Sunday political shows. That mash-up also contributes to conceiving of satire as a performative speech act in relationship to the public sphere and its reliance on informed citizens. These shows now function as news outlets for silly citizens. A significant portion of the body politic is not just entertained by the satiric send-ups these shows routinely offer; many individuals receive news first-hand from them.[4]

Developing distinctions among satire's rhetorical effects understood as displaying locutionary force, illocutionary force, and perlocutionary force enables a sorting through of the varying deployments of ridicule in the service of the public sphere within this realm of satires premised on playing with the news. An examination of specific examples could be organized along a spectrum based on Austin's categories. The spectrum highlights how satire's paradoxical structure of serious and nonserious can be manipulated with the possibility of creating not just standard satire with an illocutionary force but also a particular and less ordinary version, satiractivism. Examples of satire based on playing with the news could therefore be sorted into three groups:

1. a group that most closely functions as a locutionary act—that is, most closely resembles actual news reporting as a constative speech act—with comic techniques operating as rhetorical dressing;
2. a group that functions mainly as an illocutionary act—that is, full-blown comic presentations with clear satiric butts—sometimes complete with an explicit, serious statement of the needed action or reform; and
3. a group that moves significantly from an illocutionary function toward a perlocutionary function that goes beyond the possibility

of achieving metanoia. This last group also has full-blown comic presentations with clear satiric butts and often includes a serious announcement of the needed action or reform. In addition, this group completes its satire with an explicit call to the audience as citizens to engage in the democratic process to achieve the needed reform. Examples from this last group therefore exhibit the quasi-perlocutionary quality that distinguishes satiractivism.

One particular feature of satire in an illocutionary mode must be underlined: its ridicule of comic butts performs the basic task of making desired public sphere values visible by way of counterexample. This process has always been a feature of satire. However, a satire often does not rest with its ironically laughable presentation; it might also employ what rhetoricians call *paralipsis*, in which the desired values are explicitly stated. This move constitutes the PSA moment, wherein the satire presents the wished-for value, behavior, or reform as though a Public Service Announcement had been stuffed into the comic presentation. Paralipsis is not a recent invention. Jonathan Swift uses it in "A Modest Proposal." John Oliver's *Last Week Tonight* gains much of its special essay-like quality from its insistent educational thrust, as though he intends his satiric presentation to be consumed as an extended and comic PSA.

Satire as Locutionary Speech Act

In the first or locutionary group, closest to actual news reporting, I offer two examples, Jack Shafer's weekly column, "The Swamp Diary," appearing in *Politico*, and the blog "Politics with Charles P. Pierce" in *Esquire*. Shafer's weekly column started in May 2017 when it was clear that a true scandal about Russian interference in the 2016 election was brewing: "This was the week that the seeds of scandal and ineptitude planted over the past six months finally sprouted their first shoots, wrapping green tendrils around the president's ankles and around the throats of his aides, yanking them to earth. . . . Trump is now caught in history's grinder, and the sparks and noise emitted are lighting up the media universe" (Week 1, May 27, 2017). Shafer's forte rests upon his ability to report the news from the week before with just enough comic phrasing to a–muse, especially those readers in the body politic who cannot believe that Donald Trump occupies the oval office and who hope for cosmic justice to put things right.

Though Shafer clearly has journalistic reporting as his first goal, he fashions his column as more than reporting and thus, at times, offers something more or less reminiscent of a standup monologue in print or of *SNL*'s "Weekend Update," politically focused and repurposed for the pages of *Politico*. However, the best current comparison might be to *Last Week Tonight with John Oliver*, even though Shafer's column and Oliver's television show occupy slots in very different media, sit very nearly on opposite ends of a sarcasm range, and inhabit the very different categories of locutionary and illocutionary, with Oliver also intermittently flashing the quasi-perlocutionary force of satiractivism. Despite these differences, "Swamp Diary" and *Last Week Tonight* have at their core a reportorial intent: they first wish to inform the citizenry.

Shafer uses the trope "swamp" to organize his reporting on Trump's potentially scandalous relationship with Russia. He also at times treats the news about the Russia investigation as though it could be packaged into different kinds of movies or television genres—spy thrillers, revenge drama, reality show run amok—more evidence of discursive integration. This tactic in one column engenders "Action Hero Robert Mueller," dubbed "a Charles Bronson type, remaining silent for reel after reel." The movie trope reappears in another column: "Thanks to his shouting and warmongering, Trump has made it easy to frame him as the villain, so let's do it. Having minted his brand in gold—everything from sink fixtures to seatbelt buckles to Oval Office curtains woven an auric yellow—Trump will be this feature's Mr. Gold(short)finger. Preening, cruel and more than a little cocky. Too cocky. Compare him with Mueller, a living, walking Gary Cooper who doesn't leak, doesn't talk to the press, and has successfully sworn his posse to secrecy" (Week 20, October 7, 2017). For anti-Trump readers, such pop culture framing makes perfect sense: the unfolding scandal effectively (and sarcastically) interpreted as an easily accessible movie narrative in which The Donald plays the villain.

Shafer's consistent use of comic phrasing functions as a seasoning of lampoon and satire to the main dish of narrating actual events. Different examples illustrate the amounts of such seasoning, varying the laughter-provoking quotient. First, consider examples of his reporting with a minimalist comic tone, which occupies the default position in the weekly column, for the fundamental strength of "Swamp Diary" resides in its locutionary force of summarizing news events and compiling facts about the investigation.

What if that constitutional crisis over the subpoena or indictment of Donald Trump that every TV pundit, wringing sweaty palms, has forewarned us of never comes to pass?

By constitutional crisis, I mean an unprecedented state of affairs that contributes to a decline in the Constitution's perceived legitimacy or sends a chicken-with-its-head-cut-off emergency pleading to the Supreme Court. Looking wide and far, I see no such decline, no such headless chicken. . . .

As long as the Constitution is performing its central functions, . . . no constitutional crisis exists. The Constitution's framework appears to be operating nicely. The full heat of a criminal investigation is falling on the president almost daily and yet the sun rises and sets just the same. The best remedy for a criminal president, if it comes to that, will be impeachment. And impeachment never signifies a constitutional crisis. It is the Constitution. (Week 55, June 9, 2018)

In a sharp *Washington Post* overview of the special counsel's investigation this week, Aaron Blake wrote that the language contained in the Kilimnik "Person A" court filings indicates that Mueller might be attempting to show that Manafort actually "colluded" with the Russians during the campaign. "It doesn't say how compelling that evidence is, mind you, but it makes it crystal clear that was a focal point of the probe," Blake writes. This hunch would explain why Manafort—unlike Gates, Michael Flynn and George Papadopoulos—hasn't copped a Mueller plea. Perhaps Mueller hasn't offered him one because he's assembled a substantial, bulletproof case against him not worth trading away for cooperation. (Week 46, April 7, 2018)

In Shafer's weekly columns, eventually numbering nearly one hundred, he often directs significant slices of ridicule at specific public individuals in what should be labeled that version of satire Jonathan Swift calls *lampoons*. When the lampooning impulse predominates, the quotient of caustic phrasing goes up—sometimes way up, as this bouquet of quotes suggests:

Testifying before the House Intelligence Committee this week, Sessions offered more excuses than a high schooler who just crashed his mom's car while skipping classes and drinking behind the wheel. . . . This week, Sessions updated his original statement again: reading press accounts about Papadopoulos, recently arrested for lying to the FBI, had triggered fresh recollections about a Trump-Putin meeting Papadopoulos had proposed at a meeting Sessions chaired. The attorney general blamed his poor memory on the "chaos" of the presidential campaign, the ensuing lack of sleep, his busy Senate schedule and heavy travel. Like the D student that he is, Sessions protested that it was unreasonable for the committee to expect him to remember the conversation he had with Trump foreign policy adviser Page about a Russia trip Page had arranged. (Week 26, November 18, 2017)

If the mark of a great diplomat is the ability to speak craziness with a straight face, Tillerson earned admittance to the Dips Hall of Fame. . . . Sounding more like a therapist than the secretary of state, Tillerson said, "We're unhappy. They're unhappy," and explained that salvaging this "really important relationship" meant blotting out the recent unpleasantness. (Take a shot of amnesia and call me in the morning.) Then Tillerson produced a laugh line that topped his previous ones. "The Russians have asked for proof and evidence" of the meddling, he said. Perhaps he should buy Putin a subscription to the *Washington Post*. (Week 7, July 8, 2017)

If we've learned anything from months of scandal reporting, the Russians set their sights on two types of people wandering the halls of Trump Tower. There were the self-promoters like Michael Flynn and Paul Manafort who they knew would cooperate based on direct or potential payouts. But the Russians also shopped a second group of Tower denizens, the over-their-heads strivers often compared to the hapless Fredo Corleone. These Fredos—George Papadopoulos and Carter Page—attracted Russian agents like magnets, and were easily manipulated by direct appeals to their stooped egos. But of all the Fredos occupying Trump world, perhaps Donald Trump Jr. proved to be the easiest mark for the Russians. (Week 26, November 18, 2017)

Trump becomes the biggest comic butt for lampooning, however, as in this very derisive analogy floated by Shafer shortly after the infamous ad hoc news conference in the lobby of Trump Tower that followed days after the riot and murder in Charlottesville, Virginia, 2017:

If and when the American Kennel Club gets around to assigning a new breed for dogs that resemble President Donald Trump—portly with short paws and a chow chow mane of Clorox blond?—it should not neglect to single out the breed's primary behavioral trait: Trump is what dog handlers would call a "fear-biter," not a naturally fierce or aggressive hound, but one that snaps and chomps when frightened.

A panicky and snarling Trump toothed his way down to bone this week.... Trump's ostensible topic of the week was white supremacists, with whom he threw in at a news conference and via a tweet triptych. But the intensity of his fury could not easily be explained. Who could have known he felt this strongly about Southern "heritage" beyond the casual racism he drools from time to time? As with canine rage, Trump's fulmination was probably a matter of transference, with some other trauma setting him off. (Week 13, August 19, 2017)

Analogizing Trump's characteristic behavior to a dog breed—a very bad-tempered dog breed—illustrates the higher levels of caustic comic phrasing Shafer at times allows himself, in this case commensurate with the significant events under scrutiny and the big stakes they entail. Shafer's analogy not only enables a way to dramatize in comically degrading terms the intensity of Trump's defense of the white supremacists, but it also sets up the easy yet apt psychologizing of a transference of generalized wrath from "some other trauma," bringing the satiric analysis back to the Russian investigation as the prime motivator for Trump's snarling behavior. In another column, Shafer again mixes in a high quotient of sardonic put-down, zeroing in once more on Trump's characteristic behaviors, this time not just his chronic ire but his chronic lying too:

> By jumping up and down with the fury of a Yosemite Sam, is Trump really confirming the accuracy and potency of the [Steele] dossier?
>
> We can find a sliver of truth in Trump's "the FBI paid for the dossier" line, but it's as sturdy as a wet Kleenex.... Trump remains the guy who deliberately confuses lightning bugs with lightning to get himself out of a jam.
>
> By stitching all of these unmatched remnants into a hypothetical conspiracy [about who funded the Steele Dossier], Trump seeks to undermine not the investigators on Capitol Hill or those working for special counsel Robert S. Mueller III, but the public. He's like a kid with a box of kitchen matches riding his trail bike through a dry forest, stopping every 100 yards to play pyromaniac and then bicycling on.

He had better hope that the winds don't shift and fires end up crisping him. (Week 22, October 21, 2017)

Although these lampooning examples highlight the illocutionary staple of satire, performing the witty ridiculing of a comic butt, they also illustrate how reporting decorated with edgy and sarcastic levity should nevertheless be tabulated within the locutionary end of a spectrum of contemporary satire playing with the news. Though clearly indulging in the comic speech of satire, Shafer displays differing levels of serious public sphere speech, at times moving beyond simple reporting and donning the hat of news analyst. For example, he suggests that Trump's deeper motive centers on undermining the public's trust in its institutions (the FBI and the press), a suggestion that hints at how Trump's undermining the trust of the *dēmos* undermines democracy. The satiric engagement with the public sphere could not be stronger in such instances.

Shafer powers his column with a summarizing function, both of the ongoing investigation of Trump and company and of the reporting by other journalists on the investigation and reactions to it. Nevertheless, the comic packaging shows conspicuously throughout his column as well, notably at the outset when Shafer gave the potential Russia collusion a ridiculing name to brand it as a scandal:

> The scandal with no name took an accelerating turn this week as the *New York Times* uncoiled three stunning stories about a June 9, 2016, meeting in Trump Tower where Donald Trump's kin and campaign brain trust conferred with a Russian emissary and her entourage. The naming convention for political scandals insists that we incorporate a place name into it—Watergate, Teapot Dome, Whitewater, Chappaquiddick, My Lai, Abu Ghraib, Iran Contra, et al. In observance of this rule, the disquieting meeting in which a Russian offered dirt on Hillary Clinton to Donald Trump Jr., Jared Kushner, and then-campaign manager Paul Manafort in the Manhattan skyscraper suggests "Trump Kowtower" as the carnival's best appellation. (Week 8, July 15, 2017)

The next week, Shafer's naming suggestion brought in a host of like-minded responses (as in no pun too cheap) from readers who had the correct uptake as silly citizens—*yes, the column reports in a fundamentally locutionary* mode, but it also reports in comic mode to giggle and maybe gloat over the news—and who wanted to participate digimodern style in the fun: "Trump Tower of Babble," "Chump Tower," "The Muscovian Candidate," "Kremlin-ghazi," "Mar-Gulag-o," "Battleship Putrumpin," and "K(GB) Street." Some of the suggestions show the relish with which Shafer's readers consume his narrative fare, his locutionary reporting mixed with illocutionary satire: "The Borscht Betrayals," "The Proofs in the Putin," "Lies with that Nothingburger?," "FUBAR Burger," "McHammer and Sickle," "Junior Minsk," "Moscow Mule." These epithets suggest how silly citizenship within digimodernism works, transforming citizens into would-be satirists and editorial cartoonists.

Though "swamp" in Shafer's "The Swamp Diary" title refers to the investigation into Russian interference in the 2016 election and possible obstruction of justice, he cannot resist other scandals when he discerns them in the swamp's ethically brackish water. Thus one column focuses on the Stormy Daniels fiasco while continuing the habit of lampooning by highlighting what a horrendous job Rudy Giuliani has been doing as Trump's (then) new lead lawyer. The adult film actress sued to be released from a nondisclosure agreement about her sexual encounter with Trump, who not only denies the event but also denies the agreement exists. Shafer says that having Giuliani in the news mix is "almost as good as having two Donald Trumps," and that Giuliani almost immediately "napalmed whatever credibility he still had as a counselor, a tactician, and broker by shooting his mouth off to the press about the [Stormy Daniels] case" so that, along with Trump's "gyrations" around the truth, "Giuliani's scheming has turned a tiny turd of embarrassment into an epic dunghill." Shafer's lampooning readily moves beyond the basic motive of causing personal discomfort: "Giuliani's belly flop won't be more than a footnote when they write the history of the special counsel's investigation of Russian meddling, but it deserves our savoring if only because it demonstrates the rigor with which Trump addresses his legal problems. . . . Trump and his allies seem incapable of telling a consistent story—or even of sticking to the stories they tell" (Week 50, May 5, 2018). Here lampooning extends to the public sphere issue of the Trump administration's efforts to derail a special counsel investigation into election meddling, a topic for satire proper.

The blog that Charles Pierce writes for *Esquire*, "Politics with Charles P. Pierce," reads similarly to Shafer's column in its ability to repackage the news about civic issues into a comic smorgasbord of facts and epithets. Pierce refers to his blog as "the shebeen" (he's Irish Catholic from the Boston area), which features the Stupid Café, in which "some stupid for lunch" appears as a regular item on the menu. Another feature, "Our National Dialogue," provides roundups of wacky news items, introduced with sardonic phrasing, for example, "Welcome back to our weekly survey of Our National Dialogue which is, as we know, what Rachmaninoff would have come up with had he written the 'Quaalude In C# Minor.'" Another favorite summary phrase is "What Are The Gobshites Saying These Days?" He frequently signs off by writing, "I'll be back on Monday with god-alone-knows what kind of gobshitery. Be well and play nice, ya bastids. Stay above the snakeline."

Pierce's particular talent may be epithets in the service of lampoons, for he always has ready a generous scoop of asperity for one and all, but especially for "Punditaria" and the "Sunday Showz," his collective names for talking heads on TV and the political talk shows on Sunday. Pierce delivers these epithets dripping with sarcasm in equal-opportunity abundance. Here is a random sampling:

> *National Review* is "America's flagship journal of white supremacy."
> "the well-known conservative intellectual journal *Human Events*—or, as it's known around the magazine rack at the cigar store, *Highlights For Wingnuts*"
> "*New York Times* columnist David Brooks and the Young Fogies Club, with Moral Hazard, the Irish setter owned for photo op purposes, with Douthat, the houseboy"
> "Mika Brzezinski, half of the Squint And The Meat Puppet Morning Zoo Crew on MSNBC"
> "George Stephanopolos, host of *This Week With the Clinton Guy Shocked by Blowjobs*"
> "Butcher Bill Kristol"
> "the ancient New Right Undead, ... Morton Blackwell and Richard Viguerie"
> "Breitbart's Mausoleum For The Chronically Unemployable"

For some unknown reason, Thomas Friedman enjoys extra attention: Pierce rhetorically slaps him around as the "Blog Official Absentee Rustwater sommelier . . . Rawhide Chewer . . . Erosion Officer . . . Windburn Consultant, Friedman of the Plains"; or "flat-worlder and amanuensis of the world's taxi drivers." Perhaps he thinks Friedman the model for how not to maintain a blog. The last phrasing clearly references Friedman's book *The*

World Is Flat: A Brief History of the Twenty-First Century (2005) as well as Friedman's habit of including in his blog what taxi drivers have to say as the on-the-ground sources when he arrives in a city, as though he mimics an anthropologist quizzing an indigenous informant.

Ted Cruz enjoys multiple descriptors too: "Tailgunner Ted Cruz"; "Cruz and the original Tailgunner, Joe McCarthy"; "Ted Cruz, who says in every speech that the president [Obama] will nominate a Supreme Court justice who will order the crosses and Stars of David sandblasted off the tombstones at Arlington." Of course, Donald Trump cannot be left out of this game of inventive comic insults: "a vulgar talking yam"; "the Frankenstein's Monster of the Republican Party"; "the creature of the Republican Party Id"; "A Gong-Show caliber crank." Notably, these epithets, almost without exception, reference some feature of the comic butt as a public figure in the public sphere. The invective in these epithets and descriptors thus generally fit all the features of satire: playful, aggressive, critical, intended to induce comic laughter LOL and LOI about civic issues.

If Shafer on the comic insult meter might routinely but rather randomly reach a five or six on a scale of ten, Pierce at times storms to an eleven, as when he covers a speech by Trump in Arizona, August of 2017, but makes the crowd his satiric target as much as he mocks Trump, whose speech was a "mendacious litany of sixth-grade sneering."

> Before we get to the other stuff, and there was lots of other stuff, I'd like to address myself to those people represented by the parenthetical notation (Applause) in the above transcript, those people who waited for hours in 105-degree heat so that they could have the G-spot of their irrationality properly stroked for them. You're all suckers. You're dim and you're ignorant and you can't even feel yourself sliding toward something that will surprise even you with its fundamental ugliness, something that everybody who can see past the veil of their emotions can see as plain as a church by daylight, to borrow a phrase from that Willie Shakespeare fella. The problem, of course, is that you, in your pathetic desire to be loved by a guy who wouldn't have 15 seconds for you on the street, are dragging the rest of us toward that end, too.
>
> A guy basically went mad, right there on the stage in front of you, and you cheered and booed right on cue because you're sheep.... The President of the United States came right up to the edge of inciting you to riot and you rode along with him. You're on his team, by god.

*****

> I have no more patience, and I had very little to start with. I don't care why you're anxious. I don't care for anybody's interpretation of why you voted for this abomination of a politician, and why you cheer him now, because any explanation not rooted in the nastier bits of basic human spleen is worthless. I don't want any politicians who seek to appeal to the more benign manifestations of your condition because there's no way to separate those from all the rest of the hate and fear and stupidity. . . . I don't care why you sat out in a roasting pan since 5 a.m. Tuesday morning to whistle and cheer and stomp your feet for a scared, dangerous little man who tells you that your every bloody fantasy about your enemies is the height of patriotism. . . . [Y]our idol is a danger to the country and so are you. Own it. Deal with it. And, for the love of god, and for the sake of the rest of us who live in this country, do better at being citizens.[5]

This quote raises a basic issue for evaluating cultural artifacts that might be labeled *satire*. If one starts with the fundamental premise that satire by definition displays an aggressive comic critique, that its method of employing ridicule to advance social and civic justice displays the paradox of a comically insulting ethos, then measuring invective quotients displayed by individual instances of satire will force an analysis to moments when judging whether an example should be called *satire* or just *rant* may be a matter of taste. Moreover, that taste will not just concern who or what constitutes the satiric butt, not just concern one's political views or ethical standards; it will also concern a taste for the bitterest items to be found within the entire satiric banquet that apparently demand such labels as "Juvenalian" and "degenerative" or perhaps "black humor."

This last column by Pierce reads more like a pundit's steroid-induced rant than mere reporting, but does that mean it cannot be read as I read Shafer's columns, performing satire's ridicule yet remaining in the basically locutionary mode of reporting? Whichever way one's taste directs, at the end a proper satirist's public sphere goal notably appears—wanting the audience to be better citizens. Thus mocking them in the most acerbic terms can be read as a comic wake-up call, a satiric slap up the side of the head or blistering caustic call-out of a specific portion of the body politic. No doubt, some readers will greet it with unlaughter. In any case, Shafer's column and Pierce's blog exemplify the discursive integration that marks the aesthetic of the postmodern, mashing together the locutionary performance of reporting with comic tactics that inevitably slide toward the illocutionary performance of a satiric ridicule.

While Charles Pierce's column can be remarkable for the harshness of its ridicule, it is instructive to compare the comic rant quoted above to the more playful manner Jack Shafer uses when he mocks the overkill of support for Trump's incessant calls for investigations of Hillary Clinton and Democrats: "Given their way, Trump supporters will establish so many special counsels the offices will cease to be special. But they will have enough to field a reasonably competitive office softball team."[6]

Stephen Colbert also uses a more playful tone when he mocks Trump's supporters. The set-up for a bit about the audience in his monologue from June 21, 2018, consists of a video clip of Trump at a rally in Duluth, Minnesota, the day before, in which Trump talked about his executive order to detain families together instead of separating children from parents, as if he had solved the border crisis, even though such soft detention is illegal and thus unworkable. Colbert refers to the crisis as "the worst moral scandal in recent memory," and then mocks anyone who would support that so-called policy. He does so by suddenly putting his arms straight up in the air, head thrown back, speaking in a high-pitched voice, presumably to match the posture of someone cheering wildly, and also intermittently clapping: "Yeah! Woo! The children will go to jail with their parents. Woo! Woo! Why am I clapping? What have I become? What have I become? I have been led into a position of moral hazard, and I have failed the test. Lock me up. Lock me up. I am a danger to myself and others. Woo! Woo! Woo! Woo! I'm a cautionary tale. I'll never explain this to my grandchildren."[7] This bit registers as an excellent instance of the postmodern fusing of public sphere and comic public sphere. The question of "What have I become?" and the answer "I have failed the test . . . of moral hazard" articulate the various speculations and analyses in news stories since the 2016 election about who the Trump supporters are and why they support him—and so hint at the more explicit questioning of motive found in Pierce's blog—while the strangely pitched voice and the wild gestures rewrite those speculations and stories in a laughter-provoking fashion that does not employ the bitter phrasing of Pierce. Colbert comically imagines self-awareness ("I am a danger and a cautionary tale") and implied regret (I won't be able to explain my support to posterity) in the supporters' minds, two qualities that many citizens would say appear conspicuously absent in their fellow citizens who support the Trump administration.

Colbert has another opportunity to ruminate, again under the cover of joking, about what motivates Trump supporters when Trump in the rally bragged about his achievements as president. He also took the opportunity to brag about being better than "the other side," even though the media calls them elites, because he has a nicer apartment, he's smarter, richer, and he was elected president. Colbert calls this statement "some deep weird" because in effect Trump implies he should be considered the most elite, which Colbert immediately dramatizes with his signature imitation Trump voice: "We hate the elites, and I'm the most elite of all, so that means we hate me most of all." After this exercise in logic to mock Trump, Colbert shifts back to mocking the supporters at the rally who cheered the statement with a second mimicking of the crowd speaking collective support for its twisted logic. "Woo! Woo! Woo! Yeah! We hate you. We hate you. Yeah! Woo! Woo! But not as much as we hate ourselves. Seriously. Lock us up. No sharp objects. Take away our belt and shoelaces. This is a cry for help." The nonsensical statement from Trump about elites stands in for all the crazy and nonsensical statements and policies coming from the Trump White House, yet the crowd cheers, behavior reminiscent of what Pierce had reported during another political rally. In a nice ironic turn propelled by a reverse discourse, Colbert flips back onto Trump's supporters one of their favorite chants during the 2016 campaign, "Lock her up!," referring to "Crooked Hillary," as Trump called Hillary Clinton, when Colbert imagines them saying, "Lock me up!" The comic diagnosis, that their support actually signals an unconscious cry for help, absurdly captures the absurdity of their unthinking support, again without a bitter tone.

Colbert performs the supporters in reverse discourse fashion. Pierce rhetorically lambasts them. Colbert's performance displays a goofy or silly quality, an obvious dose of playfulness compared with Pierce's comic critique, which probably creates the biggest difference in considering the two efforts as satire, not rant. Colbert in effect says that we cannot know what motivates people to support Trump even in his worst moral moments or for his most absurd statements. Pierce may not be sure as well, but he asserts that any explanation for motive must involve "the nastier bits of basic human spleen." Colbert imagines the supporters unconsciously saying *help me out of my moral quandary*. Pierce explicitly labels them people of the political id: they attended the rally "so that they could have the G-spot of their irrationality properly stroked." Colbert imagines them admitting they failed a test of moral hazard. Pierce disparages them as "dim" and "ignorant . . . sheep [displaying] hate and fear and stupidity." Colbert's ridicule does also sound a far-from-friendly note as he indicts Trump supporters for a moral failure apparently beyond their ken. Pierce's ridicule, however, lays on the caustic with a large trowel, asserting an essential lack of reason that all but labels them barbarians or even brutes, unfit for participation in the public sphere.

Though both Colbert and Pierce apply healthy doses of caustic satire to the body politic as represented by those who continue to support Trump despite his chaotic public policy executed via Twitter, they do not remain wholly in the comic public sphere with their versions of calling Trump supporters a basket of deplorables. Instead, one can unpack Colbert's phrase, "This is a cry for help," not as easy psychologizing but rather as a reference to the desperation significant parts of the electorate have had about the deplorable state of routine politics in Washington, DC. When the capital to many citizens appears in the political imaginary as a swamp in which the moral alligators roam freely and in charge, one might become ready to try any remedy. While that does not explain support eighteen months after the election, it does acknowledge the place of Trump supporters as citizens in the public sphere. And Pierce's urging Trump supporters to "do better at being citizens" does the same, hinting that despite his acerbic tone, he has not completely lost his civic-minded patience.

Satire as Illocutionary Speech Act

The examples in the second group represent satiric artifacts in an explicit illocutionary mode—that is, featuring comic butts and possibly paralipsis (a clear statement of a value) but no explicit call to action in the public sphere. I draw the examples from *The Daily Show* to demonstrate the more standard satiric format of silly and sardonic wrapped around serious that features the illocutionary act of ridiculing a comic butt. I offer these as exemplary of how comically playing with the news in the form of mock news clearly shows satire signifying the comic public sphere, but not as being exhaustive of such examples or even of a particular type or style of satire.

In these illocutionary examples of satire, the true value to be championed or the reform to be desired must usually be inferred from how the satire ridicules the comic butt: mock Trump the inveterate liar in order to argue in comic fashion that presidents should not lie, for example. The instances I present as what one would recognize as the typical satiric fare on television today feature Jordan Klepper doing what the so-called field correspondents for *The Daily Show* do best: parodying real reporters in unreliable narrator fashion, especially when conducting interviews. Klepper's parody typically features his persona of an overly confident man foolishly excessive in his behavior so that he ironically undercuts his opinions, a different elaboration of Steven Carrell's description of the faux correspondent role. Klepper's persona inevitably joins a list of comic butts in a given instance so that the savvy viewer infers that the proper civic value opposes what he touts.

Klepper's parodic reporter persona, then, is essentially eironic.[8] When the interviewee expresses odd or bizarre ideas and perspectives, Klepper often reinforces his or her claims with his own odd behavior, thus overemphasizing their bizarre qualities in reverse discourse fashion and allowing the audience to infer the correct conclusions about the issues covered. Klepper's eironic persona marks him as painfully comic in his confidence, probably inducing cringe laughter in much of his audience, because he apparently accepts unblinkingly even the strangest claims.

For example, in a segment entitled "Internet Killed the Newspaper Star," Klepper functions as the eironic advocate for online, so-called news outlets that fail to produce good journalism, like *Gawker*. Klepper adopts the view that in the postmodern world of journalism, news being informative on important civic issues has become passé because such efforts have been routinely replaced in the digital age with sensationalized stories that are not necessarily true. Moreover, Klepper argues, such fake journalism embodies exactly what the student staffers on the University of Michigan school newspaper he interviews should adopt: that future is now. He supports this position about what should be designated twenty-first-century news by also interviewing a former editor of *Gawker*, Neetzan Zimmerman, who offers advice to the Michigan students. For Zimmerman, a story has no worth if it is not shared virally on the web. Writing headlines in a certain style guarantees success because they can then function as *clickbait*. A story's accuracy or truth is irrelevant, he asserts, as long as people click on the headline and share the story on social media or email. Zimmerman as *Gawker* editor clearly functions as a node in the media ecosystem for disseminating simulacra. As one headline example, Zimmerman offers "Meet the Man with No Ass Crack." Klepper enthusiastically champions the *Gawker* approach to the journalism students, a stance that leads to a moment when he continually interrupts Zimmerman during the interview because he cannot help but use his phone to read the kind of stories *Gawker* promotes. In effect, Klepper becomes the audience Zimmerman's tactics target, in Baudrillard's terms the audience as ecstatic consumer of stories, the media-induced schizophrenic who is "open to everything in spite of himself [and prey to] the total instantaneity of things."[9] This audience replaces the informed citizenry necessary for the public sphere with the manipulated citizenry of the anti-public sphere. The list of comic butts includes not just sites like *Gawker* but also those who patronize them.

While Zimmerman's advice exaggerates unfairly the world of digital journalism (standard practice for satire to exaggerate of course, even with unfair gibes), Klepper's treating it as the new wisdom makes the point that standard news outlets, especially in print, have to a significant extent been swamped by such digital outlets like *Gawker*, which profess a completely different idea of what matters as news. Always lead with sex, Zimmerman counsels, which results in a hilarious moment in which Klepper forces a student reporter interviewing a University of Michigan faculty scientist doing research on Alzheimer's disease to ask about her personal life. Part of the hilarity (maybe cringe laughter is again the better description here) comes from the student's obvious disdain for Klepper's bringing a *Gawker* style to the interview.

This example presents satire in an illocutionary mode, performing ridicule in its standard satiric format, implying through irony (including Klepper's eironic persona) the worthlessness of its main target *Gawker* as a reputable news source while also ironically suggesting how naive the Michigan students behave in their professing the ideals of journalistic practice. The ironic ridicule of the comic butts performs the basic task of making the desired values visible. However, the segment does not rest with its ironically laughable presentation; it also employs paralipsis, in which the desired values are explicitly stated in the midst of promoting their opposites via comic laughter, which provides a PSA moment. That moment happens at the beginning of the segment when the students assert that good journalism must be well researched, informative, and empowering for the readers.[10]

Klepper's parodic reporter persona as comic butt comes front and center again when he plays the role of investigative journalist in "Good Guy with a Gun."[11] While this segment brims with jokes, it highlights serious topics about gun ownership by illustrating the faults in gun regulations, showing for example the ease with which anyone can obtain a gun and then a gun license. However, the segment targets a bigger comic butt, taking aim at the notion that the best way to stop a bad guy with a gun is to be a good guy with a gun, an idea espoused by talking heads at the outset of the segment in numerous video clips that follow news footage of actual shooting incidents at schools and hospitals.

The central joke of the piece stems from the prospect that the Klepper persona will be the good guy with a gun. Klepper performs that role via his excessive behavior in favor of gun rights, which includes his thoughtless equation of firing an actual gun with the video game *Call of Duty*. That dangerously wacky confusion inspires him to imagine he will behave like an action movie hero when the bad guy with the gun appears. The worrisome behaviors compound. Klepper brags that he has a wild streak and the personality of a rule breaker, even as he starts the shooting instruction, gun in hand. He continuously argues with his instructors, insisting that he has the correct view on all issues and so implying that he knows more than they do and thus has an attitude beyond learning. Being a good guy with a gun for Klepper also involves moments imagining having sex with a celebrity (Cher), a fantasy to match his being a movie hero, rather than learning how to be safe in handling a gun and how to become competent in the event of an active shooter incident. When he passes the easy written test as well as the practice session that involves firing one clip of ammunition, Klepper says America can now feel safe knowing he is armed and might also have a conceal carry permit. Cringe laughter again presumably ensues.

Klepper's overly confident persona in this example also dramatizes how a citizen should not act when given information that challenges one's perspective on an issue. When Klepper enrolls in a second and more rigorous gun training program, he also acquires a copy of an FBI report, "A Study of Active Shooter Incidents in the United States Between 2000–2013," which discredits the right-wing bromide that a good guy with a gun can always take down a bad guy with a gun. A rational individual would conclude that the bromide should be logged as generally false because of the data presented: that scenario has only worked in 3 percent of all cases. However, Klepper sticks with the original claim touted by certain pundits, the NRA, and particular politicians in the opening video clips. Moreover, he attempts to discredit the report as "liberal claptrap" and as an instance of a favorite right-wing conspiracy theory, namely, as an omen that the government plans to take away guns from their rightful owners. In effect, Klepper enacts the anti-public sphere, his persona incapable of a metanoia resulting from an ongoing education and reasoned debate.

Notably, Klepper unmasks his persona near the end of the segment. The finish involves Klepper in active shooter simulations, which he fails spectacularly. Those failures evoke the first PSA moment: being successful in such scenarios, he admits, is "starting to feel way more complicated than movies, and videos, and politicians make it seem," adding "it takes a life-time commitment to training" to be that good guy with a gun. Klepper then suggests an absurd solution implied by the catchphrase that constitutes the primary target of the satire—create millions of armed good guys with life-time training to cover the millions of schools and hospitals in America (that is, to cover all of America)—before he provides a second PSA moment. That second unveiling of a sensible civic value consists of suggesting that the problem might be solved if the United States does not allow bad guys to have guns in the first place. Klepper makes the suggestion to two of the police professionals in the training exercise, and their response is "not gonna happen in our lifetime."

Klepper builds his eironic persona to unmask in comic-sphere fashion the bias and truthiness in the opinions and claims of his fellow citizens who inhabit the anti-public sphere and ignore the public sphere. In the man-on-the-street interviews for his "Jordan Klepper Fingers the Pulse" segments ("the real news is on the streets"), he leaves that persona aside in favor of another, one presenting a direct, even confrontational attitude that hides behind a mask of curiosity. The resulting dialogues mimic the public sphere at its minimal level: discussion between two (apparently) average citizens. In one installment of his series, "Conspiracy Theories Thrive at a Donald Trump Rally," Klepper plans to discover what "new truths" Trump supporters "know," a quest triggered by an initial look at clips of *Fox News* video that speculated about Hillary Clinton's health during the 2016 campaign. Because the news that she had pneumonia supposedly confirmed the wildest speculations, other new truths must be possible. For example (say some of those Trump supporters), she has AIDS courtesy of Bill, who has it courtesy of Magic Johnson; alternatively, a body double exists. Other claims sound familiar as right-wing talking points: Obama was not only not born in the United States, but he is a Muslim and a terrorist; the media lies about Trump's support in the electorate, refusing, for example, to show how much support he has in the African American community. Klepper stringing the claims together in rapid fire piles absurdity onto absurdity, compounding a sense that all Trump supporters display a mentality dubbed in the vernacular as "wingnut."

Against each claim, Klepper pushes back, sometimes to devastating effect. For example, he mocks the body double theorist by showing him identical photographs and allowing him to point out differences he claims to find. Klepper ironically agrees to the supposed differences by saying if "you kinda have a paranoid mind" and look at something long enough, you can find anything. Klepper endorses the claim that Obama is a Muslim because "besides the birth certificate, there is no evidence," to which the woman who says that there were no credible witnesses to his birth agrees. However, when Klepper questions the legitimacy of Trump's birth for the same reasons and says to her that he is "using your logic against you," she is nonplussed. When he asks a young man to show him the African Americans at the rally that the media supposedly fails to report, none can be found, and again, the interviewee is nonplussed: simple observation has instantly refuted his claim. When Klepper ironically notes that the Trump supporters have "ironclad sources," the video cuts to the woman who has already said that Obama practices Islam now admitting that her sources are Facebook and Twitter, primary nodes for a network of simulacra. She then agrees with Klepper, who characterizes her thinking as "facts and bullshit" put together: "Exactly," she responds. Another man says he has no sources, just opinions, while the woman who claims Obama has acted as a Muslim terrorist turbocharges that earlier moment of honesty when she admits, with a smile, that "my mind is made up without any information," and "nothing will change my mind," earning her first prize as the walking, babbling embodiment of the anti-public sphere.

Klepper signals his strategy of a mocking confrontation at the outset when he calls Trump supporters "crackpots," and it produces multiple PSA moments by repeatedly pointing out the main comic butt of Klepper's parodic public sphere dialogues: people blindly accept a wild claim or choose to believe false information simply because it reinforces their preexisting and uninformed beliefs. These people inhabit the realm of the anti-public sphere because truthiness as rumors and opinions dictate their beliefs and shape their arguments; they apparently have no interest in facts and reasoned debate. Their display of ignorance and prejudice as the basis for their citizenship self-indicts them as people of the political id. The best example from all the interviewees has to be the man who, after saying Hillary has AIDS, accuses Obama of complicity in 9/11 because we all (supposedly) know he was absent from the Oval Office at the time. After all, he was always taking vacations, another anti-public sphere talking point. When Klepper asks how do we know that Obama was not in the Oval Office as president on 9/11, the man responds, "I don't know, but I would like to get to the bottom of it."[12] The more level-headed and informed members of Klepper's audience can take pleasure (feel superior) in watching these interviewees exercise their First Amendment rights, but their opinions surely generate the uneasiness of cringe laughter because of how palpably sincere they are as they perform the anti-public sphere as foolish citizens, as opposed to silly citizens.

This last example from Klepper's series of encounters with fellow citizens supplies an absurd climax for the ultimate satiric target: Americans who consume uncritically the so-called news from outlets like *Breitbart* and *Fox News*, a complement to their fondness for stories from *Gawker*. Conspiracy theories and fabricated, sensationalized stories now function as the news for a significant portion of the electorate. Social media like Facebook and Twitter allow citizens to occupy a digital echo chamber for their beliefs, fed by the wildest tales, which are the ones most likely to go viral, validating Neetzan Zimmerman's theory of so-called journalism for the digital age. With the public sphere, maybe especially the digital public sphere, in such tatters factually and logically, no wonder the comic public sphere and its satire have burgeoned in the twenty-first century.

Because explaining the news with comic phrasing to create comic *parrhēsia* or truth telling has become the signature method for many satirists, the boundary between the first two groups, locutionary and illocutionary, appears blurry. My using Austin's terms for analytical purposes does not imply their functioning as categorical boxes into which one might infallibly sort examples. Rather, my use implies their status as potential metrics for where on the spectrum created by his three terms a given example might be placed, a spectrum along which writers like Shafer and Pierce slide from being professional journalists to becoming something approaching professional comics, like Stephen Colbert and Jordan Klepper, deliberate and avowed satirists.

Consider these two examples taken from the same week in June 2018, the first from Shafer's weekly column, "Swamp Diary," and the second from Colbert's monologue on *Late Night with Stephen Colbert*.

> Clutching the IG [Justice Department's Inspector General] report to his bosom, Trump has claimed it "totally exonerates" him and has "totally discredited" Mueller. The only problem with Trump's exaltations is that neither is remotely true. As for his idea that the IG report demonstrates malfeasance at the FBI, that's bunk, too. The IG explicitly states that political bias had no bearing on the FBI's handling of the case, no matter what sort of smack agents talked in messages to one another. As is his tendency, the president is making things up. Trump gets caught conjuring again whenever he slams Mueller's team as being manned by "13 hardened Democrats." It doesn't matter how many times it's pointed out that Mueller himself is a lifelong Republican appointed to his special counsel position by another Republican,

or that Republicans and independents also work for him, Trump keeps bringing up the 13 Democrats "leading the Witch Hunt" against him.[13]

At four distinct moments, Shafer speaks truth to power by more or less calling Trump a liar: "neither is remotely true"; "that's bunk, too"; "As is his tendency, the president is making things up." Shafer matches the mild tone of those phrasings with the verb used in the fourth moment, "Trump gets caught conjuring again," just as the slang in "no matter what sort of smack agents talked in messages to one another" reports facts through colloquialism. Shafer clearly exposes Trump's habitual mendacity and thus performs *parrhēsia* by citing specific facts while he gives his effort to produce good journalism a lightly comic tone.

Though this excerpt from Shafer's "Swamp Diary" registers as minimalist in its comic element, as often Shafer is, notably, he signals a chronic comic attitude by ending each column with a silly postscript about his contact platforms that always references the news. This one features a generalized comic butt: "In the late 1890s, legend has it, when a peeved railroad baron asked muckraking journalist Ambrose Bierce what his price was to stop reporting, he said $75 million. 'If, when you are ready to pay, I happen to be out of town, you may hand it over to my friend, the Treasurer of the United States.' Send your millions to Shafer.Politico@gmail.com. My email alerts take in filthy money to launder. My Twitter feed accepts only clean cash. My RSS feed prefers the arts of bribery and extortion." The silly tone of Shafer's postscripts complements whatever sarcasm exists in the column, as though he is in training to become a full-time satirist. The levels of comic invective functioning as an implicit quotient that separates locutionary reporting from becoming illocutionary satire suggests that one might hypothesize a level above which a journalist like Shafer might qualify as a satirist like Colbert or Klepper. However, Shafer and Pierce both would assuredly assert that they are fundamentally reporters reporting the news, though reporting characterized by using various tones of ridicule.

Colbert's monologue from *The Late Show with Stephen Colbert* for June 20, 2018, focused on the political firestorm over the Trump administration's policy of separating children from parents when they were trying to cross into the United States or just seeking asylum. After days of condemnation, both domestic and international, Trump signed an executive order to change the policy. Like Shafer, Colbert practices comic *parrhēsia* in this example, but in a much more obviously comic fashion. That difference indicates a frontier dividing locutionary from illocutionary satire within the comic public sphere. Nevertheless, both Colbert and Shafer start from a basic public sphere premise of the need to explain the news to their audiences using facts and evidence. Colbert begins by announcing the bit of news that determines his focus that night, while also effectively calling Trump a liar and mocking his lack of empathy. "Folks, our long national nightmare is [pause] different. Because after weeks of tearing families apart at the border and then falsely insisting that only Congress could solve the problem, this afternoon, the president looked deep into his heart and realized it was not there [laughter]."[14] Colbert's first line mimics a statement by Gerald Ford. After he took the presidential oath and was sworn in as the thirty-eighth president of the United States to replace Richard Nixon, who had resigned to escape impeachment, Ford gave a brief acceptance speech that was broadcast live on radio and television in which he said, "My Fellow Americans, our long national nightmare is over." Colbert thus hints at the potential parallel of Trump being forced to resign in disgrace, an ongoing fantasy of many citizens, and implicitly demands that his audience knows American history and catches the allusion. Colbert follows this opening sally, which has multiple comic targets, with a video clip of Trump signing the executive order in which he says, "I didn't like the sight or feeling of families being separated." Colbert wastes no time turning that statement into more ridicule about Trump's lack of empathy (he has no heart) and about his generally narcissistic behavior, mimicking Trump with his signature goofy impression while reciting a faux tweet. "And at the end of the day, we all know that everything is really about me and how it makes me feel. So much, sad. Broken-hearted. Me. So sad. Peace."

Colbert next veers back toward explaining the news, as though he were Shafer, by asking how could Trump sign such an order, then immediately paraphrasing Trump, who for weeks had said his hands were tied and who had been blaming the Democrats for the crisis at the border; there were laws preventing him from fixing the problem, he said. However, there was one thing we knew he could not do, continues Colbert. The screen image then cuts to a video of Trump saying, "You can't do it through an executive order" (which already garners a laugh as the audience is directly shown that Trump has been lying), and Colbert then follows the clip with the sarcastic and ironic comment, "There it is; can't be done. [laughter] So here he is, doing it." Cut back to the video of the signing and Trump saying, "You're gonna have a lot of happy people," to which Colbert asks after a jump cut back to him, "Happy people? Wait. Are you signing your resignation?" [big laugh and extended cheers, applause]. More fantasy that again references Nixon, the only president to resign.

Colbert continues his speaking truth to power in comic fashion when he says that Trump cannot take credit for fixing the situation because he started "the evil thing." The big signing ceremony made it look like he did something good instead of admitting his fault. "That's like wanting credit for solving the crimes you committed." Colbert continues, "This executive order is not what he wants you to think it is. Sure, he's reuniting families—in prison. He's detaining parents and children together." An inset screen shot appears of a *New York Times* article with a quote highlighted. Colbert may be explaining the news with a big helping of comic public sphere sarcasm, but he is also building an argument using evidence, in public sphere mode. Then Colbert references the Mueller probe, but with a joke, again mimicking Trump speaking: "Look, if I have to go to prison with my kids, so do you. I'm not doing this alone" [big laugh]. Colbert, however, immediately pivots from joking back to explaining by quoting a political scientist professor about the policy (again with an inset screen shot of the article from which Colbert quotes): "Family unity policy only pertains 'to the extent permitted by law,'" and the administration claims that "the law does not allow them to maintain family unity, so did anything actually change?" This quote refers to the basic legal issue at the heart of the crisis: prosecutorial discretion. Individuals attempting to enter the United States illegally can be charged in either criminal or civil court. The practice of both the Bush and Obama administrations had been to choose the civil courts because a criminal indictment requires children to be separated. Once Trump's Department of Justice chose a criminal charge, the law mandated separation, hence the lie that the Democrats had created the situation by allowing that law to stand, or blaming Congress in general for its failure to change the law. Either way, Trump elides the basic fact that his Department of Justice has made a choice at his direction, a choice that Colbert challenges.

The final part of Colbert explaining the news allows him to speak truth to power once more, this time by making the point that Trump did not change the policy because of empathy, despite what he said at the signing ceremony. Investigative journalism changed his mind, triggered by the news "last night" that babies and toddlers were being sent to "'tender age' shelters" (a third evidentiary inset screen shot with this quote appears), a euphemism for "internment camps for children," quips Colbert. Thus optics, not morality, made the difference, a point hammered home by quoting Trump again, who told House Republicans yesterday in a closed-door emergency meeting about the crisis that "crying babies does not look good politically." (Groans from the audience accompany one last inset screen shot, from CNN this time.) Yet Colbert immediately switches to being silly by saying that such optics doomed the campaign of Eustace T. Babysnatcher, then showing a cartoon poster featuring a man with a nineteenth-century suit and outlandish whiskers. Clearly, Colbert piles up the comic elements compared to Shafer, even including just plain silly to go with spiky jokes about Trump and his behavior as well as the specific policy discussion that centers the monologue. Just as clearly, Colbert, like Shafer, wants to educate his audience by explaining the news and offering facts and evidence, mostly in the form of quotes from news reports flashed as screen shots.

Notably, Colbert also tackles a related issue, explicitly taking a stand on the limits of the asperity and vulgarity that might be used in the service of satire, which can be read back against the heavily caustic comic style of Pierce. Colbert shows another video, this time of a random visitor to the Capitol rotunda who, seeing Trump leaving, "gave him a shout-out, 'Mr. President, fuck you!'" This response to Trump and his border policy elicits laughs and a cheering applause so extended that Colbert, waiting, bends to tie his shoe before saying, "Yeah, I know," which garners another laugh. However, he then adds, "I want to point out, that's not helping. Don't, don't, don't do that. That just feeds into their sense of victimhood." The audience response also suggests how the portion of the body politic that does not support Trump nevertheless can resemble the portion that does when it too apparently abandons even comic reason for mere anger. Thus everyone has the potential to behave as denizens of the political id.

Klepper's examples illustrate how a comic persona can enable a satire that not only highlights the policy issues and then provides the PSA moment in order to educate the views of the audience as citizens but also entertains them as audience. His parodic field reports execute their public sphere task by performing ridicule in illocutionary fashion against specified satiric butts. The comparison of Shafer, Pierce, and Colbert yields two points: they execute the public sphere task of educating citizens while also entertaining them as readers and audience, and thus they all might be tagged as satirists; judging them as satirists should come down to evaluating the use of comic techniques that do not just entertain with laughter-provoking insults but also connect the audience's attention to public sphere issues. Without that educating connection, the insults and denigration packed inside the invective only serve the anti-public sphere.

Satire as Speech Act, Part Two

6.

The last group of examples based on Austin's three speech act terms features a call-to-activism moment to complement the PSA moment: not just a spot in the comic presentation where a value or a position on a civic issue becomes apparent through the illocutionary force of performing ridicule, but a moment in which the satirist explicitly asks the audience to shift from passive spectator to engaged citizen. Satire then becomes satiractivism and approaches closest to the full perlocutionary force of political speech.

Having insisted on a boundary between comic political speech acts and political speech acts, I suggest that McClennen and Maisel's concept of *satiractivism* blurs that boundary.[1] This blurring entails labeling comic political speech as primarily illocutionary—that is, satire performs ridicule—while labeling political speech as strongly perlocutionary and satiractivism as *quasi-perlocutionary*. Satiractivism apparently operates beyond the weak perlocutionary force of metanoia embedded in satire but without reaching the full perlocutionary force of serious political speech acts. Within this spectrum of perlocutionary forces, the question becomes: How can satire's built-in illocutionary force of performing ridicule along with its potential for the weak perlocutionary force of metanoia (its status as comic political speech) be altered with the call for citizen action that characterizes satiractivism? That question generates a second question: Does satiractivism with its quasi-perlocutionary force function as a form of political speech?

An important, larger question has been hovering about the analysis so far: Does the performance of ridicule by any particular example of satire as a speech act promote the civic understanding necessary for the public sphere? In Habermas's terms, the practical consequence of communicative rationality is "working toward the cultivation of practices that bring us closer to the ideal of seeking to resolve conflicts through discourses where the only force is the 'force of the better argument.'"[2] The basic question—can one claim satire as a discursive practice that aids in the project of communicative rationality?—raises others. Does not the quantum state of satire—both serious (calm reason) and nonserious (unruly ridicule)—make it a problematic force for this ideal of resolving conflict? Alternatively, does satire's quantum state enable satiractivism's notable prominence in the second decade of the twenty-first century? Satirists now must insistently tout the reason and the action lodged in the midst of ridicule as a counterforce to the current phase of the postmodern condition. Satirists now must defy and frustrate the widespread embrace of a truthiness mentality discoloring and disfiguring political discourse, a mentality abetted by the faceless sign machine of the media ecosystem and its simulacra, a mentality epitomized by the Trump administration's deep debt to a deliberate regime of misdirection and lying.

Satire as Quasi-Perlocutionary Speech Act: An Example of Satiractivism

Jon Stewart provides an excellent first example of satiractivism, when he initially hosted first-responders who had become ill after the Twin Towers came down because a bill to compensate them, the "James Zadroga 9/11 Health and Compensation Act," was stalled in Congress. Within days of that *Daily Show* episode, the bill passed.[3] The follow-on for this fusion of comic and political speech occurred on December 10, 2015, when Stewart appeared on *The Late Show with Stephen Colbert* to ask people to contact their congressional representatives about the Zadroga provision up for renewal in the omnibus spending bill then before Congress.[4] Stewart did not just make an appeal, as one would at a political rally, or even as he had done for the first iteration of the bill when he featured testimony from actual first-responders. Instead, he mimicked presidential candidate Donald Trump, complete with wig and Cheeto dust smeared on his face in clown fashion—both props courtesy of Colbert—and parodied Trump's blowhard style of speaking to exhort people to express support for the renewal to their congressional representatives.

Parodying The Donald using Cheeto dust for make-up certainly qualifies as comic speech, but Stewart in that moment and in that costume explicitly asks for political action on a very specific civic issue. The comic public sphere fuses with the public sphere. Stewart exposes the real-world behavior of Trump as ridiculous by employing it as the comic technique for the PSA moment. Moreover, when he "Trumps it up" after the repeated urging of Colbert, he also mocks the media for its obsession with Trump's antics during the presidential campaign. As Colbert says, the media (and by extension the public) will not pay any attention to what someone says, however important for the public sphere, if he or she does not speak like Trump. Using the theater that Trump creates with all the media attention on him, which has become so corrosive to the public sphere, Stewart rhetorically reverses that theater from corrosive to constructive. He a–muses his audience and caps the performance with the call to action: the audience becomes a gathering of citizens.

The John Oliver Effect

Jon Stewart at particular moments in his version of *The Daily Show* demonstrated the move from the simple comic speech of satire to something approaching actual political speech that Lenny Bruce and Dick Gregory pioneered; however, very likely a thorough investigation of satiractivism would nominate John Oliver as the decisive factor in a turn toward this brand of satire, at least for cablecast TV.[5] From the outset of his program *Last Week Tonight* in 2013, Oliver has employed a different format from that of *Saturday Night Live*'s segment "Weekend Update," even departing from Stewart's tried and true formula on *The Daily Show*. Rather than providing a comic summary of news items, or even a focused yet brief segment on one topic, *Last Week Tonight* explores a topic in-depth for a significant portion of its thirty minutes. A satiric version of a news magazine format results, a comic *60 Minutes* in less than half the time. Paul Alonso claims *Last Week Tonight* has an "investigative nature [and is] not a faux newscast or a parody of TV pundits." Julia Fox considers *Last Week Tonight* to be "satiric journalism."[6]

The form for Oliver's main segment each week might simply be called *an essay that generates laughs*. Like Stewart and Colbert, or even Shafer and Pierce, Oliver uses large doses of comic insult as the entertaining delivery system for the public sphere element. However, unlike the others, Oliver's purpose does not center on laughter-provoking commentary about the latest news but instead zeroes in on explications that build context and offer nuances for a particular issue, often one that has not been the subject of recent news reports. In this comic essay format that retrieves issues from mainstream media neglect, the educative impulse that powers satire as the comic public sphere becomes particularly obvious.

For example, early in the first season, Oliver decides to focus on the issue of net neutrality, not because it represents a so-called hot button issue, but rather because it deserves the attention of the citizenry. Oliver even jokes that "net neutrality" might be the two most boring words in the English language and follows that quip with lots of other jokes about other boring things. Such joking at the outset of the focus segment puts the audience into the playful mood of the comic public sphere, but only as prelude to the serious business of educating folks about the fact that the Federal Communication Commission (FCC) appears ready to change rules about net neutrality. The essay quality of the segment then becomes apparent as Oliver marshals evidence that uncovers the corporate pressure to end net neutrality and the likelihood that its end will be the outcome of the FCC's process: Comcast is negotiating with Netflix; the lobbying budget for internet providers like Comcast is second only to defense contractors; Trump nominated a lobbyist for Comcast to head the FCC.

The segment ends with what people can do to prevent an end to net neutrality: give public comment for maintaining it to the FCC. Oliver not only urges the audience to exercise their rights as citizens; he also gives the internet address of the FCC to facilitate public comment. The FCC website crashed from the volume of public response only hours after the show.[7] However, the best part of this call to civic activism resides in the fact that Oliver directly addresses the "lovely trolls" and haters on the internet who routinely make nasty comments on all manner of topics and urges them to direct some of their bile to the FCC on the issue. Oliver does not simply interpellate his studio audience as citizens or even just his broadcast audience in general. He also interpellates trolls in either audience as citizens, persuading them to do something useful with their chronic rage and anger. Notably, when Oliver reprises the issue, again going after the FCC and net neutrality, and he again asks viewers to become citizen commentators, the volume of the citizen activism again overwhelms FCC servers—no doubt trolls and all.[8]

Satiractivism does not show up in every segment of *Last Week Tonight with John Oliver*, not even in every one of the focus segments that unfold as satiric essays. Nor is the underlying topic always political. For example, Oliver's segment "Alex Jones" creates an exposé of Alex Jones and his Infowars talk show, website, and business with multiple moments of parody, including the final touch with a phony doctor who mocks Jones and all the pharmaceuticals he sells.[9] Oliver presents Jones not so much as a talk-radio host with a lunatic style—though any number of video clips from his show demonstrate that style—but rather as a skilled salesman selling real products ("Infowars Life" brand) for imagined, contrived health problems. In his effort to educate the citizenry by providing context for Infowars as a commercial rather than ideological enterprise, Oliver exposes lies about the products amounting to fraud. As a final note, Oliver reports that Donald Trump endorsed Jones on air, one flimflam man conspiracist to another, but does not include a call to action. This example can be recorded as standard satire in an illocutionary mode.

In another example, this one tackling the fact citizens still celebrate Confederate monuments despite the ugly history they symbolize, Oliver makes an extended argument on a civic issue: why the Confederate statues in public places should come down. The segment functions as a comic essay and history lesson clearly in service to the public sphere, yet without obvious satiractivism. However, satiractivism, comic public sphere style, does exist in Oliver's symbolic substitutions. The segment ends with the unveiling of alternative statues, full-sized on pedestals, created by the show, which demonstrate what might be done instead of merely toppling the statues, or even dragging them off to be smelted into bling for rappers in a post-soul satire gesture. Oliver adds a finishing comic touch of mockery by presenting Stephen Colbert in the flesh as the substitute for a statue currently in Charleston, South Carolina, the joke being that Colbert as a native of Charleston would be a far more worthy (as a satirist) representative of the city. The basic public sphere thrust of the segment stands out due to the real people Oliver wants to substitute for statues in other cities, including Robert Smalls (born in slavery, elected to Congress) and Bessie Coleman (first female African American aviator).[10] In effect, *Last Week Tonight* does not merely urge (implicitly) the body politic to make a change; it shows how, an indirect but material model for action.

Though Oliver does not consistently present satire in the quasi-perlocutionary mode of satiractivism, he does make educating the citizenry a signature move. For example, when doing a segment featuring Rudy Giuliani entitled "Stupid Watergate," Oliver starts by spotlighting the many amazing gaffes by Giuliani as Trump's TV lawyer. Oliver sets up his satiric essay by promising an answer to the question: What happened to Rudy Giuliani, given that as mayor of New York City during and after the 9/11 event, he received so many accolades for being calm and steady? The answer is nothing happened; he has always been media crazy, so the big take-away becomes Rudy Giuliani loves the camera yet has a fingernails-on-chalkboard abrasive style. Oliver piles up the evidence with details before and after Giuliani being mayor—for example, his law firm represented corporations that were not always morally the best, and he told many lies during the 2016 campaign to support Trump. Thus the segment intends to educate by providing a biography via lampoon. The final assessment by Oliver: Rudy Giuliani should be understood as another version of Trump, a conclusion Jack Shafer also made. In Oliver's words, "They're both New Yorkers coasting on their reputations. They both had three marriages. Neither of them can shut up when in front of a camera, and perhaps most importantly, they both want to fuck Ivanka, which is weird for Trump because Ivanka is in his family, and is weird for Giuliani because she isn't."[11] This finish indicates how Oliver for most of a focus segment will sound like a public sphere essayist and then abruptly switch to locker-room vulgarian, a tactic that no other popular satirist employs, certainly not as routinely. Usually, Oliver delivers the vulgarity cheerfully, not in bitter Charles Pierce style.

The same impulse to offer the public a satiric biography happens when Oliver first turns his attention to Donald Trump as a serious candidate for the Republican Party's nomination.[12] Oliver begins his effort by saying that he tried to avoid talking about Trump in the context of the primaries because just mentioning his name gives Trump orgasmic pleasure. Oliver compares Trump to a mole on the back of a body (politic) that is no longer wise to ignore. The main part of his presentation unpacks and critiques the qualities that men and women on the street state are those that attract them to Trump (shown in video clips). Clearly, this segment will be a major effort to educate citizens because of the immediate context: Trump after winning most of the votes on Super Tuesday now looks most likely to be the Republican nominee. The qualities people cite for supporting Trump include his business acumen. Oliver thus spends a lot of time giving facts about the true nature of Trump's supposed wealth and business success, which is to say, Oliver enumerates Trump's many failed enterprises.[13]

Oliver supplements that reportorial presentation of biography with comic insults, some of them vulgar. Oliver starts with Trump's chronic problem with the truth: "I'm not even sure he knows he's lying. He just doesn't care about what the truth is. Donald Trump views the truth like this lemur [gesturing to an inset screen image of a lemur eating a banana] views the Supreme Court vacancy: 'I don't care about that in any way. Please fuck off. I have a banana.'" Oliver invites laughter about Trump's sensitivity to comic insults, for example, *Spy* magazine's famous "short-fingered vulgarian." Then Oliver adds his own punning insult: Trump resembles the gold Sharpie he uses to pen notes, "Something that gives the passing appearance of wealth, but is actually just a cheap tool."

In truthiness satire style, Oliver often uses Trump's own words from video clips to set up the ridicule, for example, "I'm very highly educated. I know words. I have the best words." This claim, with its self-defeating brag, gets a huge laugh from the audience and causes Oliver to laugh also. Trump bases an estimate of his net worth, stated in a deposition during a lawsuit he initiated, on "feelings, even my own feelings . . . and that can change rapidly from day to day," a statement that just may capture the essence of truthiness as gut feeling rather than accuracy or truth. Much more ominously, Oliver shows Trump joking (?) about committing a war crime to fight ISIS: kill the families of terrorists.

When Oliver notes that the name "Trump" was changed from the original German, "Drumpf," which in his view is far less magical as a branding tool, he then shifts to the digital activism of a hashtag, Suey Park style. If the name "Trump" has cast some sort of spell over portions of the American electorate, Oliver wants America instead to use the hashtag "#MakeDonaldDrumpfAgain" to break the spell. Moreover, in what amounts to culture jamming, Oliver has not only set up an internet domain with the same name, but the website, in addition to hats with the satiric hashtag, also sells a product that will use one's browser to change "Trump" to "Drumpf" wherever it appears on a web page. *Last Week Tonight* here interpellates its audience as consumers but also as silly citizens in a satiractivist mode.

This tactic of the show performing culture jamming as a kind of comic activism also shows up in "Trump vs. Truth," a thorough ridiculing of Trump and his shaky relationship with reality.[14] After mocking Trump's cable news mentality that focuses on Fox, Breitbart, and Infowars, thus underlining the problem of making real policy with fake facts, Oliver finishes by showing a parodic commercial that mocks Trump's ignorance as it sarcastically attempts to educate him. Oliver says that they have produced a series of mock commercials and that they will be run on stations that Trump watches. On top of that parodic pushback of Trump's anti-public sphere rhetoric, Oliver explicitly exhorts the audience to work at making sure Trump's alternative facts are challenged because the press is under attack from Trump's basic strategy of bullshitting.[15] Oliver deliberately interpellates his audience as citizens: "We all need to commit to defending the reality of facts. But it's going to take work. . . . We should make extra efforts on social media to verify stories before passing them on." In other words, be responsible citizens inhabiting a vibrant public sphere; do not join those in the electorate who believe in the Trump agenda of promoting the anti-public sphere.

Oliver uses the same tactic of parodic commercials as a form of satiractivism in his segment focused on the Obama administration's agreement with Iran about its nuclear weapons program.[16] The goal once again invokes, at bedrock, public sphere: to scrutinize the deal and its provisions and why Trump dislikes it. The lesson for the audience starts with a one-paragraph history of the relationship with Iran that began with the CIA overthrow of its government in 1953 in favor of the Shah, a move that in itself parodies the complicated history with Iran. As if to be sure his audience has caught the parodic nature of that one-paragraph summary, Oliver follows it with a mock podcast bit that parodies talking heads supposedly discussing Iran but mostly instead shouting at each other: a much-too-true satiric presentation of actual discourse in the public sphere.

After the comic beginning, Oliver settles into the public sphere essay portion of the segment, providing lots of details about Iran, explaining the elaborate and persistent diplomatic effort required to create the Iran deal, and explaining the advantages for the West from the deal. Oliver seasons this analysis with jokes, and he then walks his audience through Trump's objections one by one and refutes them. In a final move, Oliver imagines for everyone the consequences of pulling out of the deal unilaterally. Notably, he reminds the audience that no way exists for exercising the free speech of dissent other than writing the president. One cannot write to a congressperson because Trump has executive power over the deal. The public sphere action thus seems useless, for who can imagine Trump would be moved by such dissent? Instead, Oliver offers the comic public sphere option: a mock commercial to explain to Trump why he should keep the deal, with the same cowboy character featured in the earlier mock commercials sarcastically designed to educate Trump. Oliver announces that *Last Week Tonight* will buy airtime on Sean Hannity's show in the DC area because everyone knows Trump watches *Hannity*. The move represents another kind of satiractivism on a civic issue in which *Last Week Tonight* behaves as a silly citizen intervening in the public sphere. Oliver's judgment on such silly citizenship binds the show and its host to the audience: "I am not saying that it is going to change anything, but at least *we* will know *we* tried" (emphasis added). Notably for the tactics of truthiness satire, the effort entails leveraging the way in which Trump epitomizes Baudrillard's ecstatic media consumption.

Perhaps the best example of Oliver in the postmodern satiric habit of blurring the comic public sphere with the public sphere, often with satiractivism, occurs when Oliver travels to Russia to interview Edward Snowden.[17] Oliver opens the segment with a recurring trope that highlights how the public sphere component of his show always has the potential to overwhelm the entertaining and laughter-inducing part of the satire: the issue appears boring but is in fact vital to know. Oliver in this segment implies the need for public debate about renewal of section 215 of the Patriot Act, which allows for bulk storage of data. Oliver's comic public sphere presentation intends to trigger the necessary conversation. Oliver frames the current context of renewing the Patriot Act as a dilemma: citizens want both perfect privacy and perfect security. The public sphere conversation will therefore not be easy. The segment functions as an elaborate exhortation to discuss this vital issue.

Ominously, Oliver cites a poll showing that nearly half of Americans are not concerned, as though the issue does not require conversation and debate. To prove the uselessness of the poll because people are not informed, *Last Week Tonight* randomly asks people on the street who Snowden is and what famous act he did. Almost no one had a correct answer. Moreover, when they are told, the only circumstance that upsets people about the surveillance stems from the prospect of the government collecting pictures of people naked. Thus Oliver understands his first task as educative—"refresh your memory"—so he treats the audience to a history of the Patriot Act, including Snowden's role as the one who exposed the vast scope of the government's surveillance. Oliver then addresses his audience as citizens, in effect saying, *after Snowden's leak about the extent of the surveillance, we citizens cannot plead ignorance because we are informed citizens now*. Yet two years after the leak, "we've kinda forgotten to have a debate over the content of what Snowden leaked." Worse. The media has not been doing its job of informing and educating. The evidence for that claim comes from a video clip showing what happened when a congresswoman in 2014 tries to say that section 215 should be repealed: journalist Andrea Mitchell interrupts her to break in with the news that Justin Bieber has just been arrested, which indicates what counts as important for MSNBC.

So far, the Snowden segment follows the Oliver format of joking about the boring nature of a vital issue, warming the audience to the task of paying attention nonetheless by serving up a few jokes, and then proceeding to the heart of the satiric essay: an exposition of fact, context, and evidence. In this case, however, the context also includes an interview with Snowden, who was granted sanctuary by Russia when the US government tried to arrest him. Oliver flies to Russia, where Snowden now lives. Oliver starts the interview with jokes (that is, once it begins; Snowden was over an hour late, and so the first few minutes of the delayed interview function as comic material as Oliver paces up and down and curses). However, the rest is (most often) serious, Snowden defending the free press, even if it makes mistakes, and saying that the price of freedom entails the risk of mistakes, of incompetence. The public sphere overshadows the comic public sphere.

In one memorable portion of the interview, however, the comic public sphere asserts itself with a vulgar vengeance. Oliver reverts to playing the smart ass *Daily Show* field correspondent in his questioning, but Snowden remains calm and dignified, for example, when shown the video of people who do not know who he is or think he is in charge of *Wikileaks*; he says that "you can't expect everybody to be uniformly informed." Snowden maintains his composure when Oliver then embodies the public's apparently primary concern about Patriot Act surveillance—collecting images of people naked—by saying that his [Oliver's] "dick pic" would be potential data in the various programs authorized by the law. Explaining the public sphere in the often-vulgar terms of the comic public sphere yields the postmodern blurring of the two discursive realms.

Snowden says that he leaked government documents to give people a chance to decide, to have a conversation, about the kind of government they want to have. But does the public have the capacity and the desire to learn? That question about the enabling conditions for the functioning of the public sphere can be traced all the way back to Kant's essay on the nature of enlightenment. Witness the concern about the NSA collecting pictures of people naked: that worries people—not the other data.

John Oliver, then, employs the postmodern habit of mixing satire with news in a bid to expose in comic fashion the regime of simulacra. In doing so, three features stand out with *Last Week Tonight*. First, Oliver creates the quasi-perlocutionary force of satiractivism far more than any of his predecessors, and he does so in multiple and creative ways, from alternative statues to alternative commercials and on to mock hashtivism, as Colbert would say. Second, Oliver does not so much mix the news with satire, or even use the news as a pretext for satire, so much as he presents deep-dive, yet laughter-inducing, contexts for the news. In addition, Oliver frequently uses his focus segment as a long-form satire or satiric essay that explicates a civic issue. Educating citizens thus registers as important as making them laugh. More precisely, the great strength of *Last Week Tonight with John Oliver* resides in its habit of combining public sphere education with laughter to create silly citizens ready to respond to calls for civic action.

More Satiractivism: Samantha Bee and Stephen Colbert

The fallout from this practice—the John Oliver effect—has been for other satirists to routinely include exhortations for audience members to become engaged citizens. This satiractivism can be found in many places. For example, *The President Show*, a newer entry in Comedy Central's satiric stable, broadcast its Christmas special in 2017, which featured among other skits, a Broadway-style song for the episode's finish, titled "It's Not Going to Stop," in what amounts to a PSA moment in the form of a confession from "Trump" addressed to America. The song tells the audience that he will not stop being Trump; there is no miracle coming; he will not become a Christian or a populist—he does not even meet the criteria for being a good dad. In his narcissism and pettiness, he behaves the opposite of Jesus, an anti-Christ, and he will not stop being his nasty self "until you wise up." A decided dollop of satiractivism follows that soupçon of a PSA when "Trump" suddenly offers a plan of action as images of white supremacists marching in Charlottesville appear on the screen. As the song continues, "Trump" tells his audience he won't stop "unless Americans get more creative with their civil disobedience and use the Constitution as a weapon against the main person who has sworn to uphold it. And can you imagine if the Democratic Party actually rallied behind a coherent message that speaks to the working class people? They could even use my catch phrase, 'Make America Great Again.' It's the perfect slogan for whoever runs against me in 2020, because I am making America a lot of things, but great isn't one of them."[18] Defeating Trump in his bid for reelection in 2020 requires repurposing, in truthiness satire fashion, the false promise of his campaign slogan. That satiric revision anchors a call to civic action that not only imagines citizens being creative in their acts of civil disobedience but also imagines the Democratic Party being creatively hardheaded about how to defeat Trump. "Trump" ironically providing the roadmap to his own defeat dramatizes the postmodern fusion of comic public sphere and public sphere.

However, the best example of a satirist other than John Oliver who with some frequency can be called a satiractivist is Samantha Bee in her show *Full Frontal*. For example, the third segment of the September 13, 2017, episode, a few weeks after Charlottesville, focuses on the topic of white supremacy. A mock clandestine meeting with a former Homeland Security official begins the segment. His secret information: the government almost completely ignores domestic white terrorists. Bee has video clips of officials, including Trump, denying that such terrorists exist to accompany this revelation, and she then follows with a quick history lesson on the influence of white supremacists in Oregon presented in tandem with an interview of a former white supremacist from Portland, Oregon.

However, the heart of the segment features a second interview, one with a representative of an organization rehabilitating white supremacists called "Life After Hate."[19] Because the Trump administration withdrew a grant that the Obama White House had given it, the organization has turned to crowd funding, and the segment closes with an appeal to send them money via Samantha Bee's own website. When Bee interviews the founder of "Life After Hate," Christian Piccolini, a former neo-Nazi, a PSA moment of paralipsis pops up when she summarizes the work of the organization by saying that you "show them [the white supremacists] a way out with love and support" in the form of job training and mental health care. Like John Oliver's *Last Week Tonight*, Bee in this segment of *Full Frontal* dispenses facts along with comic bits but then officially allies her show with an organization dedicated to social reform and encourages her audience as citizens to support the organization too: practically a definition of the comic public sphere in its satiractivism strain.

Piccolini ends the interview saying Bee needs to hug a Nazi to emulate his PSA assertion that the way to change minds depends upon "love and support." She demurs. However, the segment immediately features a parodic PSA spot embedded as another video featuring actors from the television show *Portlandia* about white pride. The mock PSA encourages "mild pride" only, "a quick thumbs-up" for such "beautiful [white] traditions [as] pumpkin spice, the hammer dulcimer, hedge funds [and] white rappers" before dramatizing a less-than-enthusiastic hug for a Nazi. Functioning as both comic public sphere and public sphere, the PSA displays its postmodernity. Initially, the PSA conveys its public sphere message when it recapitulates what Piccolini tells Samantha Bee should be the answer to the problem of white supremacists—"hug a Nazi." However, it also parodies in comic public sphere fashion when it presents its message to white folks about having the proper amount of white pride: just a quick thumbs up, the actors say, because more than that creates the problem. The mock

PSA even features a logo of a hand with the thumb up; it conveys the serious thought comically, not by alternating information with comic insults and jokes, as Bee does in her part of the segment. Rather, the two spheres are delivered, in effect, as one utterance.

The October 4, 2017, episode, "A Primer on Puerto Rico" follows suit; it starts with a focus on Trump's visit to Puerto Rico after Hurricane Maria, mocking his dismal personal response to match the government's inadequate one while also ridiculing the media for its weak coverage of that poor treatment.[20] The segment features a lengthy history lesson about the long-standing nature of the second-class citizen treatment of the island narrated by Javier Muñoz, a star of *Hamilton* born in Puerto Rico: a sign of how *Full Frontal* again imitates the willingness of *Last Week Tonight* to significantly pause its comic attack in order to provide the factual background information needed for a proper public sphere debate. The episode ends with a website and a phone number for "Ayuda a los Pueblos," part of a disaster relief fund for Puerto Rico, so that folks can donate money to help their fellow citizens recover. Another example of *Full Frontal*'s satiractivism, the November 15, 2017, show discusses sexual predators in general and Roy Moore in particular in its opening segment, finishing with an appeal to Alabama voters to register and vote while giving the deadline for registering.[21]

The October 25, 2017, show also features satiractivism. Its first segment, "Natural Disasters: The Greatening," features several video clips of fires and hurricane and the facts Bee dispenses about how terrible 2017 was for natural disasters, for example, the first time three category-four hurricanes happened in one year. Bee says the point is not that climate change causes these problems; rather, it boosts the effects. Yet the United States ignores the problem, often arguing about cause and effect, so Mother Nature has struck back. The implicitly proper action would be enacting all possible policy changes to fix the problem. The second segment in the show, "Scott Pruitt Versus the World," continues the focus on climate change but by profiling the newly appointed head of the Environmental Protection Agency (EPA), Scott Pruitt, who, as Oklahoma's Attorney General, sued the EPA fourteen times. Now he is spearheading the Trump administration's rollback of regulations, even though that plan threatens public health, especially by the suggested rule change to abandon the Clean Power Plan. Mostly, both segments present a standard (i.e., illocutionary) satiric presentation of the topic that, among other comic butts, savages Pruitt.[22]

However, Samantha Bee finishes the comic treatment of climate change by revealing that in the name of *Full Frontal* she has sent a letter to the

EPA to request a hearing about the proposed rule change for the Clean Power Plan, the PSA moment wrapped in a call to action: "If any American submits a request for a hearing on this rule change before October 31, Pruitt has to hold one. We don't know for how long or where it will be held, but I do know that if enough patriotic Americans show up on that day, Scott Pruitt will be so fucking annoyed. And so consider this our official *Full Frontal* request for a hearing on the Clean Power Plan, you big Alaska-despoiling fuck. Warmly, Samantha Bee." The call for citizens to participate in the government's process of holding public hearings to take testimony promotes democracy at a basic level: citizens interacting with their government so that policy reflects the views of the governed. That Bee presents the call with vulgarity worthy of John Oliver and that the audience greets it with laughter signal the comic public sphere, as though a town hall meeting had decided in carnival fashion on a course of satiractivism for a particular issue.

Samantha Bee takes her satiractivism up two or three notches with *Full Frontal*'s app linked to the 2018 midterm elections featuring a title both public sphere and comic public sphere, "This Is Not a Game, The Game," with its comic exhortation for civic mindedness: "Answer Questions, Win Money, Save Democracy." The app presents a daily trivia game with a cash prize of up to $5,000. Participants try to answer ten multiple-choice questions about the midterms and current events—"and very important facts about democracy like in what 1980's vampire movie Kiefer Sutherland played POTUS." The game continues the satiractivism tactic of using comic rhetoric to engage an audience as citizens, with a basic goal: "To get people excited about the midterms, maybe even excited enough that they'll go out and vote! America's typical midterm election turnout SUCKS and we are 100% certain this game will solve everything. We want America to learn facts, register to vote, and get involved in the US election process. Isn't that beautiful? Don't answer. We know it is."[23] A digital intersection of satire with online gaming and real-world politics, the app went live on September 12, 2018, which meant that Bee devoted nearly all of the last two months before the midterms to touting the game on her show and the TBS website. In a segment on September 26, Bee made clear the main demographic being targeted with the app: the eighteen- to thirty-five-year-olds who vote at less than half the rate as citizens over sixty-five. In one of the many interviews Bee gave to promote the campaign, she said that "we're not sitting around thinking that we're going to go out and save democracy, we're really not. We're just trying to help in any way we can."[24]

Entertain and then inspire civic participation: the theory of a–musement, in this case supplemented by satiractivism.

Undoubtedly, the height of Samantha Bee's binding together the public sphere with the comic public sphere to date occurred in her 2018 Christmas special, "Christmas on I.C.E.," which focuses on immigration issues and the government agency Immigration and Customs Enforcement (ICE).[25] Bee begins the segment talking about immigration issues—for example, ICE continues to separate children from their parents and denies help for domestic abuse victims. Moreover, when a child died in ICE custody, some supporters of the Trump administration's policies blamed the parents, saying (in effect) that is why you should not attempt to enter the US: *the trek will kill your children*. Their finger-pointing implies that the inhumane treatment of migrants deliberately has deterrence as its goal, regardless of consequences.

Bee therefore worries that "we have lost our compassion" and she wants to do something about it, invoking the second imperative of postmodern core values: respect all differences. She will devote the entire show to raising money for KIND, "Kids in Need of Defense," which is partnering with *Full Frontal* to create a special fund for families separated by ICE. After showing the way the television audience can donate money with a text message, she becomes the satiractivist by exhorting them to donate. The studio audience already has, she adds, which elicits cheers and applause, both audiences interpellated as citizens.

The show then proceeds with several segments, some rather silly but all of which both mock and celebrate the holiday. One touts the message that Christmas time represents the time of year to tell the truth, which might be noted as the underlying theme of the entire show. Another, in which Bee recreates "Pee Wee Herman's Playhouse," with Sam as Pee Wee, mocks the right-wing talking point that liberals consciously conduct a campaign against Christmas by refusing to say "Merry Christmas." A third segment recreates the 1986 charity song and video, "We Are the World," but substituting spiked eggnog for Pepsi and presenting it as the true Christmas spirit. Mimicking the original video, the segment has a number of celebrities playing the singers, including Jon Stewart as Bob Dylan.

Probably the most serious segment of the episode features Bee in a prerecorded film as a field correspondent visiting McAllen, Texas, a border town where many migrants attempt either a crossing or present themselves as asylum seekers. Here, the satire targets not just immigration policies but also the way *Fox News* covers the policies and the migrants. Bee says she wants to find out what it is really like to come to America these days rather than listen to "the BS about terrorism spouted by *Fox News*." Part of the ridicule of *Fox News* involves a video clip of its correspondent hiding in the bushes near the Rio Grande River as though he were an ICE agent patrolling for illegals. (*Fox*'s title for its clip: "Griff Foils Illegal Attempt to Cross Border.") Bee then pretends to flush out three *Fox* field correspondents and chases them away. *Full Frontal* follows this slap at *Fox* and the attitude it represents by showing an animated billboard in McAllen they purchased that has Bee dancing and smiling and waving over the word "bienvenidos." The rest of the prerecorded segment features an interview with a woman at the McAllen bus station helping asylum seekers who are boarding buses to be taken to the detention centers to wait while the government processes their cases. For both Bee and the woman, their efforts to be welcoming and helpful indicate hope in the process. Bee has one more jab at *Fox News*, though, showing a clip from *Fox & Friends* claiming 98 percent of asylum seekers do not show up for their hearing, and then citing Department of Justice statistics that show exactly the opposite: about 2 percent fail to show up.

The note of hope in the McAllen segment contrasts with the general tone of the show, which begins with bitter vulgarity. Presenting the premise of the show, Bee says, "The world is dark, but tonight we are going to bukkake it with joy. It is a half hour slathered with tinsel and trees and carols and skating and celebrity cameos. Your hearts are going to swell with goodwill toward your fellow humans if it's the last fucking thing I do." Bee then breaks into a mock show tune in which she proclaims Christmas as "the least terrible season of the year." Her song segues to a young girl about nine dressed as the angel announcing the birth of Jesus to the shepherds. She begins by reciting the apt Biblical passage but abruptly breaks off when she comes to the part saying Jesus is born in the city of David. She then angrily claims that being born in the city of David rates better than being born in the city of Donald, who would have sneered at "savior of mankind" by substituting "loser of mankind." The supposedly angelic girl finishes by saying, "You know what—fuck 2018," and storms off the stage.

Two more moments of satiractivism stand out in the *Full Frontal* Christmas special, and both move well beyond asking for donations to KIND. The first one has a John Oliver, muckraking feel to it as Bee exposes a civic problem: asylum seekers have trouble finding legal representation because the detention centers tend to be far from cities, which means that very few lawyers are available. Bee again as field correspondent travels to one such center in Lumpkin, Georgia, where exactly one immigration lawyer lives, though he has some supplemental help from a few other pro bono lawyers living in a trailer at the back of his house. A lack of accommodations for family members to visit or help in the court proceedings compounds the problem: no hotels, only the nonprofit El Refugio, a nine-bed facility. In the spirit of *let's do something* with which Bee started the special, *Full Frontal* purchases a house and renovates it and donates it to El Refugio for the use of those families, creating twenty more spaces for them. Reminiscent of Oliver's tactics of buying commercial time to promulgate in comic ways public sphere ideas and opinions, Bee's show intervenes materially to act on an important and timely civic issue. The renovated house clearly counts as political action in a public sphere fashion. Of course, Bee pays for the project in comic public sphere fashion with a giant-sized credit card she inserts into a giant-sized processing machine, the props visually demonstrating the satiric exaggerations throughout the show.

This direct activism has an indirect complement, striking also for its radical quality: a segment encouraging citizens to resist ICE. Bee and her *Full Frontal* writers and staff first dedicate the segment to educating the audience as citizens; they want to be sure people know what rights they have if ICE should show up at their door. *Full Frontal* also encourages folks to use social media to record any aggressiveness by ICE agents, having billed this segment as the guide to the excesses of ICE. Most importantly, Bee says, people should vote for candidates who would abolish the agency. The entire segment mimics an ice-skating competition, with Bee and Adam Rippon, a champion ice-skater, playing the roles of commentators on the slapstick sketch-on-ice behind them dramatizing the excesses of ICE being successfully resisted by the "Abolish ICE Ice-Skaters." Public sphere information and advocacy of a position on a political issue, plus an exhortation to vote, all done up in mock Christmas fashion climaxes the ironic yuletide attitude of the entire satiric episode.

Significant portions of the show have been bitter and rude rather than celebratory, but the close of the show emphatically underscores how *Full Frontal* has used the holiday to conduct its activism. Bee manages one more dig at *Fox News*, a major satiric butt throughout the show, functioning more as cheerleader and promulgator of the administration's drastic immigration policies than a so-called news organization, by saying "Jesus loves me and hates *Fox News*." Crucially, she makes that statement after claiming that the real meaning of Christmas can be found in the message of radical kindness that Jesus represents, returning to the theme of compassion that started her Christmas special by quoting Jesus: "Whatever you did for one of the least of these brothers and sisters of mine, you did for me" (Matthew 25:40). Not exactly reverse discourse, but the tactics of the "*Full Frontal* Christmas I.C.E. Special," conducted on ice, mock trivial notions about the meaning of Christmas—saying "Merry Christmas" instead of "Happy Holidays" or drinking spiked eggnog to show true Christmas spirit—to counterpoint an endorsement of the Christian message of radical compassion. *Full Frontal* thereby not only questions government immigration policies but also advocates for a radical political action, the abolition of Immigration and Customs Enforcement, while implicitly admonishing Christians for failing to heed the radical words of Jesus.

Although *Late Night with Stephen Colbert* does not embrace satiractivism as robustly as does *Full Frontal*, Colbert does display comic *parrhēsia* and finish with satiractivism, also in the name of compassion, when he critiques the Department of Justice (DOJ) policy of separating children from parents at the border on the Thursday before Fathers' Day, 2018.[26] The monologue that night anticipated in some ways Samantha Bee's Christmas special later that year. The present for fathers on this day, Colbert says, should be to spend time with their children, thus setting up a cozy domestic contrast with the inhumane DOJ policy. Colbert next describes his job at *Late Night*, which perfectly articulates how the comic public sphere supplements the public sphere: "To give you my take on the conversation that everyone is already having. With any luck, my take is funnier than yours, or I would be watching you. But this story is different because this is the conversation that everybody should be having." In other words, *in my comic fashion, I am inviting all citizens to talk about this issue*, invoking the public sphere.

In this segment, Colbert maintains a mostly serious demeanor and tone, with only minimal comic insults here and there. For an example of such comic tactics, Colbert says, when he shows a photo of Attorney General Jeff Sessions smiling broadly, "Attorney General and man daydreaming about legally changing his name to 'Jim Crow,' Jeff Sessions." In general, however, Colbert keeps a public sphere focus, including providing evidence for his argument against the government's border policy. For example, he quotes a news report about the number of children already taken away at the border, more than two thousand. Colbert uses this fact to appeal to his audience as compassionate people: if this policy "sounds evil, then good news, your ears are working." He then appeals to his audience as ethical citizens: "Here's the bad news: the United States, that's you and me, are putting up with the government saying to immigrants, if you come to the United States, the worst thing imaginable will happen to you. We will take your children away from you, with no guarantee you'll see them again. That is using cruelty as a deterrent. That is not my interpretation; that is our stated intention." Colbert sticks with the public sphere by continuing to cite evidence for his position against the government's actions. "Three government officials said [as he quotes from a news story] 'Part of the reason for the proposal is to deter mothers from migrating to the United States with their children.'" Then comes the double dose of comic public sphere caustic: "The other part is just recreational racism. . . . Clearly, no decent human being could defend that. So Jeff Sessions did. In fact, he said separating kids from their parents is the Lord's work," quoting an Epistle from Paul (Romans 13:1) that says one should obey government laws. Colbert returns to the public sphere momentarily by directly countering Sessions's argument that God Himself would approve of the government's actions. He points out that if Sessions had just quoted Paul's epistle further along, the message would be quite different: "Love your neighbor as yourself. Love does no harm to a neighbor. Therefore love is the fulfillment of the law" (Romans 13:10). Colbert meets Sessions on his own Biblical ground and shows how un-Christian is his pretense of being righteous.

Colbert continues his counterargument against Sessions's religious defense of government by quoting Jesus, who said "suffer the children to come unto me" (Matthew 19:14), and then injecting comic *parrhēsia* by saying that "all Sessions saw was the words 'suffer' and 'children.'" Colbert continues: even if the kids were taken to a nice hotel, the United States "would still be the only country in the whole damn world doing it, because it's just plain wrong." Up to this point, the satire has been of the illocutionary sort, in a caustic tone, though not employing the vulgarity practiced by Samantha Bee or John Oliver. Then comes the satiractivist finish—garnished with vulgarity: "So, for Fathers' Day, call your elected representative and demand they do something. Because I sincerely believe that it doesn't matter who you voted for, if we let this happen in our name, we are a feckless cunt-try." This pronunciation of "country" is a nod of solidarity to Samantha Bee, referencing her recent dust-up with Ivanka Trump over the same border policy. Ivanka had released a photo of herself with her children in the midst of the debate about the government's actions. Bee took the gesture as part of the civic conversation about the morality of the policy and characterized Ivanka as a "feckless cunt" for making it. The outrage that ensued caused Bee to apologize—sort of. (More on this example later.) Colbert's speech on the issue exemplifies how the satirist in satiractivist mode mixes news with sarcasm, sometimes bitterly acerbic, but necessarily ends his or her comic *parrhēsia* with a call to civic action.

Case Study: The Saga of Jimmy Kimmel and the Debate on Health Care

An excellent instance of the way that the illocutionary force of satire in a postmodern environment can easily slide toward the quasi-perlocutionary force of satiractivism comes with Jimmy Kimmel's staging a comic public sphere debate on health care to create the engaged levity of silly citizenship.

In May of 2017, talk show host and professional comedian Jimmy Kimmel stepped into the public sphere when he told the story of his son's birth with a congenital heart condition and the first of three operations required to remedy the condition, and he then finished the story with what amounted to a PSA moment advocating for a health care bill that would continue the coverage for preexisting conditions contained in the Affordable Care Act (ACA), informally known as "Obamacare."[27] The context for that moment, which went viral: the Senate later in the week began debating proposed legislation from the House to change the ACA under the slogan of "repeal and replace."

The next week Kimmel continued interjecting public sphere discourse into his comic monologue by featuring an interview with Senator Bill Cassidy from Louisiana. Cassidy had declared in an interview at another venue during the week following the original viral video that any new health care bill must be better than the ACA or what had passed the House, must pass what he called "the Jimmy Kimmel test," that is, at a minimum allow for preexisting conditions. Given Cassidy's pronouncement, Kimmel invited him to speak on his show. Having Cassidy appear on screen from a remote location reprograms comic monologue into news interview: the public sphere appears suddenly, complete with the senator urging citizens to call their representatives to express their views on the issue. Kimmel transforms to the serious interviewer found on news networks and the Sunday political shows when he asks the senator a number of important public sphere questions.[28]

Jimmy Kimmel later reengages with the topic of health care reform when the Graham-Cassidy bill was introduced on September 13, 2017, as the latest attempt to replace the ACA. The bill, cosponsored by Senator Bill Cassidy from Louisiana and Senator Lindsey Graham from South

Carolina, would not cover preexisting conditions, which meant it violated what Cassidy had called back in May "the Jimmy Kimmel test." The next week, Kimmel devoted his opening monologue to the bill, a renewal of his effort in May to initiate a comic public sphere conversation about reforming ACA.[29] His September 19 monologue (and the others on the topic to follow) continued his deft weaving together of the public sphere with the comic public sphere, which exemplifies how recent satire has at times apparently erased the boundary between comic political speech and political speech with the quasi-perlocutionary force of satiractivism.

From the perspective of the public sphere, Kimmel clearly staked a position against the Graham-Cassidy bill by enumerating the specifics of what it does not do (e.g., prevent lifetime caps) to educate his audience, now interpellated as citizens, a change that clearly happens when there are audible groans as Kimmel says that the bill does none of what Cassidy claims he wants. He further educates the audience about the sham process: the Senate Republican leadership will not let the Congressional Budget Office score the bill, and only one hearing will be held, in the Homeland Security Committee, which has no connection to health care policy, with only two witnesses allowed, Cassidy and Graham. Kimmel also lists the many medical associations against the bill, gives polling data about how unpopular the bill is, and informs the audience of a current bipartisan effort to do better. Kimmel emphasizes the implicit conversation that marks the public sphere by addressing would-be critics who will say that he is politicizing his son's condition. He readily admits to politicizing it "because I have to," which elicits loud applause: the citizen audience in the studio apparently endorses his substituting serious commentary on Graham-Cassidy for his usual comic patter.[30]

From the perspective of the comic public sphere, Kimmel sprinkles jokes and comic insults throughout the monologue, which elicit a range of laughter, though mostly not of the hearty kind. The overall tone of the monologue projects sincerity and public sphere earnestness while retaining a comic edginess, not unlike Jack Shafer's "Swamp Diary" columns. For example, when Kimmel insults Cassidy by calling the bill "a scam," no one laughs. When he jokes that the topic of health care is "boring," evoking John Oliver, again no one laughs (this jab after working through details he calls "confusing"). And when he insults the audience, saying that the scam might work because "we're all looking at our Instagram account and liking things," definitely no one laughs—or the laughter must necessarily be of the LOI sort. When Kimmel mocks his audience about being obsessed with social media, he invokes Baudrillard's idea of the ecstasy of communication, in effect exhorting folks to reconstitute their subjectivity outside the regime of simulacra, outside truthiness, into that of an informed citizen.

However, Kimmel does elicit a bit of LOL laughter when he says that the Graham-Cassidy bill passes the Jimmy Kimmel test, but just the new version, which is, "only if Jimmy Kimmel is your father, otherwise you are screwed." Similarly, he garners some laughter asserting that Republicans count on people to be bored and pay the bill as much attention as we all do for "an iTunes service agreement." He does better still when he jokes that health care is not his area of expertise: eating pizza is his expertise (a good-sized laugh for what registers as the silliest of his sallies), and he scores a bigger laugh when he jokes that would-be critics of his position should shove their comments where the doctors will not be able to give a prostate exam "once they take your health care benefits away" (the clearest of comic insults, wrapped in vulgarity).[31]

The differing rhetorical registers of the two spheres can thus, for the most part, be readily sorted, yet how should one classify the most aggressive and provocative statement Kimmel makes, that "this guy Bill Cassidy just lied right to my face" because his bill does none of the things that Cassidy explicitly endorsed back in May with his pledge that he called "the Jimmy Kimmel test"? Should that statement be classified as comic insult? The audience does not laugh at the assertion of lying, just as it does not laugh at other moments of insult that might be received as comic, noted above. However, the audience does laugh loudly when, after replaying the video of Cassidy saying "yep" to Kimmel's asking him if he is for the provisions implied in the Jimmy Kimmel test, Kimmel says, "I guess 'yep' is Washington for 'nope.'"

Kimmel thus provides two versions of the claim about lying. The first can be logged as neither joke nor insult but an instance of *parrhēsia*, and thus the utterance takes its place squarely in the public sphere. The second version couches the claim of lying as laughable paradox, and thus the utterance takes its place squarely in the comic public sphere. This analytic oscillation between the two discursive spheres happens again when Kimmel first shows a picture of Cassidy with a smile that makes him look crazy-madcap while asking the audience, "Do you trust him" to fix health care, a comic insult that commands a big laugh, and then he says Cassidy seemed like a decent guy when he was on the show in May, and his medical expertise should be a help to the process if he joins the new bipartisan effort. These moments register as a postmodern quantum state in their indeterminate, superposition status or in the duality of a punning status, as utterances within both discursive spheres. When CNN reporter Chris Cuomo claims (just before he asked Cassidy in an interview to respond to the charge of lying) that Kimmel spoke "harsh words not apparently in jest," he fails to understand that, as a satirist, Kimmel spoke harsh words in jest—as well as not in jest.

The part comic, part serious—that is, satiric—monologue near the end turns to satiractivism with an explicit exhortation to call representatives, Kimmel supplying the phone number that will reach any representative. "You can't just click 'like' on this video" he says, addressing the television and online audiences once again as citizens. Kimmel here also speaks truth to all segments of his audience, insinuating that people have the wrong priorities, to which he had alluded earlier with the crack about everyone's noses stuck in their Instagram accounts. Kimmel finishes his September 19 monologue by insisting that if Cassidy continues to push his bill, he has to stop using Kimmel's name for the test of what constitutes good health care. He then invites Cassidy to stop by the studio to take the new Jimmy Kimmel test: a lie detector test. That utterance registers as comic *parrhēsia* via comic insult, and the studio audience laughs loudly and applauds.

Debate and dialogue underwrite the public sphere, what Habermas calls "communicative rationality," or simply the conversation of democracy. Once Kimmel reengaged with the health care debate by satirizing the Graham-Cassidy bill, his parodic comic conversation continued for the next two days. The YouTube clip from his next show, on Wednesday the 20th, reflects that basic fact in its title, "Jimmy Kimmel Fights Back Against Bill Cassidy, Lindsey Graham and Chris Christie."[32] Kimmel repeats that Cassidy must have been lying when he appeared on the show in May and again rattles off a list of medical associations opposing the bill. More interesting, he enacts a mock debate with Bill Cassidy by reciting key provisions of the Graham-Cassidy bill that would do exactly what Cassidy said should not happen for a bill to pass "the Jimmy Kimmel test." Kimmel ridicules Cassidy by showing that he debates (and contradicts) himself.

When Kimmel notes responses on social media as well as broadcast and cablecast media to his calling Cassidy out as a liar the previous night, he ridicules a different form of faux conversation, but the point remains. The proper conversation that should be happening in the public sphere has been displaced by Cassidy's hypocrisy, as well as by irrelevant charges against Kimmel, such as the insult from *Fox & Friends* host Brian Kilmeade, who dismisses Kimmel's position on Graham-Cassidy as Hollywood elite politics. The show on Thursday the 21st continues the trope of the failure of a proper public sphere conversation.[33] Trump tweeting a defense of Cassidy provides the best example of that failure. Trump says Cassidy does not lie, which means Trump knows what Kimmel has been saying. Kimmel then tweets in response, saying if Cassidy does not lie, will he "vote against the horrible bill he wrote?" Kimmel received no response from Trump, yet the satiric drama being enacted features a late-night talk-show host in the guise of a satirist comically discussing health care with pundits from news outlets and with politicians, including the president of the United States. Notably, Kimmel again shifts back and forth between the comic public sphere and public sphere when, after slamming Cassidy's bill as horrible, he shows public sphere civility when he says that he admires Cassidy for the work he has done as a physician in Baton Rouge, implying that the bill exhibits anomalous moral behavior for Cassidy.

Kilmeade's charge of elitism impugns the ethos of Kimmel, and that aspect of the debate touches everyone involved. Certainly, the underlying issue for Kimmel has been Cassidy's insincerity. Kimmel's charge of lying provokes Cassidy into implying that all comedians are dummies when he says in an interview given elsewhere on television that Kimmel just does not understand the bill. When Kimmel features a clip from an interview of former New Jersey governor Chris Christie saying Kimmel is "not a serious person," Christie raises the issue of ethos in a different way: Who is qualified to speak? Kimmel also plays a clip from an interview with the other senator from Louisiana, John Kennedy, who again plays the he-is-not-a-serious-person card, implying that no one would take advice on health care reform from him. In effect, Christie's and Kennedy's dismissals of Kimmel because he earns his living as an entertainer and professional comedian—a mere talk-show host—first seek to isolate the comic public sphere from the public sphere and then declare it does not exist as a legitimate supplement to the debate on a matter of national importance. Second, their dismissal denies Kimmel's status as a citizen with the right to speak on civic issues. Comics by definition speak foolishly (they are mere jesters), and so no warrant exists to hear their voices, Christie and Kennedy imply. Such a response may be the price to pay for the quick zigzagging movement between the comic public sphere and the public sphere as well as the postmodern compounding of the two discursive spheres Kimmel creates. Indeed, such a dismissive response can be leveled against any contemporary satirist as an easy way to dodge the serious critique lodged in his or her satire. Kimmel, however, notes what has to be the bottom line for why contemporary satirists so often feel obliged to speak their comic truth to power: because those in power refuse to tell the truth.

Kimmel may note that he gains nothing out of his advocacy for better health care, implicitly claiming a role as one who holds nothing back when he speaks, as a *parrhēsiastes*, or that because his name has been linked to the health care debate by Cassidy creating "the Jimmy Kimmel test," the link should provide on its own some license to speak. However, those arguments will not pass muster with folks like Christie and Kennedy, who eagerly flaunt their official positions in government or eagerly patronize by saying Kimmel does not understand the provisions of the bill. Kimmel's rejoinder: the real question cannot be his pretending to be an expert but rather why Kennedy and other senators refuse to listen to experts, the many medical associations that denounced the bill, as Kimmel repeatedly shows.

Kimmel's monologues on health care consistently use both discursive spheres to make a comic argument full of satiric intent. In addition, the general comic public sphere quality of the conversation generated by Kimmel's monologues switches at their close in these health care debate instances of his show to a public sphere activist mode, with a call for the ultimate duty of the citizen in the public sphere: contacting elected representatives and voicing opposition to Graham-Cassidy. In one case, Kimmel delivers the direct appeal to contact officials with yet another comic insult targeting the audiences for the shows—"stop texting for five seconds"— before supplying the phone numbers of key senators. Kimmel leans hard on his audiences because the *New York Times* had reported that Senator Susan Collins's office claimed that the volume of calls about the bill remained the same after Kimmel's first giving out phone numbers despite the video of the initial health care debate monologue having millions of online views. Kimmel as citizen directly appeals to the audience as citizens: *we have only ourselves to blame if nothing happens because we do not voice opposition*. Hence his redoubled effort to exhort his audiences to call the key senators: "It really does make a difference." The monologues in these shows, as comic events, thus display an explicit call to political action that follows satiric ridicule, creating satiractivism. Kimmel presumes that his satiric critique has provided a–musement and metanoia, though he clearly is not so sure about the audience shifting from a metanoia to an action to complete the satire two-step.

While the satire two-step outcome can be held up as the ideal of satiractivism, a danger in the comic tactics of satire must be noted. Kimmel's monologues enact dialogue (a structural joke, one might say), presenting in different forms exchanges among the various voices in the health care debate in a bid to both enact and mock public sphere conversation. In doing so, Kimmel stages the topic of who has the proper status and ethos to speak, a topic basic to the concept of the public sphere. While controversy exists about what Habermas thought created the proper status to speak (e.g., owning property or being educated), the core qualification would be the ethos of engaged citizenship. The comic public sphere alters this quality to engaged, yet silly, citizenship, with the satirist as the exemplar. Self-styled serious folks like Christie and Kennedy only choose to perceive silly, not the engaged levity of silly citizenship, in their responses, and so they dismiss Kimmel as not a serious person. Of course, a partial truth exists in that assertion, for as a satirist, Kimmel behaves both seriously and playfully, a condition visible in some of the comic insults, but the dismissal amounts to a failure to understand that satire exists as paradoxical utterance, in a quantum state of both/and.

The danger happens when the satirist returns the favor of dismissing opponents, which too easily can descend into a contest of snark insults meant merely to demean and thus degrade status, performing the anti-public sphere. However, comic insults often power the ridicule of satire to mark the comic public sphere, as examples from the Kimmel saga demonstrate. Senator Kennedy, quips Kimmel, was dragged out of a (presumably Louisiana) swamp to defend Cassidy, Kimmel also referring to him as a "lady" and "inbred." These insults come across as purely demeaning, having everything to do with personal appearance and stereotypes about poor whites and nothing to do with policy. Similarly, Kimmel goes after Christie's personal appearance, insinuating that his large girth results from absurd eating habits such that once his head became stuck in a bucket of fried chicken. Though this insult elicits a big laugh and applause, Kimmel takes it right back. Christie has the free-speech right to make fun of him, and he (Kimmel) was the one who once got his head stuck in a bucket of chicken. This supposed retrieval of the insult about Christie's weight perhaps measures some regret at such a cheap shot only meant to demean instead of further proper dialogue. The backtracking definitely indicates Kimmel's self-consciousness about the difference between the comic insults of the comic public sphere and the snarky insults of the anti-public sphere.

Kimmel's insult against Senator Graham also focuses on physical appearance. Graham had labeled Kimmel's attack on his bill as "garbage," but Kimmel says he will not punch back because Graham looks like his grandmother, supposedly demonstrated in side-by-side photos, grandma's face morphing into Graham's. The implicit charge of effeminacy echoes an insult against Kennedy (calling him "lady"), but the tone sounds much more whimsical due to the photo and Kimmel calling Graham "Grandma Lindsey." Aided by Photoshop, the joke reaps a big laugh and loud applause, but the whimsicality of the joke probably does not save it from being mere lampooning insult. However, Kimmel also says he will not attack Graham because he is one of the few Republicans who stand up to Donald Trump. That statement qualifies as a public sphere utterance, and because it precedes the photoshopped image, acknowledges Graham's worthiness in the public sphere before mocking him in a way that skates the boundary between comic insult and mere insult. Kimmel follows a similar mixed comic strategy when he ridicules Cassidy being caught out in a lie by first saying Cassidy has been exposed with his "GOPenis out," yet also wants to give Cassidy the benefit of the doubt that he nevertheless should be considered a good guy, a friendly thought immediately undercut by adding he stands ready to doubt the benefits named in the bill. Both jokes have the virtue of pointing to the civic issue being debated: the vulgar wit of "GOPenis" garners a big laugh and applause as it mocks the exposure of Cassidy as a base liar; the verbal wit in scrambling the catchphrase "benefit of the doubt" to "doubt the benefits" expressly references the Graham-Cassidy proposal. The takeaway from this closer look at comic insults: at times satirists launch them merely for comic ridicule (essentially lampoon), while at other times they serve the comic argument about the civic issue at hand. Only the latter can be rated properly satiric.

Kimmel conceives his jokes about Donald Trump in the monologues more broadly than simply the Graham-Cassidy bill. Instead, Kimmel mocks Trump's role in the process, or, more precisely, his lack of a role, because everyone knows he has not and will not read the bill. Imagining Trump reading the bill, says Kimmel, would be equivalent to imagining a dog doing your taxes, an insult about Trump's laziness and intelligence that elicits a big laugh and loud applause. Kimmel also jokes about Trump's ignorance, saying he does not know the difference between Medicare and Medicaid; he barely knows the difference between Melania and Ivanka. These jokes all reference Trump's personal qualities rather than the legislation, but they all also undercut Trump's status as a worthy speaker in the public sphere: lampoon functioning as satire. Other jokes that mention the legislation nevertheless also comically question Trump's ethos. Kimmel jokes that if "Obamacare" was renamed "Ivankacare," Trump would be happy because just getting rid of Obama's name is his true goal. Trump likes his name on things, referencing the Trump name as a market brand, so he would do anything to take Obama's name off the current health care legislation, even sign copies of the Koran at a (mythical) Barnes and Noble in Fallujah, Iraq. Kimmel's focus on the health care debate transforms the normally comic space of his monologue into a dialogue that mimics in satiric fashion the public sphere debate, a parody with serious intent, fueled by comic insults.

On September 26, 2017, *Politico* reported that Republican leadership in the Senate had decided not to put the Graham-Cassidy bill up for a floor vote, after it was clear their latest plan would fail. The opposition spearheaded by Kimmel's satiractivism appeared to contribute to that outcome.[34] Kimmel in his monologue that night does not so much take a victory lap for the demise of the bill he calls a "flaming bag of dog crap," but rather he continues his strong effort to mimic the dialogue of the public sphere process, first by thanking those who had been activated by his efforts and contacted Congress, effectively closing the loop of communicative rationality.

However, he also continues the process by again educating the audience: rehearsing facts about why Obamacare has not been improved because the GOP has tried to repeal and replace while refusing to work with Democrats to make the necessary changes; citing polling data showing how little support there was for Graham-Cassidy while he implicitly mocks the GOP for saying they are still going to try to repeal Obamacare. That last utterance (a straight statement of fact but a sarcasm in the context Kimmel builds) segues into his walking through the steps for the best way to write a bill—that is, holding public hearings and asking experts, not the crazy method that the Republicans tried with Graham-Cassidy: "By candlelight at night on the back of a Bazooka [gum] wrapper in a broom closet and then lying about what it will do." While that ridicule of the actual clandestine procedure garners a laugh, the real applause happens when he pivots to thanking those senators who stopped the bill. In this sequence, Kimmel again demonstrates how deftly he has deployed comic *parrhēsia* in his campaign against Graham-Cassidy. He then switches into satiractivism mode by once again urging everyone to tell their congressional representatives to take real action on the health care issue. He again interpellates his audiences—studio, broadcast, cablecast, online—as citizens, saying in effect *we are now paying attention, and elected officials will be hearing from us again.* As if that public sphere message were not enough, Kimmel finishes with another, saying folks also need to be "loud and engaged" about help for Puerto Rico after the double hit from hurricanes, and providing a phone number and texting code for donations to the Red Cross. The arc of the monologue starts with an acknowledgment of satiractivism, moves through the presentation of comic *parrhēsia* in classic illocutionary fashion, and returns to satiractivism.

Part of Kimmel's strategy of comic *parrhēsia* involved questioning the ethos of those who supported Graham-Cassidy. The biggest satiric target in this regard must be of course the occupant of the Oval Office. Kimmel mocks Trump about his flip-flops on many topics and issues after Trump on Twitter had mocked John McCain for supposedly changing his mind about repealing and replacing Obamacare. Kimmel executes the mockery with a video compilation of Trump's "bigliest about-faces" over the years that starts with his praise for Hillary Clinton as "a great woman," and then moves to his saying he would never lie, and he would produce his tax returns if he should run for president. The portrait of Trump via a string of edited video clips has the value of displacing the daily and weekly news cycle to reveal a core behavior of Trump in what amounts to a comic flash-documentary.

Kimmel jokes that the irony of Trump's attack on McCain registers as "richer" than Trump, "who has more flip-flops than a Jimmy Buffett concert." In another display of how Kimmel has been speaking truth to power via ridicule, enacting the comic public sphere but mixed with public sphere straight talk, he interrupts the mockery on flip-flops to educate his audience about McCain's heroism as a prisoner of war (e.g., his refusal to accept repatriation until all prisoners were released), showing footage of his return that documents his difficulty walking because of the beatings he suffered. In contrast, Trump's claim of a bone spur kept him home, a "deferment from Dr. Scholls." This phrasing raises a laugh, but what should be noted is how the sequence of joke, documentary footage, joke constitutes the comic *parrhēsia*: what appears as an interruption of mockery instead stages a tactic in building the mockery. Kimmel continues the satiric ridicule by first showing McCain exiting a bus when he finally does return home and then showing Trump exiting a bus with Billy Bush, referencing the infamous Access Hollywood tape. The entire sequence (in comic terms, the McCain bit) garners loud applause for McCain, validating Kimmel's takedown of Trump's credibility in the public sphere. Perhaps the best comic jab at the ethos of the Donald, however, comes when Kimmel implies Trump's narcissism by the manner in which he urges him to help with the bipartisan heath care reform effort led by senators Lamar Alexander and

Patty Murray. That support will give him good press because they will not only put his name on the legislation; they will put his face on all the surgical masks in all the hospitals so that patients on the operating table will see it and say "thank you" just before they go under. Nothing like comic fantasy to round out a critique of a warped reality.

As these examples from *Jimmy Kimmel Live!* suggest, Kimmel, once involved with the health care debate due to his son's birth defect, turned the usual discursive space of his comic monologue into a clever blend of public sphere and comic public sphere utterances. Kimmel swirled together jokes and comic insults with facts about health care in general and the Graham-Cassidy bill in particular, often with a satiractivism component as the finish. The entire set of monologues operates as a comic saga articulating a PSA.

Before the public demise of Graham-Cassidy, however, Kimmel for one show left out the satiractivism in favor of the classic illocutionary form for satire, using the format made most famous by Jon Stewart, adopted nightly in his opening monologues by Stephen Colbert, and elaborated by John Oliver—that is, an elaborated presentation of mock news. The topic, though, was not about health care but about the responses to his involvement in the public sphere debate as a satirist.

Kimmel begins that monologue with something of a recap. When he had first revealed that his son required multiple open-heart surgeries, Republican senator from Louisiana Bill Cassidy had promised, in a live interview on the show, that any bill he would support in the Senate health care debate would have to pass what he called "the Jimmy Kimmel test." When Kimmel opens his monologue by mentioning his entanglement in the debate on health care reform, the audience giggles and Kimmel says in response, "I know, it's ridiculous," a comment that seems to reference how foolish the debate is and how absurd it is that he has been involved, as well as the audience's awareness of the whole parodic conversation Kimmel carried on most of the previous week.[35]

However, much of the monologue (again) has a public sphere quality, Kimmel studding it with facts, as he did the previous week, such as polling data about the popularity of ACA versus the Graham-Cassidy bill. He once again presents himself as a comic version of a *parrhēsiastes*, emphasizing his explicit challenge to Cassidy's touting his current bill as passing the Jimmy Kimmel test when it does not. Though Kimmel appears to be making a serious argument in public sphere fashion, as a satirist he necessarily gives his speaking truth to power a comic edge in the way that he mixes facts and film clips in documentary fashion with witticisms and jokes exhibiting a range of comic invective. His tactics create a classic illocutionary presentation that exhibits an affinity with Jon Stewart's mock news format.

For example, when he recounts meeting people over the weekend at events he attended, he heard many anecdotes from folks that ACA saved them and their families, who said, "Mr. Fallon, thanks for speaking out." This bit manages to recount what actually happened to him over the weekend but adds a self-deprecatory joke (*Jimmy Fallon is better known than I am*), which conveys a light touch. Kimmel adds to the lighter comic tone by showing his Twitter profile picture, which has him holding a tray of chicken wings, on which he ironically comments, "Who says I am not a serious advocate for health care reform?" That utterance registers as postmodern—comic public sphere and public sphere at once—for while the photo authorizes his self-mocking comment, it also points to the fact that Kimmel actually has been a serious advocate for health care reform since May when he first talked about his son's condition.

That doubled gesture, the signature move of important parts of satire today, characterizes the way Kimmel has bound himself into the debate as satirist, the way that his contribution to the debate has spurred more conversation crossing back and forth between both spheres. His tweet to McCain thanking him for being a hero by voting against the bill (the satirist addressing the politician as equals advocating for good, not sham, reform) exemplifies that conversation and traversal, which then generates a reaction from *Fox & Friends*. Similarly, Kimmel's joke about pretending to like something his friends wrote, referencing McCain voting against his friend Lindsey Graham, implies and denies equivalence. They both have had to make a difficult choice that might offend friends, yet the stakes involved in the two contexts are radically different.

The comments in the *Fox & Friends* video clip treat Kimmel as public sphere advocate for a position on reform, not as a satirist. The *Fox & Friends* hosts are therefore sure Kimmel acts as a pawn of the Democrats. Moreover, his behavior supposedly proves a favorite narrative of the political right: mainstream media colludes with Democrats. The hosts ask Kimmel to confess to fighting the bill in the media for the Democrats, and his confession readily follows in the form of an utterance that jokes yet tells the truth: he quips that he did stop the bill, but Kimmel exposes the absurdity of colluding with the Democrats when he notes that the collusion entails first having a baby with a congenital heart condition, a sarcasm the audience clearly understands, given their big cheers for it. Kimmel then switches to a more public sphere explanation that transforms his supposed collusion to a reasoned position on the issue, reciting facts (e.g., the health organizations and charities that support his position on Graham-Cassidy) and ending with his conclusion: "The facts were on my side ...; it's just a matter of what's true and what isn't true." However, this insistence on public sphere rationality rather than collusion inevitably carries a residue of satiric comic public sphere sarcasm. The *Fox & Friends* charge that Kimmel acts as a "puppet" implies that he cannot think for himself—be enlightened—on the topic.

The *Fox & Friends* hosts claim that Kimmel proves the bias of the mainstream media, but one bit in the monologue satirizes the way that the Republicans have tried to manipulate the media in their crusade against Obamacare by repeatedly calling ACA a disaster. Kimmel suggests that the mere repetition suggests untruthfulness; he jokes that no one felt compelled to repeatedly state that Hurricane Harvey created a disaster: everyone knew. Trump features as the most prominent repeat offender, as a long compilation of video clips show: "disaster" is his only adjective for ACA, so Kimmel jokes that he needs a thesaurus. The compilation of clips repeating "disaster" displaces the news cycle, collapsing the time frame for the many moments of repetition to show how desperately insistently Republicans have been and continue to be in order to convince people of a lie. Moreover, the clips of Trump repeatedly saying "disaster" document how the media as simulacra machine works. The last clip shows Trump saying, "The disaster known as" and then waiting for the audience to finish the sentence with "Obamacare." Trump then says, "That was easy," a response that can be read as Trump inadvertently admitting to the brainwashing tactic of mindless repetition.

Kimmel in the same monologue has one more satiric swipe at Mr. Trump in the context of the health care debate, though like so much of the comic ridicule directed at Trump in the gaggle of Kimmel monologues, Kimmel targets not Trump's position on health care but Trump's standing as worthy speaker in the public sphere. Thus Kimmel implies Trump's narcissism when he refers to Trump holding yet another "masturbatory rally" where he complained about John McCain's vote. Kimmel matches the pungently vulgar sarcasm in that phrasing when he turns Trump's complaint back on him. Trump had said that the failure of Graham-Cassidy was "a horrible, horrible thing that has happened to the Republican Party," and Kimmel comments, "Said the horrible, horrible thing that has happened to the Republican Party," to which the audience responds with laughs, cheers, and applause.

Kimmel at the end of his saga of health debate monologues almost apologizes for injecting so much public sphere speech into a discursive space supposedly reserved for comic entertainment when he says, after the Graham-Cassidy bill has been defeated, "The best news of all is I can go back to talking about the Kardashians," and so leave out the comic *parrhēsia* embedded in his satire. In some measure, that joke again teases his audience about their stereotypical wish for entertainment at the expense of being informed, if not active, citizens, but the utterance also acknowledges the risk he took by embracing his accidental role as satirist on the topic of health care reform.

The revisioning of the late-night comic monologue genre demonstrated by all of these Jimmy Kimmel examples signals the incorporation of serious political speech into the realm of comic political speech. The membrane between discursive realms remains very permeable, especially in the age of Trump, or perhaps the metaphor for Kimmel's comic method should be a palimpsest, or two angles of vision come together as stereoscopic. This doubled view reveals the postmodern signature of truthiness satire in its basic illocutionary mode. Colbert does the same with his monologues, as does Oliver and Bee. The process of the comic public sphere and the public sphere appearing as one sphere often entails a discursive zigzag method on the part of the satirist, effectively blurring their boundary.

The trope of doubling can be extended. Zigzag as method points to how truthiness satire in its postmodern aesthetic gestures in two directions at once, in its dynamic of reverse discourse that intends to cancel the through-the-looking-glass effect of truthiness. A regime of simulacra compounded with discursive integration spawns that doubled quality of truthiness, which invents the alternative reality of the anti-public sphere. Truthiness satire intends a movement back to the reality of public sphere discourse, powered by ridiculing laughter. Discursive integration may enable truthiness, but it also disables it by encouraging individuals, both professional comedians and not-professional comedians, to zigzag with ease between the comic public sphere and the public sphere so that the two spheres at times manifest as one, a satiric counterweight.

The overarching version of this trope of doubling comes in terms borrowed from quantum physics: light (satire) as one phenomenon, when subjected to analysis at a subatomic level, exhibits a quantum state—that is, behaves as two entities, either as a particle (public sphere) or a wave (comic public sphere). Prominent satirists today have so routinely presented their comic efforts as light in a quantum state that one can easily miss the significance of that presentation. Playing with the news, as both format and content, has become an important method to achieve the goal of metanoia for the basic category of satire—its illocutionary mode, in Austin's terms. That practice, a habit by now, has provided the comic environment for introducing satiractivism. Audiences now are so used to the zigzag between comic public sphere and public sphere that mixing in an explicit call to political action registers as a natural outgrowth. Paradoxically, the more clever the satirist of today might be about presenting satire as both particle (public sphere) and wave (comic public sphere) in an entertaining fashion, the more easily he or she can interpellate the audience as citizens, canceling the status of audience members as consumers of funny monologues by subsuming the comic public sphere and propelling them into the public sphere *solus*—and so executing the satire two-step.

The Satire Two-Step Revisited

What does satiractivism imply about the argument over satire's efficacy in the real world and my effort to keep the comic political speech of satire in the comic public sphere separate from the political speech of the public sphere? That effort remains crucial because the argument denigrating satire's efficacy fundamentally rests upon conceptualizing comic political speech as political speech, a category error in effect. Rhetoric found in popular culture publications often vividly displays this confusion: comic butts are *destroyed, taken down, demolished, systematically picked apart, annihilated*.[36] Colossal humbugs are blown to rags and atoms in one blast. Except of course they are not. The British comedian Peter Cook once praised, ironically, "those wonderful Berlin cabarets . . . which did so much to stop the rise of Hitler and prevent the outbreak of the second world war."[37] The same logic has been applied to recent history: "A look at the developments in the period surrounding the 2016 presidential elections in the United States raises serious doubt about the effectiveness of humor and satire as political tools. If abrasive humor were really a reliable check on objectionable political actors and their programs, and if persistent ridicule did in fact have the capacity to damage and destroy the reputation of a candidate for public office, the 2016 campaign could not have resulted in the election of Donald J. Trump as president of the United States."[38] Such observations sound like mere complaints rather than persuasive analysis. The rhetoric claiming satire as an effective tool for broad political change because it annihilates its comic targets, at bottom, registers as a wish. Satire does not operate as political speech in the public sphere; it does not have the same status as speeches in favor of legislation or policy papers or resolutions emanating from debate at a town hall meeting. Satire functions as comic political speech intended to effect, ideally, metanoia, to promote what Dustin Griffin calls the "open-ended" potential of satire to discover, explore, and clarify. Even in its satiractivist strain, satire's uptake by an audience should be as comic political speech urging or demanding civic action.

This distinction explains why John Oliver has rejected being called a "journalist" in an interview on *CBS This Morning*.[39] Oliver recognizes that the so-called John Oliver Effect, insofar as it signifies a causal relationship to events in the public sphere, is illusory, despite popularized claims to the contrary.[40] Instead, his efforts to bring public attention to issues have the potential to function as the first step in the satire two-step. While Oliver refuses even the title "disruptive journalist," he is happy to answer to "disruptive comedian," in other words, *satirist*. Oliver's choice insists on keeping political speech as full, normal, and perlocutionary apart even from the quasi-perlocutionary comic speech of satiractivism, a distinction that rests upon the theory of a–musement—that is, laugh first, then think. Stephen Colbert's analysis of this more profound kind of a–musement bears repeating: "When you're laughing, you're not afraid, and if you're not afraid you can think."[41]

Colbert thus describes the two-step process: satire has a potential to change minds, which might then lead to political or social action. However, careful consideration of satire as a particular kind of speech act means that comic political speech cannot be equivalent to political speech. Once one argues that any brand of satire equates to activism, that satire functions as "a potent political weapon" or "an effective tool for broad political change," comic discourse metamorphoses into political discourse.

Discerning that transformation is not necessarily illusory. Indeed, one might say that the transformation of comic political speech to political speech describes exactly how satire might contribute to actual change. An appraisal after the fact of an instance of satire as comic political speech could be done, and if actual political action ensues, as with Jon Stewart and the Zadroga bill, one might want to claim cause and effect. However, then one has completely crossed the border of The Comic into another discursive field, canceling the quantum state of satire. The efficacy of Stewart's satire about the Zadroga bill, for example, did not depend on changing public policy, did not qualify as an intervention in real-world lawmaking. Instead, its potential to incite reform teed up the subsequently serious discussion about health issues for the first responders. Satire does not operate as a reforming public sphere mechanism per se, but it does have an embedded intent to promote such reforming mechanisms.

Robert Phiddian tackles the question of satire's real-world efficacy similarly. He sensibly opts for the middle ground between those who claim that satire has zero effect on the public sphere and the idealism of "satire's underlying fiction . . . that it provides an antidote to corruption in public life."[42] Satire does not function as an antidote, but it is integral to the rhetorical ecology even if it might register at times as part of the so-called noise of politics. Satire in his view does not possess the magical properties of a silver bullet but nevertheless might provide a breaking point for causing real effects or, in Amber Day's terms, nurturing counterpublics.

To grasp satire's peculiar communicative force, one must acknowledge its terpsichore effect: the robust defense of its reformist intent implied when satiractivism appears in truthiness satire nevertheless does not allow for a claim that it operates as political speech. Satire presents its ethically salutary possibilities via a saltatory process: the satire two-step of a–musement. However, the dance metaphor does not completely capture what happens to satire in a postmodern environment that features discursive integration and the simulacra effects of a digital sign machine, an environment that has engendered the felt need for a satire that incorporates activism. The two paradoxes structuring satire remain relevant: the methodological one of using ridicule to create social reform; the ontological one of being both serious and nonserious. While these structures, I would argue, have always defined satire in any age, in the current cultural moment the paradox of being at once earnestly serious and playfully nonserious has been sharply foregrounded by the practice of satiractivism with the result being an apparent collapse of the public sphere into the comic public sphere.

I have compared satire's ontological paradox to the way that light in a quantum state behaves as either a wave or a particle. Enabled by that analogy, one might feel authorized to analyze satire either as political speech or comic political speech because one can observe light as a particle or a wave—*but not at the same time*, mimicking Heisenberg's principle of indeterminacy when analyzing quantum states. The necessity of observing one aspect or the other of an event but not both has apparently moved from physics to culture, authorizing the complaints about satire's lack of efficacy in the public sphere. Nevertheless, light behaves as both wave and particle, not one or the other. Thus the analogy of a quantum state, a paradoxical ontology, demands one must remember that satire is not simply comic speech or simply serious speech but rather both. Keeping the paradox in mind compels analytical attention to satire's comic aspect (wave) and then its serious aspect (particle)—and thus to the satire two-step process of a–musement. Maybe that conceptual dance displays and dramatizes the fundamental point: the paradox of being comic and not-comic enables satire's participation in actual impact within the public sphere by staging a comic basis for it—yet still should not have an uptake as political speech.

My insisting on the process of an a–musement that leads to a metanoia, while working very well for satire in its standard illocutionary mode, fails to account completely for what happens when satire moves to the quasi-perlocutionary form of satiractivism. In those moments, comic political speech does not rest content with satirizing comic butts and implying proper values and behavior; it also parodies political speech, apparently dancing from its own discursive realm and into that of political speech because the satirist as rhetor interpellates his or her auditors as citizens, not as a studio or broadcast or cablecast or online audience expecting merely to be entertained. Isolating those moments analytically, an instance of satire might appear to function as political speech, a declaration that again provides an opening for those who denigrate satire as ineffective in the public sphere. Clearly, such a move denies satire's ontology as both/neither serious and nonserious, as though physicists had observed light in a quantum state behaving as wave and particle but nevertheless decided to choose one status over the other to describe its nature.

When an instance of satire incorporates an explicit call to political action, thus earning the tag *satiractivism* and gaining a quasi-perlocutionary status in its communicative force, it nevertheless remains an example of comic political speech, and so it should not be judged as political speech despite its deliberate intent to move beyond the basic consciousness-altering metanoia to a call for citizen engagement. In a postmodern environment, such engagement conjures the silly citizen: the citizen willing to respond to a public sphere call to action embedded in the comic political speech of satire. The zigzag method charted in many of the examples examined effectively weaves the public sphere into the comic public sphere, and here the analogy of light in a quantum state fails: one can comprehend the weaving of or the zigzagging between the serious and the nonserious, especially when satire becomes satiractivism, much easier than comprehending light as two different entities in the superposition of a quantum

FIG. 3 The postmodern comic. Used by permission of the original artist, Brom Glidden, aka Squidyes.

state. Nevertheless, when the distinction between public sphere and comic public sphere collapses (a most postmodern result), once again the light-in-a-quantum-state analogy works (see fig. 3). Like a pun, satire, especially in its satiractivist strain, insists on having two meanings at once, a very postmodern status.

The Limits of Satiric Ridicule

7.

The methodological paradox of promoting social good—improving civic life—through the use of ridicule creates one of the two foundational structures for satire. How does one promote a better society while indulging in comic insults? Yet doing so describes the enterprise of all satirists, which marks the enterprise as ethically fraught. Moreover, the satirist inevitably runs the risk of seeming to dispense rants rather than satire and thus runs the risk of being charged with misanthropy—or worse. What then defines the limits of comic insult and what constitutes the difference between the comic insult of the comic public sphere and the mere insult of the anti-public sphere? Trying to answer these questions, one must again consider audience reactions.

The Comic Insult Versus the Snarky Insult: Key and Peele's "Insult Comic"

This sketch is not directly about the politics dramatized by the separate ideological bubbles so prominently on display in social media. The public sphere here does not signify the Enlightenment claim of universal equality and rationality and therefore the promise or at least the possibility of emancipation. The sketch instead plays with the 1960s supplement about respect for all differences, the "politics of recognition."[1] This ethic can be read as identity politics, but within the mise-en-scène of a comedy club the issue becomes respecting a wish for inclusion in a laughter-provoking event. Jordan Peele's character wants to be included in the game of comic insult with everyone else; he too wants to play by laughing at his appearance, even though he is clearly disabled. "I can take it," he says when Keegan-Michael Key's stand-up comedian character hesitates to mock him.

Key's character premises his routine on speech that used to be ethically forbidden or at the least constrained by the dicta of philosophers, rhetoricians, and polite litterateurs, namely, freely ridiculing someone's physical attributes. Injunctions against laughing at specific physical rather than moral defects are at least as old as Plutarch. However, the ancients did not forbid all such ridicule. As Cicero says, the issue is always "the limits of license." Aristotle offers a general proscription: proper ridicule is "not productive of pain or harm to others." The maxim "do not laugh at the unfortunate" was often repeated in ancient Greek rhetorical theory and codified in Roman rhetorics under the heading of the *liberal versus illiberal jest*, its staying power indicated by Lord Bacon repeating it centuries later. Vic Gatrell provides details about proper subjects for laughter promulgated by the English Augustans, who were well aware of their classical ancestors.[2]

Such strictures from upper-class individuals did not prevent a general habit of mocking the deformed or natural fools, but that sort of mockery certainly cannot be satire because one cannot change afflictions caused by genetics. The technology of plastic surgery or botox remains irrelevant to the process of a metanoia. Satirists concern themselves with potentially reforming behaviors, not resculpting physiognomy. The physical appearance of audience members, however, becomes the target for jokes in the sketch: e.g., big ears, big breasts. Nevertheless, mocking disability and deformity caused by an accident operates on another level down from mocking outsized but natural features. The latter sort of ridicule implies deviations from social standards of beauty; the former sort ridicules misfortune and suffering.

The limits of the comic insult and its potential for satiric purpose appear in the exchange with the standup comedian (Key) and the disabled customer (Peele). Each time the performer ridicules an item associated with the disabled customer—the number of drinks he has had indicated by the number of glasses on his table, the vials of pills also on his table—the customer erases the possibility of laughter by explaining its true and thus serious meaning. That exchange of course functions as a delaying tactic because inclusion in the club of insulting laughter must be not about the contingency of what surrounds the customer; rather, the insult must be about the customer's physical appearance, as it has been with the other customers. Thus the equivalent gibe has to be about either the disability implied by the customer's wheelchair or his obviously scarred face, presumably from burns.

The joke that the standup comedian finally makes—imagining the disabled customer as the serial killer Freddy Kruger in the *Halloween* movies—has a certain wit, but the collective audience groans instead of laughs. The tearful reaction of the disabled customer as he says, "I thought I could [take it]," seals the standup comedian's fate. The rebellion of the audience climaxes with one member climbing onto the stage and knocking the performer unconscious with a beer bottle, the violence of the gesture apparently representing collective anger that had been suppressed with a supposedly comic uptake during the entire round of insults.

The sketch creates a meta-joke about comic violence—symbolic from the stand-up comedian and literal from the audience—yet neither side of the equation can escape complicity. The audience paid to enter a comedy club, a space explicitly set aside for comic speech, thus cuing the presence of the discursive domain of The Comic; they laughed initially at each joke. The disabled customer demands inclusion before he opts out, his own expectation of laughing suddenly converted to crying. No one can feel ethically superior, which seems to be the sketch's ultimate meaning. The audience members first accepted the snark and snarl of insult and ridicule as comic insult before they decided that it was simply bullying. They initially authorized that bullying as comic speech and therefore allowed it before they did not. However, if that authorization points to a failure of respect for all forms of difference, the sketch also implies that such failure dramatizes the very stuff of comic speech in that transgression at some level must be allowed to surface. However, the audience uptake will nevertheless decide if the transgression will be tolerated or even celebrated with comic laughter or if the stand-up comedian suffers the symbolic violence of *bombing*, the vernacular for infelicitous uptake. In the comic extravagance of the sketch, that symbolic violence transforms into literal violence.

The Key and Peele sketch apparently submerges the politics of identity, making physical appearance the central topic for joking instead, but the audience—in particular the disabled audience member—granting or withholding its laughing approbation reinvokes those politics, or at least dramatizes the rhetorical violence that too often blankets those politics like an obscene miasma. What seems funny to folks in one political or social camp will not be for those in another—that is, the unwritten rule that says *do not mock my political tribe and my social values* suddenly appears. The profoundly comic pain of the sketch becomes the audience mindlessly scapegoating the standup comedian and thus displacing the psychic violence of their own internal clash over what are, at bottom, ideological choices. If people cannot recognize their own ambivalence about what counts as legitimate targets for ridicule, how can they find within themselves the means to hear differences of opinion about bigger issues, about civic issues? "Insult Comic" implies that the stakes concerning legitimate comic laughter and the stakes concerning legitimate public sphere debate are more bound together than one might suppose. Everyone at both levels insistently stuck in his or her ideological bubble, with metanoia only a remote possibility, damages both the public sphere and the comic public sphere, inhibits their smooth functioning.

An obvious example in this context can be found in the habit of Stephen Colbert (*The Late Show*), Trevor Noah (*The Daily Show*), and Samantha Bee (*Full Frontal*) of mentioning an individual involved in a news story, showing his or her photo, and then mocking that person's physical features, a tactic that follows the lead of Jon Stewart when he hosted *The Daily Show*. To be fair, often the mocking concerns the moral features of the comic butt instead, and a tonal range of mockery exists in the many examples one might examine: sometimes just whimsical yet sometimes sharp or maybe cruel utterances. Like Key and Peele's sketch, these comic insults can violate the rhetorical/ethical rules constraining ridicule of physical appearance. Stephen Colbert's famous use of a canned ham to represent political operative Karl Rove might be the best example of the tactic, but here is another one from Colbert in which he parodies an interview Donald Trump had with Sean Hannity by splicing questions and statements from Colbert with actual responses from Trump:

> COLBERT: You're a bloated narcissist whose presidency is a knife in the moral heart of America, a wound in our national soul that will take generations to heal, if ever. [applause and cheers]
> TRUMP: A horrible, horrible embarrassment to our country. [more applause and cheers]
> COLBERT: Exactly.[3]

One might argue that this example mostly questions Trump's moral character, with only "bloated" referencing his physical appearance, and so could pass inspection as satire. Also, one such reference to physical appearance might be allowed, especially if it inhabits the light-hearted or whimsical end of a tonal spectrum, but if such comic insults pile up, when do they become just a mean-spirited rant or an invitation to physical violence? In Shakespeare's *Henry IV, Part One*, Prince Hal refers to Falstaff as "thou clay-brained guts, thou knotty-pated fool, thou whoreson obscene greasy tallow catch" and then continues with "this sanguine coward, this bed-presser, this horse-back breaker, this huge hill of flesh." Falstaff stands ready with his riposte: "You starveling, you eelskin, you dried neat's-tongue, you bull's pizzle, . . . you tailor's yard, you sheath, you bowcase, you vile standing tuck."[4] Hal and Falstaff sound earnest enough for fisticuffs, but the sheer number and variety of insults can delight. The exchange of epithets intends entertainment, not satire, particularly because no fight ensues and of course no one (especially Hal and Falstaff) expected one.

How are Tomi Lahren's insults in her opinion-piece segments "Final Thoughts" on *TheBlaze* different from the mocking that Colbert or Bee routinely indulge in? What of the insults from Charles Pierce discussed earlier? Then the shtick of Lewis Black, nearly always presented in a comic rant form, might be considered. When is he funny satiric? Does an audience have to sort his monologues into those with specific political or social content and those without such content so that Black can claim escape from the charge of merely reinforcing anti-public sphere discourse instead of promoting metanoia? The key to that question, always, lies in the task of identifying the comic butt, for example, when he mocks millennials for not voting: no political division there, just a comic exhortation to participate in democracy. Moreover, Black also takes down his own generation, the boomers: "I know we fucked things up for you, but we were counting on you to fix things, not finish the job." This apparent rant can be logged as funny and in service to the public sphere: satire.[5]

Dennis Miller when he was on *SNL* years ago became famous for his comic diatribes, verbal explosions laden with pop culture references. He reprised that shtick once he became part of *The Half Hour News Hour* (*Fox*, February–September 2007), but without success. When television critic Aaron Sankin reviewed the show and panned it because its jokes were not topical and thus woefully out of date, and not very clever, he makes an important distinction, which the title of his article—"The Ire in Satire"—suggests: mere anger does not a satire make.[6] Political figures on one side of the ideological spectrum always featured as the comic butts in *The Half Hour News Hour*. If one does not reside in that camp, the insults claiming to be comic will soon become tiring, even perhaps if they display the madcap inventiveness of Prince Hal and Falstaff. Worse: the show only lasted a few episodes, so it would seem that even those within the ideological camp implied by the jokes and sketches were bored. Not enough interest in satire from the political right, or just bad material? In either case, the show bombed.

Perhaps *The Late Show with Stephen Colbert* has struck a balance, and not just because its comic butts are not exclusively political. Colbert's monologues almost always feature Trump and Company, which means that his ridicule, to qualify as satire, cannot just be partisan snark (though it can be that too) but must also expose the absurdity of behaviors and specific actions that arguably threaten the institutions and *habitus* of democracy. That will not guarantee all audience members will laugh in agreement, but it does provide the opportunity for metanoia, something like Louis Black mocking both millennials and boomers. The trick must be for the satire to interpellate the audience as (silly) citizens, not partisan loyalists, while simultaneously treating them as an audience expecting to be entertained.

Here arises again the problem of the audience and its potential unlaughter, the refusal to accept an utterance as comic even if its individual members understand the intent to joke. In the Key and Peele sketch, the standup comedian struggling to manage audience reaction dramatizes the problem. Within social media, everyone behaves as both potential author and audience. This dynamic would appear to be perfect for the public sphere. Instead, social media has often performed as anti-social media, enabling a bubbles-of-information phenomenon that insulates individuals from one another and reinforces preexisting political ideologies and cultural beliefs. This effect may be a fundamental problem of the digital public sphere in its social media formats.

In J. L. Austin's terms, this problem centers on audience uptake. Should Ann Coulter or Laura Ingraham be understood as performance artists, if not as satirists, generating the right-wing, conservative brand of the counterpublics Amber Day discusses? Maybe they only intend to troll liberals; maybe the political right simply laughs because they outrage the political left.[7] Trolling of course is not satirizing—it has no public sphere value—though pranks of various comic intent might be employed to properly ridicule comic butts. Certain segments of the mockumentaries *Borat* (2006) and *Borat Subsequent Movie Film* (2020) serve that intent, and Sasha Cohen's 2018 show *Who Is America?* has also produced memorable satiric ridicule. In any case, the satirist proper crafts his or her satire to be a comic voice in an ongoing discussion and debate about a particular issue. In the postmodern mash-up of comic public sphere intimately interacting with the public sphere, the intent behind a comic insult to serve that discussion and debate emerges through that interaction. After using a canned ham to represent Karl Rove in several episodes of *The Colbert Report*, Stephen Colbert in a comic ritual pretended to kill the ham by stabbing it multiple times and feeding it to dogs. Rove showed his ability to take a joke by playfully suggesting that Colbert had anger management issues: "'I don't know whether that was working out his inner feelings, or encouraging maybe someone to maybe mimic him or just sort of being funny,' Rove joked in an interview with ABC. . . . 'But there was a little bit of anxiety in his stabs there.'"[8] Colbert's response also contained equal parts playful and serious: "There is an easy test [to tell the difference between Karl Rove and 'Ham Rove.'] Before you slice into your ham, ask it if it's ever put anti-gay marriage legislation in swing states to tip the scales in the 2004 presidential election. If it answers yes, that could be Karl Rove."

While Colbert's retort registers first as public sphere in its reference to Rove's strategy for reelecting George W. Bush, the comic absurdity of being unsure about how to tell the difference between the man and the ham remains. That persistent absurdity is crucial, for it provides the comic premise that allows Colbert not only to comment on campaign strategy but also to continue his elaborate and entertaining parody of campaign super PACs.

Case Study: Michelle Wolf at the 2018 White House Correspondents' Dinner

The explosion of reactions to Michelle Wolf's performance on April 28, 2018, reactions both in the room and after the fact, offers a useful focus for the problematic of the audience raised by Key and Peele's "Insult Comic" sketch. When does the insult of snark become comic insult? How to measure too much comic insult? What counts as mean-spirited and so illegitimate rant and what counts as caustic but legitimate satire? How does audience reactions sort individuals into . . . what categories? If only the lens of partisan left or right ideologies filters jokes, perhaps no metanoia is possible.

For a gambit, I start with a reasonable generalization by Megan Garber about Wolf's routine that captures the fractures in the audience reactions: "To some, Wolf's set was evidence of the current impossibility of civility in American discourse—a series of jokes that bit with too much bite, that crossed lines, that misunderstood the distinction between 'roasting' and 'bullying,' that conflated 'punching up' with 'punching the person sitting right next to you.' To others, it was an inspired piece of comic criticism, operating in the manner of Stephen Colbert at the 2006 Correspondents' Dinner: Wolf was speaking truth through comedy [i.e., satire]."[9] The first move in breaking down Garber's assessment should examine the statement that a comic monologue represents "the current impossibility of civility in American discourse," which clearly confuses the public sphere with the comic public sphere. Since when is a set of jokes delivered by a professional comic in a discursive moment explicitly marked as comic (she was hired to be funny) about "civility in American discourse"? Similarly, the complaint that one should not symbolically punch (mock and ridicule) the person sitting next to you (in this case White House spokeswoman Sarah Huckabee Sanders) again mistakes the situation. Michelle Wolf was hired with the expectation that she would make fun of anyone in the room, and even anyone not in the room. Why should Sarah Huckabee Sanders be exempt when George W. Bush was not the year Stephen Colbert featured as the comedian of the night? Why does she rate as special when no one else attending any of the Correspondents' Dinners has escaped comic tongue-lashings?

The favorite notion of the popular press that satire should always be about "punching up" and never "punching down" also deserves scrutiny, an idea invented in the age of political correctness. The mistake resides in demanding that a particular group *automatically* should be exempt from any potential need for comic critique. Undoubtedly, people in demographics at the margins of society are by definition economically and legally vulnerable, but if the satire does not target those vulnerabilities but instead skewers the bad habits or egregious follies of particular groups, that is not punching down but punching sideways at human nature. Those folks are people too, and thus they, like everyone else, deserve the backhanded respect that worthwhile satire implies. The question always should be: What is the comic butt? If a speaker mocks people simply because of who they (supposedly) are, stereotypically, or what they look like physically, that cannot be satire but rather should have an uptake as mere lampoon or snarky insult or perhaps even hate speech. Though the use of stereotypes in comic artifacts inevitably remains a tricky business, in principle it should be forbidden to forbid comic ridicule of any group.

Trickier still is the charge that Wolf's jokes "crossed lines" or "misunderstood the distinction between 'roasting' and 'bullying'" because folks objected not to the comic insults and mockery per se: only that Wolf dispensed too much of it, or perhaps that too much of it was caustic, "bit with too much bite." The difference between roasting and bullying remains as a serious issue, but who shall be the arbiter that draws the line that shall never be crossed? The complaint implicitly insists that satire should never punch down, making what amounts to an arbitrary decision about limiting comic speech. Let me be clear. A discussion about the possibility, the need even, for limiting comic speech should take place, just as it should for the limits of free speech in general. The comic public sphere cannot be exempt from that discussion: any individual should be allowed to make an argument about what constitutes too much or what has crossed some clearly articulated ethical line. The problem is prior restraint, just as it is with serious speech in the public sphere.

Once past the arguments explicit and implicit about the worthiness of the event or Wolf's failure to refrain from bullying, I want to examine other arguments regarding the specifics of Wolf's routine in order to tease out if and when she "crossed a line," but also in order to learn something about members of the audience, both those in the room and those watching the performance, either live or recorded. As noted before, deciding if what seems to be comic insult really should count as just snark insult always depends upon identifying the comic butt. In addition, sometimes the key involves recognizing that multiple comic butts can be targeted with a single joke.

In several instances, complaints about Wolf's performance imply that comic speech, with its inherent unruliness, should not behave as comic speech but instead should comport itself as serious speech—that is, as polite and decorous. Some folks therefore tag the routine variously as "mean spirited," "personally offensive," "rude and just plain mean," or "raw sewage." Andrea Mitchell, a veteran news correspondent, voiced such a complaint. Mitchell tweeted that the monologue clashed with the speech delivered by Margaret Talev, the *Bloomberg News* reporter serving as president of the White House Correspondents' Association, in the first half of the program devoted mainly to awards and the introduction of scholarships for college students. "Apology is owed to @PressSec and others grossly insulted by Michelle Wolf at White House Correspondents' Assoc dinner which started with uplifting heartfelt speech by @margarettalev."[10] Talev herself launched the same complaint, saying, "Last night's program was meant to offer a unifying message about our common commitment to a vigorous and free press while honoring civility, great reporting and scholarship winners, not to divide people. Unfortunately, the entertainer's monologue was not in the spirit of that mission."[11] Talev wants a "vigorous and free press," but not too free: civility (however one defines it) must be honored.

Talev had backing from Joe Scarborough, cohost of MSNBC's show *Morning Joe*, as well as Pat Buchanan, a speechwriter for Richard Nixon and right-wing pundit. Buchanan displays his judgment in the headline for his piece, "White House Correspondents' Dinner in the Gutter."[12] Buchanan's objection centers on the smut and obscenity uttered by Wolf, who "recited one filthy joke after another at the expense of President Trump and his people, using words that would have gotten her kicked out of school not so long ago." Like Talev, Buchanan invoked the dinner "as a celebration of the First Amendment and a tribute to journalists who 'speak truth to power,'" but clearly judged that a line had been crossed. Buchanan might be fine with speaking truth to power, but not done in a Rabelaisian vein: no smut allowed. A comment from Joe Scarborough also implies a need to sequester the strong stuff: "Let the great comedians perform on Netflix, where we watch Dave Chappelle."[13] Scarborough apparently wants to banish caustic satire even from cable. Perhaps that wish represents overheated rhetoric in the moment. Perhaps Scarborough would actually censor content on cable channels if given the power. In any case, his comment, along with the others, ignores that the monologue explicitly constitutes the comic segment of the program and that the tradition at the dinner includes a roast format, a format encouraging stringent satire. Many of the folks mounting objections have the same point: satire should be polite. Such an argument misunderstands satire, which is never polite. Satire might be more or less harsh in its comic critique; it might be presented with whimsy and fantasy. Polite, however, does not comport with the aggressive element of its nature.

The other agenda buried in Scarborough's comment would render any judgments about Wolf's performance moot: excise the comic segment from the dinner. Kyle Pope, the editor of the *Columbia Journalism Review*, explicitly made that suggestion in a post on Twitter stating that even journalists had had enough of the annual ritual. "The #WHCD debacle was inevitable, destined to be either sycophantic, on one extreme, or mean spirited, on the other. Neither is a good look at a time when trust in media is tenuous. Can we finally all agree to put an end to this thing?" Apparently, some news organizations displeased by the monologue were ready to follow the *New York Times* staff, who had stopped attending the dinner in 2008.[14]

When the complaints attack the event itself, the message might be formulated as *we in the press do not know how to handle satire, especially when it is directed at us*. The rationale for that message seems to be that, because Wolf's routine features criticism, we journalists should just not take the chance that some folks will be offended, a position foreclosing discussion about the nature of satire or its place in a practice of First Amendment rights.

Part of Margaret Talev's comments also points to the easiest way to dismiss Wolf's routine—viewing it through a strictly partisan lens—when she says Wolf should not "divide people." Like so much of the media discourse in the public sphere, this angle relegates Wolf's monologue to the never-ending contest of political parties, an event to score political points, in effect assuming the category error of mistaking comic political speech for political speech. Thus "Mike Allen, a prime voice of the city's establishment, declared in his newsletter [the next day]: 'Media hands Trump embarrassing win,'"[15] and Mika Brzezinski, the other cohost of *Morning Joe*, "declared the 2018 White House Correspondents' Dinner a win for President Trump after the comedian invited to perform angered many, including the president."[16]

However, Brzezinski also slammed Wolf not for being partisan but for being personal. This aspect of the negative reaction centers on Wolf's jokes about Sarah Huckabee Sanders, the White House Press Secretary, which provoked many complaints. "Andrea Mitchell, the NBC News correspondent, tweeted that an 'apology is owed' to the press secretary. Her network colleague Mika Brzezinski wrote that 'watching a wife and mother be humiliated on national television for her looks is deplorable.'"[17] Mitchell enjoyed this supporting tweet from one of her Twitter followers, "Mare": "Thank you for speaking up against Wolf who acted like a bully. No one should go after someone on their looks. We teach our kids not to [do] this but we let a rude comedian slide. Michelle Wolf was rude and just plain mean."[18] The sentiment (for it is not really an argument) that the status of being a wife and mother confers exemption from satiric ridicule may be admirable in its invocation of bourgeois respectability, but its political correctness nevertheless amounts to prior restraint.

David Frum comments on civility and places that argument into the ironic context of the Trump White House, which insists upon courtesy and respect when its occupant nevertheless often shows no respect with his habit of demeaning names: "One of the defining features of the Trump White House is that its staff members demand for themselves decencies and courtesies that they habitually deny to others. *Can't we disagree without being disagreeable?* they wonder—and then tweet that the former director of the FBI is a 'slime ball' and that Hillary Clinton should be jailed." In short, they have no basis for complaints when they are spoken of "in hurtful ways." Thus Frum mutes his attack on Wolf as he says, in effect, *What did you expect?* Wolf's speech was "hurtful" apparently, but the answer is to go "'high' when the other side goes low," quoting Michelle Obama. "So let them [Trump and company] be abused, be reviled, be humiliated. Yet if you go that way, you do not repudiate Trump. You become Trump."[19] Like so many others, Frum confuses the comic public sphere with the public sphere. Satirizing the president, even harshly, does not make Wolf equivalent to Trump. Michelle Obama's laudable dictum applies to the public sphere. Satire as comic speech ignores the distinction between high and low on some imagined scale of civility.

A close look at the transcript reveals that the jokes targeted Sanders not as a private individual, a wife and mother, but rather in her capacity as White House press secretary for the Trump administration. In addition, the jokes did not target her looks. (I will come back to this shortly when unpacking the routine.) This line of reasoning could be found from some who applauded Wolf and her routine, for example Jessica Valenti: "I have spent years defending women on both sides of the aisle from sexist attacks & digs on their appearance. Michelle Wolf did neither—she rightly blasted Sanders's character & her penchant for lying to the American people."[20] In a tweet responding to Andrea Mitchell, Becky B agrees: "Wolf used Brilliant analogy and metaphor to drop a truth bomb. SHS betraying women and providing cover for a mysoginst [sic] abuser via the WH podium."[21] Another tweet in response to Mitchell's from a user named "Largo" should be added: "Ms. Wolf did not fat shame sanders, she #factshamed her."[22]

Charles Pierce took a journalist's point of view, steeped in one of his larger tureens of sarcasm, by addressing other journalists about how the forces of complaint and defense should be evaluated and why the apology from Talev as the president of the White House Correspondents' Association should never have been uttered:

> Sarah Huckabee Sanders is not your friend. She is, professionally, the enemy. I don't care if most of the time she's a combination of Florence Nightingale, Mother Superior, and Cher. When she gets behind the podium, her job is to belittle you and your profession and, by proxy, all of us who practice it. She is a tower of contempt. That she was discomfited on Saturday night because of a comedian is part of what she gets paid for. Discomfiting the likes of Sarah Huckabee Sanders is part of what Michelle Wolf got paid for. The forces were perfectly in balance.[23]

Other journalists concurred. Glenn Greenwald criticized the event but commended Wolf for her funny routine: she "was hilarious & struck exactly the right tone from start to finish. She heaped irreverent contempt on D.C.

power centers because that's what good comedians do (& they deserve it)."[24] Megan Garber wrote that Michelle Wolf "was the one who emerged, whether you loved her set or hated it, as the person who could most obviously claim to have engaged, that evening, in journalism's enduring mandate: *to afflict the comfortable and to comfort the afflicted*."[25] Garber clearly understands the concept of comic *parrhēsia*; notably, she also mistakes Wolf's comic routine for journalism in its role as democracy's watchdog rather than understanding satire as a potential supplement to journalism.

Brian Kilmeade, a cohost of *Fox & Friends*, said in the ballroom, minutes after Wolf finished, that she intended her routine as "an attack to impress Jon Stewart and Stephen Colbert." As Michael Grynbaum notes, Kilmeade was "previewing a line of criticism that would be dominant on *Fox News* by Sunday morning. 'Congratulations, when the three of you go out to dinner. I'm sure you'll be laughing a lot. But in terms of the people here and the people at home—totally offensive, horrible choice. In fact, it's the reason why the president didn't want to go.'" The significance of the disagreement in the community of journalists about the meaning of Wolf's routine can be unpacked in a number of ways, but most obviously the disagreement indicates the dangers of speaking for an audience—"the people here and the people at home"—as though monolithic and in complete agreement, as Kilmeade does.[26]

Beyond assuming that the audience uptake will be expressed in one voice, Kilmeade's comment indicates the problem of mishearing what Wolf said. This mistake looms large in the furor over Wolf supposedly mocking Sanders's personal appearance. Here is what Wolf said:

> We are graced with Sarah's presence tonight. I have to say I'm a little star-struck. I love you as Aunt Lydia in *The Handmaid's Tale*. Mike Pence, if you haven't seen it, you would love it.
>
> Every time Sarah steps up to the podium, I get excited, because I'm not really sure what we're going to get—you know, a press briefing, a bunch of lies or divided into softball teams. "It's shirts and skins, and this time don't be such a little bitch, Jim Acosta!"
>
> I actually really like Sarah. I think she's very resourceful. She burns facts, and then she uses that ash to create a perfect smoky eye. Like maybe she's born with it, maybe it's lies. It's probably lies.
>
> And I'm never really sure what to call Sarah Huckabee Sanders, you know? Is it Sarah Sanders, is it Sarah Huckabee Sanders, is it Cousin Huckabee, is it Auntie Huckabee Sanders? Like, what's Uncle Tom but

for white women who disappoint other white women? Oh, I know, Aunt Coulter."[27]

Erik Wemple explains the Jim Acosta joke embedded in the riff on Sanders.[28] Some months earlier, Sarah Huckabee Sanders had been afraid that Acosta would ask Trump a question as he was signing the National Defense Authorization bill in the Roosevelt Room about his snarky tweet impugning the morality of Sen. Kirsten Gillibrand (D-NY). The context for Sanders's intervention was a "pool spray," a limited group of White House–covering journalists witnessing an official event while perhaps throwing out a question or two. Before the signing, Sanders pulled Acosta aside and (in Acosta's words) "warned me that if I asked the president a question at this pool spray... that she could not promise that I would be allowed into a pool spray again," obviously a direct threat coming from the White House press secretary. The joke implies that Acosta routinely whines and complains ("a little bitch," says Wolf) while refusing to take orders from Sanders. Because this joke follows the reference to Sanders as "Aunt Lydia" from *The Handmaid's Tale*, Wolf's performance of this line in a tone of nasty command represents Sanders as Aunt Lydia.

The joke implies the thought that Sanders, like the character Aunt Lydia, the cruel sadistic enforcer/mother of the handmaids, behaves as an unfeeling cog in a system of repressive patriarchy. Here is how Emily Nussbaum puts it: "Her job is *exactly* like Aunt Lydia: she is the frowning female enforcer for a fascist patriarchal society, punishing those who resist her lies. It has a tinge of the looks element, but that's not the point of the joke, at all—it's aimed at her job. It was a literal imitation of how she acts—she yells at people like a bossy disciplinary teacher. It has nothing to do with her looks. She DOES this, it's not a made-up thing. It's practically her brand."[29] As Nussbaum insists, nowhere in Wolf's segment about Sanders can one find a comic blow against her looks (unlike some of Kimmel's jokes in the health care debate or the routine gibes about appearances that Colbert, Noah, or Bee pass out). No doubt that charge comes from the line about Sanders's makeup, specifically her eye shadow made from the ash of burnt facts. Wolf very briefly toys with Sanders's "perfect smoky eye" being natural but quickly moves away from the thought: "Like maybe she's born with it, maybe it's lies. It's probably lies." Photos show that Sanders often chooses a very dark color for her eye shadow. While Wolf clearly references Sanders's appearance, the detail ultimately references a fashion choice, not a physical characteristic. However, the real butt of the joke highlights Sanders's job, which too often entails lying for the president as she destroys facts. The lies coming from smoky eyes cleverly draws on an association with moral darkness and obscurity, hinting at the darkness within Sanders—that is, her complicity with those lies and their intent to obfuscate. In terms of tone, the joke sits a very long way from Key and Peele's "Insult Comic" sketch or even Colbert's canned ham joke about Karl Rove. However, the line about Sanders's name sets up one of the hardest hitting jokes anywhere in Wolf's routine by suggesting that a woman working for or defending a serial sexual harasser like Trump betrays all women, while also managing comic disdain for another such betrayer, Ann Coulter.

A curious omission exists in the backlash about the eye shadow: people completely ignored the jokes that did target someone's physical appearance, which comes in a bit ridiculing a string of Republican politicians: "Republicans are easy to make fun of. It's like shooting fish in a Chris Christie." Translation: Chris Christie's physique resembles a big barrel. This joke follows another that also turns on physical appearance, extravagantly metaphorical: "Mitch McConnell isn't here. He had a prior engagement. He's finally getting his neck circumcised." Translation: Mitch McConnell is a big dick. The wit in both instances wobbles, but the McConnell joke perhaps has the virtue of obliquely shaming him for his legislative behavior as Senate Majority leader. The Christie joke simply mocks the former New Jersey governor's girth.

One thing becomes clear with a comparison of Wolf's performance to Kimmel's comic *parrhēsia* on health care: he may have used comic insult that did not always pertain to the public sphere issue, but Wolf almost never strays from satire about politics in any of her jokes, nor does she play favorites: "Just a reminder to everyone. I'm here to make jokes. I have no agenda. I'm not trying to get anything accomplished. So everyone that's here from Congress, you should feel right at home."

Wolf does spend a large portion of her time ridiculing Republicans, but she does not excuse the Democrats, starting with Hillary Clinton: "It is kind of crazy that the Trump campaign was in contact with Russia when the Hillary campaign wasn't even in contact with Michigan. It's a direct flight; it's so close." Here Wolf references a common factor offered in analyses of why Clinton lost the 2016 election, namely, a failure to campaign vigorously in some historical, so-called blue states, like Michigan, Wisconsin, and Pennsylvania.

Wolf also makes it clear that the #MeToo movement pertains not just to Trump but also to Democrats past and present: "No, things are changing.

Men are being held accountable. You know, Al Franken was ousted. That one really hurt liberals. But I believe it was the great Ted Kennedy who said, 'Wow, that's crazy; I murdered a woman.' *Chappaquiddick* in theaters now." That joking thrust might serve as the definition of a nasty woman being nasty, but not in the way Pat Buchanan thinks. Another robust put-down follows Wolf's comment that she finds Republicans easy to mock: "But I also want to make fun of Democrats. Democrats are harder to make fun of because you guys don't do anything. People think you might flip the House and Senate this November, but you guys always find a way to mess it up. You're somehow going to lose by 12 points to a guy named Jeff Pedophile Nazi Doctor."

Sexual harassment constitutes a major theme in the routine, authorized by Donald Trump as the harasser-in-chief, a comic riff that begins with the first jokes in the monologue, and in effect foreshadows all the raunchiness to follow:

> Good evening. Good evening. Here we are, the White House Correspondents' Dinner: Like a porn star says when she's about to have sex with a Trump, let's get this over with.
>
> Of course, Trump isn't here, if you haven't noticed. He's not here. And I know, I know, I would drag him here myself. But it turns out the president of the United States is the one pussy you're not allowed to grab. He said it first. Yeah, he did. Do you remember? Good.
>
> Now, I know people really want me to go after Trump tonight, but I think we should give the president credit when he deserves it. Like, he pulled out of the Paris agreement, and I think he should get credit for that because he said he was going to pull out and then he did. And that's a refreshing quality in a man. Most men are like, "I forgot. I'll get you next time." Oh, there's going to be a next time? People say romance is dead.

Buchanan and others might well complain about Wolf's coarse language, but Wolf in her opening jokes explicitly reminds her audiences that Trump introduced such language into the public sphere, not to mention his lewd behaviors: adultery with an adult film actress and with a Playboy Playmate as well as accusations of sexual harassment from at least twenty women.[30]

The charge that Wolf indulged in smut creates another big complaint, of course, a complaint functioning as the turbocharged version of calling her rude. And there can be little doubt that Wolf's persona often spoke obscene (raunchy, smutty, lewd) sentences, but, it must be noted, she performs rudely in all those ways almost always as a tactic to hit specific comic butts entangled in the prominent civic issue of sexual harassment such as Harvey Weinstein and Roger Ailes: "Which, of course, brings me to the #MeToo movement; it's probably the reason I'm here. They were like, 'A woman's probably not going to jerk off in front of anyone, right?' And to that, I say, 'Don't count your chickens.' There's a lot of party [left]."

Arguably, Mr. Trump takes the lion's share of Wolf's satiric shafts. Her most caustic arrow targets him presumably where it hurts most by ridiculing his bragging pride about being rich, though the sharp point for her poisoned dart references Trump's legendary ignorance:

> People call Trump names all the time. And, look, I could call Trump a racist, a misogynist, or xenophobic, or unstable, or incompetent, or impotent, but he's heard all of those, and he doesn't care. So, tonight, I'm going to try to make fun of the president in a new way—in a way that I think will really get him. Mr. President, I don't think you're very rich. Like, I think you might be rich in Idaho, but in New York, you're doing fine. Trump is the only person that still watches *Who Wants to be a Millionaire?* and thinks, "Me." Although, I'm not sure you'd get very far. He'd get to, like, the third question and be, like, "I have to phone a Fox & Friend."

Wolf turns the joke about not being so rich into a call-and-response format, with the audience participating, responding *How broke is he?* when Wolf calls out *Trump is so broke*. Here are some punchlines:

> "Trump is so broke. He has to fly failed business class."
> "Trump is so broke. He looked for foreign oil in Don Jr.'s hair."
> "Trump is so broke. How broke is he? He grabs pussies 'cause he thinks there might be loose change in them."

The best satiric punchline, however, has to be—"Trump is so broke. He had to borrow money from the Russians, and now he's compromised and susceptible to blackmail and possibly responsible for the collapse of the republic"—because it voices basic concerns about the Trump presidency in the proverbial nutshell and thus speaks most succinctly comic truth to power.

The joke noted before about Sarah Huckabee Sanders's name implies her betrayal of women and infers a blisteringly caustic critique by suggesting that any woman working for or defending a serial sexual harasser like Trump betrays all women, while also slamming another such betrayer, Ann Coulter. Later, Wolf returns to women in the Trump administration, starting with Kellyanne Conway, but also manages a bit of self-deprecation as well as a swipe at the media. "Man, she has the perfect last name for what she does: Conway. It's like if my name was Michelle Jokes Frizzy Hair Small Tits. You guys gotta stop putting Kellyanne on your shows. All she does is lie. If you don't give her a platform, she has nowhere to lie. It's like that old saying: If a tree falls in the woods, how do we get Kellyanne under that tree? I'm not suggesting she gets hurt, just stuck. Stuck under a tree." The comic violence in that joke seems tame, however, when Wolf turns to Ivanka Trump: "She was supposed to be an advocate for women, but it turns out she's about as helpful to women as an empty box of tampons. She's done nothing to satisfy women. So, I guess, like father, like daughter. Oh, you don't think he's good in bed. Come on. She does clean up nice, though. Ivanka cleans up nice. She's the Diaper Genie of the administration. On the outside, she looks sleek but the inside—it's still full of shit." In its raunchy and sexualized and smutty packaging, the satire in this bit may be the best candidate in the routine for an award of bad taste, but Wolf clearly does not use smut for the sake of using smut; rather, she returns the audience to the theme of women betraying women and the incompetence, corruption, and hypocrisy of the Trump administration.

Finally, because the event celebrates journalism, Wolf targets the media, the biggest satiric butt after the political parties or the Trump administration. Here she clearly rates as an equal opportunity comic insult artist, though she provides a range of comic tones. Her jab at the print media would seem to be good-humored and sympathetic: "There's a lot of print media here. There's a ton of you guys, but I'm not going to go after print media tonight because it's illegal to attack an endangered species. Buy newspapers." MSNBC's portion of Wolf's jeering does not sound quite as friendly, though still in a teasing vein: "MSNBC's news slogan is, 'This is who we are.' Guys, it's not a good slogan. 'This is who we are' is what your mom thinks the sad show on NBC is called. 'Did you watch 'This Is Who We Are' this week? Someone left on a Crockpot, and everyone died.'" However, if MSNBC can be teased about its slogan being confused with *This Is Us*, which is something like a friend kidding about the weird color combination of a shirt or blouse, Wolf lashes more than teases CNN, given that her jab implies a failure to practice good journalism. "You guys love breaking news, and you did it. You broke it. Good work. The most useful information on CNN is when Anthony Bourdain tells me where to eat noodles." Fox News, however, must suffer the strongest tongue-lashing for the media when Wolf targets their morally corrupt workplace: "Fox News is here. So, you know what that means, ladies: Cover your drinks. Seriously." The theme of sexual harassers returns, invoking Roger Ailes but also Bill Cosby.

Another gibe, however, ups the stakes with a broadsword slash of derision at the media:

> You guys are obsessed with Trump. Did you used to date him? Because you pretend like you hate him, but I think you love him. I think what no one in this room wants to admit is that Trump has helped all of you. He couldn't sell steaks or vodka or water or college or ties or Eric, but he has helped you. He's helped you sell your papers and your books and your TV. You helped create this monster, and now you're profiting off of him. And if you're gonna profit off of Trump, you should at least give him some money because he doesn't have any.

Some people expressed outrage that Wolf had the temerity to satirize Sarah Huckabee Sanders as she sat a mere few feet away, but Wolf did the same thing to the media folks in the room, saying right out loud that what they imagine exists—a fourth-estate adversarial relationship with the government and politicians in general—in practice amounts to a fantasy because the entire enterprise should be understood as one big entertainment channel. Wolf spoke truth to power there too.

Some critics who attacked the dinner as the culprit implicitly agreed with the complicity of the press. Megan Garber argues that those in charge of the dinner should consider "scaling back to become something smaller, more intimate, more meaningful—less about celebrity, less about comedy, and more about journalism. A smaller dinner would be more boring, definitely, but also more in line with journalism's own best vision of itself: as a watchdog, as a safeguard, as an extension of the curiosity of the American people."[31] Because *the press* has now become *the media*, because reporters work in a discursive system that swirls together news and entertainment, because many journalists double as celebrities, the event must change. The mixed reviews on the worth of the event itself and how it represents the profession of journalism echo the mixed reviews on Wolf's performance. The negative side has had its say. Professional writer and comic Adam Conover comes down on the positive side. Notably, like Megan Garber,

Conover conflates the role of the satirist with the role of the journalist in that both at their best challenge centers of power. The satirist, however, also must challenge journalists in all media:

> Comedy has no rules, per se. But in my fifteen years of writing and performing, I've come up with a few guidelines that I find helpful: 1) Be funny; 2) Tell the truth; 3) Make people in power uncomfortable. By that math, in her performance at the White House Correspondents' Association dinner on Saturday night in Washington, Michelle Wolf did exactly what a great comic [i.e., satirist] is supposed to do. She made the crowd of assembled journalists, politicians and guests laugh; she made them squirm; and she made them gasp in astonishment (and yes, a little delight) when a sharp sliver of the truth cut a little closer to the bone than they were expecting. In other words, she killed.[32]

A tweet from a viewer agrees: "Michelle Wolf . . . killed it, in every way possible. Her jokes were original and nasty, as she roasted Sanders herself, who was seated nearby at the head table at the invitation of the WHCA itself; she did stuff about vaginas, stuff about President Trump and hookers, stuff about the day's news."[33]

Many of the complaints and comments about Wolf's routine confuse the public sphere with the comic public sphere. This confusion comes across as particularly egregious given the roast as a comic form in which a celebrity allows him- or herself to be subjected to a sustained onslaught of comic barbs. This laugh-a-minute shellacking intends to amuse the celebrity as well as the audience. The roast thus parodies the encomia of funeral orations, ironically honoring a specific individual with comic dismemberment. The speaker(s) is allowed to say the most outrageous comic insults about the target(s). Presumably, the jokes have some basis in reality, maybe even in the physical appearance of the target, supposedly off-limits in other formats. However, a roast apparently allows for making some things up or fantasizing situations in detail. And of course the target(s) supposedly laughs along with the audience, maybe especially for the imaginative coloring the speaker has put onto events, habits, behaviors, looks. The issue of too much may remain in analyzing Wolf's performance, but, given the roast format, past experience implies a broad license that some folks somehow did not expect, including Margaret Talev, president of the White House Correspondents' Association. Trump fears the White House Correspondents' Dinner as a public event not because of fantasy but because of reality, because the standup comedian performing satire will almost certainly refer to what Trump has actually said and done. His physical appearance would not be off-limits, yet that topic would probably be secondary, given how much potential material exists about policy and behavior.

The problem of the roast as comic format, then, centers on the issue of too much: when has a line been crossed beyond which comic insults register as unacceptable? In the roast format, no such line exists, so the standup comedian at the White House Correspondents' Dinner necessarily talks like a cap-and-bells troublemaker if s/he actually indulges the form. When the trouble making consists of comic *parrhēsia*, the disturbance reverberates loudly and in the public sphere. Michelle Wolf's performance only highlights an always-present potential, the *too much question*, which of course returns to the problem of audience reception. Katherine Timpf points out this basic issue, how an audience can understand that a satirist intends a particular speech act as a joke but can decide its uptake as only outrageous and not a bit funny. In particular, if the jokes involve politics, then the speech act will almost surely be judged first through the filter of political affiliation and then as a joke:

> Many of those same people [who were outraged about Wolf's jokes about Sanders] have absolutely no problem with it when President Trump makes fun of people, no matter how low the blow. The way it appears now is that when Trump makes fun of Mika's face [Trump once said when he saw Mika Brzezinski, she was "bleeding badly from a face-lift"], the Right says "Chill, it's just a joke!" and the Left says it's an outrage. When Michelle Wolf says Sarah Huckabee Sanders's eyeshadow is made of lies, the Left says "Chill, it's just a joke!" and the Right says it's an outrage. There's certainly an element of hypocrisy on this issue on both sides, but there's also one difference: Michelle Wolf is a comedian, not the leader of the free world, so she does deserve a bit more leeway when it comes to making jokes.[34]

Adam Conover breaks down the audience issue in a different way, distinguishing between the audience in the ballroom, which showed little appreciation for the routine, and those who watched at home. For Conover, the brilliance of Wolf's performance resides in her intention to speak mostly to the other audience, the cablecast and online audiences not in the room.

Every performer who has done comedy on television knows that the people in the studio don't really matter. They're uncomfortable, they're tense, and they have to be polite because they're sitting six inches away from Chris Christie. You're never getting a real laugh out of them. Instead, you focus on the audience that counts: the folks at home. And the folks at home don't want comedy that's polite and tasteful, and secures them access to an interview next Wednesday—they want comedy that stands on the rooftop and calls out hypocrisy and deceit at the top of its lungs.[35]

Conover means they want worthwhile, robust, timely satire. Michelle Wolf's standup routine—clearly the satire of the comic public sphere—effectively destroyed the tradition of the roast at the Correspondents' dinner, thus creating a historic consequence in the public sphere, a dynamic that marks what we might call *the age of Trump* and its postmodern environment.

Case Study: Samantha Bee and Roseanne Barr

Michelle Wolf's performance highlights an important issue for probing the nature of satire: the difference between the comic insults that help to power the entertainment in satire and the mere snarky insults that are found in a rant or even as part of hate speech. How caustic can an instance of satire be without becoming simple anger because the satirist loses the element of play? This question relates to being too earnest. In other words, insults might serve the public sphere and not be part of a rant or hate speech but also not be part of any form of comic speech.

For example, Donald Trump revoked the security clearance of former CIA director John Brennan because of Brennan's criticisms of Trump, which partly come in the form of insults. "When the full extent of your venality, moral turpitude and political corruption becomes known, you will take your rightful place as disgraced demagogue in the dustbin of history"; or, "Mr. Trump grandstands like a snake-oil salesman, squandering his formidable charisma and communication skills in favor of ego, selfishness, and false promises."[36] Brennan means his remarks to take their place in a public debate on the fitness of Mr. Trump to be president. Placed into Michelle Wolf's standup routine, these statements could be part of a lampoon or satire targeting the president. Some citizens may even have laughed at them in their bare context, or applauded them as instances of *parrhēsia*, while other citizens would simply note their insulting tone and dismiss them. In any case, I doubt that anyone could make a good case that Brennan intended to utter jokes.

Clearly, the status of such utterances as Brennan's involve the twin problems of speaker intent and audience uptake when trying to characterize them. As a point of comparison, consider comedienne and actress Roseanne Barr's tweet about Valerie Jarrett, an African American woman who was a senior adviser to Barack Obama throughout his presidency and considered one of his most influential aides: "Muslim brotherhood & planet of the apes had a baby=vj." The racist stereotype of black people looking like apes, of being less than human, apparently renders the tweet unambiguously racist. As Chauncey DeVega has argued about a similar example, intent for such utterances does not matter because they "spring forth from a deep well of global racism and white supremacy.... Individual intent and agency are of little importance here because institutional racism works through individuals, regardless of the latter's intent."[37] Barr no doubt intended her reference to the Muslim Brotherhood to remind an audience that Jarrett was born in Shiraz, Iran, where her father, James E. Bowman, a pathologist and geneticist, ran a hospital for children—as well as hint at the conspiracy theory that Obama is Muslim. Both her parents are American, of European and African descent. Barr, however, claimed she intended the tweet as a joke and therefore it constitutes allowable speech, though later she tweeted: "I apologize to Valerie Jarrett and to all Americans. I am truly sorry for making a bad joke about her politics and her looks. I should have known better. Forgive me—my joke was in bad taste."[38] The apology and explanation did not work: the Twitter #flashmob did its thing and ABC canceled the successful reboot of *Roseanne*.[39]

If Barr wants her insult to register as a joke in poor taste, Brennan wants his caustic comments to register as the plain truth, as *parrhēsia*. Brennan's earnestness signals that he intends his piquant quips to be part of public debate about the Trump presidency and its negative effects on American democracy, while Barr's tasteless joke trades on a long-standing racist trope. Insofar as Barr's tweet relates to public sphere issues, it recirculates a discredited theory about Barack Obama's birthplace. If one judges the tweet as satiric, the Muslim Brotherhood reference serves as the serious part of the utterance, while the idea of sex between the Brotherhood and "planet of the apes" becomes the comically fantastic, nonserious part. The paradoxical structure for satire can be found: Barr's tweet entails playfulness, it can be argued, and Brennan's comments do not. For anyone who continues to believe that Barack Obama is a Muslim, the joke as satire could be successful, be felicitous in its uptake with such citizens, who would also be guilty of countenancing a racist trope.

Part of the media uproar over Barr's tweet and its consequences included complaints that Bill Maher's epithet for Trump in 2013 when he was stirring up the birther controversy about Obama—"spawn of an orangutan"—was the same sort of utterance, so why wasn't he fired too?[40] In his response, Maher not only condemned Roseanne Barr's tweet as racist by acknowledging what DeVega said about the historical context of the ape trope, but he also brought up the fundamental problem of too much, of comedians "crossing the line," by referencing Samantha Bee's epithet on her show that week for Ivanka Trump, "feckless cunt," as accompaniment to Barr's tweet.[41] Maher did not defend Bee but instead gave his attention to the charge against him that his orangutan comment about Donald Trump should be judged on par with Barr's tweet. Maher referred to his explanation as "Explaining Jokes to Idiots," a phrase that appears on the screen as a banner. The key point in that explanation: Maher connects the orangutan comment to Trump's birther activity at the time. The joke satirized the absurdity of the birther conspiracy by demanding that Trump produce his birth certificate to prove he was not half ape. In other words, the joke can qualify as satire because Maher comically critiques an ongoing issue in the public sphere. The choice of orangutan references Trump's oddly orange tan: Maher ridicules physical appearance based on a cosmetic choice, not on a natural feature, similar to Michelle Wolf's joke about Sarah Huckabee Saunders's eye shadow. There can be no valid comparison to a joke using a historically racist trope.

Like Brennan, Maher understands his insult as taking part in the public debate—but as a satirist would, as its supplement. Much of Maher's response monologue mocked Trump for various reasons so that Maher structures the entire bit as part comic public sphere, part public sphere in the manner seen in many other instances of contemporary satire. Thus the first reason that Maher cites to ostensibly prove that his comment should not be rated equivalent to Barr's tweet: Trump *is* an orangutan. In other words, he has no reason other than comic reason, so he doubles down on the absurdity of the initial claim, mimicking the behavior of the birther conspiracists like Trump who continue to assert Obama not only professes Islam but was not born in the United States despite offering no proof and despite Obama's providing proof to the contrary. He even ties Barr's mental health issues to the policies of the Republican Party: "It is also not a mystery to me how a person with mental illness can be being taken in by a party that has lost its mind." In addition, Maher uses the dust-up about Samantha Bee to insult Trump, joking that Trump was "furious," because "I'm the only one who gets to talk dirty about my daughter." However, this very personal insult exhibits its satiric quality when Maher continues, "Yes, the man who put 'grab them by the pussy' into grade school history books is very upset about the coarsening of the culture." Maher mocks the hypocrisy of Trump and his supporters, whereas Barr's tweet mocks in racist fashion African Americans in general and Valerie Jarrett in particular while reviving discredited claims about a president in a bid to delegitimize him.

Notably, Maher does not defend Samantha Bee's epithet for Ivanka Trump. After Ivanka posted a picture of herself blissfully hugging her son amid news of children being forcibly removed from their parents by Immigration and Customs Enforcement (ICE), Bee called her a "feckless cunt." Bee issued an apology, of sorts. Part of her response centered on the way that the media handles such events, namely, focusing on the vulgar language rather than the government's border enforcement policies. The media and individuals worried about the use of vulgar language as a comic tactic rather than worrying about the inhuman public policy that the epithet spotlighted.

How to read Bee's insulting phrase? Maher characterized it as over-the-line in his segment about calling Trump an orangutan. Nevertheless, the basic issue remains. Does such vulgarity within what Bee intended as an instance of very caustic satire maintain the playfulness needed to avoid being a mere rant and maintain the link to the public sphere needed to ensure the utterance has a potential uptake as satiric? Bee's epithet had defenders who claimed its appropriateness to its target, for example Josephine Livingstone.[42] Livingstone claims that the c-word is not the n-word: no oppression involved. Moreover, no misogyny is involved if a woman says it: "While an American man who calls a woman a 'cunt' in anger or mockery is drawing upon a tradition of misogyny, a woman calling another woman a cunt is simply summoning the strongest language she can think of. This is why Donald Trump's objection to Bee's language not only smacks of hypocrisy but also makes no sense." Ivanka deserves such language because she is "a crude villain in dainty designer clothing who panders to a father who boasts of grabbing women 'by the pussy.'" Livingstone clearly believes that Bee's attack qualifies as satiric by linking the epithet to the public sphere. "The Trump era is one of indelicacy, profanity, and real—not imagined—misogyny, and its flacks [i.e., those speaking for the administration] deserve a language that matches up. A joke is nothing compared to policy. After all, it's not the word "pussy" that is so enraging about Trump's *Access Hollywood* tape; it's the action that he's gloating about, the actual violence done to women and the pride with which he relays it. The word itself is innocent." Livingstone's argument rests in part on the theory of a–musement: Samantha Bee's epithet should make an audience think about Ivanka's troubling behavior in the context of what is happening at the border with children because of the Trump administration's harsh immigration policies; presumably, the ensuing laughter is of the LOI variety. As so often happens, Bee explains the news to her audience, educating them about practices done in their name as citizens and molding their possible responses by, in this case, dramatizing the harshest reaction possible via an inflammatory epithet.

Rebecca Traister also defended Samantha Bee, making a comparison with Roseanne Barr: "Barr's utterance mirrored and reinforced abuses being enacted by more powerful people against less powerful people, while Bee's challenged those abuses."[43] Ivanka Trump behaves complicitly with a presidential administration doing grievous harm to the bodies, families, and lives of human beings, while Bee acts on behalf of less powerful people and speaks out against the barbaric policy of taking children from parents. Traister then zeros in on the word itself. "Bee was not reinforcing or replicating the crude harm that 'cunt' has been used to inflict historically: the patriarchal diminishment and vilification of women. In fact, Bee was using it to criticize a woman precisely because that woman is acting on behalf of that patriarchy." Traister finishes by referencing Sarah Huckabee Sanders and returning to the very reason that Michelle Wolf compared the press secretary to Aunt Lydia in *The Handmaid's Tale*. Sanders can say "with a straight face that a comedian being mean to Ivanka Trump on television is 'vile,' 'vicious,' 'appalling,' and 'disgusting,' but she will never apply those apt descriptors to the administration she's fronting for: one that is led by a man who brags about grabbing women by their pussies."

None of this parsing of utterances as comic insult in the service of satire and the comic public sphere versus mere snark insult in the service of the anti-public sphere can guarantee or predict audience reception or uptake, which is why Maher tags his monologue as "Explaining Jokes to Idiots." One might say that any comedian will refer to audience members who fail to comprehend their jokes as "idiots." Moreover, in the context of failing to manage a felicitous uptake of an utterance as satire and thus recognize its link to the public sphere, "idiots" points to the original Greek meaning of *idiōtēs*, "private person, layman, ignorant person," and gathers up the connotation that it is selfish and foolish not to participate in public life by being ignorant of civic issues, or invokes "the basic sense of one who represents his own interests as compared with the official or public interest."[44] They say you can't fix stupid, but perhaps one can rescue idiots, though the problem of variable audience reception inevitably presents an obstacle.

Screeds or Satires?

Former CIA director John Brennan's harsh judgments of Donald Trump as president spotlighted how such utterances in a satire would threaten its necessary playfulness through a too-earnest effort to describe and report in caustic terms, a spotlight useful for distinguishing harsh language and insulting utterances by Samantha Bee and Roseanne Barr as satire or screed. A specific set of utterances might use irony and even bitter sarcasm, and so in the aggregate only resemble satire. Thus what appears to be comic public sphere satirizing nevertheless not only fails to be satire but also, at times, might even register as the mere snark insult of the anti-public sphere.

Writings from Andrew Sullivan and Charles Pierce allow for more exploration of the issue: not of too much comic (yet harsh and vulgar) insult, as with Michelle Wolf, but of too much earnest insult, as with John Brennan. Both writers assess the state of civic life since Donald Trump became president in a similar way, not just evaluating Trump's performance and temperament but also critiquing Republican Party leaders and that portion of the electorate that votes Republican and supports Trump. The theme for both critiques centers on the perceived strengthening power of Trump in the public sphere. The tone for both demonstrates profound alarm, conveyed by harsh words and insulting epithets meant to wake the general public with a bare-knuckle symbolic thrashing of the principal actors in the current moment of civic drama.

In his essay "This Is What the Trump Abyss Looks Like," Sullivan first notes the shift in the Senate that signals Trump's growing power approximately a year after taking office: "Flake is quitting; Corker is retiring; McCain is mortal. Sasse, Murkowski, Collins, and Paul remain, but the odds are mounting against them [because] a new slew of Bannonite candidates is emerging from under various rocks and crannies to take their places."[45] The sarcastic comment about slithering candidates to imply the ascendency of the alt-right reveals Sullivan's political viewpoint for those who are new to his writings. A former editor of the *New Republic*, Sullivan is usually described by the media as a conservative political commentator, but perhaps he garners most of his fame as a pundit for making an argument in May 2016 that Trump could win the election.[46] Sullivan in his 2017 column rehearses a number of factors about the present state of American politics meant to justify his metaphor of Trump as an abyss.

> The discourse has been coarsened to sub-tabloid levels; the courts' authority has been weakened by their own over-reach and Trump's refusal to follow core Constitutional norms. The neutral institutions that might be capable of bringing the president to heel, such as the FBI, are now being trashed by their ultimate boss. The possibility of a shared truth, about which we can have differing opinions, has evaporated in a blizzard of web-fueled distraction and misdirection, aided and abetted by a president for whom reality is whatever he wants it to be at any given moment, and always susceptible to change.

Unlike Jack Shafer, whose weekly column mostly reports the news, Sullivan offers an extended evaluation of political events, caustic in its way, though without comic ridicule. The concluding judgment about Trump's aversion to reality has been noted not just by Shafer's reporting but John Oliver's essay-form satire too, and of course Stephen Colbert consistently mocks Trump's wobbly relationship with facts. Sullivan tacks closer to Brennan than any of the others in his earnest public sphere approach.

Charles Pierce's attempt some eight months after Sullivan to raise an alarm about the country's situation deploys *dictator* instead of *abyss* as the controlling metaphor. Pierce wrote "Trump Has Access to Everything a Dictator Could Want" after the news that the White House sent a memo to Special Prosecutor Robert Mueller claiming that Trump could not be prosecuted for any wrongdoing while in office.[47] The memo from Trump's legal team plainly states that it believes he "literally is a law unto himself." Moreover, his TV lawyer Rudy Giuliani asserted publicly that Trump could commit murder and not be indicted while in office. Pierce appears to signal the comic tenor of his blog entry when he describes Giuliani's assertion this way: "Rudolph Giuliani, legal rodeo clown, is dispatched to the media to make that case in his own, inimitable drunk-uncle fashion."

Pierce warns that Trump "is consolidating power based on deceit at an alarming rate, and getting more popular as he goes," echoing Sullivan's abyss metaphor when he provides two main contextual points to warrant the alarm that the country is "hurtling toward the destruction of its most basic ideas about itself."[48] First, Pierce offers his history of the Republican Party in the last four decades, which has led to Trump. Second, he laments the Democrats' being historically useless as opposition. However, the claim that Trump behaves like a dictator does not indicate the worst of the situation according to Pierce: a recent poll reveals that 87 percent of Republicans approve of Trump's behavior and of the "slow-rolling catastrophe that is only now really picking up speed."

Because understanding Trump and the current state of affairs requires context, Pierce also has harsh words for those who work for Trump as well as other elected officials: "He has a tight, loyal cabal of flunkies who'd be chasing ambulances if it weren't for their talents as sycophants. He has a largely impotent political opposition and a largely supine congressional majority."[49] These barbs stud the opening for the blog entry, dispense a caustic judgment not unlike Sullivan's assertions, and set the stage for the heart of the argument: how the United States arrived at this political moment.

In many previous blog entries, Pierce favors a specific analogy to explain the current Republican Party—its supposed infection with a prion disease—which involves mutation and creates cognitive dysfunction such that a victim cannot maintain equilibrium. In one version, the disease manifests in people living in New Guinea who eat the brains of dead people.[50] Pierce names the origin of the problem. "The prion disease began when the party ate the monkey brains provided by Ronald Reagan, who served up crackpot economics leavened with a cynical alliance with splinter American Protestantism."[51] Pierce continues by providing a bumper-sticker history merely listing various manifestations of the disease since the Reagan administration, a list suggesting how particularly apt the acrid metaphor is: "Iran-Contra. Willie Horton. Atwater. Rove. Falwell. Graham. Luntz. Bauer. Gingrich. The Impeachment Kabuki. Florida. The lies undermining the Iraq War. Gay-baiting in the 2004 elections. The U.S. Attorneys scandal. Phony charges of voter fraud. The barbaric use of Terri Schiavo for political gain. The unprecedented obstruction, based in overt racism, of Barack Obama. The tolerance of Louie Gohmert, Steve King, Blake Fahrenhold, and Michele Bachmann. The endless flogging of the events at Benghazi." Thus the "genuine, uncut, unfiltered, un-consulted authoritarianism" of Trump cannot be a surprise for Republican leaders, represented by Speaker of the House Paul Ryan, "the zombie-eyed granny starver from the state of Wisconsin," who is part of "the largely anesthetized elite political class." After these insults linked to civic issues, the blog's uptake as satire should be obvious.

While the Republicans have gone all wobbly cognitively and morally in Pierce's estimation, the Democrats rate their own satiric tongue-lashing, making the mistake of "wasting time and money and political credibility wooing people so far gone with the prion disease that they no longer recognized the reality of their own lives." The party's diseased ideology has impaired the portion of the electorate that has voted for Republicans such that they have voted repeatedly against their own interest because, "for too long, there was nobody [in the Democratic Party] capable of explaining that they were doing that." Diseased Republicans. Incompetent Democrats. Pierce's talent for epithets makes him an equal opportunity insult maven, a talent important for earning the status of caustic satirist.

Like Pierce, Sullivan recognizes that the truly alarming fact about Trump's consolidation of power stems from the rabid support he enjoys from a significant portion of the body politic. "But by far the most important development in all this, the single essential rampart, is how . . . Trump has tightened his grip on 35 percent of the country. . . . No scandal, however great, will dislodge it because he has invaded his followers' minds and psyches as profoundly as he has the rest of ours. He is fused with them more deeply now, a single raging id, a force that helps us understand better how civilized countries can descend so quickly into barbarism."[52] Trump, then, is "total master of an enormous mob." Given Trump's assertion during the presidential campaign that his supporters were so loyal he could commit murder and not lose votes, neither Sullivan's description of "raging id" and Pierce's metaphor of a prion disease, which Sullivan echoes with his notion that Trump has fused his psyche with supporters, read as rhetorical overstatement.[53] But does the rhetoric deserve the label *satiric*? And if the rhetoric seems overstated, does that merely signal the comic exaggeration of satire? The sarcastic portrayal by Sullivan of alt-right candidates emerging from under rocks or Pierce referring to Giuliani as a rodeo clown and Ryan as a zombie who starves senior citizens—all could fit easily into comic routines from Colbert or Bee, for example, and help build a satiric critique. Those bits work as comic bits, but assigning a satiric quality to the general assessment of the public sphere by Pierce and especially to the one by Sullivan implies that merely describing current political reality generates a satiric tone. Aggressive critique may ring true, but without a playful presentation that implies some form of laughter, satire operating as generative supplement to the public sphere will be difficult to claim.

Pierce spends a significant portion of his blog on disparaging both political parties. Sullivan's take on them sounds no less dire, and that may be the problem. Because their theme is nothing short of apocalypse (the country is "hurtling toward the destruction of its most basic ideas about itself"; "a president for whom reality is whatever he wants it to be at any given moment"), the invective quotient must be commensurate just to describe the felt absurdity of the moment. Thus for Sullivan "there is no one in our political life capable of matching this [Trump's] power. Name one, if you can. And when you look at the Democratic field of 2020, no one seems up to it at all. Among the few responsible Republicans left, what we see is . . . utter cowardice in the face of an enraged base. . . . There are a few exceptions: Senators Collins and Murkowski in particular, doggedly playing their Constitutional roles and not quitting. The rest? The only thing we have to slow this assault is already Congressional roadkill."[54] The invective quotient for both writers already registers high enough to wonder if *screed* should be the most accurate label for both essay and blog, and once they describe Trump directly, the problem of choosing *satire* or *screed* decidedly compounds. Other pundits have made arguments about Trump similar to Pierce and Sullivan, but their (very-nearly-the-same) characterization of the president stands out due to the intensity each projects, often with trenchant epithets. Despite Pierce's talent for epithets, noted earlier, he delivers but one sentence directly attacking Trump, though it manages to pack a big explosive charge of vituperation: "He has combined an instinctive contempt for democratic government with a swindler's nose for easy cash and a junkie knifepoint robber's reckless disregard for consequences."[55]

Sullivan unloads on Trump in two separate moments, with both barrels as it were—or more like firing two cannons loaded with bitter grapeshot than a mere mocking shotgun. His premise: he considers Trump "psychologically disordered."

> His psyche cannot actually follow the instructions of anyone but himself. This is also why, after failing to repeal, replace or amend Obamacare, he has not faithfully executed the law, but actively sabotaged it. If he does not have his way, he will either sulk and refuse to do his constitutional duty, or he will simply smash whatever institution or law that obstructs his will.
>
> . . . [T]his president is so psychologically disordered he cannot behave in any other way. His emotions control his mind; his narcissism overwhelms even basic self-interest, let alone the interest of the country as a whole. He cannot unite the country, even if, somewhere in his fathomless vanity, he wants to. And he cannot stop this manic

defense of ego because if he did, his very self would collapse. This is why he lies and why he cannot admit a single one of them. He is psychologically incapable of accepting that he could be wrong and someone else could be right. His impulse—which he cannot control—is simply to assault the person who points out the error, or blame someone else for it.[56]

These paragraphs may be understood as *parrhēsia*, but if they are comic *parrhēsia*, if one logs them as satiric critiques, Sullivan has time-warped his audience back to the black humor territory of the 1960s, diving deep for the sources of the political and social dis-ease besetting the body politic, even if the trenchant lampooning risks the charge of character assassination. Sullivan's humor here might then register as a gallows humor for the collective subjectivity of the body politic, seeming to say: *look with open eyes at how absurdly bad is our political reality and then try to laugh it off*.

Pierce has but the one solo shaft loosed at Trump because his main target is not Trump but what has enabled him: the Republican Party and his supporters. Pierce therefore has little else to say about Trump. Instead, at the end of his blog entry, he strikes the alarm bell hard once last time for those citizens who do not fall into those two categories by saying, "This administration is the obvious culmination of 40 years of conservative Republican politics. A crude culmination, truly, but if you can't see the through-line from Reagan's assertion in November of 1986 that he had not 'traded arms for hostages,' through the blizzard of untruth behind the push to invade Iraq, to this president's casual disregard of even a head-fake toward the truth, it's because you're not looking for it."[57] This appeal to that part of the electorate not infected with prion disease surely contributes to marking the blog entry as public sphere speech even if the mordant tone of its ridicule leaves one in doubt about its possible status as comic political speech or drives one to label it degenerative satire or black humor along with Sullivan's analysis.

However, if considering Sullivan's column as satire invokes the black humorists, the column also registers as even more obviously public sphere speech than Pierce's blog. Sullivan does not finish his essay by directly addressing the electorate as Pierce does; rather, its trajectory arcs toward explicit policies for specific problems and seems more directed at political leaders, reinforcing the essay quality of the piece and rescuing the column from the charge against the black humorists' so-called degenerative satire that they offered no alternative values to their unblinking assessments: "If the Democrats were smart, they would propose something like this [a tax cut for the working poor and middle-class paid for by doubling the estate tax or adding a new tax bracket for those earning over $1 million a year] themselves—and get ahead of the GOP, using it as a platform for 2018. And if the Republicans could abandon zombie Reaganism, they could rescue themselves from the electoral oblivion they so richly deserve. There's a win-win here for both parties and the country."[58] The earnest nature of both writers' conclusions cannot be missed, so that trenchant ridicule by Pierce such as "Giuliani, legal rodeo clown" and "zombie Reaganism" or Sullivan's "Congressional roadkill" evinces only a modest seasoning of caustic wit to accompany the earnestness rather than leaven it with the comic playfulness necessary for satire. Compare those moments with the silliness and absurdity of Colbert's Ham Rove depiction of Karl Rove or of Key and Peele's whimsical critique of black masculinity.

Consider again Pierce's one sentence directly attacking Trump: "He has combined an instinctive contempt for democratic government with a swindler's nose for easy cash and a junkie knifepoint robber's reckless disregard for consequences." How different is that string of insults from one Stephen Colbert delivers? "You're a bloated narcissist whose presidency is a knife in the moral heart of America, a wound in our national soul that will take generations to heal, if ever." Does performance versus cold print give Colbert an edge in conveying the necessary playfulness? Possibly. What clearly separates the two sentence-length attacks, however, is context. Colbert's line forms part of a parody of Trump's interview with Sean Hannity, comprising snippets from the interview alternating with Colbert asking questions so that an audience understands that *The Late Show* has obviously altered the video and thus created a patently comic fraud. When Trump apparently responds to Colbert's insult by saying, "A horrible, horrible embarrassment to our country," and Colbert then says, "Exactly," so that Trump appears to agree with Colbert's caustic assessment, the sentence full of insults suddenly has a discernible comic packaging, becomes part of a mock candid moment. The audience meets every line in the parodic exchange with applause, laughter, and cheers, signaling a delight in Trump's faux confession, the fantasy of Trump admitting what so many in the electorate believe, thus providing a laughter-provoking absurdity.[59]

The earnestness that gives both the Sullivan and the Pierce examples the general feeling of a public sphere essay—Pierce gives us a history lesson and Sullivan specific policy suggestions—does not automatically render these examples as noncandidates for satire. In some ways, neither resides far from the comic neighborhood inhabited by Jack Shafer's "Swamp Diary" and its often-sarcastic summaries of the week's events involving the Mueller investigation. John Oliver routinely provides comic essays, and both he and Samantha Bee routinely provide history lessons to contextualize the civic issue being presented. Nevertheless, the wickedly barbed descriptions of political parties, portions of the electorate, and Trump (especially of Trump), without being accompanied by more instances—by more elaborate instances—of obvious comic playfulness, read as too earnest and thus more deserving of being called elements in a screed rather than in a satire. The mood of earnest citizenship overwhelms the moments of silly citizenship. Sullivan's extended psychologizing of Trump in particular fails to display the paradox of satire being both aggressive and playful. Political speech, not comic political speech, would seem to be the best overall description. Nevertheless, both examples might instead earn the label *black humor*—or *Juvenalian satire*—from some readers. David Denby offers a third option by calling Juvenal the master of the almost-satire he calls high snark. In J. L. Austin's terms, all of these possibilities could be felicitous uptakes once one considers all the various demographics of the body politic.

8. Satiric Intent and Audience Uptake

Trying to decide when an instance of ridicule should either be rated as the snark of anti-public sphere speech or the comic insult of satire brings us back to the vexed questions of author intent and audience reception. As we have seen in the examples discussed in the previous chapter, these questions can entail issues of style (too much comic insult) as well as the issue of an earnest aggressiveness that engenders screeds and rants rather than satire because playful elements are lost. In J. L. Austin's speech act theory, intent is always assumed, but because the reaction to comic material by an interlocutor or an audience or a reader can vary widely, audience reception—the "uptake" in Austin's terms—takes on a particularly troublesome aspect. That trouble is multiplied for satire not only because ridicule can both serve and degrade the public sphere but also because the playful elements of satire can be exploited to obscure intent harmful to the communicative rationality of the public sphere. Finally, the problem of audience uptake means that utterances not meant to induce laughter are nevertheless rated as comic.

The Buffoon Presidency

For many people, Donald Trump is a notoriously humorless individual. However, Trump does routinely dish out ridicule.[1] In his definition of a ready-witted gentleman, Aristotle opposes that figure with the boor who has no humor and the vulgar buffoon who constantly makes jokes, even when inappropriate. The Donald behaves as a combination of the boor and the buffoon, though he manages in particular to create laughter at himself, invoking Susanne Langer's idea of a modern buffoon, a clown who creates laughter inadvertently yet carries on in an indomitable fashion.[2] Both as boor and buffoon, Mr. Trump sets himself up as a conspicuous target of ridicule. For example, after his July 2018 trip to England, Europe, and Russia, it became clear how much the English had been mocking Trump—trolling him. The Trump baby balloons that greeted him in London only provided the most obvious example. Queen Elizabeth's brooch worn on the first day of Trump's visit provided the most subtle; it was a gift from the Obamas.[3]

Trump routinely makes himself a big target for comic mockery even though the intent behind his speech and behavior is most often anything but comic. This habit marks him as Aristotle's boor but it also makes him Langer's stumbling and bumbling buffoon. The name of the tour that Stormy Daniels conducts as she so publicly sues Trump to be released from her nondisclosure agreement about their sexual encounter explicitly displays his condition of being an everyday target for ridicule: "Make American Horny Again." The title of the tour mocks Trump's signature campaign phrase, "Make America Great Again," while reminding everyone of his sexual peccadilloes.

If one wanted to create a catalog of Trump-as-buffoon examples, the first item probably has to be his not knowing most of the words to "God Bless America" when the song was played at a ceremony touted as celebrating America. The buffoonery of Trump clearly not knowing the lyrics has a whipped-cream topping of irony in that the event functioned as the backup to the cancelled Philadelphia Eagles' visit as Super Bowl champions when most of them refused to attend. Trump vilified the players on Twitter as part of the rash of supposedly unpatriotic kneeling during the national anthem in the NFL. Then there is the "covfefe" incident. When Trump tweeted, at 12:06 a.m. on May 31, 2017, "Despite the constant negative press covfefe," media of all stripes, social and mainstream and not-so-mainstream, exploded with speculations trying to decided what "covfefe" signified.[4] Next example would be a word salad at a rally in July 2018. Trump talking about the huge crowds that come to hear him speak creates the lead-in to his rambling riff.

> I have broken more Elton John records, he seems to have a lot of records and we beat—and I, by the way, I don't have a musical instrument. I don't have a guitar or an organ. No organ. Elton has an organ and lots of other people help him. You know we've broken a lot of records. We've broken virtually every record because you know, look, I only need this

space. They need much more room for basketball, for hockey, for all the sports. They need a lot of room. We don't need it. We have people in that space, so we break all these records. But really we do it without like the musical instruments. This is the only musical, the mouth, and hopefully the brain attached to the mouth, right? The brain, more important than the mouth is the brain. The brain is much more important.[5]

Trump manages unconscious irony in this instance when he says that the record-breaking crowds he brags about happen because "I guess I speak well. You know, we turned away thousands of people [from the rally]. They [the mainstream press] never say I'm a great speaker. Why the hell do so many people come? Why—I don't think—it's true, why do they come? Why?" Why indeed? The very question one would ask after hearing the scrambled brag about setting records.

The question points from a different direction to the problem of audience reception. In the previous chapter, I argued that whether or not a piece of writing can be logged as a screed or a satire, or whether or not an epithet or insult should be understood as comic or merely insulting ultimately rests upon choosing one of the various uptakes possible for an utterance. Though the intent of the writer or speaker to be satiric may be clear, an audience will almost assuredly fracture over a given joke or performance. Certainly, that fracturing happened with the performance of Michelle Wolf at the White House Correspondents' Dinner in 2018. With these examples of Donald Trump, the problem of audience reception becomes relevant again, for they give citizens an opportunity to judge his comments as jokes, to have an uptake that understands the utterances as utterances that might provoke laughter of all sorts, regardless of intent.

Trump's address to the United Nations General Assembly on September 25, 2018, provides another example for this topic. Trump early in the speech trotted out a favorite claim used at rallies for his supporters: "In less than two years, my administration has accomplished more than almost any administration in the history of our country." The line garnered consistent applause at his campaign rallies, but the General Assembly responded with audible laughter. Trump at first tried to deflect the laughter by insisting the claim was "So true," but he was clearly caught by surprise. Then he added, "I didn't expect that reaction, but that's OK," to more laughter and some applause. The applause seemed to be for the apparently good-natured manner, complete with a smile, with which he accepted the laughter. Though Trump delivered the line earnestly and surely expected a sober reaction, he subsequently claimed that world leaders did not laugh at him during his remarks but were, in fact, laughing with him. "The fake news said people laughed at President Trump. They didn't laugh at me. People had a good time with me. We were doing it together. We had a good time; they respect what I have done." The ambiguity of the phrase "People had a good time with me" underlines the always-present, potential disconnect between speaker intent and audience uptake. Trump can claim that the General Assembly was laughing with him, but that "good time" can also be construed as happening at his expense. His reaction in the moment showed that he and the audience were not "doing it together."[6]

Probably the best example of Trump as inadvertent buffoon is his proclamation that "Our great American companies are hereby ordered to immediately start looking for an alternative to China," which provoked the Twitter-sphere into a viral spate of ridicule. The range of people mocking the order is notable. The memes with dogs are hilarious.[7]

Judging Donald Trump as a buffoon president whose utterances can be taken as unintentional jokes would be simply good entertainment if he were not the president of the United States and so the ostensible leader of the free world. However, given that all utterances of the US president are by definition part of the public sphere, the buffoonery thesis implies more than pleasurable guffaws. Apparently, Mr. Trump's utterances often generate an uptake not so much self-deprecating as self-satirizing in the ironic mode of a dramatic monologue.

The Troll in Chief

If Trump as buffoon fulfills one part of Addison and Steele's definition of a humorist—being the target of a ridiculing humor—he also fulfills the other part with his capacity and penchant for being the creator of ridiculing humor. Maybe one should say that, in place of a sense of humor, he has an elaborated case of *schadenfreude*. In the digital public sphere, such turbocharged schadenfreude makes Mr. Trump the troll in chief.[8] Indeed, Trump has shown from the beginning of his political career that he excels in disparagement humor with his insult epithets for his political opponents: "low-energy Jeb" (Jeb Bush), "Lying Ted" (Ted Cruz), "Little Marco" (Marco Rubio), "Pocahontas" (Elizabeth Warren), and "Crooked Hillary" (Hillary Clinton). He famously referred to Kim Jong Un, the leader of North Korea, as "Little Rocket Man," and he routinely mocks the *New York Times* by referring to the newspaper as "the failing *New York Times*" while routinely disparaging the investigation of Special Counsel Robert Mueller as "seventeen angry Democrats." Since Trump became president, he has continuously used his Twitter account to mock any and all who oppose or question him, including tweets attacking witnesses at impeachment hearings in real time.

At the basic level of simple ridicule, these epithets apparently function in the same way as does Charles Pierce's habit of using disparaging nicknames for almost any public figure. The difference lies in what precisely the epithets ridicule: as always, the question must be—what constitutes the butt of the ridicule? Pierce at least sometimes mocks public figures with epithets that reference roles in the public sphere—that is, political beliefs and actions—while Trump's nicknames often launch merely personal attacks. Thus Pierce names *New York Times* columnist David Brooks head of the Young Fogies Club, while David Gregory becomes the "Dancin' Master [who] pretend[s] not to have noticed anything that has happened in Washington for the past 20 years," and George Stephanopolos "host of *This Week With the Clinton Guy Shocked by Blowjobs*." While one might accurately say that other Pierce monikers sound random if not personal—author and columnist Thomas Friedman must suffer as the "Official Absentee Rustwater sommelier"—Trump's "Low-energy Jeb" and "Little Marco" reference physical aspects and "Pocahontas" mocks Elizabeth Warren's claim of Native American ancestry. "Crooked Hillary" originally referenced Clinton's misuse of a server to store official emails, thus involving the public sphere. However, Trump continued to refer to Clinton as "Crooked Hillary" even after the FBI determined that she broke no laws and compromised no classified information; he used the epithet in a more general way to characterize without warrant her public sphere behavior. Similarly, Trump used "Lying Ted" as a general slam against Ted Cruz. However, these nicknames did not involve policy nor even ideology, but were intended as personal slurs against Secretary of State Clinton and Senator Cruz. The irony about his epithet for Ted Cruz of course is that Trump routinely lies about almost any topic that comes up, for example, the *New York Times* is not failing and Robert Mueller is a life-long Republican. Moreover, Trump's business empire has been riddled with dubious practices that certainly would earn him the sobriquet "Crooked Donald," including cheating contractors on payments, an ethically suspect pattern that has continued since Trump became president: refusing to release tax returns, provoking suspicion of fraud; emoluments from deals with Russians and Saudis; emoluments from Trump Tower bookings, the last item engendering lawsuits.[9]

As mere disparagement, Trump's epithets cannot be rated as comic insults in service to a satiric critique intended to further discussion and debate in the public sphere; rather, they rate as snarky insults intended to short-circuit discussion with the laughter of the anti-public sphere. Granted, Pierce as a political blogger whose reporting sometimes carries a satiric edge can skate close to the fissure of writing rants and screeds so that his epithets might be marked down as anti-public sphere insults too. Such is always the danger of satire because it uses ridicule to power its engine of critique. However, Trump's humor of insult—humor in the old sense that his habit of insult has become so ingrained as to be his fundamental temperament—appears to have no other purpose than disparagement of political opposition or derailment of public sphere critiques of him or his policies.

A particularly jarring example of Trump's humor of insult happened during the Senate hearings for the confirmation of Judge Brett Kavanaugh to be a Supreme Court justice. Once Christine Blasey Ford accused Kavanaugh of sexual assault when they were in high school, no one could dispute the brutality of the public scrutiny of both Kavanaugh and Ford. Moreover, few could doubt that the Republicans were determined not to have a full investigation of Ford's allegations nor of the other allegations of sexual misconduct that surfaced after Ford's story became public. That determination only added to the hurricane fury of the media coverage. Trump at first remained balanced in his reaction to Ford's accusation, saying he thought Kavanaugh was a good man but Ford's story should be heard. Late in the process, however, his humor of snark insult took over during a campaign-style rally in Mississippi, Trump imitating Ford giving testimony, mocking her for not knowing the answers to specific questions. Though Trump's mocking parody of Ford's memory could have an uptake with supporters as a satire of her claims based on a fuzzy memory of long-ago events, it also effectively mocked the trauma of all victims of sexual assault. From Trump's point of view, that trauma could not be recognized seriously because it endangered the nomination. Rather than advancing the process of discovering truth, Trump's mockery contributed to the anti-public sphere and its obfuscation of truth, an obfuscation Trump compounded with his remarks about sons being in danger of phony accusations, a false choice for the public. Yes, that danger exists, but it cannot erase the danger of sexual assaults against daughters. Like his mockery, this comment intends to deflect and discourage discussion about Ford's experience, not encourage it. The crowd reacted to Trump's mockery with laughter and applause.[10]

The crowd's reaction is noteworthy, for it demonstrates the anti-public sphere in action. Their applause and laughter did not signal the a–muse-ment of a satiric critique. Trump did not use ridicule to enable a focus on the issues before the public: the accusations of sexual assault by a nominee for the Supreme Court and the Republican senators' refusal to search for the truth of the accusations. Instead, Trump's mocking performance dispar-aged and deflected those issues as a tactic to transform satiric a–musement into anti-public sphere entertainment. Trump performed for the crowd as he does so often on Twitter, as the troll in chief, or as an insult comic, like Andrew Dice Clay, who once complained that Trump was stealing his act.[11]

That the crowd in Mississippi consumed Trump's performance as the polar opposite to the comic insults of satire, as the mere snarky insults of the anti-public sphere, also became apparent at another Trump rally later in October of 2018, this one in Montana. Trump traveled there to support the candidacy of Greg Gianforte for Congress. Gianforte, a wealthy busi-nessman, replaced Interior Secretary Ryan Zinke as Montana's congressman in a May 2017 special election. The race took a strange turn in its final day "when audio emerged of Gianforte grabbing and body-slamming a political reporter for *The Guardian* named Ben Jacobs."[12] Trump endorsed Gian-forte with more performance: "'And by the way, never wrestle him. Do you understand that? Never,' Trump deadpanned, pausing for a moment to soak in the roaring crowd. 'Any guy who can do a body slam—he's my kind of guy,' the president continued, using his hands to mimic a body flip-ping onto the ground."[13]

As Chris Cillizza pointed out, the context for Trump praising Gian-forte for a criminal assault against a reporter (Gianforte pleaded guilty to a misdemeanor assault charge and was sentenced to a 180-day deferred sentence, forty hours of community service, twenty hours of anger manage-ment, and a $300 fine) focused on the disappearance of *Washington Post* journalist Jamal Khashoggi inside the Saudi Arabian consulate more than two weeks before the rally.[14] The world would later learn that Khashoggi had been murdered. Apparently, that context could not override the crowd's appetite for base entertainment:

> Peter Gianna, a retired law enforcement officer wearing a cowboy hat and a rain jacket, was chuckling as he relived the body slam jokes with a friend, expressing disbelief that Trump had gone there [that is, prais-ing the body-slam].
>
> "Some of the things he says just make me laugh," he said.

> ... For his supporters and allies, Trump's irreverent jokes, which have become a central part of his increasingly frequent rallies across the country, are a feature, not a bug.
>
> Inside Thursday night's rally, Kendrick Richardson, 18, a student at Washington State University who came to Montana to see the president, repeatedly laughed at Trump's zingers.
>
> "Donald Trump's a funny guy," he said. "That's a part of his charisma. That's one of his best features."
>
> A group of people waiting in line for Trump's speech recounted the president's recent mockery of Stormy Daniels. "What did he call her? Horseface?" one woman remarked. Nearby, a married couple—Freddy Martinez, 36, a student, and Sarah Martinez, 35, a truck driver—burst out laughing.[15]

Trump insults to entertain and to erase public sphere discussion. The uptake from at least some members of the rally's audience validates those insulting utterances as funny ha-ha, but their response signals the presence of the anti-public sphere and thus the insults fail to be part of satiric speech.

Iowa GOP Chairman Jeff Kaufmann does not shy away from the thought that Trump's rallies do not feature policy ideas or the political future of the United States: "These individuals come to these rallies to be entertained [and] in many ways he's giving these supporters and attendees exactly what they want."[16] Writing up the event, Andrew Restuccia and Ben Schreckinger came to the same conclusion, referring to Trump's speech as "stand-up shtick." The audience uptake of Trump's speech renders it standup by a professional insult comic. Asked about the tone at the rallies, a former White House official said, "It's performance art. He's putting on a persona and he's going through a routine of sorts." Brian O. Walsh, president of the pro-Trump group "America First Action," provides a friendly description of that persona: "the unpolished everyman" who rejects political correctness and says what he thinks. Moreover, Trump's advisers say that "the president's crass sense of humor is at the core of his appeal to a conservative base . . . and they're betting that his jokes, paired with his broader say-anything attitude, will help deliver a repeat of the success he saw in 2016."

If ever any doubt existed that postmodern discursive integration marks today's public sphere, then the embrace by political advisors and the Republican Party—as well as a significant portion of the body politic—of Trump's performance of an insulting and crass brand of humor as substitute for policy and vision should put that doubt to rest. Nevertheless, even that description does not capture the effect of that substitution, in which the rhetoric of the anti-public sphere masquerades as the rhetoric of the public sphere. Discursive integration and a regime of simulacra have opened the door to satire as the sign of the comic public sphere, functioning as a laughter-inducing supplement to the current public sphere. Trump's performance art, however, does not feature that supplementing function but rather intends a through-the-looking-glass effect: substitute the anti-public sphere for the public sphere and pretend no one can tell the difference.

The Just Joking Defense

In the regime of simulacra, intent appears like a smudged and so indecipherable signature. When everything registers as a copy, what happens to intention beyond the intent to reproduce something by posting it on Facebook or retweeting it with a hashtag to create a trend? Who can be held responsible for an utterance or an image in such an environment? Similarly, the anonymity provided by internet pseudonyms and avatars attenuates responsibility. Social media in particular countenances all forms of obscurity. On the other hand, the #flashmob outrage of social media in particular scours away attempts to be obscure and thus evade a charge of intent. From that angle, an audience, when it can, ruthlessly constructs a rhetorical ethos for a speaker or author regardless of intent. Just joking as a defense about intent has no perlocutionary force in those instances.

Justine Sacco knows all too well about the potentially terrible consequences of #flashmob outrage in an environment of rampant reproduction that creates the phenomenon of a viral post. While the senior director of corporate communications at IAC (InterActiveCorp), Sacco tweeted her idea of a joke as she traveled from the United States to South Africa to visit family during the holidays in 2013: "Going to Africa. Hope I don't get AIDS. Just kidding. I'm white!" By the time she had finished her eleven-hour flight, she was the number-one worldwide trend on Twitter as people, including her corporate bosses, lambasted her for her apparent insensitivity to the problem of AIDS in Africa. Worse. People in the Twittersphere were eager to see her reap harsh repercussions for her so-called joke. As Jon Ronson puts it, "The furor over Sacco's tweet had become not just an ideological crusade against her perceived bigotry but also a form of idle entertainment."[17] Sacco was fired. The tweet had upended her life, a consequence that Ronson shows lasted long after losing her job.

The #flashmob phenomenon relates to what Baudrillard calls the "ecstasy of communication" in which all functions are "abolished in a single dimension, that of communication,"[18] enabled by the networking of televisions and computers. In this brave new world, the physical body becomes a component in the system, plugged in and wired, so that the brain operates as a node, merely receiving and relaying information. Conscious reflection becomes the casualty for this behavior, while intent evaporates. Here one finds the root of the sci-fi fantasy of downloading and uploading a human consciousness as though it were a digital file as well as the fantasy of the eye recording 24/7 like a camera, the triumphant tyranny of the visual. In this economy of behaviors, Baudrillard posits a saturation of images and words as signs, a kind of communicative promiscuity. The defense of just joking or kidding should be understood as part of this promiscuity, the need for the defense an effect of someone running his or her mouth, reflection disengaged, or more precisely, digits on keyboards often mindlessly relaying what appears on a screen.

Sacco may have thought her tweet should be taken as a joke, but it flippantly comments on AIDS as a long-time public health scourge in multiple African countries, so that the "just kidding" phrase reads as a racist joke that AIDS cannot affect white populations. Similar to Roseanne Barr's supposed joke about Valerie Jarrett looking like an ape, Sacco's comment tying race and AIDS together has too much preexisting context for her joking intent to matter to the social media #flashmob. Sacco might simply echo Barr and say her tweet as a speech act should have the less ethically fraught uptake of a joke in poor taste, not the more ethically fraught uptake of racism, but the just joking defense, especially when invoked for hot-button social issues, does not solve the issue of intent for either the public sphere or the comic public sphere. Instead, the just joking defense underscores the ethical dilemma of satire, especially when speakers deliberately confuse the comic public sphere with the public sphere. Justine Sacco may not have intended such confusion, but Roseanne Barr apparently did, showing how hate speech can hide behind supposedly comic political speech when a speaker exploits the ambiguity of comic playfulness in order to disguise such speech. The just joking defense in that way threatens to corrode the peculiar nature of satire as a speech act entailing ridicule to persuade.

Perhaps the following stories come under the heading of *you can't make this up*, but like the Justine Sacco tale, they illustrate the basic problem with the just joking defense. Consider first the case of Mitchell Langbert, a sixty-four-year-old associate professor of business at Brooklyn College. In the middle of the confirmation hearings for the nomination of Brett Kavanaugh to the Supreme Court, Langbert wrote a blog post saying, "If someone did not commit sexual assault in high school, then he is not a member of the male sex." Langbert later apologized and claimed he intended the post as a parody to protest constraints on speech uttered by conservatives. He framed the post in a new entry by claiming he was modeling Swift's "A Modest Proposal" and by reproducing a key paragraph from Swift. "I was trying to be satirical, but I guess I'm no Jonathan Swift. I appreciated that it may have been in bad taste."[19] The original blog is three paragraphs and has no paralipsis for the statements, though Langbert surely managed to capture the outrageous rather than ironically modest quality of Swift's proposal with his idea that the allegations of sexual assault count merely as "a series of supposed spin-the-bottle crimes during Kavanaugh's minority, which they [Democrats] characterize as rape, although no one complained or reported any crime for 40 years." Langbert also had some insulting comments for Democrats in the original post: "a party of tutu-wearing pansies, totalitarian sissies who lack virility, a sense of decency, or the masculine judgment that has characterized the greatest civilizations." Without a paralipsis to signal irony, without elements of playful silliness or whimsy, and read in the larger context of Langbert's blog, which clearly shows his partisan politics, the original post and its insults could be understood as the earnest rant of someone voicing what self-styled real men think about the effeminate Democrats. This example may not stoop to the level of hate speech, but Langbert's bungled satire has trivialized, misunderstood, and dismissed women's accounts of sexual assault with his spin-the-bottle image. The ethical use of satiric ridicule would further a public sphere conversation about sexual assault and/or the way that the process of confirming nominees to the Supreme Court has become a mud-slinging contest that shows the world American-style democracy at its most uncomic.

Another example involves a Florida middle school teacher who called her podcast supporting white supremacy satire.[20] Dayanna Volitich was a social studies teacher at Crystal River Middle School in Crystal River, Florida. Online, she was "Tiana Dalichov" and the host of a white supremacist podcast called "Unapologetic." Her Twitter account bristled with racist and anti-Semitic posts. Volitich "claimed her comments were 'political satire and exaggeration' and the persona was a 'hobby.'" Hate speech in this instance clearly hides behind satire. Her just joking defense, like those offered by Sacco and Barr, did not prevent her from being fired from her job.

As a professional commentator, Alex Jones cannot claim his persona rates as a hobby, but he has claimed that the behavior on his Infowars shows creates the fiction of a persona. Jones found himself embroiled in a custody battle with his estranged wife, Kelly Jones, with whom he has three children, when she said Mr. Jones's on-air rants—for which he is renowned—prove he is "not a stable" father. However, Randall Wilhite, Mr. Jones's attorney, said the behavior was merely an act. Wilhite argues that, because Jones is a "performance artist," anything he said should be understood as just kidding, or in Austin's terms as parasitic speech.[21]

Notwithstanding Jones's claim, most of his audience members take him and his utterances seriously.[22] Moreover, his effort to say otherwise is itself eminently open to being taken as unintentionally hilarious because Jones's performance shows no sign of the irony required to qualify his speech as comic, let alone satiric. Unlike Stephen Colbert, who playfully explained the irony of his persona playing another persona during the #CancelColbert controversy (a Chinese spokesperson for a mock charity), Jones performs his persona with intense earnestness. In addition, paralipsis cannot be found—no PSA moment, just staying in character. That intense earnestness establishes the signature wild-eyed affect in his performance, which has encouraged Colbert to mock him with his over-the-top parody, Tuck Buckford, host of Colbert's parody of Infowars, BrainFight. As Jay Willis notes, Jones behaves so absurdly already that satirical mocking becomes difficult, which highlights a core problem in the postmodern media ecosystem: the blur between news and fake news threatening to make the satire of mock news moot.[23]

The problem cannot simply be reduced to which audience uptake seems proper for a given utterance. The man who shot up a pizza parlor demonstrated the perlocutionary effects of the Infowars's mash-up of news and fake news: "A North Carolina man was arrested Sunday after he walked into a popular pizza restaurant in Northwest Washington carrying an assault rifle and fired one or more shots, D.C. police said. The man told police he had come to the restaurant to 'self-investigate' a false election-related conspiracy theory involving Hillary Clinton that spread online during her presidential campaign."[24] Jerry Palmer's argument can be most useful here: a joke cannot be a joke until a listener's uptake renders it a joke: the circuit of sender, message, and receiver must be completed. In James Carey's terms, a communion between speaker and listener must exist, otherwise, unlaughter might ensue, as Michael Billig names the most negative of responses.[25] Billig's idea demonstrates J. L. Austin's notion of "uptake," that is, a statement being successful in conveying intent: "felicitous" Austin would say. Underneath this theorizing about joking utterances and utterances in general, one finds the problem of the inevitably fractured audience for comic artifacts lodged within a regime of simulacra and discursive integration. On the one hand, audience members might insist that a joke in bad taste deserves the punishment of public shaming and being fired. Perhaps Roseanne Barr deserved that consequence, but what of Justine Sacco or Dayanna Volitich? Did not all three circulate hate speech, whatever their intent? On the other hand, the speaker of any utterance within the regime of simulacra and discursive integration can claim that he or she was just kidding. However, as the instances of all three women show, the audience has the last word on the status of the utterance.

Clearly, the problem for the comic public sphere, as many examples discussed already have shown, remains how to sort legitimate satire from mere rants and hate speech, how to sort the comic insults of the comic public sphere from the snarky insults of the anti-public sphere. The imperative to discern irony and other comic techniques in the service of satire becomes particularly fraught when a satirist employs the strategy of reverse discourse. While the stakes within the comic public sphere today entail understanding how satire operates within a postmodernist aesthetic, the potential damage in the public sphere stands out equally clear, as the man self-investigating the pizza parlor vividly demonstrates.

In discussing Alex Jones's just joking defense that he merely plays a comic persona, Todd Gitlin makes the connection to the public sphere and to the regime of simulacra and discursive integration, what Gitlin calls "a reality-show culture": "But I bring this sordid business up because Alex Jones's lawyer is not original. He parrots a theme that ricochets through American culture. If you've heard it recently, odds are you've heard it from the president of the United States or one of his band of idiots."[26]

Donald Trump does not apologize; he says he was "kidding." During the campaign, after insisting that Barack Obama was "the founder of ISIS," and having garnered all the mileage possible from a flat-out lie that it would be merciful to call insane, he tweeted a morning-after tweet that he'd been "sarcastic." Gitlin's analysis continues:

> The practitioners of strategic insincerity do not retract or apologize. They "walk a statement back." They "regret" having "misspoken." They issue nonapology apologies, as in: "I apologize if anyone was offended."

> If any more evidence were needed that we inhabit a reality-show culture, here it is. A reality show is to reality as sarcasm is to irony. This is, not awesomely, a no-accountability culture. It traffics in smears harnessed to smirks that follow along just behind to collect the poop. It will say anything, anything, for effect and deny you the right to object without playing the fool.[27]

Donald Trump as the reality TV president epitomizing the theme of just joking would seem to refute any argument that the office of the presidency would transmute the Donald from his New York tabloid persona that he parlayed into being the host of *The Apprentice* to a responsible commander in chief who recognizes the public sphere weight of his speech.

Examples to support Gitlin's contention beyond Trump's claim that Obama founded ISIS are, sadly, easy to come by. Candidate Trump was just joking—it was a gaffe or misstatement—when he called on his gun-owning supporters to assassinate Hillary Clinton.[28] Trump supporters insist it rates as a bad joke.[29] Candidate Trump requested during the campaign that Russia hack and release Hillary Clinton's emails. The campaign later attempted to clarify Trump's remarks, saying he wanted Russia to hand over the emails if they had them. White House press secretary Sean Spicer later still said Trump was "joking" when he asked Russia to hack Hillary Clinton's emails.[30] Some Trump surrogates made the same claim. For example, Newt Gingrich tweeted that "The media seems more upset by Trump's joke about Russian hacking than by the fact that Hillary's personal server was vulnerable to Russia."[31] Trump as president may be the king of anti-public sphere snark insults and misinformation, but that habit leaves the White House staff to explain many of his tweets as jokes. Thus, Sarah Huckabee Sanders alleged Trump was "making a joke" when he said police officers should be able to rough up those in custody.[32] Similarly, stalwart Trump ally Jim Jordan says Trump was joking when he said China should investigate Joe Biden.[33] Trump surrogates even maintained a just joking defense in the midst of the coronavirus pandemic when Trump stated that he asked officials to slow down testing rates because the resulting positive outcomes look bad, though he later said he was serious.[34]

Trump said that Democrats behaved treasonously because they failed to clap during his first State of the Union address.[35] Just joking? A pattern underlies these utterances: say something seriously (e.g., the United States wants to buy Greenland) and when it blows up in his face (many Danes thought the offer to buy the island was a joke) act as though it was a joke all along or (in this last case) turn the original utterance into a joke.³⁶ Trump appears as the buffoon unsure when he is joking.

Earlier, I offered the "covfefe" incident as an example of Trump being unintentionally comic. When Trump tweeted, "Despite the constant negative press covfefe," the chattering class chattered earnestly about finding a meaning. The moment seemed perfect to say *just kidding*, just a joke, just some elaborate pun or acronym, or just a mistake. Apparently, nothing of the sort. Sean Spicer explained the tweet this way: "I think the president and a small group of people know exactly what he meant."³⁷ Nevertheless, Trump's tweet in response to the bewilderment and mocking reactions for the original tweet was surely in jest, as though a riddle had been delivered from the Oval Office: "Who can figure out the true meaning of 'covfefe'??? Enjoy!' @realDonaldTrump."³⁸ When I say "surely," of course, I mean *who knows*?

What should be the public uptake for the video aired in 2017 showing Trump body-slamming a man on WWE's *WrestleMania* that had been doctored so that the CNN logo covers the man's head? Trump retweeted the video. Just joking? All speech acts require context to be fully understood, so perhaps it matters that Trump routinely refers to the press as "the enemy of the people." Trump's speech acts, however, register as designed to create a context full of contradictions that enable the just joking defense whenever convenient. On December 28, 2017, Trump was interviewed by the *New York Times*. At one point he said this:

> We're going to win another four years for a lot of reasons, most importantly because our country is starting to do well again and we're being respected again. But another reason that I'm going to win another four years is because newspapers, television, all forms of media will tank if I'm not there because without me, their ratings are going down the tubes. Without me, the *New York Times* will indeed be not the failing *New York Times*, but the failed *New York Times*. So they basically have to let me win. And eventually, probably six months before the election, they'll be loving me because they're saying, "Please, please, don't lose, Donald Trump."

The astonished reaction from Ezra Klein, the author of the article, vividly underscores the basic issue entailed by simulacra and discursive integration: "What is one even to say about this? Is it a joke? If so, why is Trump taking this opportunity to make it? Is it an attack on the media? Is it Trump finding another way to compliment himself, to give himself credit for the media's success? Imagine how we would react to literally any other president speaking like this." Klein goes on to highlight the problem for the public sphere: "Trump has bludgeoned us into becoming accustomed to these kinds of comments."[39] The uptake for these kinds of comments could be, or could not be, as jokes. I have been arguing that the comic public sphere functions as a supplement to the public sphere, nestled inside its discursive realm, as it were, but nevertheless theoretically distinct. Trump represents the efforts of the anti-public sphere to erase the distinction and replace both with its discursive chaos.

Of course, the just joking defense does not get someone off the ethical hook, if one follows Freud's conception of jokes and their relation to the unconscious. Jokes reveal one's innermost thinking. Max Boot understands this point, one necessary for all citizens to learn.[40] Trump appears as representative of the verbiage game (logorrhea?) that marks the public sphere today, a game that too often presents merely a ramble of thoughts loosely linked—a feedback loop gone awry, perhaps, bits and phrases repeated and riffed on, tracing a wobbly precession of meanings. The supposed joke appears somewhere in Trump's broken syntax and faulty grammar, but not marked as joke in any conventional form, and certainly not taken as such in the moment by many citizens as well as many individuals in the media. Aides must "walk back" a given statement by saying Trump was only joking or just kidding; they must walk back the statement from the public sphere and try to pin it within the comic public sphere, the spatial metaphor of *back* denoting the mendacity that underlies the utterance *just joking*. As Baudrillard notes, such language games as Trump plays always risk vertigo.[41]

Trump-jokes (we seem to need a name to denote this specific class of utterances) form part of Mr. Trump's habit of bullying and name-calling; he thinks he can say whatever he wants. Claiming a statement of ill will should be understood as just a joke simply indicates his after-the-fact way of deflecting criticism. Trump does not risk vertigo; he intends it. Thus his many statements claimed either before or after-the-fact as jokes have no intent to induce the laughter of the comic public sphere, but rather he plots division within the public sphere and therefore plots an invocation of the anti-public sphere. Trump-jokes circulate as utterances meant to divide an audience into those who agree (symbolically, they laugh at the so-called joke) and those who refuse the uptake (symbolically, they react with cringe laughter or unlaughter).

Maybe it is not enough to conclude that Donald Trump behaves as a reality TV show star rather than a president. Maybe one should add that he also performs as an unconscious standup comedian, if not an unintentional buffoon. Maybe the body politic must understand some of his utterances, tweets or otherwise, as jokes because they so often register as objectively preposterous. Given Trump's attenuated or narrow sense of humor, the hypothesis that he jokes intentionally loses credibility to the theory that many of his utterances are unintentional jokes either because they make no sense or because they are so nakedly self-serving. Conversely, to the extent that he intends to be funny, those utterances encourage disparaging laughter from a humor based on the worst kind of low snark.

According to Graydon Carter, America has long ago moved past the need to admit that Trump himself behaves like some sort of joke. "It can reasonably be said that our dear leader is now the most ridiculed man on the planet. In fact, he may well be the most ridiculed man in history." Whatever kind of laughter Trump generates—cringe laughter and unlaughter from many citizens, surely, even as others just as surely laugh with him— Carter insists that the resulting chaos cannot be a laughing matter at all because "no amount of spin is going to change the fact that the Trump White House, like the company its inhabitant has run for the past four decades, continues to be a shambolic mess."[42]

The just joking defense indicates the bad-faith communication plaguing the public sphere today and suggests the difficulty sorting utterances apparently part of the comic public sphere. Arpad Szakolczai offers the idea of a "commedification of politics," using the tradition of *commedia dell'arte* to explain a performative turn that features an interpenetration of theatrics, masking, and liminality within the public sphere and contemporary politics that has enabled discursive strategies like the just joking defense. This analysis presents a special version of Baym's discursive integration, one in which the borderline between reality and theater has dissolved. In this view, Habermas's concept of the public sphere and his ideal speech situation that entails a communicative rationality does not explain modernity or the current postmodern cultural condition. Instead, for Szakolczai, the public sphere has become an arena in which one achieves dominance not by the force of the best argument, as Habermas claims, but rather by "the force of laughter through mocking and ridicule."[43]

In this regime of commedification, loss of authenticity and loss even of a grasp on reality informs the media-saturated contemporary environment. Politics registers as farce. Szakolczai's commedification theory renders

Trump a reality TV star who has moved his show from an NBC sound stage to the White House, shifting his role as the boss of apprentices to play the president of the United States in the guise of a figure somewhere between a mountebank and a *commedia dell'arte zanni*. This new show, let's call it *Trump's Presidency Show*, presents absurdity as a norm, truth and morals as irrelevant. *Trump's Presidency Show* does not intend for its audience to laugh in any positive way, and indeed many citizens cheer rather than giggle. *Trump's Presidency Show* claims its speech acts as constatives, subject to validation, yet their uptake by many citizens renders them jokes or just fake statements. In what can only be described as Orwellian, Trump declares those fake statements and false claims of all sorts to be truth, while any news report that dares to challenge White House narratives cobbled together from them, he labels "fake news." As David Graham says, Trump as president behaves "like a funhouse George Washington; he cannot tell a truth."[44] Like Harpo in a Marx Brothers movie, Trump the *zanni* creates chaos.

That chaos creates the chaos of the anti-public sphere, with its features of obfuscation and gut feelings—its truthiness.[45] The just joking defense signifies a use of supposed comic speech the exact opposite of how satire functions, not for clarity but merely to confuse. The depths to which Donald Trump will go are perhaps best demonstrated in a speech in Charlotte, North Carolina, the day that FBI agents arrested a man for sending pipe bombs in the mail to prominent Democrats, CNN, and critics of the administration. After condemning such violence in the name of politics, Trump began "a lengthy rhetorical barrage against the press, as though it were the mainstream media and not him that had celebrated and incited violence."[46]

Szakolczai's erudite reading of the long-term effects of *commedia dell'arte* on the functioning of the public sphere in Western democracies would make perfect sense to Jeet Heer, though Heer's version of discursive integration stems from a more vernacular view, insisting that political speech, professional wrestling, and standup comedy have been swirled together into a toxic mash-up of a discourse. "Trump is the latest in a long line of carnival barkers, sports impresarios, and insult comics who have exploited America's racial anxieties to build large audiences in the service of a quick buck. He's brought the mores of the taboo-pushing performer and the boxing hype-man into the political arena in ways that Ronald Reagan, Jesse Ventura, and Arnold Schwarzenegger never dreamed of. In the process, he's cannily exploited the license given to entertainers to talk about race in offensive ways, benefitting from the forgiveness that's extended more readily to clowns than to politicians."⁴⁷ Heer quotes John Podhoretz from the *National Review* to draw a direct line from Trump's performance in *Trump's Presidency Show* to a tradition in American entertainment—the insult comic—"Trump the heir to Howard Stern and Andrew Dice Clay, those ace purveyors of the (white) American id."

Trump understood as a buffoon or *zanni* uncovers another irony: the self-proclaimed master of the art of the deal has proved so inept at legislative negotiations that he was left out of discussions about budget and immigration when those goals were front-and-center topics during January 2018. Certainly, his malaprop style of negotiation proved disastrous in the 2018–19 shutdown of the government, first creating the crisis by suddenly refusing to sign the continuing resolution to fund the government after he said he would support it, and then failing to attain his stated goal of border wall funding before agreeing to reopen the government after thirty-five days. His tweets, too often the equivalents of Harpo honking his horn insofar as any discernible meaning can be found, merely disrupt conversation. In effect, those tweets can all be reduced to "covfefe." Trump might as well be in Wonderland, dueling with the hookah-smoking caterpillar about using words to mean what he wishes them to mean, regardless of audience uptake.

The answer to the question *does Trump know what he is doing?* is *maybe*, but that should not be understood as implying some crafty rhetorical and political plan. Trump behaves as an idiot savant wandering in the regime of simulacra, brilliant at channeling the worldviews of conspiracy theorists and white nationalists. He can play the Twitter machine like a meme virtuoso—indeed, Trump has claimed that talent made him president—but its narrowness, expression reduced to 280 characters, defines his abilities.⁴⁸ When his Twitter mentality partners with his narcissism and bullying, he creates for all citizens to see an absurd pattern of destructive behavior that includes himself, despite his claim that he is a "very stable genius. . . . Actually, throughout my life, my two greatest assets have been mental stability and being, like, really smart."⁴⁹

Find the Punchline

9.

Satire as the Comic Public Sphere: Postmodern "Truthiness" and Civic Engagement makes a postmodern contribution to the study of The Comic by investigating the limits of satire functioning as the comic public sphere as well as discerning its frontiers with discourse constituting the public sphere; it traces the outer edges of the comic laughter generated by satire, distinguishing LOL and LOI laughter while pointing toward cringe laughter and unlaughter as likely features for some instances. In addition, the book investigates the unstable differences between screeds or rants and satire (i.e., the limits of comic license), continues the work of troubling distinctions between satire and journalism begun by Geoffrey Baym and Jeffrey Jones, and throws out for more consideration a theme Amber Day's work pursues: that only thin conceptual membranes differentiate satire, satiractivism, and activism. *Satire as the Comic Public Sphere* accomplishes this work by placing notable examples of contemporary satire into the context of the postmodern condition.

The postmodern condition does not abandon truth, or feature some idea about so-called post-truth, but rather represents a profound skepticism toward claims of universal and transcendent Truth. Within postmodernity, truth matters, but its version results from a negotiation necessarily a part of its skepticism. Rather than *Truth*, the postmodern embraces *truths*, a constellation of values in Richard Bernstein's metaphor. Not a single sun lighting the way, but two suns orbiting around each other, a doubled truth: every individual should be treated equally, with unalienable rights; every individual's difference should be respected. These two solar truths apparently contradicting each other signify postmodernity. Thus the device of a pun with its doubled meaning epitomizes the postmodern in a comic mode: that is why irony has permeated the postmodern comic aesthetic; that is why the reverse discourse prevalent in truthiness satire, with its habit of being ironic and sincere simultaneously, has become prominent. The postmodern features the limits of knowing, liminality, and the Heisenberg uncertainty of language lodged in the structure of a pun. Limits and uncertainty—these elements condition the public sphere today and enable not just truthiness satire but also the liminality of satiractivism. The Enlightenment as the birth of modernity, modern satire's entanglement with the public sphere, and the twenty-first century digital version of the public sphere all enable satiractivism—a strain of satire that apparently functions on the discursive frontier between political speech and comic political speech. Satire as a performative speech act has always meant performing ridicule to force metanoia, but satiractivism as a performative, in some cases—like Jon Stewart as clown Trump exhorting his audience to testify as citizens on the Zadroga bill—also describes a political action executed though laughter-inducing means.

Satire in a postmodern environment, then, has two innovations, mainly featured in the twenty-first century: truthiness satire and satiractivism. Satire now has a capacity to become truthiness satire because a discursive integration mash-up of narrative genres and a regime of simulacra mark the (digital) public sphere. Discursive integration has compounded news and entertainment genres, bringing into prominence the mock news format that has proved so amenable to satire. The regime of simulacra has revised *the real* into *the apparently real* and *the hyperreal*, allowing the (digital) public sphere to become a discursive space in which the truthiness of fake news and conspiracy theories competes equally with rules of evidence and metrics for rationality and transparency. The comic logic of truthiness satire and satiractivism repurposes discursive integration and a regime of simulacra within a postmodern aesthetic. Truthiness satire is thus generative within a postmodern contingency.

Postmodern discursive integration can manifest in a positive way—satire at times apparently functions as political discourse insofar as satiractivism operates—but it also enables a dark side, seen in Donald Trump's insult humor, which substitutes for policy and vision at his campaign rallies. The uptake from some citizens renders anti-public sphere insult and fake news accusations as public sphere discourse, so that disparagement operates as political speech. That disparagement ultimately expresses a politics of *ressentiment*—a discourse speaking the political id. Trump's multiple claims of fake news, convenient and politically expedient because the public record so often contradicts him, register as an ultimate insult against the public sphere, as *the* insult delivered by the anti-public sphere. The regime of simulacra expressed by his claims sustains the anti-public sphere. Digital technology and the faceless anonymity inherent in the internet encourage the dissemination of fake news, metastasizing memes, and conspiracy theories that populate the anti-public sphere.

Trump's style of political speechmaking epitomizes the way that the process of discursive integration has swept up the production of comic artifacts. In effect, Trump's political speeches at rallies function as standup shtick—a humor of cruelty, snarky insult, and mean-spirited vulgarity—performance art for the anti-public sphere that seeks divisiveness as a goal rather than communicative rationality or metanoia or positive peace. Jokes create a community of insiders by ridiculing those deemed outside, and Trump has exploited that process with a toxic vengeance.[1] Satire reveals falsehoods with witty language and clever dramatization, potentially creating a community dedicated to civic engagement. The pseudo-satire of the anti-public sphere so prominent at Trump's political rallies and so easily found on the internet consists of put-downs without critical thinking, without implying conclusions useful to the public sphere about what is being ridiculed and why.[2] Instead, Trump offers plainly nasty snark, often as an end in itself and certainly without civic virtue, or as a means to a goal of—not furthering the conversation of the public sphere—but rather to end that conversation with the triumph of a domineering ideology.

A full history of satire would reveal important pivots, but starting with the rise of the public sphere in eighteenth-century England, that history demonstrates satire's modernity, which is still visible in the postmodern condition. In the Western tradition, satire is always generative in that it implicitly evokes values and principles by ridiculing its targets, its comic butts. Satire also always implies metanoia—that is, the consciousness of an alert and a–mused reader of or audience for satire might alter. The rise of the public sphere amplifies this generative metanoia by emphasizing civic life in an impulse to reform. Samuel Johnson codifies this emphasis with his definition of satire in his *Dictionary* (1755) after Jonathan Swift had expounded it in his essay "A Vindication of Mr. Gay and *The Beggar's Opera*" (1728) and dramatized it in "A Modest Proposal" (1729) with its embedded paralipsis PSA moment. The early scholarly consensus about satire in the United States after World War II is that this (by then) traditional reforming role in the public sphere arena weakened to a point of feebleness so as to seem to disappear, earning the label *degenerative*. Nevertheless, ridicule implied values as comic butts were identified. Indeed, the ridicule of this so-called degenerative satire arguably assumed epic proportion, taking aim not just at human nature and individuals as well as institutions but also at the very processes of thought and representation upon which such ridicule—and the status quo under comic assault—is built. *Degenerative* references the critique of foundational concepts, thus earning that style of satire the more apt label *(early) postmodern*. Because ridicule of foundational concepts cannot present alternatives, the satire was read as self-immolating, also earning the label *black humor* as well as charges of despair and cynicism and moral relativity. Though postmodernity altered the cultural terrain for the production of satire, suggesting another pivot in satire's history, postmodern satiric ridicule nevertheless engaged then-current social issues as well as long-standing conceptual foundations so that values are implied and metanoia remains possible. The Enlightenment value of satire being educative remains too, albeit the education entails a notable degree of skepticism, the always-now critique, that insists on limits.

Postmodern satire in its contemporary phase has reaffirmed the educative function of satire and its impulse to reform insofar as it has emphasized the tactic of the PSA moment in the tradition of Swift and the discursive presence of a comic public sphere; it has actively reclaimed the generative function of satire, though its postmodern aesthetic emphasizes rational skepticism leavened with affective optimism. Moreover, that reaffirmation has spawned not just new versions of generative satire but also satire more avowedly public sphere. This postmodern mash-up of comic public sphere and public sphere can be found in the satiractivism of mock news shows and the comic monologues of late-night hosts, and in the work of satiric documentarians and political activists that Amber Day has investigated and explained, in the hashtag activism of citizens like Suey Park. This mash-up of comic political speech and political speech, then, has created political activists who use satire to complement satirists who advocate political action.

Though the postmodern condition does not decouple satire from its Enlightenment relationship to the public sphere, the material condition of a particular technology has been crucial to demarcating a modernist from a postmodernist aesthetic: television. For mock news shows, postmodern discursive integration has a peculiar quality because they weave "real news footage or the actions of real public figures into the satirist's narrative,"[3] a process that sets them apart from other examples of political satire. The element of "real news footage" operates as the quintessential *real* for the technology of television: that footage provides images that reflect a reality in what Baudrillard calls the first order of the image. Satire before the existence of television could always reference *the real* insofar as actual events could be narrated or pictured, and actual people could be named and described or caricatured in the satire. However, the technology of recording moving images with sound has rendered that older version of *the real* weak in that its mediation appears much more obvious than the illusion of immediacy that video provides. According to Jane Feuer, "the medium [of TV] seems to insist more and more upon an ideology of the live, the immediate, the direct, the spontaneous, the real."[4] Television insists because a sense of immediacy distinguishes it from other communication media, and the paradigm for that sense is news footage.

Including lots of news footage in a mock news show highlights its satiric engagement with actual events. Moreover, the ability to search video archives means that the traditional satiric functions of exposé and speaking truth to power can easily be fulfilled. Recalling *the real* with news footage against a background of truthiness operates as a boon to satire in a mock news format in that a public figure's previous words can be matched to current deeds. The lying lies of politicians, their chronic hypocrisy, can thus be routinely exposed to ridicule. While this process has probably not slowed down the lies and hypocrisy, it does alert those citizens who are paying attention to the extent of the corruption of public sphere discourse and who can be blamed for it. When, in contrast, the images provided by news footage fall within Baudrillard's order of the simulacrum, satire's tradition of exposé targets this degeneration of representation; that is, when the news to be reported is only that of other news reports, the news functions as a self-perpetuating image-generating machine and *the real* becomes the *hyperreal*, making possible the truthiness of the anti-public sphere. Truthiness satire then steps forward to call to account this through-the-looking-glass effect. As Robert Tally says, "Real news ... presents the false representations but insists on their representative accuracy, and the fake [i.e., mock] news of *The Daily Show* and *The Colbert Report* ... provides the authentic fakery of the hyperreal."[5] This formulation captures not only the through-the-looking-glass effect of truthiness but the postmodern pushback of truthiness satire.

However, such formulations turn satire into hybrid journalism, similar to saying that mock news shows represent an "injection of politics into previously nonpolitical spaces."[6] The concept of hybridity, spawned by the postmodern condition's discursive integration and regime of simulacra, therefore also unfortunately enables a habit of misreading the nature of satire when discussing examples of mock news, which are said to "provide some of the best examples of the melding of satire with the world of serious political discourse."[7] Such misreadings create a category error. Satire does not meld with the world of serious political discourse, although by definition it participates in that world, because the public sphere is not the comic public sphere. Satire, especially in mock news formats, performs as a *supplement* to, not a melding with, the public sphere of serious political discourse.

Thus the formulation *satire that plays with the news* describes mock news shows more accurately than saying they are "actually an alternative form of reporting."[8] Satire in these shows performs as a comic speech act that mimics reporting—not alternative reporting but mock reporting. On the most basic level of representation, mock reporting presents what satire has always done. Thus satire does not operate as a mirror held up to society, copying an original in the way that reporting claims to be objective, but describes a society instead within the comic distortions of a fun-house mirror. Satire's built-in claim to civic fame is the irony that such distortion can "reveal a sort of higher truth."[9] News reporting with its video footage encodes reality: its narrative and images endeavor to reflect a reality, even though it must necessarily be partial and framed. The satire created by mock-news parody should not be understood as alternative news, even if the audience uptake treats it as such, because that is tantamount to unraveling satire's serious aspect and setting aside its nonserious aspect, a process mimicking wave function collapse when analyzing quantum states. Such uptake remains an audience's prerogative, of course, but then satire itself collapses and its status as comic political speech disappears. Satire that plays with the news remains outside the realm of reporting because its comic quality alters whatever measure of a serious quality it includes.

Efforts to define satire as political action also include a defense of it from a "most damning" criticism, one conspicuously leveled at the so-called black humorists: it offers no positive or alternative vision. Satire merely obsesses with social wrongs and thus can "do little toward articulating what an alternative might look like. This would seem to be a serious limitation, particularly for explicitly political material."[10] If one conceptualizes satire as "explicitly political material," then the limitation indeed sounds serious. However, satire is not political material. The exhortation that satire should somehow move beyond the simple opposition of its comic criticism to reach an explicit agenda for concrete changes misunderstands the nature of satire by expecting it to function as political speech. A somewhat more nuanced version of this mistake happens when "TV satire ... reimagine[s] the possibilities of the genre by adopting advocacy journalism practices [so that] comedic criticism ... would transpire into audience political action."[11] Though saying satire adopts "advocacy journalism" rather than invoking satiractivism again implies the category error, *transpire* captures the momentum of the satire two-step when the comic criticism of satire transmutes into political action. The mistake in such formulations is not about detecting public affairs discourse embedded in satire, or about uncovering a measure of potential political efficacy in nurturing counterpublics. The mistake resides in failing to understand the dynamic of the comic public sphere and the public sphere as process, to understand that the hybridity discerned in postmodern satire operates via speech acts fluid in their performative force.

Using J. L. Austin's speech act categories provides a method for separating satire as comic political speech from political speech, thus clarifying its relationship to the public sphere and countering efforts to define satire as political action. The use of Austin's speech act categories can prevent the categorical confusion of one kind of utterance with another, as Mark Rolfe does when he says that mocking tactics from well-known Augustan satirists were not "idealized and gentlemanly political debate" because their satire "aimed at destroying an opponent's credibility through making an audience laugh."[12] Rolfe first implies that satire should be conceptualized as a form of political debate (exactly the categorical confusion) before denigrating that status by asserting that satire instead foments aggressive destruction (viciously snarky and nasty, no doubt) of a political opponent's credibility. That formulation of satire's goal offers a very narrow use of its comic methods that conjures the tactics of Mr. Trump. Indeed, it is not immediately clear that using such methods constitutes satire in any meaningful way—that is, in a comic public sphere way. Rolfe's formulation returns to the difference between rant and satire as well as the limits of satire as a vehicle to promote the communicative rationality of the public sphere. How to measure the danger of an audience feeding only on the comic insults of satire, the danger of an audience behaving as citizens of the political id? How to discern the difference between affects of anger and disgust channeled to the potentially useful comic purposes of satire and just more of the anti-public sphere—between comic insult versus mere insult? As Kirby Olson says, invoking a politics of carnival, "laughter takes thinking out of the hands of the divine, and thus out of the hands of the rulers, and places it in the hands of the unruly."[13]

Stephen Colbert makes the point about comic political speech versus political speech this way: "People might perceive it (*The Colbert Report*) as substantive because the jokes happen to be political. But I guarantee you that it has no political objective. I think it's dangerous for a comedian to say 'I have a political objective.' Because then they stop being a comedian and they start being a politician. Or a lobbyist."[14] Not politician or lobbyist with a specific political objective, the satiric truth teller instead functions as gadfly buzzing around the body politic, stinging it when necessary, and saying *wake up and act as enlightened citizens.*

Why is this widespread category error so consequential? Because treating instances of satire as though they are political speech rather than comic political speech enables the argument that satire results in chronic failure to execute the civic reform it might claim for itself, an argument that continues to open satire to the charge that it has no discernible effect in the public sphere.

On this vexed issue of does satire make a difference, a decided gulf in thinking exists, among both scholars and commentators in popular culture publications. The discussion over Suey Park's "#CancelColbert" event provides a clear pop culture example of the critique that satire does nothing to affect the real-world policy issue at stake. As Jay Kang notes, "Much of the debate about #CancelColbert has been about the efficacy of hashtag activism and whether the act of dissent has been cheapened by the ease, and sometimes frivolity, of Twitter protests."[15] Robert Tally articulates the affirmative view: "What sets the two Comedy Central shows apart, from other news programs and from other comedy programs, is their profoundly critical spirit. As both Jon Stewart and Stephen Colbert have proved, . . . [the] movement from political satire, as ancient as comedy itself, to this immanent critique of the mainstream media itself has real-world effects."[16] Amber Day's argument about satire and counterpublics aligns with Tally's viewpoint. Indeed, she remains adamant about the mistake of the opposing argument to chastise satirists for failing to "single-handedly cause tangible political change," calling "that sort of causality . . . absurd."[17] Yet the opening provided by the category error clearly persists.

A variety of commentators and theorists, literary and otherwise, exploit that opening, asserting that satire has little political effect or no ability to produce actual change. John Gilmore states the most radical version of this position, saying that even the notion that satire actually intends reform is "open to question."[18] Instead, satire in his view operates as Saturnalia or carnival, staging a reversed world but only temporarily, like a safety valve that ultimately supports status quo when the ritual moment of carnival ends. If radical change can be linked to "considerable satirical activity,"[19] it might be a mere reflection of broader change than a cause. Conservative satire is much more common. Gilmore's challenge that satire does not have an embedded intent to reform would seem to be focused on satire before the rise of the public sphere and Jonathan Swift's 1728 defense of Gay's *The Beggar's Opera* or Samuel Johnson's 1755 definition of satire as explicitly having that intent. Gilmore premises his challenge on a division of satire into radical and conservative strains, which obscures the idea of reform by linking it only to the radical strain. The argument that, historically speaking, satire mainly supports conservative viewpoints (a claim echoed by Theodor Adorno) does not rule out an intent to reform: rather, reform moves in another direction, back to some position within the status quo, not forward to a new one that changes it. Nevertheless, Jonathan Greenberg agrees with Gilmore's pessimism about the efficacy of satire: its moral purpose "rarely" spurs any "magical, instantaneous" reform and can seem "wholly inadequate" in the face of large-scale problems.[20]

When examined closely, the claim that satire rarely or never creates reforms or is wholly inadequate against big problems displays a confused logic in its hyperbolic negativity. Satire has no actual consequences or efficacy in the real political or social world, these arguments go, because it maintains a detached attitude. The premise of that assertion insists that satire *ought* to be attached to or engaged with, not detached from, the real political or social world, otherwise noting its failure makes no sense. But why that negative judgment? Why should satire as a form of comic artistry be castigated for its supposed failure to produce actual consequences in the real political or social world any more than other forms of art? The answer springs from a second claim about satire that has been around at least since Swift's essay or Johnson's dictionary definition: its impulse or intent to reform the political or social world. Yet is not that second claim tantamount to saying that satire does in fact have an attachment to the real world? Does not an intent to reform constitute its attachment—that is, its primary engagement? First, the attack on satire declares its detachment and therefore its lack of power in the real political or social world and then touts its attachment, an intent to engage, but also its failure in following through on it. A confused argument to be sure.

Perhaps the root of the problem centers on what is meant by *detached*. If that means satire is not quite the same as political discourse, the relationship of distance or separation implied apparently makes sense. However, that implication can mislead in two ways. First, it misleads because it assumes too much of a separation in that satire's paradoxical nature ensures inevitable imbrication in the real political or social world through its references to actual people and actual events, even before one speaks of an intent to reform that those references might signify. Second, it misleads because it does not assume enough of a separation in that a satiric artifact as an instance of a comic political speech act has a fundamentally different status from an instance of a political speech act. Satire's comic concern with a civic issue cannot be rated as political discourse in the same way as a policy paper advocates an intervention on that same civic issue. Saying satire is detached misunderstands its role in the real political and social world. Saying satire has little or no effect misunderstands its nature as comic supplement to political discourse. As supplement, satire always implies a basic engagement while any claim of its intent to reform implies a next level of engagement, though not at a level one should necessarily call activism.

The argument that satire has no efficacy not only displays confusion about satire's supposed detachment from the political and social world; it also makes the mistake of assuming a one-to-one relationship between audiences consuming satire and political action. Amber Day puts it this way: "Efficacy is [thus] analogous only to material returns. The problem with defining political effect so narrowly is that it risks reducing all democratic politics to what one does at the polls, ignoring the political groundwork that precedes any type of change. It negates the much lengthier process of altering structures of feeling, . . . and it elides the importance of building political communities."[21] Building political community happens, for example, via Michael Moore's films featuring guerilla theater tactics.[22] Moore remains engaged beyond the films, not detached, and so his level of efficacy can be measured, producing consequences in the real political and social world. Moore's films and the comic guerilla theater of the Yes Men activist group, for example, demonstrate a civic activism on the part of Moore and the actors that are similar to stunts Stephen Colbert pulled at the FCC and in a congressional hearing that Marcus Paroske calls "participatory satire."[23] Their satires perform a comic civic activism, an engagement beyond satire's symbolic link to the world of real people and events and even its implied intent to reform. Change in the public sphere happens at many levels, and satire potentially fosters it. Such change begins with metanoia:

satire first has the potential to change minds, for someone either to adopt another point of view, to modify an existing point of view, or to decide to become part of active counterpublics about specific civic issues.

The charge that satire has no discernible effect in the public sphere or on politics in general, then, can be refuted on two counts. First, such indictments amount to a categorical error, mistaking comic political speech for political speech. Traditional satire in an illocutionary mode does not intend to directly induce material changes in the public sphere or politics; rather, it constitutes a first step toward such change as the audience is a–mused and experiences metanoia. In addition, Amber Day argues that although satire may not trigger a cause-and-effect sequence, it has an important potential to aid in the building of political community. This incremental process of change in the public sphere aligns with the postmodern notion of change advocated by Foucault and Lyotard, partial and local rather than radical or global transformations.

Satire has also been attacked on two other fronts, both related to the issue of efficacy and the possibility of changes in the public sphere. The second charge asserts that satire produces negative effects on the processes of democracy—for example, fostering cynicism. However, significant research by Baym, Day, Jones, McClennen and Maisel, among others, suggests otherwise: satire has a positive effect on democracy. Satire can facilitate political activism and boost civic participation, despite its ridicule and sarcasm and the possibility of producing negative emotions about politics or being mistaken as anti-public sphere snark.[24]

The third charge asserts that satire merely preaches to the converted; therefore, no change would be discernible. "If we think of the satirist as a sort of resistance fighter in a cultural guerrilla war against forces of conservatism and oppression, . . . [if] the purpose of satire is to change the world, or at least change the ways in which we think about it, do [satirists] do more than elicit complacent smiles from those who already share their points of view?"[25] Help on this charge can be found in Samuel Johnson's definition of modern satire proper, which intends reform, rather than a lampoon that ridicules personal traits but not necessarily in service to the public sphere. Satirists criticize and ridicule always, though premodern instances of satire generally target private moral behavior rather than tout reform in a public arena: a healthy mind for the individual rather than the health of the body politic and social as primary goal. Satire before the Enlightenment was therefore much more likely to be conservative than modern examples, though its metanoia was always possible, theoretically, in both private and public realms. The impulse to reform Johnson has in mind for modern satire should be understood as tied to the notion of public sphere discourse. His definition sets out the modern view of satire, one that emphasizes a reforming impulse comically supplementing the public sphere. That process ensures the satirist's addressing the whole public, not just the hypothetically already-converted, and functions as the source for any image of a satirist as resistance fighter or fearless *parrhēsiastes*.

More help can be found in the goals of the activist groups Day examines. Billionaires for Bush and the Yes Men as well as the satiric documentarians she profiles employ irony "not only to attract attention to the cause, but to actively call upon audiences' shared assumptions and predilections in an attempt to make members of existing discursive communities present to one another and, ideally, to turn those communities into actively politicized ones."[26] These goals differ from those of satirists, though satirists recently, at times, reach the level of engagement labeled *satiractivism*. Political activists begin at that level, explicitly calling on the audiences to become actively political. Metanoia at that level centers on audiences becoming conscious of already existing values, rather than altering values and then deciding to become political active. Members of those audiences "may still be apathetic, or unconnected to a larger movement, or simply in need of some validation. Passively holding a particular opinion or assumption is not analogous to acting on it or even to privileging it as particularly pressing."[27] In other words, the satire consumed by such audiences can play an important role in the public sphere.

Day's insight about satire as dissent, about satire's potential for inspiring the overt engagement of political activism, emphasizes the metanoia that awakens, affirms, and reinforces preexisting values and principles and insists on the potential real-world effects of that change in consciousness. That metanoia can "fulfill an integral community-building function [and] slowly shift debate by turning laughter over a shared joke into anger and engagement."[28] The existence of that potential for metanoia awakening, affirming, and reinforcing preexisting values and principles is precisely why the people she calls "ironic activists" employ satire's tools of irony and parody and ridicule, its comic political speech, to influence public sphere discussions of civic issues. Even preaching to the converted has value for the public sphere.

Satire as the Comic Public Sphere examines satirists and theorizes how they build their apparent political engagement on the poetics of satire's a–musement, its aesthetics that please and entertain but critique too: a–musement designed with a rhetorical potential to create metanoia. Satire has a built-in level of engagement via its parody of the public sphere. Day's analysis suggests that my claim for satire's metanoia signifies a layered process with more than one level of potential change. The change might be a consciousness awakening to preexisting values and principles, as she argues, or it might be a new consciousness altering preexisting values and principles. Either version of change in thought or perception or belief signals a basic affective and cognitive engagement with the civic issue at hand. Once a–mused—that is, once one laughs at satire's ridiculed butt and then muses on the value or principle implied in the ridicule—one then *might* be moved to the overt engagement of political activism: the satire two-step. That dance pinpoints what one composition teacher reports when using satire as a classroom focus: a student "transforms her awareness of injustice into aims for its amelioration or eradication."[29] In the comic public sphere, satire's rhetorical power creates the silly citizen who experiences metanoia, either causing an alteration in an individual's beliefs or perceptions or a reaffirmation of an individual's existing community—or even an individual's decision to switch communities. Either layer of metanoia functions as precondition for the appearance of the active citizen within the public sphere.

While the arguments and issues concerning satire's efficacy, its potential effects in the public sphere, apply to modern satire in general, the innovations for satire in the twenty-first century, truthiness satire and satiractivism, have particular elements that configure their poetics.

Truthiness satire targets, as a fundamental comic butt, the claim that the postmodern condition translates into the cynicism of fake news in which truth does not matter, only the viral reproduction of its falsehood. Donald Trump's litany of charges about fake news against mainstream publications like the *New York Times* epitomizes that cynicism, ironically highlighting his mendacity, as though his tweets function as a one-man Ministry of Truth for the anti-public sphere. A second fundamental comic butt for truthiness satire, then, must be the truthiness of the anti-public sphere. Satire as the sign of the comic public sphere has become the most important comic enterprise in the postmodern digital twenty-first century because of the sustained assault in the public sphere on truth, facts, and civility. The discourse of politics in the United States has become so corrupt, venal, and vitriolic that only the comic ridicule of satire can mount the harsh and mordant critique it deserves.

Satiractivism of all sorts operates as an emergent tactic (in Raymond Williams's sense) because discursive integration and the regime of simulacra have vitiated for a significant portion of the electorate the trust needed to sustain journalism's traditional role as democracy's watchdog. The hyperreality of the news has rendered it as an ideological battleground instead of a primary source of information to underpin the communicative rationality of the public sphere. Moreover, the incivility of the discourse that accompanies political action has short-circuited the process of debate and deliberation necessary for the smooth functioning of the public sphere. Not always content with satirizing those conditions, some satirists now are ready to bring the comic speech of satire into the public sphere by directly exhorting their audiences to act as citizens after making them laugh about the follies and iniquities of the media and the political class. Most of the comic critiques deserving the name *satire* remain in the more traditional rhetorical mode of aiming to induce metanoia, a change of mind, but the postmodern environment of truthiness has encouraged some satirists to add civic action to the goal of metanoia, interpellating audiences looking to be entertained as silly citizens ready to be engaged.

Given the postmodern cultural environment, some satirists have developed a poetics of comic critique premised on a process of reverse discourse in which they turn back on itself the ridiculous nature of anti-public sphere truthiness.[30] In this aesthetic, satirists retool discursive integration and the regime of simulacra, transforming them from structures that all too often organize discourse in the public sphere into the primary comic butts of their satire. Whatever may be the specific topic or issue at hand, satirists creating truthiness satire build their comic critiques by appropriating those structures to demonstrate in mocking fashion their false natures and pernicious effects. Stephen Colbert's concept of truthiness functions as a reverse discourse, mocking the alternative-facts crowd and their anti-public sphere agenda. Reverse discourse parodies its source. When parody's iteration intends mockery (for it does not always), then the process of a comic reverse discourse resembles reaching into a sock and turning its inside into its outside: the butt of the process does not disappear but instead its signifiers reappear rescripted for ridiculing laughs.

The process of that reverse discourse rescripting can be a simple one. The digital public sphere now imagines the recording of everything, which can result in a regime of simulacra. However, it also creates a vast archive of recorded events and speeches that allows for a comic butt's own words to be easily retrieved to demonstrate hypocrisy and lying and thus create laughter-provoking self-condemnation. The distinct comic tactic of using the comic butt's own words in the building of a satiric tongue-lashing was in a more limited way always a potential in the print world. Digital technology, however, has magnified exponentially that potential, which Jon Stewart routinely exploited on *The Daily Show*. That archival power becomes particularly useful when the media ecosystem that produces the archive becomes the comic butt. Stringing together in rapid-fire video clips that show how the media is covering (or not covering) a particular story can very quickly reveal biases, a particular kind of comic turn within digimodernism.

My employing categories from J. L. Austin's speech act theory provides a way to distinguish the poetics of a special strain of satire—satiractivism—from a more traditional form in which the goal centers on making values clear via paralipsis and metanoia. However, the liminal nature of satiractivism obscures the boundary between political speech and comic political speech, a drawback because it encourages the category error of speaking of certain instances of satire as a kind of journalism. Similarly, when I recounted at the beginning of the book the anecdote about the laughter of Desiree Fairooz at a public hearing, I ignored the implied question of whether the laughter ought to be logged as comic political speech or actual political speech, regardless of how it functioned in the moment for the government's uptake. The idea of a comic public sphere implies that laughter generated by satire functions as a kind of political speech—that is, a comic kind—just as it suggests that citizenship has morphed into silly citizenship. These distinctions are not just semantic hair-splitting, given the argument that satire and its laughter have no efficacy, cannot change anything in the public sphere. The premise of that argument classifies satire and its laughter as political speech and then scorns its supposedly discernible lack of material effect in the public sphere. However, if one understands satire and its laughter as comic political speech, the metric for efficacy shifts dramatically. Rather than saying satire cannot actually make a difference in the sociopolitical world,[31]—in effect saying that satire is useless because no cause and effect can be established—satire's function as *comic supplement* to political speech becomes clear. Fairooz's laughter signaled a judgment on the claim that Senator Jeff Sessions treated all American citizens equally under the law. In the public sphere, Fairooz might have provided evidence of Sessions's record to disprove factually the claim. In the comic public sphere, she laughs, which does not disprove the claim but rather voices doubt about it, a potential prelude to factual proof and a supplemental tactic for making the case and even perhaps encouraging citizens to act on the conclusion.

Demonstrating the postmodern features of limits, frontiers, and edges, *Satire as the Comic Public Sphere* worries about the aesthetics (and ethics) of comic insults versus mere insults because satire has a family resemblance to cursing, to apotropaic goals of scaring off evil spirits.[32] At some level, citizens want their satirists to ward off metaphoric evil spirits, and if that takes caustic epithets, occasional vulgarity, and harsh ridicule that approaches plain cursing, so be it. However, citizens also do not want their favorite satirists to behave as misanthropes, to become Timon of Athens. Famous historical satirists who seem to flirt with misanthropy—Juvenal, Swift, or Pope, for example—probably could not garner popular approbation in their day from the average citizen. Satire today, then, appears paradoxical, if not schizophrenic, in its comic qualities: working to promote the public sphere yet trafficking in comic insults, thus apparently working against the rational communication of the public sphere it wants to serve. With their comic ridicule, satirists court an audience always potentially in danger of yielding to the worst angels of its nature. Similarly, the postmodern laughter generated by comic artifacts today operates as strangely fluid, even schizoid, potentially serving both the political left and the political right, a possible sign of trolling or cringe laughter or unlaughter as well as LOI and LOL, with little or no linkage to the public sphere. In short, satire and the various kinds of comic laughter it generates indicate an inevitable audience ambivalence.

While my idea of metanoia and Amber Day's elaboration of satire as dissent both help to dispel the negative arguments about satire—that it lacks any significant efficacy for the public sphere, encourages cynicism, or merely preaches to the converted—a more intractable issue for investigations of satire involves audience uptake and the problem of laughter.[33]

The issue of audience and readers presents a fundamental difficulty when trying to understand the nature of satire and how it operates in a given society at a particular historical moment. What to make of authorial intention? For satire, authorial intention apparently often must give way to audience interpretation. A reader could say that a text might have been intended as a satire, or simply can be read as such regardless of any intention by the author. The issue becomes particularly fraught if an audience also serves as the satire's target, or part of the target. In any case, results can be unintended (in Austin's terms, "infelicitous") because "satire is, or seems to be, in the eye of the beholder."[34] The just joking defense exploits these ambiguities, which are inherent in Austin's notion of audience uptake. As news anchor Brian Williams says, Jon Stewart's audience "gets to decide if they like the serious Jon as much as they do the satirical Jon."[35]

Austin insists on intent in speech acts, and one of the best theorists on irony, Linda Hutcheon, insists on intent in the use of irony.[36] Ironies may be stable or unstable, but either way intent is embedded. If one agrees on embedded intent in irony and/or satire—or for that matter, in jokes and all manner of comic artifacts—that still leaves the choice (or capacity) to read an ironic statement with the audience/reader. The audience/reader either uptakes the ridicule of satire, or fails to uptake ridicule, or refuses to uptake ridicule and reads satire as a serious assertion.

The problem with audience uptake points to the performative quality of satire as a speech act, which in turn recalls Day's argument that satires "bring into being a public that not only shares its worldview but will continue to circulate its discourse." In particular, the activist groups she examines want to turn "shared understanding into sustained circulation and communication."[37] Assuming a felicitous uptake of satire entails two cognitive steps at the level of engagement Day highlights: a counterpublic acknowledged and then active recirculation of its discourse. Felicitous uptake, then, necessitates more elaboration of metanoia: a second two steps in addition to satire's a–musement communicative force. The four steps would be, first *metanoia as a–musement* (the fun side of satire entertains and provokes laughs, which activates and/or creates a discursive community—that is, folks who laugh agree with the implicit values of the satiric ridicule; that community thinks about, muses on, the public sphere issue embedded in the satire); and then next *metanoia as inspiration* (the community recognizes itself as a preexisting discursive community; the community actively recirculates the shared understanding implicit in its laughter). The second two steps move the audience from the comic public sphere toward the public sphere.

The problem with audience uptake and authorial intention becomes particularly fraught in the context of memes on the internet, or in the context of the internet in general. This complication is compounded because the symbolic violence of the comic public sphere inevitably tangles with the violence verbal and actual in the public sphere.

For example, in October 2019, the *New York Times* reported on a video shown at a pro-Trump conference, American Priority, that "appears to be an edited scene of a church massacre from the 2014 dark comedy film *Kingsman: The Secret Service*." The video is arranged as a series of internet memes that includes the logo for Trump's 2020 reelection campaign. "The most violent clip shows Mr. Trump's head superimposed on the body of a man opening fire inside the 'Church of Fake News' on parishioners who have the faces of his critics or the logos of media organizations superimposed on their bodies." Besides journalists, other targets depicted include the late John McCain, California representatives Adam Schiff and Maxine Waters, Utah senator Mitt Romney, and former presidents Bill Clinton and Barack Obama.[38]

This video from Trump supporters features a tough-guy Trump persona and apparently promulgates the idea, a favorite trope for Mr. Trump, that news media are enemies of the people. The origin of the video by a pro-Trump group calling itself "The GeekzTeam, . . . part of a loose network of right-wing provocateurs with a direct line to the White House," would support this supposition.[39] The video was first uploaded to YouTube in 2018 and was not the group's first such endeavor.

Given that origin, what can be said about its intent? Clearly, someone thought the year-old video would entertain the conference attendees. Some individuals probably were entertained, surely the primary intent, but I doubt one could make a blanket statement about everyone being comfortable with the level of graphic violence against not just news organizations but actual public figures. I will come back to the issue of violence, but first I want to consider how the video as text and its consumption might be read beyond simple entertainment.

Charlie Warzel argues not just that the authors of the video intended to be playful and entertaining for a certain segment of the body politic, but that a secondary intent can also be discerned: trolling the liberals. "The memes' creators and sharers can giddily watch the president dispatching his enemies while claiming the video is just a funny gag. When confronted, they can throw hands up in the air and cry, 'Snowflake!' In their version of reality, the uproar over this video is more proof that overly sensitive liberals are 'triggered.' Indeed, MAGAland began relentlessly mocking the *Times* report on the video within minutes of its publishing. '23 paragraphs, about a meme lol. Yikes this is psychotic,' someone wrote on Twitter. 'These types of articles is [sic] why the meme was made,' another replied."[40] Multiple levels of intent, then, are easily discerned: "use what are known as 'spicy memes' to fire up the president's base online, stir outrage among his opponents and provoke coverage by the mainstream media."[41]

Logan Cook claimed yet another intent for the meme, saying that "the video showing Mr. Trump shooting, stabbing and punching his foes was 'clearly satirical.'" Cook maintains a website, MemeWorld, a centralized meme repository that "acts as a clearinghouse for offensive memes and videos, allowing users to post homemade videos that often depict Mr.

Trump as a crusader or superhero who uses violence to suppress news outlets, individual journalists and political opponents."[42] The charge of being offensive coupled with the claim of being satirical evokes *Charlie Hebdo* and its reputation as a satiric magazine that often provokes the indictment of its being tasteless and offensive. Suppose, however, one takes seriously Cook's claim of an intent to be satiric. What would be the comic butts of the satire and what public sphere values does the ridicule then implicitly advocate?

The answer could begin by noting that the violence takes place in "The Church of Fake News," implying that the mainstream media operates like a cult in its reporting, marching in the lockstep of a religious fanaticism that constantly denounces Trump. The video, then, satirizes perceived failings of corporate media. The exaggerated violence of the video could also be understood as more satiric ridicule of the media if it is read as a parody of a meme casting Trump supporters as stereotypically violence-prone deplorables. From this angle, the pleasure for some who watched the video would not simply be a question of trolling the liberal snowflakes but would also consist of mocking them via the satiric tactic of exaggeration: *You think we would behave this way so this video mimics and mocks that belief with what clearly counts as an over-the-top fantasy*. Tasteless, sure. Offensive, no doubt. Satire, *Charlie Hebdo* style?

Yet, if one can make a case for Cook's claim, a counterreading is readily available: the video parodies Trump supporters and the rhetoric of violence that Trump spreads against the news media, thus redirecting the mocking from the media to those supporters and Trump. This reading acknowledges the exaggeration, but rather than restricting the public sphere context for that exaggeration to the media's ostensibly biased coverage of Trump and his supporters, the new context starts with another video Trump tweeted in July 2017, similar in style, "in which he is shown at a wrestling match body slamming CNN's logo and beating it up. The president was roundly criticized for encouraging violence against journalists by posting that clip, but his supporters enjoyed it, and helped make the tweet viral."[43] In this second reading, the fantasy of satiric violence in the Church of Fake News fails to comically dispel and overlook the president's public sphere rhetoric of violence.

Turning the parodic mocking both for and against Trump's supporters demonstrates Gilmore's point that satire appears in the eye of the beholder, an operation of reading rather than an internal feature of a text, but it also underlines how context matters for any reading. The paradox of satire being at once serious and nonserious means that public sphere context must always be involved in interpreting satiric intent. In addition, that paradox implies that the symbolic violence of satire's comic public sphere will always be entangled with the violence rhetorical and actual that occurs in the public sphere.

One might therefore simply laugh at the crazy fantasy of the massacre in the video and be done. One might instead laugh at the fantasy and understand it as a mocking commentary on a media stereotype that cuts two ways, satire either ridiculing the media or ridiculing those who would laugh at the video. Either way, a counterpublic laughs and so becomes visible to itself and decides to act on its sense of community either by disseminating the video or condemning its dissemination.

However, once the public sphere context predominates in a reading, satire as comic political speech evaporates, or rather, gives way to the political speech of the public sphere. "While the president and those in his orbit are distancing themselves from the video, it's impossible not to draw lines between Trump's rhetoric and things like this, and it's not so surprising that a video like this would exist—and be shown at a pro-Trump conference. Media bashing is a feature of Trump's presidency, not a bug."[44] Noting the similarity in comic style between the Church of Fake News fantasy and the WWE fantasy Trump retweeted only begins the process of moving away from the comic public sphere because Trump has on multiple public occasions incited violence against the media, referring to them as "enemies of the people." That phrase adds a historical context with its echoes of totalitarianism, *enemies of the people* having been used by the Nazis and Mao and being particularly associated with Joseph Stalin.[45] Indeed, Trump has even hinted that his supporters would react violently to his losing his reelection bid, invoking a specter of civil war street violence that some supporters have repeated.[46]

Moreover, the fuller public sphere context deepens this gulf between the symbolic violence of satire and the rhetorical violence of political speech when actual violence in the name of an ideology ensues, as was the case with a shooting in El Paso in August 2019. The same process is on display in the attempted murder via pipe bombs in the mail of media staff and political figures in October 2018, exactly the targets in the Church of Fake News video, what Trump has called an "unholy alliance of corrupt Democrat politicians, deep-state bureaucrats and the fake news media."[47] In both cases, the perpetrators explicitly referenced Trump's violent rhetoric.[48] Once arrived at this thick-description public sphere context, one cannot plausibly maintain that the video rates as satire or simply enjoy its so-called entertaining fantasy.

The example of the Church of Fake News video demonstrates the problem of audience uptake, but also the way in which reading an instance of purported satire involves more than authorial intent and comic targets; it shows how public sphere context can negate a claim to be satire by insisting that a text operates as political speech, not as comic political speech. Migrating memes as deliberate anti-public sphere nastiness seem to be particularly difficult cultural artifacts to interpret because often they claim their hate speech as satire's comic political speech, the just joking defense.

Viveca Greene addresses this topic by suggesting that when examining memes, one should elide authorial intent and audience reception in favor of context. The example of the Church of Fake News video shows how each of those foci for interpretation can change an evaluation of purported satire. In a response to Greene's argument, Dale Tracy asks if the focus on context to interpret memes and tweets will fail to completely discount intention and reception, even if interpreting satire might require "movement away from individuals and into subject positions . . . [so that satire must] involve identity categories more than it does individuals . . . [and] operate more clearly at the level of power relations than do other texts."[49] Greene's essay and Tracy's response suggest that much more work remains to understand this internet segment of comic artifacts and the perennial topics for satire it highlights: its audience uptake, authorial intention, and symbolic violence.

The felt need for a satiric supplement to the public sphere that has powered the recent efflorescence of satire has arisen, in part, because twenty-first-century journalism has become vitiated by corporate insistence on entertainment and profit such that it apparently cannot adequately report the problems inherent to the digital public sphere. In the postmodern environment of discursive integration, that inadequacy has given rise to the idea of satiric journalism.[50] *Satire as the Comic Public Sphere* acknowledges that development by examining locutionary forms of satire—that is, news reporting that veers toward a low level of satire in its employment of comic insult. News for corporate profit and mass entertainment—as commodity—indicates the ascendency of popular culture within the public sphere. As one of the most profitable products in popular culture today, satire necessarily takes its place within the debate and discussion of the public sphere to manifest the comic public sphere. Thus something like a postmodern comic *parrhēsia* (commodity as truth-telling vehicle) can happen in the pop culture arena of mock news.[51]

The public tolerates the comic schizophrenia of satire—its use of insult and ridicule to further communicative rationality—because some faith in its truth-telling capability remains. However, comic *parrhēsia* in a postmodern and late-capitalist environment does not often evoke a Juvenal or a Lenny Bruce. The pop satirists of today cannot strictly be said to evoke the idealism in the Greek concept of *parrhēsia*, revived as a topic by Michel Foucault, with its notion that speaking out entails the risk of personal danger, except for the possible and obvious example of the editors of *Charlie Hebdo*.[52] No such thing as a television satirist fitting the definition of being truly fearless and without any constraint exists. Nor can television satirists be organic intellectuals: they are creatures of the media ecosystem, not organic in the sense of grassroots. *Organic* these days seems instead mostly to emanate from the dark corners of the web: the vitriol of (anti-)social media or 4chan and 8chan or the memes of the alt-right to be found in Alan Kirby's digimodernism frame and Viveca Greene's analysis. No doubt the same could be said for any extreme positions on either side of the political spectrum. Such examples of fearless speech via ridicule only sound fearless in the sense of being unreflective and thus constitutive of the anti-public sphere. Moreover, what would establish the credentials of such unconstrained speakers as intellectuals? Expressions of the political id, the speech of such individuals registers as anything but intellectual.

The rants of the anti-public sphere and the dark, unrestrained speech to be found on the web and in so-called social media formats implicitly argue for a need of some restraint. The ideal of free speech does not mean that anything can be said in all contexts. Rather than lamenting the censorship and Nielsen ratings hedging even the more incisive comic *parrhēsia* on television today, those conditions should remind everyone of the basic process of the public sphere (and thus the comic public sphere): debate and discussion. The problematic of free speech to one side, the Foucauldian *parrhēsiastes* represents an ideal, like Habermas's public sphere and its communicative rationality. However, if the risk is not the same, truth telling still happens. Satire delivered by television (or in print or digitally) remains a valuable commercial property yet has the potential to be anti-capitalistic.[53] Postmodern truth tellers exist—that is, satirists enabled by corporate media and making lots of money, at least those on national television, yet mocking the news media—but rarely corporate entities. They operate in punning fashion, as two things at once: truth tellers and employees. That contradiction may be the meaning of claiming a comic form of *parrhēsia* within a postmodern aesthetic. The pop satirists in the

United States today are not so much subversive rebels (they operate within a capitalist system) as comic trouble makers. Like all satirists, they are provocateurs, troubling the public's consciousness in that they have the potential of a–musing the masses.

Parrhēsia happening in the postmodern marketplace often employs a reverse discourse process. The satiric monologues of Kimmel and Colbert and Oliver and Bee, for example, arrest and reverse the sign machine of hyperreality as the ultimate pop culture engine: their very pop culture nature, their being embedded in the economics of broadcast television, cablecast, or streaming services, enable them as twenty-first century comic *parrhēsiastes*. Their apparently compromised positions give them a purchase in the cultural and therefore political discourse. Moreover, their circulation within broadcast and cablecast and narrowcast digital technologies gives them an advantage over satirists in print. That would be the glass half full. The more cynical, glass half-empty version would note that the masses consume all television satire via media conglomerates and then insist that consumerism wins out even over political ideology. Is media *parrhēsia* no comic *parrhēsia* at all? *Satire as the Comic Public Sphere: Postmodern "Truthiness" and Civic Engagement* suggests that the answer to that question is *No!*—in thunder. The discourse satiric and otherwise that surrounded impeachment proceedings in the House and the trial in the Senate as well as the 2020 presidential campaign all suggest that the need for the comic parrhēsia of truthiness satire will not soon abate, even as that set of historically specific circumstances gives way to another.

Notes

INTRODUCTION

1. Julia Manchester, "Woman Arrested for Laughing in Sessions Hearing Heading Back to Trial," *Hill*, September 1, 2017, http://thehill.com/blogs/blog-briefing-room/news/348857-woman-arrested-for-laughing-in-sessions-hearing-heading-back-to; Laurel Wamsley, "DOJ Drops Case Against Woman Who Laughed During Sessions Hearing," NPR, November 8, 2017, https://www.npr.org/sections/thetwo-way/2017/11/08/562823691/charges-dropped-against-woman-who-laughed-during-sessions-hearing; David Emery, "Was a Woman Prosecuted for Laughing During Jeff Sessions' Confirmation Hearing?," Snopes, updated November 8, 2017, originally published May 3, 2017, https://www.snopes.com/fact-check/woman-prosecuted-laughing-sessions.

2. Mark Twain, *The Mysterious Stranger Manuscripts*, ed. and introduction by William M. Gibson (Berkeley: University of California Press, [1969] 2005), 166. For a look at joking in repressive regimes, see Elliott Oring, *Joking Asides: The Theory, Analysis, and Aesthetics of Humor* (Boulder: University Press of Colorado, 2016), chapter 7; see also John Otis, "It's No Joke: Venezuela Cracks Down on Comedians," NPR, May 5, 2015, https://www.npr.org/sections/parallels/2015/05/05/404443837.

3. David Atkins, "Trump Wants 'Retribution' Against Comedy Shows," *Washington Monthly*, February 17, 2019, https://washingtonmonthly.com/2019/02/17/trump-wants-retribution-against-comedy-shows; see also Geoff Herbert, "Alec Baldwin Ready to Make *SNL* History as Ratings Soar: 'Oh, It's a Big Deal,'" syracuse.com, February 9, 2017, https://www.syracuse.com/tv/2017/02/alec_baldwin_snl_ratings.html; Frank Pallotta, "Baldwin Gets *SNL* Its Biggest Ratings in Six Years, Outdraws Trump's Host Stint," CNN, February 12, 2017, http://money.cnn.com/2017/02/12/media/saturday-night-live-ratings-alec-baldwin-donald-trump/index.html; Stephen Battaglio, "*Saturday Night Live* Ratings Soar Thanks to Baldwin's Trump and McCarthy's Spicer," *Los Angeles Times*, February 14, 2017, http://www.latimes.com/business/hollywood/la-et-st-snl-ratings-up-20170214-story.html.

4. Jürgen Habermas, *The Structural Transformation of the Public Sphere: An Inquiry into a Category of Bourgeois Society*, trans. Thomas Burger (Cambridge: MIT Press, [1962] 1989).

5. Conway's "alternative facts": https://www.youtube.com/watch?v=VSrEEDQgFc8. Matthew Yglesias, "11 House Republicans Call for

Prosecutions of Clinton, Comey, Lynch, and Others," *Vox*, April 18, 2018, https://www.vox.com/policy-and-politics/2018/4/18/17252290.

6. Jean-François Lyotard, *The Postmodern Condition: A Report on Knowledge*, trans. Geoff Bennington and Brian Massumi (Minneapolis: University of Minnesota Press, 1984), 51.

7. "Our Dishonest President," *Los Angeles Times*, http://www.latimes.com/projects/la-ed-our-dishonest-president. For the dubious nature of the quote, see https://quoteinvestigator.com/2015/12/18/live.

8. Jean Baudrillard, *Simulacra and Simulation*, trans. Sheila Faria Glaser (Ann Arbor: University of Michigan Press, 1994), 6. See also Robert T. Tally Jr., "I Am the Mainstream Media (and So Can You!)," in *The Stewart/Colbert Effect: Essays on the Real Impacts of Fake News*, ed. Amarnath Amarasingam (McFarland: Jefferson, NC, 2011), 149–63.

9. Rachel Paine Caufield, "The Influence of 'Infoenterpropagainment': Exploring the Power of Political Satire as a Distinct Form of Political Humor," in *Laughing Matters: Humor and American Politics in the Media Age*, ed. Jody C. Baumgartner and Jonathan S. Morris (New York: Routledge, 2008), 3–20; Rob King, "Retheorizing Comedic and Political Discourse, or What Do Jon Stewart and Charlie Chaplin Have in Common?," *Discourse* 34, nos. 2–3 (2012): 263–89. See also Leonard Freedman, "Wit as a Political Weapon: Satirists and Censors," *Social Research* 79, no. 1 (2012): 87–112.

10. See Judith Yaross Lee, *Twain's Brand: Humor in Contemporary American Culture* (Jackson: University Press of Mississippi, 2012).

11. See Rebecca Krefting, *All Joking Aside: American Humor and Its Discontents* (Baltimore: Johns Hopkins University Press, 2014), and Linda Mizejewski, *Pretty/Funny: Women Comedians and Body Politics* (Austin: University of Texas Press, 2014). For international interest, see Geoffrey Baym and Jeffrey P. Jones, eds., *News Parody and Political Satire Across the Globe* (New York: Routledge, 2013); Marijke Meijer Drees and Sonja de Leeuw, eds., *The Power of Satire* (Amsterdam: John Benjamins, 2015); and Paul Alonso, *Satiric TV in the Americas: Critical Metatainment as Negotiated Dissent* (Oxford: Oxford University Press, 2018).

12. Geoffrey Baym, "Serious Comedy: Expanding the Boundaries of Political Discourse," in Baumgartner and Morris, *Laughing Matters*, 21–37, at 22, original emphasis. See also Baym's "*The Daily Show*: Discursive Integration and the Reinvention of Political Journalism," *Political Communication* 22, no. 3 (2005): 259–76, and his book, *From Cronkite to Colbert: The Evolution of Broadcast News* (Oxford: Oxford University Press, 2009), 18.

13. Though some scholars have referred to TV shows such as *The Daily Show with Jon Stewart* and *The Colbert Report* as "fake news" shows, following Stewart's own designation, I will employ "mock news" for them and similar cultural artifacts and reserve "fake news" for entities like the Drudge Report, Breitbart, and Infowars. This distinction emphasizes the parodic nature of *The Daily Show* and its ilk while pointing to the alternative-facts quality of Breitbart and its ilk. Amber Day uses the term "parodic news show"; see Day, *Satire and Dissent:*

Interventions in Contemporary Political Debate (Bloomington: Indiana University Press, 2011), 44.

14. The recent rise of mock news shows has a global reach, documented in Baym and Jones, *News Parody and Political Satire*.

15. Colbert coined the term *truthiness* in a segment called "The Wørd" during the pilot episode of *The Colbert Report* on October 17, 2005.

16. Jeffrey P. Jones, *Entertaining Politics: Satiric Television and Political Engagement*, 2nd ed. (Lanham, MD: Rowman and Littlefield, 2010); Baym, *From Cronkite to Colbert*, chapter 8; Day, *Satire and Dissent*, especially chapter 2.

17. Sophia A. McClennen and Remy M. Maisel, in *Is Satire Saving Our Nation? Mockery and American Politics* (New York: Palgrave Macmillan, 2014), offer the term "satiractivism." For their presentation of empirical data, see chapter 8; see also Jones, *Entertaining Politics*, chapter 2; Day, *Satire and Dissent*, 87–96.

18. Bruce Michelson unpacks the scholarship usually denoted by *humor studies* and contrasts it with *humor research*. See Michelson, "The Year's Work in American Humor Studies, 2013," *Studies in American Humor*, ser. 4, vol. 1, no. 1 (2015): 41–105, at 41–43. I use *humor studies* here as a shorthand distinction from *media studies*. My preference for an umbrella term to denote all scholarship about comic cultural artifacts is *The Comic*, which I introduce below.

19. Jones, *Entertaining Politics*, 65.

20. Baym, *From Cronkite to Colbert*, 20; Jones, *Entertaining Politics*, 190.

21. Day, *Satire and Dissent*, 12–13, 19.

22. See Allaina Kilby, "Provoking the Citizen," *Journalism Studies* 19, no. 13 (2018): 1934–44.

23. Jonathan Greenberg offers the idea that satire should be seen from two other conceptual angles besides as a mode applied to a broad range of culture: as a genre and as a practice. Satire from this last angle requires a context of expectation and interpretation, an understanding of its deeply embedded nature, its potential for intervention in a public arena, and its functioning as a specific kind of cultural capital. Jonathan Greenberg, *The Cambridge Introduction to Satire* (Cambridge: Cambridge University Press, 2019), 11.

24. Greenberg, *Cambridge Introduction to Satire*; John T. Gilmore, *Satire*, New Critical Idiom Series (London: Routledge, 2018).

25. David Denby, *Snark, A Polemic in Seven Fits* (New York: Simon and Schuster, 2009).

26. Quoted in Gilmore, *Satire*, 7–8.

27. Jonathan Swift, "A Vindication of Mr. Gay and *The Beggar's Opera*," *Intelligencer III*, in *The Prose Works of Jonathan Swift*, ed. Temple Scott (London: George Bell and Sons, 1902), 9:318, https://archive.org/details/proseworksjonatoojacogoog. This issue was published May 25, 1728.

28. Jürgen Habermas, "Modernity Versus Postmodernity," trans. Seyla Ben-Habib, *New German Critique*, no. 22 (1981): 3–14, at 9.

29. Richard J. Bernstein, *The New Constellation: The Ethical-Political Horizons of Modernity/ Postmodernity* (Cambridge: MIT Press, 1991).

30. Greenberg, *Cambridge Introduction to Satire*, 160.

31. For example, President Trump questioning the World Health Organization's estimate of deaths from the coronavirus, based on his "hunch": "Exclusive: President Trump Addresses Coronavirus Concerns on 'Hannity,'" Fox News, March 5, 2020, https://video.foxnews.com/v/6138542348001; see also Stephen Collinson, "Backlash over White House Virus Response Builds," CNN, March 6, 2020, https://www.cnn.com/2020/03/06/politics/coronavirus-mike-pence-donald-trump-politics-congress/index.html.

32. J. L. Austin, *How to Do Things with Words* (Cambridge: Harvard University Press, 1962).

33. The concept of satiractivism should be compared to Krefting's formulation for charged humor: always ready "to incite social change, develop community, and lobby for civil rights and acknowledgment" (*All Joking Aside*, 25), and Alonso's term, "critical metatainment" (*Satiric TV in the Americas*, 15). Day explores the "much finer line between news and entertainment, satire and political argument" (*Satire and Dissent*, 43) that some satiric examples exhibit. I am concerned with professional examples of satiractivism, not the average citizen's efforts implied in Alan Kirby's concept of digimodernism. See *Digimodernism: How New Technologies Dismantle the Postmodern and Reconfigure Our Culture* (London: Continuum, 2009).

34. Stephen Halliwell, *Greek Laughter: A Study of Cultural Psychology from Homer to Early Christianity* (Cambridge: Cambridge University Press, 2008). See also Lydia Amir, "Taking the History of Philosophy on Humor and Laughter Seriously," *Israeli Journal of Humor Research* no. 5 (2014): 43–87.

35. Quoted in Jones, *Entertaining Politics*, 68.

36. Jones, *Entertaining Politics*, 70, 81 (emphasis added); Baym, *From Cronkite to Colbert*, 125.

37. Jeffrey P. Jones, Geoffrey Baym, and Amber Day, "Mr. Stewart and Mr. Colbert Go to Washington: Television Satirists Outside the Box," *Social Research* 79, no. 1 (2012): 33–60, at 35, even though the second half of their title says, "Television Satirists."

CHAPTER 1

1. Sarah Bishop, "'I'm Only Going to Do It If I Can Do It in Character': Unpacking Comedy and Advocacy in Stephen Colbert's 2010 Congressional Testimony," *Journal of Popular Culture* 48, no. 3 (2015): 548–57, at 556.

2. I follow Henri Bergson's 1899 treatise, *Laughter: Essay on the Significance of the Comic (Le Rire: Essai sur la signification du comique)*; and Umberto Eco, "The Comic and the Rule," in *Travels in Hyperreality*, trans. William Weaver (San Diego: Harcourt & Brace, 1986), 269–78.

3. The Western tradition underpins my reading of comic artifacts, but theory from sources outside that tradition should always be understood as part of the discourse of The Comic as well. On the last point about human nature, see my article, "From Ethology to Aesthetics: Evolution as a Theoretical Paradigm in Research on Laughter, Humor, and other Comic Phenomena," *Humor: International Journal of Humor Research* 15, no. 3 (2002): 245–81.

4. Eco, "Comic and the Rule," 272.

5. Michael Coffey, *Roman Satire* (London: Methuen, 1976), 3–18; Daniel M. Hooley, *Roman Satire* (Malden, MA: Blackwell, 2007), 1–11; Gay Sibley, "*Satura* from Quintilian to Joe Bob Briggs: A New Look at an Old Word," in *Theorizing Satire: Essays in Literary Criticism*, ed. Brian A. Connery and Kirk Combe (New York: St. Martin's Press, 1995), 57–72; Gilmore, *Satire*, chapter 3; Greenberg, *Cambridge Introduction to Satire*, chapter 3.

6. Conal Condren makes this point in "Satire and Definition," *Humor: International Journal of Humor Research* 25, no. 4 (2012): 375–99. See also the introduction, Drees and de Leeuw, *Power of Satire*, 1–15.

7. See, for example, Jonathan Rossing, "An Ethics of Complicit Criticism for Postmodern Satire," *Studies in American Humor*, ser. 4, vol. 5, no. 1 (2019): 13–30.

8. See Michel Foucault, *History of Sexuality*, trans. Robert Hurley (New York: Pantheon Books, 1978): "Homosexuality began to speak in its own behalf, to demand that its legitimacy or 'naturality' be acknowledged, often in the same vocabulary, using the same categories by which it was medically disqualified" (101). See also Yasser Fouad Selim, "The Making of Identity in Arab American Stand-Up Comedy," in *Who Defines Me: Negotiating Identity in Language and Literature*, ed. Yasser Fouad Selim, Eid Mohamed, and Kevin Lacey (Newcastle upon Tyne: Cambridge Scholars, 2014), 19–31; Homi K. Bhabha, "Of Mimicry and Man: The Ambivalence of Colonial Discourse," in *The Location of Culture* (London: Routledge, 1994), 85–92; Nancy Walker, *A Very Serious Thing: Women's Humor and American Culture* (Minneapolis: University of Minnesota Press, 1988).

9. George A. Test, *Satire: Spirit and Art* (Tampa: University of South Florida Press, 1991).

10. Test, *Satire*, 15.

11. Plato, *Philebus*, in *Plato: Complete Works*, trans. Dorothea Frede, ed. with introduction and notes by John M. Cooper (Indianapolis: Hackett, 1997), 398–456. For the issue of an ethical ridicule, see Anthony Ashley Cooper, Third Earl of Shaftesbury, "*Sensus Communis*: An Essay on the Freedom of Wit and Humor," in *Characteristics of Men, Manners, Opinions, Times*, ed. Lawrence E. Klein (Cambridge: Cambridge University Press, [1709] 2000), 29–69. See also Jure Gantar, *The Pleasure of Fools: Essays in the Ethics of Laughter* (Montreal: McGill-Queen's University Press, 2005); Brian Bergen-Aurand, ed., *Comedy Begins with Our Simplest Gestures: Levinas, Ethics, and Humor* (Pittsburgh: Duquesne University Press, 2017).

12. Roger Caillois, *Man, Play, and Games*, trans. Meyer Barash (New York: Schocken Books, [1958] 1979).

13. Contemporary examples of the always punch up claim: Alison Dagnes, *A Conservative Walks into a Bar: The Politics of Political Humor* (New York: Palgrave Macmillan, 2012); CM, "In the Wake of *Charlie Hebdo*, Free Speech Does Not Mean Freedom from Criticism," *Hooded Utilitarian*, January 7, 2015, http://www.hoodedutilitarian.com/2015/01/in-the-wake-of-charlie-hebdo-free-speech-does-not-mean-freedom-from-criticism/; Saree Makdisi, "How 'Je Suis Charlie' Makes Matters Worse," *Los Angeles Times*, January 16, 2015, https://www.latimes.com/opinion/op-ed/la-oe-0118-makdisi-je-suis-charlie

-makes-things-worse-20150118-story.html; and Garry Trudeau, "The Abuse of Satire," *Atlantic*, April 11, 2015; http://www.theatlantic.com/international/archive/2015/04/the-abuse-of-satire/390312. Theodor Adorno claims satire was the realm of the powerful until Voltaire in "Juvenal's Error," *Minima Moralia: Reflections from a Damaged Life*, trans. E. F. N. Jephcott (London: NLB, [1951] 1974), 209–12, at 210. Both John Gilmore, *Satire*, and Jonathan Greenberg, *Cambridge Introduction to Satire*, stress the conservative side of satire before the Enlightenment. Paul Michael Johnson's distinction between *satire* and *schadenfreude* is useful in this context: "Don Quixote, Charlie Hebdo, and the Politics of Laughter: From Satire to Schadenfreude," *Dissident Voice* no. 29 (2015): http://dissidentvoice.org/2015/04/don-quixote-charlie-hebdo-and-the-politics-of-laughter. For a recent example of status quo power doing the punching, see James Nixon, "'You Think I'm joking': Examining the Weaponized Comedy of President Obama's Stand-Up Addresses at the White House Correspondents' Association Dinner," *Studies in American Humor* ser. 4, vol. 5, no. 1 (2019): 103–23.

14. Robert C. Elliott, *The Power of Satire: Magic, Ritual, Art* (Princeton: Princeton University Press, 1960); see also Jerome Neu, "Insult Humor," in *Sticks and Stones: The Philosophy of Insults* (Oxford: Oxford University Press, 2008), 215–41.

15. For Aristophanes, see Kenneth Reckford, *Aristophanes' Old and New Comedy* (Chapel Hill: University of North Carolina Press, 1987). For ritual clowns, see Kimberly A. Christen, ed., *Clowns and Tricksters: An Encyclopedia of Tradition and Culture* (Denver: ABC-Clio, 1998); Vilsoni Hereniko, *Woven Gods: Female Clowns and Power in Rotuma* (Honolulu: University of Hawai'i Press, 1995); Louis A. Hieb, "Meaning and Mismeaning: Toward an Understanding of the Ritual Clown," in *New Perspectives on the Pueblos*, ed. Alfonso Ortiz (Albuquerque: University of New Mexico Press, 1972), 163–95; and William E. Mitchell, ed., *Clowning as Critical Practice: Performance Humor in the South Pacific* (Pittsburgh: University of Pittsburgh Press, 1992).

16. I have argued for Charlie Chaplin as a modern version of a ritual clown and suggested that Sam Clemens as Mark Twain at times functions as another version, the Citizen Clown. See James E. Caron, "Silent Slapstick Film as Ritualized Clowning: The Example of Charlie Chaplin," *Studies in American Humor* ser. 3, no. 14 (2006): 5–22; "The Satirist Who Clowns: Mark Twain's Performance at the Whittier Birthday Celebration," *Texas Studies in Literature and Language* 53, no. 4 (2010): 433–66; James E. Caron, *Mark Twain, Unsanctified Newspaper Reporter* (Columbia: University of Missouri Press, 2008).

17. Dustin Griffin, *Satire: A Critical Reintroduction* (Lexington: University Press of Kentucky, 1994), 39. Griffin links this idea to Bakhtin's analysis of Menippean satire: it tests truths rather than embodies them.

18. Day, *Satire and Dissent*, 99, 108.

19. The phrase "rail agreeably" is from *Tatler #242*, in Joseph Addison and Richard Steele, *The Tatler*, ed. with introduction and notes by George A. Aitken, 4 vols., 1898, facsimile reprint (Hildesheim: Georg Olms Verlag, 1970), 4:234–38, at 436. See also Joseph Addison's dictates on the temperament of

s/he who would rail agreeably: *Spectator #23* (1:97–100), and *Spectator #35* (1:145–48), in Joseph Addison and Richard Steele, *The Spectator*, ed., introduction, and notes by Donald F. Bond, 5 vols. (Oxford: Clarendon Press, 1965). The figure of the satirist for this sort of satire I have elsewhere called "the gentleman humorist." See James E. Caron, "Comic *Belles Lettres* and a Literary History of the American Comic Tradition," *Studies in American Humor* ser. 3, no. 29 (2014): 13–34; and "Comic Laughter in *The Blithedale Romance*: Miles Coverdale and the Idea of the Gentleman Humorist," *Nathaniel Hawthorne Review* 39, no. 2 (2013): 4–35.

20. Keegan-Michael Key and Jordan Peele, "I Said Bitch," *Key and Peele*, season 1, episode 1, January 31, 2012, https://www.youtube.com/watch?v=5LGEiILL1__s.

21. See Derek C. Maus and James J. Donahue, eds., *Post-Soul Satire: Black Identity After Civil Rights* (Jackson: University Press of Mississippi, 2014).

22. Laughter from tickling or pathological laughter falls into categories other than comic laughter.

23. An experimental design study makes the point. See Alison O'Connor, "The Effects of Satire: Exploring Its Impact on Political Candidate Evaluation," in *Satire and Politics: The Interplay of Heritage and Practice*, ed. Jessica Milner Davis (London: Palgrave Macmillan, 2017), 193–225.

24. James W. Carey, *Communication as Culture: Essays on Media and Society*, rev. ed. (London: Routledge, 2009).

25. See Jerry Palmer, "The Limits of Humor," in *Taking Humour Seriously* (London: Routledge, 1994), 147–74. In Freud's model, that evaluation is about pleasure derived from an instance of *witz*, which has an aesthetic structure. Sigmund Freud, *Jokes and Their Relation to the Unconscious*, trans. James Strachey (New York: Norton, [1905] 1960), 95, 135, 143–45.

26. Frances McDonald argues for the complicated nature of "laughter without humor" in "'Ha-Ha and Again Ha-Ha': Laughter, Affect, and Emotion in Nathanael West's *The Day of the Locust*," *American Literature* 88, no. 3 (2016): 541–68, at 542. Steven Weisenburger, in *Fables of Subversion: Satire and the American Novel, 1930–1980* (Athens: University of Georgia Press, 1995), argues for West being a precursor to recognized postmodernists like Pynchon. Peter Schmidt suggests a family of similar texts appearing since the 1960s, what he characterizes as a harsh form of Menippean satire, generating "interpretive and formal instability, brokenness, and ambiguity . . . with no 'safe space' available." See Peter Schmidt, "Menippean Satire in the Digital Era: Gary Shteyngart's *Super Sad True Love Story*, in *Teaching Modern British and American Satire*, ed. Evan R. Davis and Nicholas D. Nace (New York: MLA, 2019), 277–85, at 278.

27. Michael Billig, *Laughter and Ridicule: Towards a Social Critique of Humour* (London: Sage, 2005).

28. For efforts to understand audiences, see Moira Smith, "Humor, Unlaughter, and Boundary Maintenance," *Journal of American Folklore* 122, no. 484 (2009): 148–71; Toshiaki Furukawa, "Localizing Humor Through Parodying White Voice in Hawai'i Stand-Up Comedy," *Text&Talk* 35, no. 6 (2015): 845–69; Jane Fife, "Peeling *The Onion*: Satire and the Complexity of Audience Response," *Rhetoric Review* 35, no. 4 (2016): 322–34; Zohra Fatima,

"Humor, Satire and Verbal Parody in *The Hitchhiker's Guide to the Galaxy*: A Relevance Theoretic Approach," *NUML Journal of Critical Inquiry* 14, no. 2 (2016): 38–53. For two examples of MRI research, see Dean Mobbs et al., "Humor Modulates the Mesolimbic Reward Centers," *Neuron* 40, no. 5 (2003): 1041–48; Angela Bartolo et al., "Humor Comprehension and Appreciation: An fMRI Study," *Journal of Cognitive Neuroscience* 18, no. 11 (2006): 1789–98.

29. Michael M. Grynbaum, "Michelle Wolf Sets Off a Furor at White House Correspondents' Dinner," *New York Times*, April 29, 2018, https://www.nytimes.com/2018/04/29/business/media/michelle-wolfs-routine-sets-off-a-furor-at-an-annual-washington-dinner.html; Patrick J. Buchanan, "White House Correspondents' Dinner in the Gutter," *American Conservative*, May 1, 2018, http://www.theamericanconservative.com/buchanan/white-house-correspondents-dinner-in-the-gutter; Common Dreams staff, "Comedian Michelle Wolf Delivers 'Scathing' Roast of Trump and His Cronies at Correspondents' Dinner," *Common Dreams*, April 29, 2018: https://www.commondreams.org/news/2018/04/29/comedian-michelle-wolf-delivers-scathing-roast-trump-and-his-cronies-correspondents.

30. Iser alludes to the "minimal hypothesis" of anthropologist Eric Gans when explaining his idea: the originary scene is "a blank . . . an energizing source, which can never be filled." Richard Van Oort, "The Use of Fiction in Literary and Generative Anthropology: An Interview with Wolfgang Iser," *Anthropoetics: The Journal of Generative Anthropology* 3, no. 2 (1997/98): 1–10, at 5, http://www.anthropoetics.ucla.edu/ap0302/Iser_int.htm.

31. Georges Bataille, "Un-Knowing: Laughter and Tears," trans. Annette Michelson, *October* no. 36 (1986): 89–102, at 90, original emphasis; see also Lisa Trahair, "The Comedy of Philosophy: Bataille, Hegel, and Derrida," *Angelaki: Journal of the Theoretical Humanities* 6, no. 3 (2001): 155–69.

32. John Morreall, "Comic Vices and Comic Virtues," *Humor: International Journal of Humor Research* 23, no. 1 (2010): 1–26. The claim for a fundamental unruliness has support from Anca Parvulescu, "The Civilizing of Laughter," in *Laughter: Notes on a Passion* (Cambridge: MIT Press, 2010), 23–58, and Robert Bernard Martin, "The Dangers of Laughter," in *The Triumph of Wit: A Study of Victorian Comic Theory* (Oxford: Clarendon Press, 1974), 1–16. For a claim of laughter's inherent "positivity," see James Nikopoulos, "The Stability of Laughter," *Humor: International Journal of Humor Research* 30, no. 1 (2017): 1–21.

33. Remy Tumin, "Stephen Colbert Uses Profanity to Describe President Trump's 'Soul,'" *New York Times*, October 5, 2017, https://www.nytimes.com/2017/10/05/arts/television/stephen-colbert-trump-michael-moore.html.

34. Quoted in Richard Bernstein, "The Rage Against Reason," in *The New Constellation: The Ethical-Political Horizons of Modernity/Postmodernity* (Cambridge: MIT Press, 1991), 31–56, at 55n35.

35. Aaron Sankin, "The 'Ire' in 'Satire,'" *San Francisco Bay Guardian* 41, no. 23 (March 7, 2007), http://sfbgarchive.48hills.org/sfbgarchive/2007/03/07/ire-satire. Carson S. Kay traces a

tradition of right-wing satire in print and in particular on radio, while arguing it has failed on television: "More Like Jon: Humor Technique, Medium, and Ideology in Televised Satire of the Post-Stewart Era," unpublished paper.

36. See "Colbert's Super Pac: Ham Rove's Secrets," *The Colbert Report*, season 7, episode 124, September 29, 2011, http://www.cc.com/video-clips/ivvzeu/the-colbert-report-colbert-super-pac-ham-rove-s-secrets.

37. Quoted in Bernstein, "Rage Against Reason," 46.

CHAPTER 2

1. Stephen Eric Bronner, in *Reclaiming the Enlightenment: Toward a Politics of Radical Engagement*, Ebook (New York: Columbia University Press, 2004), argues for the contemporary relevance of the Enlightenment values that underpin the concept of the public sphere.

2. Jürgen Habermas, "The Public Sphere," *New German Critique* no. 3 (1974): 49–55, at 49; quoted in Geoff Eley, "Nations, Publics, and Political Cultures: Placing Habermas in the Nineteenth Century," in *Habermas and the Public Sphere*, ed. Craig Calhoun (Cambridge: MIT Press, 1992), 289–339, at 289.

3. Andreas Gestrich, "The Public Sphere and the Habermas Debate," *German History* 24, no. 3 (2006): 413–30, at 415.

4. James Van Horn Melton, *The Rise of the Public in Enlightenment Europe* (Cambridge: Cambridge University Press, 2001), 4.

5. Micheline Frenette and Marie-France Vermette, "Young Adults and the Digital Public Sphere: A Cross-Cultural Perspective," *Comunicação e Sociedade* 23 (2013): 36–55, at 46.

6. Axel Bruns, "Life Beyond the Public Sphere: Towards a Networked Model for Political Engagement," *Information Polity* 13, no. 1–2 (2008): 65–79. In effect, digital platforms enhance the argument in Michael Warner, *Publics and Counterpublics* (New York: Zone Books, 2005). See also John Michael Roberts, *New Media and Public Activism: Neoliberalism, the State, and Radical Protest in the Public Sphere* (Bristol, UK: Policy Press, 2014).

7. Frenette and Vermette, "Young Adults and the Digital Public Sphere," 39.

8. Baym, *From Cronkite to Colbert*.

9. Jean-François Lyotard, "Re-Writing Modernity," *SubStance* 16, no. 3 (1987): 3–9, at 9.

10. Kirby, *Digimodernism*, 101.

11. Ibid., 51.

12. "Everyone in China Is Getting a 'Social Credit Score,'" *The Late Show with Stephen Colbert*, May 7, 2018 (#536), CBS, https://www.cbs.com/shows/the-late-show-with-stephen-colbert/video/4RPSPANR2VYKF6ijYSMPDphMqUFWy2uK/everyone-in-china-is-getting-a-social-credit-score-. #Flashmob activism is notable in the case of Justine Saccho, not satire but malicious glee: Ali Vingiano, "This Is How a Woman's Offensive Tweet Became the World's Top Story," *BuzzFeed*, December 21, 2013, https://www.buzzfeed.com/alisonvingiano/this-is-how-a-womans-offensive-tweet-became-the-worlds-top-s. See also Jon Ronson, "How One Stupid Tweet Blew Up Justine Sacco's Life," *New York Times Magazine*, February 12, 2015, https://www.nytimes.com/2015/02/15/magazine/how-one-stupid-tweet-ruined-justine

-saccos-life.html; and Ronson's book, *So You've Been Publicly Shamed* (New York: Riverhead Books, 2015).

13. Bronner, *Reclaiming the Enlightenment*, 66, 15.

14. Gilbert Highet, *Anatomy of Satire*, 235, quoted in Greenberg, *Cambridge Introduction to Satire*, 63.

15. Gilmore, *Satire*, 47, 61–63.

16. Greenberg, *Cambridge Introduction to Satire*, 104; Vic Gatrell, *The City of Laughter: Sex and Satire in Eighteenth-Century London* (New York: Walker, 2006), 171.

17. Gilmore, *Satire*, 71.

18. Greenberg, *Cambridge Introduction to Satire*, 13, 104.

19. Quoted in ibid., 13.

20. Ibid., 106.

21. Ibid., 17.

22. Ibid., 106.

23. Ibid.

24. Mark Rolfe, "The Populist Elements of Australian Political Satire and the Debt to the Americans and Augustans," in *Satire and Politics: The Interplay of Heritage and Practice*, ed. Jessica Milner Davis (London: Palgrave Macmillan, 2017), 37–71, at 38.

25. Layne Neeper, "'To Soften the Heart': George Saunders, Postmodern Satire, and Empathy," *Studies in American Humor* ser. 4, vol. 2, no. 2 (2016): 280–99, at 281.

26. Adorno, "Juvenal's Error," 210. See also Northrop Frye in "The Nature of Satire": a satirist could "not speak for the twentieth century" because the mode itself had "gone stale and moldy," quoted in Weisenburger, *Fables of Subversion*, 9; and Ihab Hassan, "Laughter in the Dark: The New Voice in American Fiction," *American Scholar* 33, no. 4 (1964): 636–38, 640, at 637.

27. Melton, *Rise of the Public in Enlightenment Europe*, 8.

28. Immanuel Kant, "Answer to the Question: What is Enlightenment?," trans. Thomas K. Abbott, in *Basic Writings of Kant*, ed. and introduced by Allen W. Wood (New York: Modern Library, [1784] 2001), 135–41, at 135. Subsequent references will appear in the text. For a good account of Enlightenment thinking, particularly for its battle against what Foucault calls "countermodernity," see Bronner, *Reclaiming the Enlightenment*.

29. Michel Foucault, "What is Enlightenment?," trans. Catherine Porter, in *The Foucault Reader*, ed. Peter Rabinow (New York: Pantheon Books, 1984), 32–50, at 32, 35. Subsequent references will appear in the text. See also Habermas's remarks in "Modernity Versus Postmodernity."

30. Lyotard, *Postmodern Condition*, xxiv.

31. Habermas, "Modernity Versus Postmodernity," 9.

32. Lyotard, "Re-Writing Modernity," 4. Subsequent references will appear in the text.

33. Habermas, "Modernity Versus Postmodernity," 7. See also "'Post'-ing Modernity," John Paul Jones III, Wolfgang Natter, and Theodore R. Schatzki, in *Postmodern Contentions: Epochs, Politics, Space*, ed. John Paul Jones III, Wolfgang Natter, and Theodore R. Schatzki (New York: Guilford Press, 1993), 1–15, who understand "enlightenment thought [as] the most significant context within which contemporary thought operates" (10); and Edward W. Soja, "Postmodern Geographies and the Critique of Historicism," in Jones, Natter, and Schatzki, *Postmodern Contentions*, 113–36.

34. Lyotard, *Postmodern Condition*, 65–66, 73, 79. Thomas Docherty quotes Michel Serres, who offers the automobile as a concrete example of such simultaneity because the ensemble of its various technical achievements can be dated either recently, at the start of the twentieth century, or, in the case of the wheel, the neolithic age. Thomas Docherty, "Just Events," in *Postmodern Times: A Critical Guide to the Contemporary*, ed. Thomas Carmichael and Alison Lee (DeKalb: Northern Illinois University Press, 2000), 53–66, at 60.

35. Richard J. Bernstein and the editors, "Postmodernism, Dialogue, and Democracy: Questions to Richard J. Bernstein," in Jones, Natter, and Schatzki, *Postmodern Contentions*, 99–112, at 100. See also Bernstein, "An Allegory of Modernity/Postmodernity: Habermas and Derrida," in *New Constellation*, 199–229. Kirby Olson reformulates Bernstein's metaphor of a constellation to describe the modern/postmodern relationship into the image of "a three-ring circus, or Circus Maximus, in which classical liberal, Marxist, and postmodern ideas are fighting with each other simultaneously," in *Comedy After Postmodernism: Rereading Comedy from Edward Lear to Charles Willeford* (Lubbock: Texas Tech University Press, 2001), 21. Other examples of this inextricable interrelatedness include the introduction to *Supplanting the Postmodern: An Anthology of Writings on the Arts and Culture of the Early 21st Century*, ed. David Rudrum and Nicholas Stavris (New York: Bloomsbury Academic, 2015), xi–xxix; Bronner, *Reclaiming the Enlightenment*; Mike Gane and Nicholas Gane, "The Postmodern: After the (Non) Event," in *Postmodernism: What Moment?*, ed. Pelagia Goulimari (Manchester: Manchester University Press, 2007), 127–38, at 136.

36. Linda Hutcheon, "Epilogue: The Postmodern . . . in Retrospect," in *The Politics of Postmodernism*, 2nd ed. (London: Routledge, 2002), 165–81, at 167.

37. The phrase "a politics of recognition" is quoted from Charles Taylor by Charles Jencks in Alison Lee, "Post-Modernism: A Whole Full of Holes, an Interview with Charles Jencks," in Carmichael and Lee, *Postmodern Times*, 245–63, at 249.

38. Lyotard, *Postmodern Condition*, 41.

39. Habermas, "Modernity Versus Postmodernity," 8.

40. See Carey, *Communication as Culture*, 55.

41. Ibid., 61.

42. Jacques Derrida, "Structure, Sign, and Play in the Discourse of the Human Sciences," in *The Structuralist Controversy: The Languages of Criticism and the Sciences of Man*, ed. Richard Macksey and Eugenio Donato (Baltimore: Johns Hopkins University Press, 1970), 247–72, at 271.

CHAPTER 3

1. Baym, *From Cronkite to Colbert*, 5. Subsequent references will appear in the text.

2. Quoted in Frenette and Vermette, "Young Adults and the Digital Public Sphere," 40.

3. Helena Sousa, Manuel Pinto, and Elsa Costa e Silva, "Digital Public Sphere: Weaknesses and Challenges," *Comunicação e Sociedade* 23 (2013): 9–12, at 9; Avery E. Holton and Seth C. Lewis, "Journalists, Social Media, and

the Use of Humor on Twitter," *Electronic Journal of Communication* 21, nos. 1–2 (2011), http://www.cios.org/EJCPUBLIC/021/1/021121.html.

4. Olson, *Comedy After Postmodernism*, 10.

5. John Hartley, "Silly Citizenship," *Critical Discourse Studies* 7, no. 4 (2010): 233–48, at 241.

6. For a specific example of how digital platforms can enable silly citizenship, see Emily Regan Wills and André Fecteau, "Humor and Identity on Twitter: #muslimcandyheartrejects as a Digital Space for Identity Construction," *Journal of Muslim Minority Affairs* 36, no. 1 (2016): 32–45.

7. Hartley, "Silly Citizenship," 236.

8. Baym, "*Daily Show*: Discursive Integration," 262.

9. Jeff St. Onge, "'Comedy Before Country': Engaged Levity and Absurdist Critique in *Mad* Magazine," *Studies in American Humor* ser. 3, no. 30 (2014): 155–67, at 160.

10. Kenneth Burke, *Attitudes Toward History*, 1937, 2nd ed. rev. (Los Altos, CA: Hermes, 1959), 39–44. For *communitas*, see Victor Turner, *The Ritual Process: Structure and Anti-Structure* (Ithaca: Cornell University Press, [1969] 1977).

11. Quoted in Bernstein and the editors, "Postmodernism, Dialogue, and Democracy," 111.

12. Kirby, *Digimodernism*, 54.

13. Northrop Frye provides this distinction between levels of values implied by a satiric butt in "The Nature of Satire," in *"The Educated Imagination" and Other Writings on Critical Theory, 1933–63*, ed. Germaine Warkentin, vol. 21 of *The Collected Works of Northrop Frye* (Toronto: University of Toronto Press, 2006), 39–57, at 44.

14. Aristotle, *Poetics*, in *Complete Works*, ed. Jonathan Barnes, 2 vols. (Princeton: Princeton University Press, 1984), 2:2316–40, at 2319.

15. Bruce Jay Friedman, ed., *Black Humor* (New York: Bantam, 1965); see also Drew Friedman, http://drewfriedman.blogspot.com/2011/05/black-humor.html. Friedman's book includes excerpts from American writers Thomas Pynchon, Joseph Heller, John Barth, and Terry Southern.

16. Olson, *Comedy After Postmodernism*, 4. See also Gillian Pye, "Comedy Theory and the Postmodern," *Humor: The International Journal for Humor Studies* 19, no. 1 (2006): 53–70; Susan Purdie, *Comedy: The Mastery of Discourse* (Toronto: University of Toronto Press, 1993); Jerry Aline Flieger, *The Purloined Punchline: Freud's Comic Theory and the Postmodern Text* (Baltimore: Johns Hopkins University Press, 1991).

17. Pye, "Comedy Theory and the Postmodern," 55, emphasis added.

18. Olson, *Comedy After Postmodernism*, 5. Thus "the comic" in these analyses signifies ideas about postmodern comic texts, while "The Comic" as my umbrella term signifies an encompassing discursive realm.

19. Weisenburger, *Fables of Subversion*. Subsequent references will appear in the text. See also Patrick O'Neill, *The Comedy of Entropy: Humour, Narrative, Reading* (Toronto: University of Toronto Press, 1990).

20. Roland Barthes, *The Empire of Signs*, trans. Richard Howard (New York: Hill and Wang, 1982), originally published in French in 1970.

21. James Agee and Walker Evans, *Let Us Now Praise Famous Men* (New York: Houghton Mifflin, [1941] 1988), 11.

22. Weisenburger, *Fables of Subversion*, 121; Olson, *Comedy After Postmodernism*, 5.

23. The relationship of black humor to satire is ambiguous, not just in Friedman's 1965 presentation of the term, but even in its original use by André Breton, who says black humor must eschew satire's didactic goals, but claims Jonathan Swift as "the first black humorist." See André Breton, *Anthologie de l'humour noir* (1940, revised 1950), ed. and and introduction by Mark Polizotti (London: Telegram, 2009), 29. Friedman conceptualizes black humorists having "to sail into darker waters somewhere out beyond satire" (x).

24. Bronner, *Reclaiming the Enlightenment*, 19, 51, passim.

25. Quoted in Lee, "Post-Modernism," 248–49. This overlap has been explored, for example, by Jack DeRochi in "'What Have You Learned': Considering a New Hermeneutic of Satire in *Family Guy*," *Studies in American Humor* ser. 3, no. 17 (2008): 35–48; by Kerry D. Soper in *Garry Trudeau: Doonesbury and the Aesthetics of Satire* (Jackson: University Press of Mississippi, 2008); and in Baym's idea of the neo-modern in *From Cronkite to Colbert*.

26. Baudrillard, *Simulacra and Simulation*, especially the first essay, "The Precession of Simulacra."

27. Benedict Anderson, *Imagined Communities: Reflections on the Origin and Spread of Nationalism*, revised ed. (London: Verso, 1991).

28. Baudrillard, *Simulacra and Simulation*, 2.

29. "Postmodernism," *Stanford Encyclopedia of Philosophy*, September 30, 2005; substantive revision, February 5, 2015, https://plato.stanford.edu/entries/postmodernism.

30. Jean Baudrillard, "The Ecstasy of Communication," in *The Anti-Aesthetic: Essays on Postmodern Culture*, ed. Hal Foster (Port Townsend, WA: Bay Press, 1983), 126–34.

31. For example, Wills and Fecteau, "Humor and Identity on Twitter."

32. John Oliver, "Trump vs. Truth," *Last Week Tonight*, February 12, 2017, season 4, episode 1. Posted on YouTube, https://www.youtube.com/watch?v=xecEV4dSAXE.

33. Veronica Stracqualursi, "*Washington Post*: Trump Was the One Who Altered Dorian Trajectory Map with Sharpie," CNN, September 6, 2019, https://www.cnn.com/2019/09/06/politics/trump-sharpie-hurricane-dorian-alabama/index.html; Emily Stewart, "The Incredibly Absurd Trump/CNN SharpieGate Feud, Explained," *Vox*, September 6, 2019, https://www.vox.com/policy-and-politics/2019/9/6/20851971/trump-hurricane-dorian-alabama-sharpie-cnn-media.

34. John Oliver, "Trump's Wiretap Claim," *Last Week Tonight*, March 5, 2017, season 4, episode 4.

35. D. R. Tucker, "Antisocial Media: The Threat of Trump on Twitter," *Washington Monthly*, March 18, 2017, https://washingtonmonthly.com/2017/03/18/antisocial-media-the-threat-of-trump-on-twitter. Edward W. Soja refers to such claims as evidence of a postmodern right: "Postmodern Geographies," 122. See also Jack Shafer's comment, "Trump thrives in environments of the moment where he can pitch whatever version of reality that best suits his needs and temperament": "Swamp Diary, Week 64: Trump's Not Afraid of Lying to Mueller. Just Telling the Truth,"

Politico, August 11, 2018, https://www.politico.com/magazine/story/2018/08/11/trump-mueller-interview-perjury-truth-219350.

36. Rebecca Morin and David Cohen, "Giuliani: 'Truth Isn't Truth,'" *Politico*, August 19, 2018, https://www.politico.com/story/2018/08/19/giuliani-truth-todd-trump-788161.

37. Amanda Robb, "Anatomy of a Fake News Scandal," *Rolling Stone*, November 16, 2016: https://www.rollingstone.com/feature/anatomy-of-a-fake-news-scandal-125877; Marc Fisher, John Woodrow Cox, and Peter Hermann, "Pizzagate: From Rumor, to Hashtag, to Gunfire in D.C.," *Washington Post*, December 6, 2016, https://www.washingtonpost.com/local/pizzagate-from-rumor-to-hashtag-to-gunfire-in-dc/2016/12/06/4c7def50-bbd4-11e6-94ac-3d324840106c_story.html.

38. Kirby, *Digimodernism*, 53.

39. Joshua Topolsky, "The End of Twitter," *New Yorker*, January 29, 2016, https://www.newyorker.com/tech/elements/the-end-of-twitter.

40. M. W. Smith, *Reading Simulacra: Fatal Theories for Postmodernity* (Albany: State University of New York Press, 2001), 3.

41. Results can also be ramped up with formulated methods and coordinated efforts. See Benjamin T. Decker, "What a Kamala Harris Meme Can Teach Us About Fighting Fake News in 2020," *Politico*, March 3, 2019, https://www.politico.com/magazine/story/2019/03/03/what-a-kamala-harris-meme-can-teach-us-about-fighting-fake-news-in-2020-225515.

42. Baudrillard, *Simulacra and Simulation*, 16, emphasis in the original.

43. The Urban Dictionary features the term as slang for any sexy Muslim woman. The last image mentioned is a stock photo in a series for sale, https://www.canstockphoto.com/muslim-woman-with-machine-gun-armed-41885871.html; see also an image of real Muslim women in Lyari, Karachi, with automatic weapons, https://www.pinterest.com/pin/267823509060481720. For Isis recruiting, see Brian Todd, "ISIS Using 'Jihotties' to Recruit Brides for Fighters," CNN, January 20, 2016, https://www.cnn.com/videos/world/2016/01/20/jihotties-isis-recruiting-brides-todd-dnt-tsr.cnn. CNN was mocked for pushing the jihottie tag: "CNN roasted for 'jihotties' segment detailing online push to promote ISIS bachelors," *news.com.au*, January 22, 2016, http://www.news.com.au/technology/online/social/cnn-roasted-for-jihotties-segment-detailing-online-push-to-promote-isis-bachelors/news-story/9fc8624d78e819d96c4da953ed686139.

44. For examples, see John Atlas, "Fake ACORN Pimp Pleads Guilty; the *New Yorker* Adds Its Voice to the Anti-ACORN Story," *HuffPost*, May 27, 2010, Updated May 25, 2011, https://www.huffingtonpost.com/john-atlas/fake-acorn-pimp-pleads-gu_b_591708.html; Tommy Christopher, "Andrew Breitbart's Video 'Evidence' of Lying Congressmen Is Anything But," *Mediaite*, August 6, 2010, https://www.mediaite.com/online/andrew-breitbarts-video-evidence-of-lying-congressmen-is-anything-but; Paul Kane, "'Tea Party' Protesters Accused of Spitting on Lawmaker, Using Slurs," *Washington Post*, March 20, 2010, http://www.washingtonpost.com/wp-dyn/content/article/2010/03/20/AR2010032002556.html.

45. This point is made by Thomas Docherty in "Just Events," 58–59.

46. Ibid., 63.

47. Baudrillard, *Simulacra and Simulation*, 30.

48. For more on the through-the-looking-glass effect of the anti-public sphere, see Joe Conway, "After Politics/After Television: *Veep*, Digimodernism, and the Running Gag of Government," *Studies in American Humor*, ser. 4, vol. 2, no. 2 (2016): 182–207.

49. Anderson Cooper, "Nikki Haley Said Trump Is Truthful: Cooper Rolls the Tape," CNN, November 12, 2019, https://www.cnn.com/videos/politics/2019/11/13/nikki-haley-trump-truthful-ridiculist-ac360-vpx.cnn.

50. *MAD About Trump: A Brilliant Look at Our Brainless President*, with a forward by Jake Tapper (New York: E. C. Publications, 2017); "Trump's Response to Puerto Rico," *MAD*, February 2018, 28.

51. *The Late Show with Stephen Colbert*, July 26, 2018.

52. "Seth Meyers' Statement on Charlottesville," *Late Night with Seth Myers*, August 14, 2017, https://www.nbc.com/late-night-with-seth-meyers/video/seth-meyers-statement-on-charlottesville/3568768; Jimmy Fallon, "Opening Monologue," *The Tonight Show*, August 14, 2017, https://www.youtube.com/watch?v=E9TJsw67OmE.

53. Hartley, "Silly Citizenship"; McClennen and Maisel, *Is Satire Saving Our Nation?*; Day, *Satire and Dissent*; Baym, *From Cronkite to Colbert*.

54. This phrasing reworks a definition of "reverse humor" from Simon Weaver, "The 'Other' Laughs Back: Humour and Resistance in Anti-Racist Comedy," *Sociology* 44, no. 1 (2010): 31–48.

55. "'Frontline'—Clayton Bigsby," *Chappelle's Show*, season 1, episode 1, January 22, 2003, Comedy Central, https://www.cc.com/video/7nn0sh/chappelle-s-show-frontline-clayton-bigsby-pt-1-uncensored

56. Weaver, "'Other' Laughs Back," 33.

57. Ibid., 31.

58. Jessyka Finley, "Black Women's Satire as (Black) Postmodern Performance," *Studies in American Humor* ser. 4, vol. 2, no. 2 (2016): 236–65; Lisa Guerrero, "Can I Live? Contemporary Black Satire and the State of Postmodern Double Consciousness," *Studies in American Humor* ser. 4, vol. 2, no. 2 (2016): 266–79.

59. The strategy gains an international cast with comic PSAs coming from New Zealand, for example. See Charlotte Graham-McLay, "New Zealand Disappears from World Maps, and a Viral Video Is Born," *New York Times*, May 4, 2018, https://www.nytimes.com/2018/05/04/world/asia/new-zealand-video.html.

60. Originally aired on March 26, 2014, https://www.youtube.com/watch?v=MBPgXjkfBXM.

61. "Who's Attacking Me Now?: #CancelColbert," *The Colbert Report*, March 31, 2104, https://www.youtube.com/watch?v=MBPgXjkfBXM.

62. Maddy Foley, "There's More to 'Woke' Than You Think," *Bustle*, January 11, 2016, https://www.bustle.com/articles/134893-what-does-woke-mean-theres-more-to-the-slang-term-than-you-think.

63. Jay Caspian Kang, "The Campaign to 'Cancel' Colbert," *New Yorker*, March 30, 2014, https://www.newyorker.com/news/news-desk/the-campaign-to-cancel-colbert.

64. Ibid.

65. Prachi Gupta, "#CancelColbert Activist Suey Park: 'This Is Not Reform,

This Is Revolution,'" *Salon*, April 4, 2014, https://www.salon.com/2014/04/03/cancelcolbert_activist_suey_park_this_is_not_reform_this_is_revolution.

66. Gupta, "#CancelColbert Activist Suey Park."

67. Jonathan Rossing examines such reactions to such satire with a focus on the #CancelColbert controversy in "Ethics of Complicit Criticism."

68. Gupta, "#CancelColbert Activist Suey Park."

69. Weaver, "'Other' Laughs Back," 44.

70. Kang, "Campaign to 'Cancel' Colbert."

71. Ibid.

72. Samuel Beckett, *The Unnameable* (New York: Grove Press, 1958), 179.

73. Judith Butler, "Gender Is Burning: Questions of Appropriation and Subversion," in *Bodies That Matter: On the Discursive Limits of "Sex"* (London: Routledge, 1993), 121–40. See also Butler, "From Parody to Politics," in *Gender Trouble: Feminism and the Subversion of Identity* (New York: Routledge, 1990), 142–49, at 146: "There is a subversive laughter in the pastiche-effect of parodic practices in which the original, the authentic, and the real are themselves constituted as effects."

CHAPTER 4

1. David Gorman, "The Use and Abuse of Speech-Act Theory in Criticism," *Poetics Today* 20, no. 1 (1999): 93–119.

2. Austin, *How to Do Things with Words*, 60, original emphasis. Further references will appear in the text. See also John R. Searle, *Speech Acts: An Essay in the Philosophy of Language* (Cambridge: Cambridge University Press, 1969).

CHAPTER 5

1. The British version of *That Was the Week That Was* ran for thirty-seven episodes from November 24, 1962, to April 27, 1963, and September 28, 1963, to December 28, 1963. The American version lasted only twenty episodes, January 31, 1964, to May 4, 1965, intermittently.

2. Amber Day also notes *Rowan and Martin's Laugh-In*, *The Flip Wilson Show*, and the Canadian show *Seven Days* as predecessors to "Weekend Update" in *Satire and Dissent*, 49–50, 54–57; see also Amber Day and Ethan Thompson, "Live From New York, It's the Fake News! *Saturday Night Live* and the (Non)Politics of Parody," in Baym and Jones, *News Parody and Political Satire*, 169–81.

3. Chris Smith, *The Daily Show (The Book): An Oral History as Told by Jon Stewart, the Correspondents, Staff and Guests* (New York: Grand Central, 2016), xvi. Subsequent references will appear in the text. See also Paul Alonso, "*Last Week Tonight with John Oliver* and the Stewart/Colbert Impact on U.S. Political Communication in the Post-Network Era," in *Satiric TV in the Americas*, 22–50.

4. Data on this claim is mixed. See Castro Duvall, "Comedy or Cable: Where Do Americans Get Their News?," *Law|Street*, January 2, 2015, https://lawstreetmedia.com/issues/entertainment-and-culture/comedy-cable-americans-get-news; Jeffrey Gottfried and Monica Anderson, "For Some, the Satiric 'Colbert Report' Is a Trusted Source of Political News," *Pew*

Research Center, December 12, 2014, http://www.pewresearch.org/fact-tank/2014/12/12/for-some-the-satiric-colbert-report-is-a-trusted-source-of-political-news; Alex Weprin, "Comedy Central Study: A Majority of Millennials Still Get News from TV," *TVNewser*, October 18, 2012, https://www.adweek.com/tvnewser/comedy-central-study-a-majority-of-millennials-still-get-news-from-tv/151887; David Niven, S. Robert Lichter, and Daniel Amundson, "Our First Cartoon President: Bill Clinton and the Politics of Late Night Comedy," in Baumgartner and Morris, *Laughing Matters*, 151–70; Paul Brewer and Xiaoxia Cao, "Late Night Comedy Television Shows as News Sources: What the Polls Say," in Baumgartner and Morris, *Laughing Matters*, 263–77; Dannagal G. Young and Russell M. Tisinger, "Dispelling Late-Night Myths: News Consumption Among Late-Night Comedy Viewers and the Predictors of Exposure to Various Late-Night Shows," *International Journal of Press/Politics* 11, no. 3 (2006): 113–34.

5. Charles Pierce, "I Have No More Patience for Trump Supporters," *Esquire*, August 23, 2017, https://www.esquire.com/news-politics/politics/news/a57164/trump-arizona-speech.

6. "Swamp Diary," *Politico*, Week 30, December 16, 2017.

7. "The Late Show with Stephen Colbert," *CBS*, June 21, 2018, https://www.cbs.com/shows/the-late-show-with-stephen-colbert/video/xygeVZjfzztzkCgt9_OuGlDPYPQ1QzEp/the-late-show-6-21-18-don-lemon-mike-colter-death-cab-for-cutie-.

8. Naming Klepper's persona "eironic" evokes the classic Greek comic figure of the *eiron*, who seems less than he is but often bests his opposite, the braggart *alazon*.

9. Baudrillard, "Ecstasy of Communication," 133.

10. "Internet Killed the Newspaper Star," *The Daily Show with Jon Stewart*, July 30, 2014, http://www.cc.com/video-clips/izsb2o/the-daily-show-with-jon-stewart-internet-killed-the-newspaper-star.

11. "Jordan Klepper: Good Guy with a Gun," *The Daily Show with Trevor Noah*, posted on *YouTube*, December 11, 2015, https://www.youtube.com/watch?v=MCI4bUk4vuM.

12. "Jordan Klepper Fingers the Pulse: Conspiracy Theories Thrive at a Donald Trump Rally," *The Daily Show with Trevor Noah*, September 20, 2016, http://www.cc.com/video-clips/e9z0ej/the-daily-show-with-trevor-noah-jordan-klepper-fingers-the-pulse-conspiracy-theories-thrive-at-a-donald-trump-rally.

13. Jack Shafer, "Swamp Diary, Week 57: Mueller Plays Defense as Trump Pounds His Credibility," *Politico*, June 23, 2018, https://www.politico.com/magazine/story/2018/06/23/week-57-mueller-plays-defense-as-trump-pounds-his-credibility-218893.

14. "The Late Show with Stephen Colbert," *CBS*, June 20, 2018, https://www.cbs.com/shows/the-late-show-with-stephen-colbert/video/VYp4t10CqMK6smjbcBC_mJoxBjITSoAE/the-late-show-6-20-18-trevor-noah-liza-koshy-two-feet-.

CHAPTER 6

1. Rebecca Krefting's concept of "charged humor" also straddles this conceptual boundary, as does Amber Day's analysis of satire as an ironic form

of dissent. See Krefting, *All Joking Aside*; and Day, *Satire as Dissent*.

2. Bernstein, "Allegory of Modernity/Postmodernity," 205.

3. *The Daily Show*, August 4, 2010, http://www.cc.com/episodes/zmh1y9/the-daily-show-with-jon-stewart-august-4-2010-bruce-henderson-season-15-ep-15098; and December 16, 2010, http://www.cc.com/episodes/0eekn4/the-daily-show-with-jon-stewart-december-16-2010-mike-huckabee-season-15-ep-15161.

4. Jon Stewart, "Jon Stewart Crashes Stephen's Monologue," *Late Night with Stephen Colbert*, posted on YouTube December 10, 2017, https://www.youtube.com/watch?v=jHHQ9WdFekc.

5. See, for example, a *CBS This Morning* interview, referencing consequences after particular shows: "John Oliver: I'm Not a Journalist," January 18, 2018, https://www.cbsnews.com/video/john-oliver-im-not-a-journalist. See also Victor Luckerson, "How the 'John Oliver Effect' Is Having a Real-Life Impact," *Time*, updated July 10, 2015, originally published, January 20, 2015, http://time.com/3674807/john-oliver-net-neutrality-civil-forfeiture-miss-america; and Brian Steinberg, "And Now This: John Oliver Just Might Be a Journalist," *Variety*, February 16, 2018, https://variety.com/2018/tv/news/john-oliver-journalist-hbo-last-week-tonight-1202702144.

6. Alonso, *Satiric TV in the Americas*, 40; Julia R. Fox, "Journalist or Jokester? An Analysis of *Last Week Tonight with John Oliver*," in *Political Humor in a Changing Media Landscape: A New Generation of Research*, ed. Jody C. Baumgartner and Amy B. Becker (Lanham, MD: Lexington Books, 2018), 29–44, at 29.

7. "Net Neutrality in America," *Last Week Tonight*, May 31, 2014, season 1, episode 5. See Amanda Holpuch, "John Oliver's Cheeky Net Neutrality Plea Crashes FCC Website," *Guardian*, June 3, 2014, https://www.theguardian.com/technology/2014/jun/03/john-oliver-fcc-website-net-neutrality.

8. "Net Neutrality," *Last Week Tonight*, May 7, 2017, season 4, episode 11. See Jeff John Roberts, "John Oliver Gets Fired Up Over Net Neutrality—and FCC's Site Goes Down," *Fortune*, May 8, 2017, http://fortune.com/2017/05/08/john-oliver-net-neutrality.

9. "Alex Jones and Infowars," *Last Week Tonight with John Oliver*, July 30, 2017, season 4, episode 19.

10. "Confederate Monuments," *Last Week Tonight with John Oliver*, October 8, 2017, season 4, episode 26. Posted on YouTube, https://www.youtube.com/watch?v=J5b_-TZwQoI.

11. "Rudy Giuliani," *Last Week Tonight with Jon Oliver*, May 6, 2018, season 5, episode 10.

12. "Donald Trump Presidential Campaign, 2016," *Last Week Tonight with John Oliver*, February 28, 2016, season 3, episode 3. Posted on YouTube, https://www.youtube.com/watch?v=DnpO_RTSNmQ.

13. See Russ Buettner and Susanne Craig, "Decade in the Red: Trump Tax Figures Show Over $1 Billion in Business Losses," *New York Times*, May 8, 2019, https://www.nytimes.com/interactive/2019/05/07/us/politics/donald-trump-taxes.html.

14. "Trump vs. Truth," *Last Week Tonight with John Oliver*, February 12, 2017, season 4, episode 1. Posted on

YouTube, https://www.youtube.com/watch?v=xecEV4dSAXE.

15. See Harry G. Frankfurt, "Donald Trump Is BS, Says Expert in BS," *Time*, May 12, 2016, http://time.com/4321036/donald-trump-bs; and Quinta Jurecic, "On Bullshit and the Oath of Office: The 'LOL Nothing Matters' Presidency," *Lawfare*, November 23, 2016, https://www.lawfareblog.com/bullshit-and-oath-office-lol-nothing-matters-presidency. See also Frankfurt's book, *On Bullshit* (Princeton: Princeton University Press, 2005).

16. "Iranian Nuclear Deal," *Last Week Tonight with John Oliver*, April 22, 2018, season 5, episode 9.

17. "Government Surveillance," an interview with Edward Snowden in Russia, *Last Week Tonight with John Oliver*, April 4, 2015, season 2, episode 8. Posted on YouTube, https://www.youtube.com/watch?v=XEVlyP4_11M.

18. "It's Not Going to Stop," *The President Show, Christmas Special*, December 1, 2017, posted on YouTube, https://www.youtube.com/watch?v=QkdPCHMLGNM.

19. "Life After Hate," *Full Frontal*, September 13, 2017, season 2, episode 18. Posted on YouTube, https://www.youtube.com/watch?v=w-n3qiLeVqg.

20. "A Primer on Puerto Rico," *Full Frontal*, October 4, 2017, season 2, episode 21. Posted on YouTube, https://www.youtube.com/watch?v=658YZO_CmOk.

21. "We Can All Do Better Than Roy Moore," *Full Frontal*, November 15, 2017, season 2, episode 26. Posted on YouTube, https://www.youtube.com/watch?v=t1shnJT8NCY.

22. "Natural Disasters: The Greatening," and "Scott Pruitt Versus the World," *Full Frontal*, October 25, 2917,

season 2, episode 23. Posted on YouTube, https://www.youtube.com/watch?v=dSyRlCr_lsk; and https://www.youtube.com/watch?v=hrDeKfiCpbo.

23. Samantha Bee, "Answer Questions, Win Money, Save Democracy," *TBS*, September 6, 2017, https://www.tbs.com/shows/full-frontal-with-samantha-bee/articles/thisisnotagame.

24. Ryan Reed, "Samantha Bee Unveils New Civic Engagement Trivia App on *Full Frontal*," *Rolling Stone*, September 13, 2018, https://www.rollingstone.com/tv/tv-news/samantha-bee-full-frontal-civic-engagement-trivia-app-723633.

25. Samantha Bee, "Christmas on I.C.E.," *Full Frontal*, December 19, 2018, season 3, episode 31, https://www.tbs.com/shows/full-frontal-with-samantha-bee/season-3/episode-31/christmas-on-ice.

26. "Jeff Sessions Cites the Bible in Separating Children from Parents," *Late Night With Stephen Colbert, CBS*, June 14, 2018. Posted on YouTube, https://www.youtube.com/watch?v=j4KaLkYxMZ8.

27. "Jimmy Kimmel Reveals Details of His Son's Birth and Heart Disease," *Jimmy Kimmel Live!*, May 1, 2017. Posted on YouTube, https://www.youtube.com/watch?v=MmWWoMcGmoo.

28. "Jimmy Kimmel on Response to Emotional Monologue About Baby and Health Care Debate," *Jimmy Kimmel Live!*, May 8, 2017. https://www.youtube.com/watch?v=SToeM55KMzU (video no longer available at this site).

29. "Jimmy Kimmel on Bill Cassidy's Health 'Care' Bill," *Jimmy Kimmel Live!*, September 19, 2017. Posted on YouTube, https://www.youtube.com/watch?v=cOlibbx5sx0. See Scott Lemieux, "Repeal and Replace Is Back, and

Scarier Than Ever," *Los Angeles Times*, September 19, 2017, http://www.latimes.com/opinion/op-ed/la-oe-lemieux-cassidy-graham-20170920-story.html.

30. Much of the monologue is transcribed in Emily Yahr, "Jimmy Kimmel Gets Heated About Health-Care Bill, Says Sen. Bill Cassidy 'Lied Right to My Face,'" *Washington Post*, September 20, 2017, https://www.washingtonpost.com/news/arts-and-entertainment/wp/2017/09/19/jimmy-kimmel-gets-heated-about-health-care-bill-says-bill-cassidy-lied-right-to-my-face.

31. For another take on the serious quality of this show, see Elahe Izadi, "How Jimmy Kimmel, of All People, Became One of the Most Influential Voices on Health Care," *Washington Post*, September 20, 2017, https://www.washingtonpost.com/news/arts-and-entertainment/wp/2017/09/20/how-jimmy-kimmel-of-all-people-became-one-of-the-most-influential-voices-on-health-care.

32. "Jimmy Kimmel Fights Back Against Bill Cassidy, Lindsey Graham and Chris Christie," *Jimmy Kimmel Live!*, September 20, 2017. Posted on YouTube, https://www.youtube.com/watch?v=wB5Hek7Z2b8.

33. "Round 3 of Jimmy Kimmel's Health Care Battle," *Jimmy Kimmel Live!*, September 21, 2017. Posted on YouTube, https://www.youtube.com/watch?v=KUH0KQ1qMiw&index=3&list=RDcOlibbx5sx0.

34. "Jimmy Kimmel Grateful Health Care Bill Is Dead," *Jimmy Kimmel Live!*, September 26, 2017. Posted on YouTube, https://www.youtube.com/watch?v=DV8REy2AgCo; Seung Min Kim, Jennifer Haberkorn, and Burgess Everett, "Senate Won't Vote on Last-Ditch Obamacare Repeal Bill," *Politico*, September 26, 2017, https://www.politico.com/story/2017/09/26/obamacare-repeal-failure-republican-senate-243148; Elahe Izadi, "How Jimmy Kimmel," documents the way that Kimmel's satire affected the public sphere.

35. "Jimmy Kimmel's Emotional Weekend over Health Care Battle," *Jimmy Kimmel Live!*, September 25, 2017. Posted on YouTube, https://www.youtube.com/watch?v=jtx7aTdaVzM.

36. Adam Felder, "The Limits of the Late-Night Comedy Takedown," *Atlantic*, April 17, 2017, https://www.theatlantic.com/entertainment/archive/2016/04/late-night-comedy/475485.

37. Quoted in Holger Kersten, "Mark Twain's 'Assault of Laughter' and the Limits of Political Humor," *Studies in American Humor*, ser. 4, vol. 4, no. 2 (2018): 171–182, at 176. See also Amir Ahmadi Arian, "The Ubiquitous, Ineffective Laughter," *openDemocracy*, April 10, 2017, https://www.opendemocracy.net/en/north-africa-west-asia/trump-satire-comedy-night-show.

38. Kersten, "Mark Twain's 'Assault of Laughter,'" 176. For a similar argument, see Ralph M. Rosen, "Efficacy and Meaning in Ancient and Modern Political Satire: Aristophanes, Lenny Bruce, and Jon Stewart," *Social Research* 79, no. 1 (2012): 1–32.

39. *CBS This Morning*, "John Oliver: I'm Not a Journalist," January 18, 2018.

40. Lauren Holter, "5 Times John Oliver Made a Real Impact and Proved That Late-Night Shows Aren't All Fun and Games," *Bustle*, February 8, 2016, https://www.bustle.com/articles/140358-5-times-john-oliver-made-a-real-impact-proved-that-late-night-shows-arent-all-fun; Kate Hohenstatt, "The John Oliver Effect: When a Satirical

News Show Actually Sparks Change in Society," *Odyssey*, March 7, 2016, https://www.theodysseyonline.com/john-oliver-effect. See also Luckerson, "How the 'John Oliver Effect' Is Having a Real-Life Impact"; and Steinberg, "And Now This: John Oliver Just Might Be a Journalist."

41. Tumin, "Stephen Colbert Uses Profanity."

42. Robert Phiddian, "Have They No Shame? Observations on the Effects of Satire," in *Satire and Politics: The Interplay of Heritage and Practice*, ed. Jessica Milner Davis (London: Palgrave Macmillan, 2017), 251–63, at 254.

CHAPTER 7

1. Keegan-Michael Key and Jordan Peele, "Insult Comic," *Key and Peele*, October 23, 2013, season 3, episode 6. Posted on YouTube, https://www.youtube.com/watch?v=RlTbJZ64sVM.

2. See Mary A. Grant, *The Ancient Rhetorical Theories of the Laughable* (Madison: University of Wisconsin, 1924), 28, 36–37, 76–87; Cicero, *De oratore*, Loeb Classical Library, trans. E. W. Sutton, 2 vols. (Cambridge: Harvard University Press, 1948), 375; Aristotle, *Poetics*, 2:2319. See also Halliwell, *Greek Laughter*, chapter 6, especially his reading of Aristotle's proscription, 326–31; for Lord Bacon and the liberal versus illiberal jest, see Grant, *Ancient Rhetorical Theories of the Laughable*, 14, and Gatrell, *City of Laughter*, 172–76.

3. *The Late Show with Stephen Colbert*, October 12, 2017. Posted on YouTube, https://www.youtube.com/watch?v=h9ga9lHtcXM.

4. *Henry IV, Part One*, Act II, scene iv, ll. 227–29, 244–50.

5. Lewis Black, "Back in Black—Getting Out the Millennial Vote: *The Daily Show*," October 6, 2016. Posted on YouTube, https://www.youtube.com/watch?v=HaU70Qeb0Cc.

6. Sankin, "'Ire' in 'Satire.'" See also Geoffrey Baym, "Rush Limbaugh with a Laugh-Track: The (Thankfully) Short Life of the 1/2 Hour News Hour," *Cinema Journal* 51, no. 4 (2012): 172–78; Alex Nichols, "Dennis Miller's New Podcast Is an Incoherent Marvel," *Outline*, June 7, 2018, https://theoutline.com/post/4835/dennis-miller-option-podcast-really-bad?zd=1&zi=fv5gdsko.

7. See Viveca S. Greene, "'Deplorable' Satire: Alt-Right Memes, White Genocide Tweets, and Redpilling Normies," *Studies in American Humor*, ser. 4, vol. 5, no. 1 (2019): 31–69; Justin Peters, "Public Impeachment Sneering: Laura Ingraham Is Laughing Through the Ukraine Affair," *Slate*, November 14, 2019, https://slate.com/news-and-politics/2019/11/laura-ingraham-impeachment-fox-news.html.

8. Brett Logiurato, "Stephen Colbert Responds to Karl Rove's Charge That He Has 'Anger Management' Problems," *Business Insider*, March 26, 2013, https://www.businessinsider.in/Stephen-Colbert-Responds-To-Karl-Roves-Charge-That-He-Has-Anger-Management-Problems/articleshow/21225864.cms.

9. Megan Garber, "The Slow, Awkward Death of the White House Correspondents' Dinner," *Atlantic*, April 29, 2018, https://www.theatlantic.com/entertainment/archive/2018/04/what-happened-at-the-white-house-correspondents-dinner/559232.

10. Erik Wemple, "The President Is Seeking to Destroy Journalism. Now Let's Debate Dinner Entertainment!,"

Washington Post, April 30, 2018, https://www.washingtonpost.com/blogs/erik-wemple/wp/2018/04/30/the-president-is-seeking-to-destroy-journalism-now-lets-debate-dinner-entertainment.

11. Wemple, "President Is Seeking to Destroy Journalism."

12. Patrick J. Buchanan, "White House Correspondents' Dinner in the Gutter," *American Conservative*, May 1, 2018, http://www.theamericanconservative.com/buchanan/white-house-correspondents-dinner-in-the-gutter.

13. Mairead McArdle, "Mika Brzezinski: White House Correspondents Dinner a Big Win for Trump," *National Review*, April 30, 2018, https://www.nationalreview.com/news/mika-brzezinski-white-house-correspondents-dinner-a-big-win-for-trump.

14. Michael M. Grynbaum, "Michelle Wolf Sets Off a Furor," *New York Times*, April 29, 2018, https://www.nytimes.com/2018/04/29/business/media/michelle-wolfs-routine-sets-off-a-furor-at-an-annual-washington-dinner.html.

15. Grynbaum, "Michelle Wolf Sets Off a Furor."

16. McArdle, "Correspondents Dinner a Big Win for Trump."

17. Grynbaum, "Michelle Wolf Sets Off a Furor."

18. Wemple, "President Is Seeking to Destroy Journalism."

19. David Frum, "Michelle Wolf Does Unto the White House as It Has Done unto Others," *Atlantic*, April 30, 2018, https://www.theatlantic.com/politics/archive/2018/04/whca-sanders/559253. Original emphasis.

20. Common Dreams staff, "Comedian Michelle Wolf Delivers 'Scathing' Roast of Trump and His Cronies at Correspondents' Dinner," *Common Dreams*, April 29, 2018: https://www.commondreams.org/news/2018/04/29/comedian-michelle-wolf-delivers-scathing-roast-trump-and-his-cronies-correspondents.

21. Wemple, "President Is Seeking to Destroy Journalism."

22. Ibid.

23. Charles P. Pierce, "The Forces Were Perfectly in Balance at the White House Correspondents' Dinner," Esquire, April 30, 2018, https://www.esquire.com/news-politics/politics/a20100406/michelle-wolf-sarah-huckabee-sanders-white-house-correspondents-dinner.

24. Common Dreams staff, "Comedian Michelle Wolf Delivers 'Scathing' Roast of Trump." Greenwald says "comedians" but of course he really means "satirists."

25. Garber, "Slow, Awkward Death," original emphasis. Garber is paraphrasing Peter Finley Dunne's comic character, Mr. Dooley.

26. Grynbaum, "Michelle Wolf Sets Off a Furor."

27. https://www.vox.com/policy-and-politics/2018/4/30/17301436/michelle-wolf-speech-transcript-white-house-correspondents-dinner-sarah-huckabee-sanders.

28. Wemple, "President Is Seeking to Destroy Journalism."

29. Common Dreams staff, "Comedian Michelle Wolf Delivers 'Scathing' Roast of Trump."

30. Lucia Graves and Sam Morris, "The Trump Allegations," *Guardian*, November 29, 2017, https://www.theguardian.com/us-news/ng-interactive/2017/nov/30/donald-trump-sexual-misconduct-allegations-full-list.

31. Garber, "Slow, Awkward Death."

32. Adam Conover, "Michelle Wolf Did What Comedians Are Supposed to

Do," *New York Times*, April 30, 2018, https://www.nytimes.com/2018/04/30/opinion/michelle-wolf-white-house-correspondents-dinner.html. See also Emily Stewart, "The Michelle Wolf White House Correspondents' Dinner Controversy, Explained," *Vox*, April 30, 2018. https://www.vox.com/policy-and-politics/2018/4/29/17298834/michelle-wolf-jokes-sarah-huckabee-sanders-whcd-maggie-haberman-press-aunt-lydia.

33. Wemple, "President Is Seeking to Destroy Journalism."

34. Katherine Timpf, "Don't Be Mad at Wolf's Sanders Jokes If You've Never Been Mad at Trump," *National Review*, April 29, 2018, https://www.nationalreview.com/2018/04/michelle-wolf-jokes-no-worse-than-trump-attacks-on-opponents.

35. Adam Conover, "Michelle Wolf Did What Comedians Are Supposed to Do."

36. Jack Shafer, "John Brennan's Trumpian Turn," *Politico*, August 16, 2018, https://www.politico.com/magazine/story/2018/08/16/trump-john-brennan-feud-219368. See also David Frum, "The Shame and Disgrace Will Linger," *Atlantic*, August 10, 2019, https://www.theatlantic.com/ideas/archive/2019/08/trumps-conspiracy-theory-about-clintons-and-epstein/595915.

37. Chauncey DeVega, "Ron DeSantis and the 'Monkey' Comment: Here's Why Conscious Intent Doesn't Matter," *Salon*, August 31, 2018, https://www.salon.com/2018/08/31/ron-desantis-and-the-monkey-comment-heres-why-conscious-intent-doesnt-matter. See also P. R. Lockhart, "Republican Ron DeSantis Says Electing Black Opponent Andrew Gillum Would 'Monkey This Up,'" *Vox*, August, 29, 2018, https://www.vox.com/policy-and-politics/2018/8/29/17796112/ron-desantis-andrew-gillum-monkey-racism-language-florida-governors-election.

38. Antoinette Bueno, "Roseanne Barr Leaves Twitter, Apologizes After Racially Charged Tweet Sparks Outrage," *Entertainment Tonight*, May 29, 2018, https://www.etonline.com/roseanne-barr-leaves-twitter-apologizes-after-racially-charged-tweet-sparks-outrage-103150.

39. John Koblin, "After Racist Tweet, Roseanne Barr's Show Is Canceled by ABC," *New York Times*, May 29, 2018, https://www.nytimes.com/2018/05/29/business/media/roseanne-barr-offensive-tweets.html; Robert Mackey, "ABC Fires Roseanne Barr After Her Apology for Her Racist Tweet Confirmed It Was Racist," *Intercept*, May 29, 2018, https://theintercept.com/2018/05/29/roseanne-barrs-apology-racist-islamophobic-tweet-confirms-racism-islamophobia.

40. Elizabeth Nolan Brown, "*Roseanne* Reboot Is Dead. Will *Real Time with Bill Maher* Be Next?," *reason*, May 30, 2018, https://reason.com/blog/2018/05/30/roseanne-cancellation-snags-bill-maher; Matt Wilstein, "Bill Maher Rips Right-Wing 'Snowflakes' for Equating Him with Roseanne," *Daily Beast*, June 2, 2018, https://www.thedailybeast.com/bill-maher-rips-right-wing-snowflakes-for-equating-him-with-roseanne.

41. Madeleine Aggeler, "The Samantha Bee and Ivanka Trump C*ntroversy, Explained," *Cut*, May 31, 2018, https://www.thecut.com/2018/05/samantha-bee-ivanka-trump-say-feckless.html.

42. Josephine Livingstone, "What's So Bad About the C-Word," *New Republic*, June 5, 2018, https://newrepublic.com/article/148713/whats-bad-c-word.

43. Rebecca Traister, "Samantha Bee and the War of Words," *Cut*, May 31 2018, https://www.thecut.com/2018/05/samantha-bee-ivanka-trump-full-frontal.html.

44. Eric Anthamatten, "Trump and the True Meaning of 'Idiot,'" *New York Times*, June 12, 2017, https://www.nytimes.com/2017/06/12/opinion/trump-and-the-true-meaning-of-idiot.html. Quote is from A. W. Sparkes, "Idiots, Ancient and Modern," *Australian Journal of Political Science* 23, no. 1 (1988): 101–2, at 101.

45. Andrew Sullivan, "This Is What the Trump Abyss Looks Like," *Intelligencer*, October 27, 2017, https://nymag.com/intelligencer/2017/10/this-is-what-the-trump-abyss-looks-like.html. https://nymag.com/intelligencer/2017/10/this-is-what-the-trump-abyss-looks-like.html.

46. Andrew Sullivan, "Democracies End When They Are Too Democratic," *New York Intelligencer Magazine*, May 2, 2016, http://nymag.com/daily/intelligencer/2016/04/america-tyranny-donald-trump.html. See also Jacob Weisberg, "Is America's Democracy Ripe for a Dictatorship? Why Andrew Sullivan Thinks Trump May Defeat Clinton for the U.S. Presidency," *Slate*, May 20, 2016, http://www.slate.com/articles/news_and_politics/politics/2016/05/andrew_sullivan_thinks_donald_trump_may_defeat_hillary_clinton.html.

47. Charles Pierce, "Trump Has Access to Everything a Dictator Could Want," *Esquire*, June 4, 2018, https://www.esquire.com/news-politics/politics/a21070090/trump-consolidate-power-lies-authoritarianism.

48. Pierce, "Trump Has Access."

49. Ibid.

50. "Prion Disease," *Wikipedia*, https://simple.wikipedia.org/wiki/Prion_disease.

51. Pierce, "Trump Has Access."

52. Sullivan, "Trump Abyss."

53. Jeremy Diamond, "Trump: I Could 'Shoot Somebody and I Wouldn't Lose Voters,'" CNN, January 24, 2016, https://www.cnn.com/2016/01/23/politics/donald-trump-shoot-somebody-support/index.html.

54. Sullivan, "Trump Abyss."

55. Pierce, "Trump Has Access."

56. Sullivan, "Trump Abyss."

57. Pierce, "Trump Has Access."

58. Sullivan, "Trump Abyss."

59. *The Late Show with Stephen Colbert*, October 12, 2017; Hannity interview took place on October 11.

CHAPTER 8

1. Bret Stephens, "A Presidency Without Humor," *New York Times*, December 7, 2018, https://www.nytimes.com/2018/12/07/opinion/trump-bush-memorial-humor-president.html; Nell Scovell, "Can Donald Trump Get a Laugh?," *New York Times*, April 28, 2018, https://www.nytimes.com/2018/04/28/opinion/donald-trump-jokes-laughs.html; Eddie Scarry, "Actually, Bret Stephens, Trump Is Funny," *Washington Examiner*, December 10, 2018, https://www.washingtonexaminer.com/opinion/columnists/actually-bret-stephens-trump-is-funny; and Joanna Weiss, "Trump Pokes Fun at Himself. Why Do Only Some People See It?," *Politico*, November 9, 2019, https://www.politico.com/magazine/story/2019/11/09/trump-pokes-fun-at-himself-why-do-only-some-people-see-it-229908.

2. Aristotle, *Nicomachean Ethics*, in *The Complete Works of Aristotle*, ed.

Jonathan Barnes, 2 vols. (Princeton: Princeton University Press, 1984), 2:1729–867, at 1780–81. Susanne K. Langer, "The Great Dramatic Forms: The Comic Rhythm," in *Feeling and Form: A Theory of Art Developed from Philosophy in a New Key* (London: Routledge and Kegan Paul, 1953), 326–50, at 342–44.

3. S. E. Cupp, "The Best Week Ever for Throwing Shade at Trump," CNN, July 23, 2018, https://www.cnn.com/2018/07/19/opinions/trolling-trump-queen-richard-marx-dictionaries-cupp-opinion/index.html.

4. Angela Watercutter, "The Internet Defines 'Covfefe,'" *Wired*, May 31, 2017, https://www.wired.com/2017/05/internet-defines-covfefe. See also Jessica Estepa, "Covfefe, One Year Later: How a Late-Night Trump Tweet Turned into a Phenomenon," *USA Today*, May 31, 2018, https://www.usatoday.com/story/news/politics/onpolitics/2018/05/31/covfefe-one-year-anniverary-donald-trumps-confusing-tweet/659414002.

5. *Factbase*, "Speech: Donald Trump Holds a Political Rally in Great Falls, Montana—July 5, 2018," https://factba.se/transcript/donald-trump-speech-make-america-great-again-rally-great-falls-montana-july-5-2018.

6. Chris Cillizza, "Donald Trump Bragged About Himself to the United Nations. The UN Laughed," CNN, September 25, 2018, https://www.cnn.com/2018/09/25/politics/donald-trump-un-speech-laugh/index.html; David A. Graham, "The World Just Laughed at Donald Trump," *Atlantic*, September 25, 2018, https://www.theatlantic.com/international/archive/2018/09/trump-unga-laughter/571267; Rebecca Morin, "Trump on World Leaders: 'They Didn't Laugh at Me,'" *Politico*, September 26, 2018, https://www.politico.com/story/2018/09/26/trump-on-unga-they-didnt-laugh-at-me-845025.

7. Luke O'Neil, "'I Hereby Order': Trump Mocked for Highly Formal, Meaningless Decree," *Guardian*, August 23, 2019, https://www.theguardian.com/technology/2019/aug/23/trump-hereby-order-response-president-mocked-decree.

8. Chris Cillizza, "Donald Trump, Internet Troll," CNN, November 28, 2018, https://www.cnn.com/2018/11/28/politics/donald-trump-internet-troll/index.html.

9. David A. Fahrenthold and Jonathan O'Connell, "D.C., Maryland Can Proceed with Lawsuit Alleging Trump Violated Emoluments Clauses," *Washington Post*, March 28, 2018, https://www.washingtonpost.com/politics/dc-maryland-may-proceed-with-lawsuit-alleging-trump-violated-emoluments-clause/2018/03/28/0514d816-32ae-11e8-8bdd-cdb33a5eef83_story.html; Katie Benner, "Judge Denies Trump's Request to Dismiss Emoluments Lawsuit," *New York Times*, September 28, 2018, https://www.nytimes.com/2018/09/28/us/politics/trump-emoluments-democrats-lawsuit.html; Larry Buchanan and Karen Yourish, "Tracking 29 Investigations Related to Trump," *New York Times*, updated September 25 2019, originally published May 13, 2019, https://www.nytimes.com/interactive/2019/05/13/us/politics/trump-investigations.html.

10. Allie Malloy, Kate Sullivan, and Jeff Zeleny, "Trump Mocks Christine Blasey Ford's Testimony, Tells People to 'Think of Your Son,'" CNN, October 3, 2018, https://www.cnn.com/2018/10/02/politics/trump-mocks-christine-blasey

-ford-kavanaugh-supreme-court/index.html.

11. "Andrew Dice Clay: Trump Stole My Act," *Conan on TBS*. Posted on YouTube, https://www.youtube.com/watch?v=tYu67ByKThc.

12. Chris Cillizza, "What Donald Trump Did Thursday Night in Montana Is Really Dangerous," CNN, October 20, 2018, https://www.cnn.com/2018/10/19/politics/trump-montana-gianforte/index.html.

13. Andrew Restuccia and Ben Schreckinger, "In MAGA World, Trump's Jokes Always Land," *Politico*, October 19, 2108, https://www.politico.com/story/2018/10/19/trump-rallies-comedy-916795.

14. Cillizza, "What Donald Trump Did."

15. Restuccia and Schreckinger, "In MAGA World."

16. All quotes in this paragraph: Ibid.

17. Ronson, "How One Stupid Tweet Blew Up Justine Sacco's Life." In the article, Ronson details other recipients of #flashmob outrage. Ronson traces the exposure of the tweet to Sam Biddle, the editor of *Valleywag*, Gawker Media's tech-industry blog. He retweeted it to his 15,000 followers and eventually posted it on *Valleywag*.

18. Baudrillard, "Ecstasy of Communication," 131.

19. This apology was subsequently taken down and replaced: the blog was "intended to be taken in the same light as Swift's claim that Irish children should be eaten. I was surprised to learn that some readers took me literally, claiming that I advocate rape." Mitchell Langbert, "Kavanaugh: A Modest Proposal," September 27, 2018, http://mitchell-langbert.blogspot.com/search?q=Kavanaugh; Tony Marco and Steve Almasy, "Professor Implied Committing Sex Assault Is a Rite of Passage for Men. Now He Says That Was Satire," CNN, October 4, 2018, https://www.cnn.com/2018/10/03/us/brooklyn-college-professor-kavanaugh-comments-protests/index.html.

20. Cleve R. Wootson Jr., "A Middle School Teacher Led a Double Life as a White Nationalist Podcaster," *Washington Post*, March 5, 2018, https://www.washingtonpost.com/news/education/wp/2018/03/05/a-middle-school-teacher-led-a-double-life-as-a-white-nationalist-podcaster; A. J. Willingham, "Middle School Teacher Secretly Ran White Supremacist Podcast, Says It Was Satire," CNN, March 6, 2018, https://www.cnn.com/2018/03/05/us/dayanna-volitich-white-nationalist-florida-school-podcast-trnd/index.html.

21. Will Worley, "*InfoWars*' Alex Jones Is a 'Performance Artist Playing a Character,' Says His Lawyer," *Independent*, April 17, 2017, https://www.independent.co.uk/news/infowars-alex-jones-performance-artist-playing-character-lawyer-conspiracy-theory-donald-trump-a7687571.html. See also Jason Abbruzzese, "Alex Jones Plays a Character on *Infowars* Named 'Alex Jones,' Says Lawyer for Alex Jones," *Mashable*, April 17, 2017, https://mashable.com/2017/04/17/alex-jones-defense-performance-artist.

22. Twitter took his statements seriously too when it banned Jones permanently from the social media platform. See Sara Salinas, "Twitter Permanently Bans Alex Jones and Infowars Accounts," *CNBC*, September 6, 2018, https://www.cnbc.com/2018/09/06/twitter-permanently-bans-alex-jones-and-infowars-accounts.html;

Kate Conger and Jack Nicas, "Twitter Bars Alex Jones and Infowars, Citing Harassing Messages," *New York Times*, September 6, 2018, https://www.nytimes.com/2018/09/06/technology/twitter-alex-jones-infowars.html.

23. Jay Willis, "Stephen Colbert's Conspiracy Theorist Character 'Tuck Buckford' Needs a Podcast Immediately," *GQ*, April 18, 2017, https://www.gq.com/story/stephen-colbert-tuck-buckford-brain-fight.

24. Faiz Siddiqui and Susan Svrluga, "N.C. Man Told Police He Went to D.C. Pizzeria with Gun to Investigate Conspiracy Theory," *Washington Post*, December 5, 2016, https://www.washingtonpost.com/news/local/wp/2016/12/04/d-c-police-respond-to-report-of-a-man-with-a-gun-at-comet-ping-pong-restaurant. See also "Pizzagate Conspiracy Theory," *Wikipedia*, https://en.wikipedia.org/wiki/Pizzagate_conspiracy_theory; Cecilia Kang and Adam Goldman, "In Washington Pizzeria Attack, Fake News Brought Real Guns," *New York Times*, December 5, 2016, https://www.nytimes.com/2016/12/05/business/media/comet-ping-pong-pizza-shooting-fake-news-consequences.html; Matthew Haag and Maya Salam, "Gunman in 'Pizzagate' Shooting Is Sentenced to 4 Years in Prison," *New York Times*, June 22, 2017, https://www.nytimes.com/2017/06/22/us/pizzagate-attack-sentence.html.

25. Palmer, "Limits of Humor"; Carey, *Communication as Culture*; Billig, *Laughter and Ridicule*.

26. Todd Gitlin, "Alex Jones's Defense," *Huffington Post*, April 19, 2017, https://www.huffingtonpost.com/entry/alex-jones-defense_us_58f7cfd2e4b01d4eb1e168d7.

27. Gitlin, "Alex Jones's Defense." See also Noland D. McCaskill, "Trump Backs Off His Backpedal on Obama Terror Claim," *Politico*, August 12, 2016, https://www.politico.com/story/2016/08/trump-obama-islamic-state-sarcasm-226947; Andrew Buncombe, "Donald Trump Says He Was Being Sarcastic About Barack Obama Being the Founder of Isis," *Independent*, August 12, 2016, http://www.independent.co.uk/news/world/americas/us-elections/donald-trump-says-he-was-being-sarcastic-about-barack-obama-being-the-founder-of-isis-a7186936.html.

28. Paul Waldman, "Trump's Latest Outrageous Statement Wasn't a 'Gaffe.' It Was Something Much Worse," *Washington Post*, August 10, 2016, https://www.washingtonpost.com/blogs/plum-line/wp/2016/08/10/trumps-latest-outrageous-statement-wasnt-a-gaffe-it-was-something-much-worse.

29. Robert Costa, "Ryan: Trump Second Amendment Remarks a 'Joke Gone Bad,'" *Washington Post*, August 10, 2016, https://www.washingtonpost.com/news/powerpost/wp/2016/08/10/ryan-trump-second-amendment-remarks-a-joke-gone-bad.

30. Dan Merica, "Spicer: Trump Was 'Joking' When He Asked Russia to Hack Clinton," *CNN*, June 26, 2017, https://www.cnn.com/2017/06/26/politics/trump-clinton-russia-hacking-email-joking/index.html; Jack Holmes, "You Decide: Was Trump Joking When He Asked Russia to Hack Hillary's Emails?," *Esquire*, June 26, 2017, http://www.esquire.com/news-politics/videos/a55893/trump-russia-hack-hillary. Trump repeated this claim in 2019. See Marshall Cohen, "Trump Says He Joked About Wanting Russian Help in 2016. The Facts Tell a Different Story," *CNN*,

March 5, 2019, https://www.cnn.com/2019/03/05/politics/trump-emails-joke/index.html.

31. Michael Crowley and Tyler Pager, "Trump Urges Russia to Hack Clinton's Email," *Politico*, July 27, 2016, https://www.politico.com/story/2016/07/trump-putin-no-relationship-226282.

32. Francesca Chambers, "'It Wasn't a Directive, It Was a Joke': White House Says Speech Where Trump Said It's OK for Police to 'Rough' Up Thugs Wasn't Intended as a Police Brutality Endorsement," *Daily Mail*, August 1, 2017, http://www.dailymail.co.uk/news/article-4751254/Trump-making-joke-endorsed-police-brutality.html; Melanie Arter, "WH Defends Trump's Remarks on How to Treat MS-13 Gang Members: He Was Joking," *CNSNEWS.COM*, August 2, 2017, https://www.cnsnews.com/news/article/melanie-arter/wh-defends-trumps-remarks-how-treat-ms-13-gang-members-he-was-joking.

33. Rishika Dugyala, "Jim Jordan: Trump Not Serious in Calls for China to Investigate Biden," *Politico*, October 6, 2019, https://www.politico.com/news/2019/10/06/jordan-trump-china-investigate-biden-032972.

34. Tara Subramaniam, "Trump's Claim That He Wants to Slow Coronavirus Testing Is the Latest in a Pattern of Supposed Jokes and Sarcasm," CNN, June 23, 2020, https://www.cnn.com/2020/06/23/politics/trump-claim-coronavirus-slow-testing-pattern-joking-sarcasm/index.html; Quint Forgey, "'I Don't Kid': Trump Says He Wasn't Joking About Slowing Coronavirus Testing," *Politico*, June 23, 2020, https://www.politico.com/news/2020/06/23/trump-joking-slowing-coronavirus-testing-335459.

35. David A. Graham, "He Dares Call It Treason," *Atlantic*, February 6, 2018, https://www.theatlantic.com/politics/archive/2018/02/one-dares-call-it-treason/552395. See also Dan Merica and Jim Acosta, "Trump Was 'Joking' When He Accused Democrats of Treason, White House Says," CNN, February 6, 2018, https://www.cnn.com/2018/02/06/politics/treason-donald-trump-joking/index.html; Gregory Krieg, "The Truth About Donald Trump's 'Jokes,'" CNN, February 6, 2018, https://www.cnn.com/2018/02/06/politics/donald-trump-jokes/index.html.

36. Martin Selsoe Sorensen, "In Denmark, Bewilderment and Anger Over Trump's Canceled Visit," *New York Times*, August 21, 2019, https://www.nytimes.com/2019/08/21/world/europe/greenland-denmark-trump.html.

37. Jessica Estepa, "Sean Spicer Says 'Covfefe' Wasn't a Typo: Trump Knew 'Exactly What He Meant,'" *USA Today*, May 31, 2017, https://www.usatoday.com/story/news/politics/onpolitics/2017/05/31/sean-spicer-says-covfefe-wasnt-typo-trump-knew-exactly-what-he-meant/102355728. A former White House aide, Cliff Sims, said that Trump sent Spicer to the podium with that answer: Anderson Cooper, "Ex-Trump Aide Explains President's 'Covfefe' Tweet," CNN, January 30, 2019, https://www.cnn.com/videos/politics/2019/01/30/cliff-sims-former-trump-aide-covfefe-tweet-ac360-sot-vpx.cnn.

38. Brian Bennett, "All Jokes Aside, Trump's 'Covfefe' Tweet Sparks Questions Too," *Los Angeles Times*, May 31, 2017, http://www.latimes.com/politics/la-na-pol-trump-tweet-20170531-story.html; Matt Flegenheimer, "What's a 'Covfefe'? Trump Tweet Unites a Bewildered Nation," *New York Times*, May 31,

2017, https://www.nytimes.com/2017/05/31/us/politics/covfefe-trump-twitter.html.

39. Ezra Klein, "Incoherent, Authoritarian, Uninformed: Trump's *New York Times* Interview Is a Scary Read," *Vox*, Dec 29, 2017, https://www.vox.com/policy-and-politics/2017/12/29/16829806/trump-interview-new-york-times.

40. Max Boot, "President Trump's 'Jokes' Are No Laughing Matter," *Washington Post*, March 7, 2017, https://www.washingtonpost.com/news/global-opinions/wp/2018/03/07/president-trumps-jokes-are-no-laughing-matter/?noredirect=on.

41. Baudrillard, *Simulacra and Simulation*, 16, 145.

42. Graydon Carter, "The Trump Presidency Is Already a Joke, But It's No Laughing Matter," *Vanity Fair*, March 22, 2017, https://www.vanityfair.com/news/2017/03/graydon-carter-trump-presidency-is-already-a-joke.

43. Arpad Szakolczai, *Comedy and the Public Sphere: The Rebirth of Theatre as Comedy and the Genealogy of the Modern Public Arena* (London: Routledge, 2013), 5; see also 24ff.

44. David A. Graham, "Trump's Incoherent Rally in Charlotte," *Atlantic*, October 27, 2018, https://www.theatlantic.com/politics/archive/2018/10/trumps-charlotte-rally-after-cesar-sayocs-arrest/574168.

45. Sarah Zhang, "Trump's Most Trusted Adviser Is His Own Gut," *Atlantic*, January 13, 2019, https://www.theatlantic.com/politics/archive/2019/01/trump-follows-his-gut/580084.

46. Graham, "Trump's Incoherent Rally."

47. Jeet Heer, "Divide and Conquer," *New Republic*, September 16, 2016, https://newrepublic.com/article/136321/divide-conquer.

48. Chris Baynes, "Donald Trump Says He Would Not Be President without Twitter," *Independent*, October 22, 2017, https://www.independent.co.uk/news/world/americas/us-politics/donald-trump-tweets-twitter-social-media-facebook-instagram-fox-business-network-would-not-be-a8013491.html; Mathew Ingram, "The 140-Character President," *Columbia Journalism Review*, Fall 2017, https://www.cjr.org/special_report/trump-twitter-tweets-president.php; Chris Cillizza, "Twitter Made Trump. Will It Un-make Him?," CNN, July 26, 2018, https://www.cnn.com/2018/07/26/politics/twitter-trump-analysis/index.html.

49. Daniella Diaz, "Trump, I'm a 'Very Stable Genius,'" CNN, January 6, 2018, https://www.cnn.com/2018/01/06/politics/donald-trump-white-house-fitness-very-stable-genius/index.html. See also Morgan Gstalter, "Trump Again Labels Himself a 'Very Stable Genius,'" *Hill*, July, 12, 2018, http://thehill.com/homenews/administration/396628-trump-calls-himself-a-stable-genius.

CHAPTER 9

1. Sophia A. McClennen, "The Joke Is on You: Satire and Blowback," in Baumgartner and Becker, *Political Humor in a Changing Media Landscape*, 137–56.

2. See, for example, Greene, "'Deplorable' Satire," as well as St. Onge, "Engaged Levity."

3. Amber Day, *Satire and Dissent*, 54.

4. Quoted in ibid., 71.

5. Tally, "I Am the Mainstream Media," 153; See also Jones, *Entertaining Politics*, 10.

6. Baym, *From Cronkite to Colbert*, 173.

7. Day, *Satire and Dissent*, 57.

8. Jones, *Entertaining Politics*, 10.

9. Gilmore, *Satire*, 177.

10. Day, *Satire and Dissent*, 189. See also Jones, Baym, and Day and their critique of Stewart and Colbert's "Rally to Restore Sanity and/or Fear" in "Mr. Stewart and Mr. Colbert Go to Washington": "If there was a weakness to the rally, it was that neither Stewart nor Colbert asserted an alternative interpretive framework to direct meaning-making" (42).

11. Kilby, "Provoking the Citizen," 1942.

12. Rolfe, "Populist Elements," 41, 43.

13. Olson, *Comedy After Postmodernism*, 14.

14. Deborah Solomon, "Funny About the News," *New York Times Magazine*, September 25, 2005, https://www.nytimes.com/2005/09/25/magazine/funny-about-the-news.html.

15. Kang, "Campaign to 'Cancel' Colbert."

16. Tally, "I Am the Mainstream Media," 154.

17. Day, *Satire and Dissent*, 21.

18. Gilmore, *Satire*, 8.

19. Ibid., 185.

20. Greenberg, *Cambridge Introduction to Satire*, 16. See also Kersten, "Mark Twain's 'Assault of Laughter,'" 171–82. Amber Day adds Leonard Fineberg (1967), Charles Schutz (1977), Edward and Lilian Bloom (1979), and Dustin Griffin (1994) to this negative viewpoint.

21. Day, *Satire and Dissent*, 138–39. More research that supports Day's basic point about differing levels of efficacy would include Caty Borum Chatoo, "A Funny Matter: Toward a Framework for Understanding the Function of Comedy in Social Change," *Humor: International Journal of Humor Research* 32, no. 3 (2019): 499–523; and Lauren Feldman and Caty Borum Chatoo, "Comedy as a Route to Social Change: The Effects of Satire and News on Persuasion About Syrian Refugees," *Mass Communication and Society* 22, no. 3 (2019): 277–300. Other examples documenting some level of efficacy include a play that promotes public engagement with climate change debates (Inger-Lise Kalviknes Bore and Grace Reid, "Laughing in the Face of Climate Change? Satire as a Device for Engaging Audiences in Public Debate," *Science Communication* 36, no. 4 [2014]: 454–78) and Twitter posts that enact meaningful political work (Jenny L. Davis, Tony P. Love, and Gemma Killen, "Seriously Funny: The Political Work of Humor on Social Media," *New Media and Society* 20, no. 10 [2018]: 3898–3916). Satire also educates students in public administration classes (Nina Hayes, "Satire as an Educative Tool for Critical Pedagogy in the Public Affairs Classroom," *Administrative Theory and Praxis,* no. 38 [2016]: 251–66), promotes political participation (Srđan Mladenov Jovanović, "'Balm for the Soul': Serbian Political Satire as a Critical Hub for Citizens," *Media Studies: Journal for Critical Media Inquiry* 13, no. 1 [2019]: 28–44), and creates community solidarity (Berenice Pahl, "Pussy Riot's Humour and the Social Media: Self-irony, Subversion, and Solidarity," *European Journal of Humour Research* 4, no. 4 [2016]: 67–104).

22. Day, *Satire and Dissent*, 129.

23. Marcus Paroske, "Pious Policymaking: The Participatory Satires of Stephen Colbert," *Studies in American Humor*, ser. 4, vol. 2, no. 2 (2016): 208–35.

24. See Hoon Lee and Nojin Kwak, "The Affect Effect of Political Satire: Sarcastic Humor, Negative Emotions, and Political Participation," *Mass Communication and Society* no. 17 (2014): 307–28; Amy B. Becker, "Playing with Politics: Online Political Parody, Affinity for Political Humor, Anxiety Reduction, and Implications for Political Efficacy," *Mass Communication and Society* 17, no. 3 (2014): 424–45; Robert Hariman, "Political Parody and Public Culture," *Quarterly Journal of Speech* 94, no. 3 (2008): 247–72.

25. Gilmore, *Satire*, 98–99.

26. Day, *Satire and Dissent*, 145.

27. Ibid., 146.

28. Ibid.

29. Robin Runia, "Satire in Composition: Writing Toward Social Justice," in Davis and Nace, *Teaching Modern British and American Satire*, 307–13, at 313.

30. See Rossing, "Ethics of Complicit Criticism."

31. Kersten, "Mark Twain's 'Assault of Laughter.'"

32. Elliott, *Power of Satire*.

33. See James E. Caron, "Satire and the Problem of Comic Laughter," *Comedy Studies* (March 6, 2020), DOI: 10.1080/2040610X.2020.1729485.

34. Gilmore, *Satire*, 14.

35. Quoted in Jones, Baym, and Day, "Mr. Stewart and Mr. Colbert Go to Washington," 57.

36. Linda Hutcheon, *Irony's Edge: The Theory and Politics of Irony* (London: Routledge, 1994).

37. Day, *Satire and Dissent*, 183.

38. Michael S. Schmidt and Maggie Haberman, "Macabre Video of Fake Trump Shooting Media and Critics Is Shown at His Resort," *New York Times*, October 13, 2019, https://www.nytimes.com/2019/10/13/us/politics/trump-video.html; David Cohen, "Press Organization Condemns Fake Massacre by Trump Depicted at Pro-Trump Event," *Politico*, October 13, 2019, https://www.politico.com/news/2019/10/13/violence-against-journalists-trump-event-046541.

39. Annie Karni, Kevin Roose, and Katie Rogers, "Violent Video Was Product of Right-Wing Provocateurs and Trump Allies," *New York Times*, October 14, 2019, https://www.nytimes.com/2019/10/14/us/politics/trump-shooting-media-video.html.

40. Charlie Warzel "The Violent Trump Video Is Dumb, and That's the Point," *New York Times*, October 14, 2019, https://www.nytimes.com/2019/10/14/opinion/trump-shooting-video.html.

41. Karni, Roose, and Rogers, "Violent Video."

42. Ibid.

43. Schmidt and Haberman, "Macabre Video."

44. Emily Stewart, "A Pro-Trump Conference Showed a Fake Video of Trump Shooting the Media and His Opponents," *Vox*, October 14, 2019, https://www.vox.com/policy-and-politics/2019/10/14/20913686/fake-trump-shooting-video-media-nytimes-cnn.

45. Emma Graham-Harrison, "'Enemy of the People': Trump's Phrase and Its Echoes of Totalitarianism," *Guardian*, August 3, 2018, https://www.theguardian.com/us-news/2018/aug/03/trump-enemy-of-the-people-meaning-history.

46. Thomas B. Edsall, "Will Trump Ever Leave the White House?," *New York Times*, October 2, 2019, https://www.nytimes.com/2019/10/02/opinion/trump-leave-white-house.html.

47. Quoted in Schmidt and Haberman, "Macabre Video."

48. Jelani Cobb, "How the Trail of American White Supremacy Led to El Paso," *New Yorker*, August 6, 2019, https://www.newyorker.com/news/daily-comment/how-the-trail-of-american-white-supremacy-led-to-el-paso; Jon Swaine and Juweek Adolphe, "Violence in the Name of Trump," *Guardian*, August 28, 2019, https://www.theguardian.com/us-news/ng-interactive/2019/aug/28/in-the-name-of-trump-supporters-attacks-database.

49. Greene, "'Deplorable' Satire"; Dale Tracy, "On Second Thought," *Studies in American Humor*, ser. 4, vol. 5, no. 2 (2019): 287.

50. Jeffrey P. Jones and Geoffrey A. Baym, "A Dialogue on Satire News and the Crisis of Truth in Postmodern Political Television," *Journal of Communication Inquiry* 34, no. 3 (2010): 278–94.

51. Timothy M. Dale, "The Revolution Is Being Televised: The Case for Popular Culture as Public Sphere," in *Homer Simpson Marches on Washington: Dissent Through American Popular Culture*, ed. Timothy D. Dale and Joseph J. Foy (Lexington: University Press of Kentucky, 2010), 21–36; Jamie Warner, "The Daily Show and the Politics of Truth," in Dale and Foy, *Homer Simpson Marches on Washington*, 37–58.

52. Michel Foucault, "Parrēsia," trans. Graham Burchell, *Critical Inquiry*, no. 41 (2015): 219–53.

53. Lee, *Twain's Brand*.

Index

absurdity, 70–71, 105, 160, 178, 186
Acosta, Jim, 167–68
"Action Hero Robert Mueller" (column), 95, 96
activism, 39–40, 217–19, 221
　See also hashtag activism; satiractivism
Addison, Joseph, 27
Adorno, Theodor, 42–43, 46, 236n13
Affordable Care Act (ACA), 136–48
Agee, James, 61
aggression, comic, 25, 103, 164, 184
　See also violence, comic
AIDS, 197–98
Alexander, Lamar, 145–46
Allen, Mike, 165
Alonso, Paul, 119, 234n33
alternative facts, 3–5, 34, 51, 64–67
ambiguity, 78–79, 198–99
a-musement, 14, 24, 32–33, 151–53, 180, 219–20
anger, 157, 159
Anon (film), 29–30, 39
anonymity, 67, 197
anti-public sphere, 8–10, 12, 23, 27, 34, 48, 54, 108, 116, 155, 159, 228
　definition of, 56–57
　enabling of, 58
　and truthiness satire, 70, 79–80
　as entertainment, 192–97
　as hyperreality's truthiness, 63–69, 149, 206, 212, 220–21
　as snark insult, 180–81, 189, 201, 202, 214, 218
　as masked comic public sphere, 196–97, 204, 209–10
　performance of, 109–11, 123–24, 142
　restraint on, 229–30
　See also counterpublics; id, political
Appearance. *See* physical appearance
argument, 118, 121
　See also debate
Aristotle, 156, 189, 251n2
artifacts, comic, 19–35, 78, 228, 234n3
assault. *See* sexual assault; violence
attachment, 216–17
Auden, W. H., 41
audience, 9, 13, 131, 237–28
　active role of, 29, 80, 221
　interpretation, 74–75, 160
　reception, 175–76, 191
　uptake, 85–86, 156–57, 160–61, 176–77
　See also under intent, speaker; laughter
Aunt Lydia (*The Handmaid's Tale*), 167–68
Austin, J. L., 13, 85–88, 200–201, 214

Baldwin, Alec, 2
barbarism, 57–58
Barr, Roseanne, 176–79, 180, 198
Bataille, Georges, 31
Baudrillard, Jean, 4, 38–39, 63–65, 68, 198
Baym, Geoffrey, 5, 52–54
Bee, Samantha, 4, 6, 127–34, 178–81
Bernstein, Richard, 11, 47
Billig, Michael, 200–201
Billionaires for Bush, 219
Bishop, Sarah, 19–20, 22
Black, Lewis, 159
black humor, 60–63, 103, 211, 243n23

black humorists, 60–63, 71
Black Lives Matter, 87
Black Mirror (series), 29–30, 39–40
Blake, Aaron, 96
boor, 189–92
Boot, Max, 204
Bowman, James E., 177
Breitbart, 3, 8, 232n13
Brennan, John, 176–78
Bronner, Stephen, 40
Bruns, Axel, 37
Brzezinski, Mika, 101, 165, 175
Buchanan, Pat, 163–64
buffoon, 189–92
bullying, 157, 161–63, 204
    See also epithets; roasting; trolling
butts, comic, 26, 62, 92–93, 221–22, 242n13
    identifying, 78, 159, 162–63, 193

#CancelColbert, 74–79, 200, 215, 246n67
Carey, James, 51
Carrell, Steve, 91
Carson, Johnny, 14
Carter, Graydon, 205
Cassidy, Bill, 136–46
Caufield, Rachel, 4
Chapelle, Dave, 73–74
Chaplin, Charlie, 236n16
Chase, Chevy, 90
Chodikoff, Adam, 91
Christie, Chris, 140–42, 169
"Christmas on ICE" (episode), 131–34
Cicero, 156
Cillizza, Chris, 195
citizens
    dividing of, 204–5
    engaged, 120, 124, 127, 130, 141–42, 144–45
    informed, 39, 56, 112, 120, 125, 137–38
    silly, 55–57, 73, 93, 99–100, 123–24, 142, 242n6
    See also audience; citizenship
citizenship, 55–56, 72–73, 108, 111

rights of, 120, 140–43
    See also citizens
civility, 161–62, 165, 221, 238n32
Clayton Bigsby (skit), 73–74
climate change, 129–30, 260n21
Clinton, Hillary, 67–68, 105, 110, 169, 193, 200, 202
clown, 25, 118, 182, 209,
    ritual, 236n15–16
    See also buffoon
CNN, 71–72, 172–73, 203, 226
cognitive engagement, 218–20
Colbert, Stephen, 6, 33, 34, 121, 187
    uniting comic public sphere and public sphere, 72–73, 104–6, 215
    monologues of, 113–16, 134–35, 179
    See also #CancelColbert; *Colbert Report, The*; Ham Rove (skit); *Late Show with Stephen Colbert, The*; truthiness: Colbert coinage of
Colbert Report, The, 6, 53–55
Coleman, Bessie, 121
comedians, 14–15
    dismissal of, 140–42, 147–48
    See also satirists
Comic, The, 10, 14, 19–35, 233n18, 242n18
comic discourse, 7, 74, 151
comic political speech, 2, 8, 33, 52, 55
    See also under political speech
comic public sphere, 2, 7, 20, 34, 221
    See also public sphere, comic public sphere relationship to; anti-public sphere: acting as comic public sphere; Colbert, Stephen: uniting comic public sphere and public sphere
comic speech, 59, 86–87, 162–76
    See also comic political speech
commedification of politics, 205–6
commercials, mock, 123–24
communication, digital, 63–68, 198
communicative rationality, 47, 118, 139, 144
community building, 217–18, 219–21

complicity, 157
Confederate monuments, 121
Conover, Adam, 173–74, 175–76
consensus, 4, 47
conspiracy theories, 67, 112
"Conspiracy Theories Thrive at a Donald Trump Rally" (segment), 110–12
constatives, 85–88, 93
constellation metaphor, 11, 50, 208, 241n35
Conway, Kellyanne, 3, 172
Cook, Logan, 225–26
Cooper, Anderson, 71
coronavirus, 234n31
counterpublics, 26, 214–18, 224
See also anti-public sphere
covfefe, 190, 203
critique, 24–25, 58, 103, 185–86, 194
always-now, 44, 49, 55
See also ridicule
Cruz, Ted, 102, 193
Cuomo, Chris, 139
cursing, 223
cynicism, 218
cyst metaphor, 58

Daily Show with Jon Stewart, The, 6, 53–55, 90–93, 232n13
Daniels, Stormy, 100, 190, 196
Day, Amber, 7, 26, 74, 215, 217–20, 224, 232n13, 234n33
debate, 38, 47–48, 58, 161, 221, 229
Declaration of Independence, 47–48
Defoe, Daniel, 42
degenerative satire, 11, 60–63, 103, 186–87, 210–11
See also black humor
democracy, 37, 160, 218
Democratic party, 184–85
Denby, David, 9–10, 188
detachment, 216–17
determining judgment, 69
DeVega, Chauncey, 177–78
différance, 80

difference, respect for, 48–50, 131, 155–58, 208
digimodernism, 38–39, 56–58, 67, 234n33
See also communication, digital; digital public sphere
digital public sphere, 37–40, 55–56, 63–64, 112, 221–22, 239n6
See also communication, digital; digimodernism; digitized media; discursive integration
digitized media, 37–40, 56–58
See also news media; social media
disability, 156–58
discourse, 38, 47, 58
See also comic discourse; political discourse; reverse discourse
discursive integration, 5, 56, 95, 103–4, 196–97, 206
creating truthiness, 209–10, 221
See also digital public sphere
discursive spheres, 57
discussion. See discourse
dissent, 55, 124, 219, 247–48n1
Drudge Report, 3, 8

earnestness, 24, 34, 176–77, 181–83, 187–88, 200
Eco, Umberto, 21
emancipation, 43–44
Empire of Signs, The (Barthes), 61
engaged levity, 56–57
Enlightened Public Sphere 2.0. See digital public sphere
Enlightenment, 6, 10–11, 36–37, 40–51, 239n1, 240n29
"Entire History of You, The" (*Black Mirror* episode), 39
Environmental Protection Agency (EPA), 129–30
epithets, 101–2, 165, 192–94
See also bullying; ridicule; trolling
essay, comic, 119–21, 124, 126–27
everyday life, 61, 64–65
exaggeration, 28, 108, 184

facts, 65, 111, 115, 123–24
    See also alternative facts; truth
Fairooz, Desiree, 1, 32, 222
Fallon, Jimmy, 72–73
Falstaff (*Henry IV*), 159
Federal Communication Commission (FCC), 120
Feuer, Jane, 212
field correspondent, faux, 90–92, 106–12, 126, 131–33
Finley, Jessyka, 74
First Amendment rights, 111, 164, 229
#flashmob, 39–40, 49, 75, 177, 197–98, 239–40n12, 256n17
    See also hashtag activism
Ford, Christine Blasey, 194
Ford, Gerald, 90, 114
Foucault, Michel, 43–45
Fox, Julia, 119
Fox & Friends, 147–48
Fox News, 65, 66, 131–33, 173
Frankfurt, Harry, 54
Frenette, Micheline, 38
Freud, Sigmund, 29, 31, 204, 237n25
Friedman, Thomas, 101–2
friendly satire, 27–28
Frost, David, 89–90
Frum, David, 165–66
Full Frontal with Samantha Bee, 8, 128–34
funny, 29–30

Garber, Megan, 161–62, 167, 173
Gatrell, Vic, 41, 156
Gawker, 107–8
GeekzTeam, 225
generative satire, 11, 61–63, 211
    See also degenerative satire
gentleman humorist, 237n19
Gianforte, Greg, 195
Gianna, Peter, 195–96
Gilmore, John, 40–41, 215–16
Gingrich, Newt, 202
Gitlin, Todd, 201–2
Giuliani, Rudy, 67, 100, 121–22, 182

"God Bless America" (song), 190
"Good Guy with a Gun" (segment), 108–9
government surveillance, 125–26
Graham, David, 206
Graham, Lindsey, 136–37, 142–43
Graham-Cassidy bill, 136–46
Greenberg, Jonathan, 11, 40–41, 216, 233n23
Greene, Viveca, 228
Greenwald, Glenn, 166–67
Griffith, Dustin, 26
Grynbaum, Michael, 167
guerilla theater tactics, 217–18
Guerrero, Lisa, 74

Habermas, Jürgen, 2–3, 4, 33–34, 36–37, 45, 205
Haley, Nikki, 71
Half Hour News Hour, The, 159–60
Hall, Joseph, 40
Halliwell, Stephen, 14
Ham Rove (skit), 34, 158, 161
Handmaid's Tale, The, 167–68
Hannity, Sean, 124
Hartley, John, 55–56
hashtag activism, 75–79, 123, 126, 215
    See also #flashmob
hate speech, 62, 176, 198–99
health care, 136–50
Hebdo, Charlie, 26, 226, 229
Heer, Jeet, 206–7
Henry IV (Shakespeare), 159
high-modern ideals, 52–54
homosexuality, 235n8
humor, 19–20
humor studies, 6–7, 233n18
Hutcheon, Linda, 47
hyperreality, 63–70, 212, 220–21
    See also under reality
hypocrisy, 137–40, 165, 175, 212, 221–22

id, political, 65, 105, 111, 207–9, 214
    See also anti-public sphere
identity construction, 64–66

identity politics, 155–58
idiocy, 178, 180–81
illocutionary speech acts, 86–88, 93–94, 106–16, 121
imaginary, the, 31
Immigration and Customs Enforcement (ICE), 131–34
incredulity, 49–50
Infowars, 3, 8, 120–21, 200
innocent relief, 19
insult, comic, 119, 142, 147, 176, 181–83
    See also under snark
insult, humor of, 194, 209–10
"Insult Comic" (sketch), 155–58
intent, speaker, 86, 160–61, 176
    vs. audience uptake, 167, 176–77, 187, 191, 189–207, 223–24
internet, 5, 38, 61, 224
    See also digital public sphere
"Internet Killed the Newspaper Star" (segment), 107–8
ironic authenticity, 74
irony, 42, 56, 71, 108, 201, 224
    unconscious, 191
"I Said Bitch" (sketch), 27–28
"It's Not Going to Stop" (comic song), 127

Jacobs, Ben, 195
Jarrett, Valerie, 177–78, 198
Javerbaum, David, 91
Jefferson, Thomas, 47–48
Jencks, Charles, 63
Jesus, 133–34, 135
Jihotties, 68–69, 244n43
Jimmy Kimmel Live!, 72–73
Jimmy Kimmel test, 136–37, 141, 146
Johnson, Samuel, 10, 210, 218–19
joking, just, 197–207, 223
Jones, Alex, 120–21, 200, 201, 256–57n22
Jones, Kelly, 200
Jordan, Jim, 202
"Jordan Klepper Fingers the Pulse" (segment), 110

journalism, 52–53, 174, 214, 220–21
    hybrid, 212–14
    See also political journalism
Juvenal, 9–10, 188

Kang, Jay, 79, 215
Kant, Immanuel, 43–44, 64
Kaufmann, Jeff, 196
Kavanaugh, Brett, 194–95, 198–99
Kennedy, John, 140–42
Key, Keegan-Michael, 27–28, 155–58
Khashoggi, Jamal, 195
"Kids in Need of Defense" (organization), 131
Kilborn, Craig, 90
Kilmeade, Brian, 139–40, 167
Kimmel, Jimmy, 72–73, 136–50, 169
King, Rob, 4
Kirby, Alan, 38–39, 58
Klein, Ezra, 203–4
Klepper, Jordan, 106–12, 116
knowledge, 3, 50–51
Kubrick, Stanley, 29–30

Lahren, Tomi, 159
lampoon, 10, 96–101, 121–23, 143, 162
    See also insult, comic; ridicule; Trump, Donald, lampooning of
Langbert, Mitchell, 198–99, 256n19
lanx satura, 22
Last Week Tonight with John Oliver, 8, 65–66, 92, 94, 119–27
Late Show with Stephen Colbert, The, 72, 113–16, 118–19, 134–36, 160
laughability, 14, 20–21, 29
laughter, 1–2, 20–21, 28–32, 61–62, 88, 126, 237–38n28
    absence of, 31–32, 137–38
    cringe, 30, 32, 107
    humorless, 237n26
    laugh-on-inside (LOI) 32, 137, 180
    laugh-out-loud (LOL) 30–32, 138
    problem of, 1–2, 78–79, 222–23, 158
    withholding, 157
    vocal, 29–32, 191

laughter (*continued*)
    See also intent, speaker: vs. audience uptake; laughability; unlaughter
license, comic, 7, 25–26
    limits of, 13, 155–88
"Life After Hate" (organization), 128
liminality, 208–9, 222
Livingstone, Josephine, 170–80
locutionary speech acts, 86–88, 93–106
ludicrous, the, 21–22, 27
lying, 121, 138–40, 167–69, 221–22
Lyotard, Jean-François, 3, 38, 44, 45–47, 49–508

MAD magazine, 56, 71–72
Maher, Bill, 178–79
Manafort, Paul, 96
Margolis, Jim, 91
Martin, Millicent, 89–90
Marx, Harpo, 206, 207
McCain, John, 145, 147, 225
McConnell, Mitch, 169
Media. *See* news media
media, mass, 4–7, 37
    See also digitized media
media studies, 6–8, 233n18
Melton, James Van Horn, 37
memes, 192, 224–29
MemeWorld, 225–26
Menippean satire, 236n17, 237n26
metanoia, 9, 26–27, 87, 210–11, 219–21, 224
    See also satire, functions of: as change agent
metaphorical zero, 31–32
metaphors, 25–26, 58, 69, 181–82
#MeToo movement, 169–71
Meyers, Seth, 72–73
micrologies, 46
Miller, Dennis, 159–60
minimal hypothesis, 238n30
misogyny, 171, 179
Mitchell, Andrea, 163, 165–66
mockery. *See* commercials, mock; insult, comic; mockumentaries; news, mock; ridicule

mockumentaries, 160
modernity, 36, 40–51, 69–70
    rewriting of, 38, 45–50
    See also project of modernity
"Modest Proposal, A" (Swift), 42, 75, 94, 199
Moore, Michael, 217
Morin, Robert E., 1
MSNBC, 172
Mueller, Robert, 95, 96, 193
Murray, Patty, 145–46

"Natural Disasters: The Greatening" (episode), 129
Neeper, Layne, 42
neoclassical values, 41
neo-Enlightenment, 55
net neutrality, 120
news, fake, 6, 8, 23, 65–66, 123, 206, 220, 232n13
news, mock, 8, 90–92, 146–47, 200, 212–13, 232n13, 233n14
news media, 12, 147–48
    footage, 211–12
    playing with, 76, 89–94, 213
    ridiculing, 119, 172–73, 225–27
    types of, 3, 8, 34, 52–53, 93
    See also news, fake; news, mock; violence: toward media; *and individual names*
New York Times, 192–93, 203
Nixon, Richard, 114, 115
non-knowing, 31
"Nosedive" (*Black Mirror* episode), 40
Nussbaum, Emily, 168

Obama, Barack, 124, 143–44, 177–78
Obama, Michelle, 165–66
Oliver, John, 8, 65–66, 119–27, 151
    See also *Last Week Tonight with John Oliver*
Olson, Kirby, 60–62, 214–15
O'Neil, Chuck, 91
opposition, 38, 69
    See also anti-public sphere

Our Dishonest President, 4

paidia, 25, 32
Palmer, Jerry, 200
Papadopoulos, George, 96–97
paralipsis, 94, 108, 199
parasitic language, 87–88
Park, Suey, 75–79
parody, 70–72, 74–78, 90
parrhesia, comic, 2, 33, 59–60, 93, 135–36, 144–45, 229–30
    See also truth; truth telling
partial transformations, 44–46
partisanship, 160, 163, 165, 175
    Patriot Act, 125–26
Peele, Jordan, 27–28, 155–58
performatives, 81, 85–88
perlocutionary speech acts, 86–88, 93–94
personas, 76, 107–10, 200, 201, 225–27, 247n8
    unmasking of, 109–10
Phiddian, Robert, 152
Philadelphia Eagles, 190
physical appearance, 142–43, 155–58, 162, 168–69, 193
Piccolini, Christian, 128
Pierce, Charles, 94, 100–106, 166, 182–87, 193–94
Pizzagate, 67, 68, 200
play, 24, 25, 34
playfulness, comic, 22, 24–25, 55, 77, 105, 120, 187, 200
Podhoretz, John, 207
politeness, 164, 176
political correctness, 162, 165
political discourse, 3, 7
    satire as supplement to, 213–14, 217, 222
political journalism, 7, 37, 53–55, 248n5
    See also journalism
political speech, 52, 55, 59, 86–87
    relationship to comic political speech, 117, 119, 137, 149–54, 165, 215, 227

political talk shows, 92, 101
Politico, 144
politics of recognition, 48, 155, 241n37
"Politics with Charles P. Pierce" (blog), 94, 100–104
pop culture, 61, 229–30
Pope, Kyle, 164
postmodernity, 11, 36, 40–51, 53–54, 69–70
precession of a model, 68–69
President Show, The, 127
"Primer on Puerto Rico, A" (episode), 129
Prince Hal (*Henry IV*), 159
prion disease metaphor, 183–84
prior restraint, 165
project of modernity, 9–11, 45–47, 53, 70
public service announcements (PSAs), 24, 62, 94, 128–29
    See also paralipsis
public sphere
    definition of, 2, 36–51
    neo-modern, 53–54, 243n25
    rationality in, 56–57
    relationship to satire, 2–3, 4, 41–42
    See also anti-public sphere; comic public sphere; public sphere, comic public sphere relationship to; Trump, Donald: worthiness in public sphere
public sphere, comic public sphere relationship to, 56–58, 152, 166, 174, 211, 213
    blurring lines between, 125–26, 138–40, 178
    zigzag between, 72–73, 77, 104–6, 136–50
    See also comic public sphere; public sphere
punch ups, 25, 90, 161–62, 235–36n13
puns, 45, 209
putting down, 45
Pye, Gillian, 60
Pynchon, Thomas, 29–30

qualification to speak, 140, 143–46, 148–49
quantum state, 48, 49, 142
    of light, 149–50, 152–54
quasi-perlocutionary speech acts, 117–54

racism, 74–78, 135, 177–78, 198–99
rail agreeably, 27–28, 236–37n19
rant, 13, 27, 103, 105, 158–59, 201
reader. *See* audience
Reaganism, 186–87
reality, 64–65, 69
    devolving into hyperreality, 63–65, 209–10
    See also Trump, Donald: relationship to reality
reality tv. *See* Trump, Donald: reality tv presidency of
reasoning, 37–38, 43, 48–50
    capacity for, 42, 48
reflective judgment, 69, 198
reform, 5, 8–11, 33–35, 151–52, 216
    See also satiractivism; satire, functions of: as change agent
repetition, 64, 148
reporting, in-depth, 119–20, 126
representation, 61, 69
reproducibility, 63–68, 197
Republican party, 182–87
ressentiment, politics of, 209–10
reverse discourse, 12, 70, 73–79, 105, 107, 149, 221
"Re-Writing Modernity" (essay), 45
Richardson, Kendrick, 196
ridicule, 25, 27, 32, 74, 90, 108, 211
    ethical, 235n11
    self-, 147, 172
    See also critique; insult, comic; news media: ridiculing; Trump, Donald: ridiculing others
"Ridiculist, The," 71
ridiculous, the, 21–22, 27, 58
rights, universal, 47–48, 50
roasting, 174–75
    See also bullying

Robb, Amanda, 68
Rolfe, Mark, 42, 214
Ronson, Jon, 197
Rove, Karl, 34, 66–67, 158, 161
Russian investigation, 67, 95–100, 112–13
Ryan, Paul, 183

Sacco, Justine, 197–98, 239–40n12
Sanders, Sarah Huckabee, 162, 165–69, 180, 202
Sankin, Aaron, 159
satiractivism, 6, 8–9, 27, 73, 209, 222, 233n17, 234n33
    as quasi-perlocutionary, 117–54
    and truthiness satire, 79–81, 209, 220–21
    See also reform; satire, functions of
satire, 1, 32, 35, 42–43
    conservative, 9, 40, 236n13, 238–39n35
    definition of, 10, 22, 26, 52, 210–11, 233n23
    efficacy of, 150–54, 215–18, 222
    ethical issues of, 13, 22–23, 25, 33–34, 74, 198
    failings of, 22, 26, 41, 214–15, 240n26
    paradoxical nature of, 22–23, 33–35, 153, 223
    as serious and nonserious, 22–24, 33–34, 87–89, 93, 152, 226–27
    See also comic political speech; degenerative satire; friendly satire; generative satire; Menippean satire; political discourse: satire as supplement to; public sphere: relationship to satire; satire, functions of; truthiness satire; two-step, satire
satire, functions of, 236n117
    as call to action, 119–20, 144–45
    as change agent, 7, 22, 33, 40–43, 103, 151–53, 158, 215–18
    to educate, 5, 95, 120–25, 128, 137, 144, 260n21

See also metanoia; parrhesia; comic; reform; satiractivism; satire
satirists, 4, 14–15, 32, 62–63, 151, 174, 218–23, 229–30
   See also black humorists; comedians; and individual names
Saturday Night Live (SNL), 2, 90, 92
Scarborough, Joe, 163–64
schadenfreude, 192, 236n13
"Scott Pruitt Versus the World" (segment), 129–30
screed, 182–87
   See also rant
self-reflection, 43–44
Sessions, Jeff, 96–97, 134–35, 222
sexual assault, 170–71, 194, 199
Shafer, Jack, 94–96, 102–3, 112–13
Shaftesbury, Lord, 25
Shelby, Richard, 1
Shortest Way with Dissenters, The (Defoe), 42
signifiers, 64, 68–75, 80
signs, 64–65, 198
silly citizens. *See under* citizens
simulacra, regime of, 5, 12–14, 61, 64–66, 70, 209–10
simulation, regime of, 63–70
skepticism, 50, 53–54
Smalls, Robert, 121
Smith, M. W., 68
snark, 9–10, 27, 57, 176
   vs. comic insult, 34, 161–76, 194, 210
Snowden, Edward, 125–26
Snyder, Dan, 75–79
social codes, 21–22, 42, 60–61
social media, 5, 38–40, 112, 160
   See also digitized media; Twitter
speech act theory, 13, 85–88, 214
Spicer, Sean, 202–3
Steele, Richard, 27
Stewart, Jon, 6, 7, 90–92, 223
   See also Daily Show with Jon Stewart, The; Zadroga bill
St. Onge, Jeff, 56
"Stupid Watergate" (segment), 121–22

subversiveness, 41–42, 61, 245n73
Sullivan, Andrew, 181–87
Structural Transformation of the Public Sphere, The (Habermas), 36–37
surface, 61, 69
surface/depth metaphor, 69
"Swamp Diary, The" (column), 94–96, 112–13
Swift, Jonathan, 10, 29–30, 94, 199, 210, 243n23
Szakolczai, Arpad, 205–6

Talev, 163–65
Tally, Robert, 212
Tapper, Jake, 71, 72
television, 61, 211–12, 229
Terms of My Surrender, The, 33
Test, George, 23–32
That Was the Week That Was, 89–90
"This is Not a Game, The Game" (app), 130
"This Is What the Trump Abyss Looks Like" (essay), 181–82
through-the-looking-glass effect, 66, 68–71, 212, 245n48
   See also truthiness
Tillerson, Rex, 97
totality, 49
Tracy, Dale, 228
Traister, Rebecca, 180
trolling, 120, 160, 192–97, 225
   See also bullying; epithets
Trump, Donald, 2, 9, 165, 220
   not apologizing, 201–7
   bragging, 190–91, 204
   reality tv presidency of, 69, 202, 205–7
   relationship to reality, 63, 65–67, 122–23, 148, 234n31, 243–44n35
   rhetoric in public sphere, 170–71, 179–81, 224–28
   ridiculing others, 189–97, 210
   speechmaking performance art, 191–92, 195–97, 210
   worthiness in public sphere, 143–46, 148–40

Trump, Donald (*continued*)
  See also covfefe; Russia investigation; Trump, Donald, lampooning of; Trump supporters
Trump, Donald, lampooning of, 2, 71–72, 102, 112–16, 127, 148, 173, 190
  abyss metaphor, 181–82
  as boor and buffoon, 189–92
  as clown, 118–19, 209
  as dictator, 182–83
  as dog breed, 97–98
  as Drumpf, 122–23
  failed enterprises, 122, 171
  fitness, 176, 185–86
  laziness and ignorance, 143–46, 171
  as orangutan spawn, 178–79
  See also Trump, Donald
Trump, Ivanka, 172, 178–81
"Trump Has Access to Everything a Dictator Could Want" (essay), 182–83
Trump's Presidency Show, 206–7
Trump supporters, 104–6, 110–12, 182–87
"Trump's Response to Puerto Rico" (*MAD* magazine), 71–72
Trump Tower meeting, 97, 99
"Trump vs. Truth" (segment), 123–24
truth, 11, 68, 194, 213
  versions of, 64–66
  relevance of, 107, 111
  universal, 63, 208–9
  See also truthiness; truth telling
truthiness, 48
  Colbert coinage of, 6, 7, 11, 23, 54, 221, 233n15
  See also discursive integration: creating truthiness; truthiness satire
truthiness satire, 11–14, 23, 63, 70–73, 123, 220
  doubled quality of, 149–50, 153–54
  See also under satiractivism
truth telling, 229–30
Tuck Buckford (skit), 200
Tucker, D. R., 66–67

Twain, Mark 236n16
Twitter, 63–64, 67, 75–76, 207
two-step, satire, 32–33, 80, 141–42, 150–54, 220

United Nations General Assembly, 191–92
"Unite the Right" rally, 72–73
"Universal Declaration of Human Rights," 48
uncertainty, 41–42, 208–9
unlaughter, 30, 103, 160, 205
  See also laughter
Uptake. See under audience; intent, speaker
utterances, 85–86
  refusing, 77–79, 204–5
  See also intent, speaker: vs. audience uptake

Valenti, Jessica, 166
values, shared, 41, 42, 62
Vermette, Marie-France, 38
violence
  rhetoric causing, 180, 200, 224–28
  celebrating, 195, 203
  toward media, 195, 203
  violence, comic, 22–23, 25–26, 60, 157, 172
  ritualized, 25, 224–28
Volitich, Dayanna, 199
voting, illegal, 65–66
vulgarity, 122–23, 126, 135–36, 148
  allowability of, 164, 170, 179

Walsh, Brian O., 196
Warzel, Charlie, 225
Washington Redskins, 75–79
Weaver, Simon, 74, 78
"Weekend Update" (segment), 90, 92
Weisenburger, Steven, 60–62
Wemple, Erik, 168
whimsy, 27, 143, 164, 199
White House Correspondents' Dinner (2018), 23, 31, 161–76

white supremacy, 128, 177
Wilhite, Randall, 200
Williams, Brian, 223
Wittgenstein, Ludwig, 50–51
witz, 19, 31, 237n25
Wolf, Michelle, 23, 31, 161–76, 180, 191
World Is Flat, The (Friedman), 101–2

Yes Men, 217, 219
Yglesias, Matthew, 3
YouTube, 38

Zadroga bill, 118–19, 151–52, 209
Zelensky, Volodymyr, 87
Zimmerman, Neetzan, 107–8

Printed in the USA
CPSIA information can be obtained
at www.ICGtesting.com
CBHW020514280624
10717CB00002B/21